Adobe® AIR™ 1.5 Cookbook™

David Tucker, Marco Casario, Koen De Weggheleire, and Rich Tretola

Beijing · Cambridge · Farnham · Köln · Sebastopol · Taipei · Tokyo

Adobe® AIR™ 1.5 Cookbook™

by David Tucker, Marco Casario, Koen De Weggheleire, and Rich Tretola

Published by O'Reilly Media, Inc., 1005 Gravenstein Highway North, Sebastopol, CA 95472.

O'Reilly books may be purchased for educational, business, or sales promotional use. Online editions are also available for most titles (*http://safari.oreilly.com*). For more information, contact our corporate/institutional sales department: (800) 998-9938 or *corporate@oreilly.com*.

Editor: Linda Laflamme
Production Editor: Molly Sharp
Copyeditor: Kim Wimpsett
Technical Editors: Peter Elst, Ikezi Kamanu, and Aaron Brownlee
Proofreader: Kim Wimpsett

Indexer: Fred Brown
Cover Designer: Karen Montgomery
Interior Designer: David Futato
Illustrators: Robert Romano and Jessamyn Read

Printing History:

November 2008: First Edition.

RepKover™

This book uses RepKover, a durable and flexible lay-flat binding.

ISBN: 978-0-596-52250-6

[M]

1225410254

Adobe
Developer
Library

Adobe Developer Library, a copublishing partnership between O'Reilly Media Inc. and Adobe Systems, Inc., is the authoritative resource for developers using Adobe technologies. These comprehensive resources offer learning solutions to help developers create cutting-edge interactive web applications that can reach virtually anyone on any platform.

With top-quality books and innovative online resources covering the latest tools for rich-Internet application development, the *Adobe Developer Library* delivers expert training, straight from the source. Topics include ActionScript, Adobe Flex®, Adobe Flash®, and Adobe Acrobat® software.

Get the latest news about books, online resources, and more at *adobedeveloperlibrary.com*.

Table of Contents

Foreword

Since coming to Adobe, I've spent a great deal of time supporting the release of Adobe AIR. To help developers get up to speed on the new technology, the On AIR Bus Tour visited 18 cities across the United States and a similar AIR tour crisscrossed Europe. Over the course of those many miles and months, we reached a huge number of developers and did our best to help get them started building their own AIR applications.

The community has responded. As of this writing there are over 25,000,000 installs of Adobe AIR and a steady stream of new applications being released. With Adobe AIR 1.5, developers now have access to all of the amazing new features in Flash Player 10, including native 3D support, dynamic sound generation, and Pixel Bender.

To harness this new power, however, developers need learning resources. Although novice developers can get up to speed using the articles and tutorials at the Adobe AIR Developer Center (*http://www.adobe.com/devnet/air*) as well as a few introductory books, intermediate and advanced developers have been largely on their own. There hasn't been a more advanced resource that focuses on providing solutions and code snippets for real-world AIR development—until now. This is why I'm so excited about the *Adobe AIR 1.5 Cookbook*. I've always been a fan of the O'Reilly cookbook series.

Many aspects of this book make it a great reference. To begin with, *Adobe AIR 1.5 Cookbook* is the first book to cover Adobe AIR 1.5, so you can be sure that you will have an up-to-date reference. You couldn't ask for a better group of authors to help teach you the ins and outs of AIR development. An active member of the Flash community, David Tucker has created great video training on AIR for Lynda.com. A frequent speaker on the conference circuit, Marco Casario is an authority on all things Flash, Flex, and AIR. Koen De Weggheleire is a highly energetic Flash Platform expert from Belgium who is also extremely active in the community. Rich Tretola has been involved with AIR from the beginning and is a recognized Flex expert.

Packed with advice from such a trusted team, *Adobe AIR 1.5 Cookbook* will find a permanent home beside my keyboard whenever I'm doing any AIR development.

—Lee Brimelow
Platform Evangelist
Adobe Systems, Inc.

Credits

Author Bios

David Tucker is a software engineer with Universal Mind (*http://www.universalmind .com*) and is located in Savannah, Georgia. David's current focus is developing the next generation of rich Internet applications with Adobe AIR, Flex, and Flash. David is the author of the *AIR for Flash Developers* video training series (Lynda.com, 2008). David has worked on a variety of development platforms including ColdFusion and PHP. When David does not have a computer in front of him, he is probably playing guitar. David writes regularly at *http://www.insideria.com*, and his blog can be found at *http: //www.davidtucker.net*.

Marco Casario is the founder and CTO of Comtaste (*http://www.comtaste.com*), a company dedicated to exploring new frontiers in rich Internet applications in the enterprise field. He's an Adobe Community Expert, an Adobe Master Instructor for Flex, and a professional speaker at international conferences like Adobe MAX, Flash on the Beach, 360Flex, FITC, AJAXWorld, and Web 2.0 Expo. Marco is the author of *Flex Solutions: Essential Techniques for Flex 3 Developers* (friends of ED, 2007) and *The Essential Guide to AIR with Flash* (friends of ED, 2008), as well as a coauthor of *Advanced AIR Applications* (friends of ED, 2009). He runs his well-known personal blog at *http://casario.blogs.com*.

Koen De Weggheleire is a faculty member of the Technical University of West-Flanders (HOWEST) where he teaches Flash Platform solutions (Flash, Flex, and AIR) with a smile. As the Adobe User Group manager for Belgium (*http://www.adobeu sergroup.be*) and Adobe Community Expert for Flash, Koen is heavily addicted to the community; he inspires the community by his blog at *http://www.newmovieclip.com* and by speaking at several events (Adobe MAX, FITC, 360 Flex, Flashbelt, Flash in the Can, and Flash on the Beach). Koen also is a coauthor of *Foundation Flex for Developers* (friends of ED, 2007). When there is still some time left, you can find Koen at his company, Happy-Banana, together with Wouter Verweirder doing Flash Platform consultancy on advanced, award-winning rich Internet applications. When Koen is not talking ActionScript, you can find him producing music, collecting goodies, eating pizza, or renovating his 100-year-old house.

Rich Tretola currently is the rich applications technical lead at Herff Jones. An award-winning Flex developer, he is the lead author of *Professional Flex 2* (Wrox, 2007) and the sole author of *Beginning AIR* (Wrox, 2008). Rich has been building Internet applications for more than 10 years and has worked with Flex since the original Royale beta version of Flex in 2003. Other than Flex, Rich builds applications using ColdFusion, Flash, and Java. Rich is highly regarded within the Flex community as an expert in RIA and is also an Adobe Community Expert. He runs a popular Flex and AIR blog at *http://everythingflex.com*, is the community manager of *http://insideria.com*, and was also a speaker at the Adobe MAX 2007 conference in Chicago. Rich will be speaking at MAX 2008 in San Francisco. For a nontechnical escape, Rich is also a co-owner of a company that manufactures chocolate bars located on Maui named WowWee Maui.

Technical Editor Bios

Ikezi Kamanu is a senior technical consultant at Adobe Systems and longtime RIA enthusiast, with more than 10 years of experience with Adobe technologies. His career in software and multimedia development has been centered on rich, innovative user experiences and overall cool factor. An aspiring "efficiency architect," Ikezi can be seen near his New York home studying checkout counter queues, taxi patterns, or favorable flight routes for his next great escape. His website is *http://www.efficiencyarchitect.com*.

Aaron Brownlee is a senior technical consultant for Adobe Systems and makes his home in Oakland, California. He started doing web development in 1997, spent a decade orienting objects using Java, and currently dazzles the clients of Adobe Consulting using Flex and AIR. When not causing his MacBook to overheat, he enjoys family, bicycles, and motorcycles. His blog can be found at *http://blogs.adobe.com/viab*.

Peter Elst is an Adobe Community Expert, is a certified instructor, and is active in the Adobe User Group Belgium. As a freelance Flash Platform consultant and respected member of the online community, Peter has spoken at various international industry events and has published his work in leading journals. Most recently, Peter was lead author of *Object-Oriented ActionScript 3.0* (friends of ED, 2007).

Community Contributor Bios

Luca Mezzalira is an Italian Adobe Certified Expert and Adobe Certified Instructor for Flash and Flash Lite. Luca is the owner of M.art3, the first Italian Flash Platform agency that works exclusively on Flex, Flash, AIR, and Flash Lite. M.art3 is based in Padova near Venice, Italy. Luca works with national and international companies on many types of projects utilizing the Flash Platform, from mobile devices to touch screens. He also created a training project, called Let's Course, with other Italian companies that organize courses and important events in Italy. In May 2008, Luca became a consultant for Adobe Italy on the Flash Platform. He writes for national and international technical magazines, and he is a staff member of actionscript.it, the Italian

Adobe User Group. In addition, Luca is a speaker for national and international conferences and community events.

Marin Todorov is a software engineer with experience in building web applications and desktop software going back to the mid-90s. Professionally as a developer and manager, he has utilized various technologies, mostly focusing on the server programming side of the Web. In addition to his career as a developer, he has also been an associate university teacher, and he has written many technical articles and published a book about Perl. Marin started using Flash with version 4 and has been developing desktop software in Adobe AIR ever since its early betas. In his free time, Marin fancies composing music and studying languages.

Jeff Tapper has over a decade of experience developing Internet applications for many clients, including Condé Nast, IBM, and Morgan Stanley. He is an Adobe Certified Instructor for all of their Flex, ColdFusion, and AIR development courses. Jeff has worked as an author on ten books, including *Flex 3: Training from the Source* (Adobe Press, 2008) and *Breaking Out of the Web Browser with Adobe AIR* (New Riders Press, 2008). He sits on the editorial board of Flex Developer's Journal. Jeff is a senior consultant at Digital Primates IT Consulting Group.

Matt Poole is a freelance Flash platform consultant and developer working in London, United Kingdom and is active in the London Flex and Flash Platform user groups. Matt has consulted on making the most of breaking Flash Platform features in the social networking and online gambling arenas, and has more recently been involved in the high profile BBC iPlayer.

Greg Jastrab is a Flex/Flash/AIR developer working at SmartLogic Solutions, LLC, in Baltimore, Maryland. He has been using Flash since Flash 5 and Flex since 1.5. When not coding, Greg enjoys playing poker, guitar, video games, and relaxing with his wife and dog.

Ryan Stewart is a Platform Evangelist for Adobe and lives in Seattle, Washington. He has been doing Flex development for almost five years and has a passion for all things rich Internet application. He has had speaking engagements at industry conferences like Adobe MAX, Web 2.0 Expo, and Web Design World. He also has an industry-leading blog on ZDNet, where he covers all aspects of the RIA space. In his free time, he hikes, goes mountaineering, and codes.

Preface

AIR is a powerful application runtime that lets developers build cross-platform desktop applications in multiple development environments: Flex, Flash, and JavaScript. AIR applications have all the features you would expect from a web application, but in addition, they provide functionality you would expect from a desktop application, including file system access, network monitoring, and an embedded database.

The *Adobe AIR 1.5 Cookbook* exists to help you solve problems. It is not here to explain everything about AIR but rather to be a guide and reference during your AIR development. Like every developer, you will inevitably encounter roadblocks during development, and this book will help you get over the hump.

The challenge in writing this book was to adequately discuss as much of the AIR APIs as possible for each of the three development environments: Flash, Flex, and JavaScript. Because of this, we have chosen to tackle specific areas of AIR development that we think are useful for developers. This book is meant to provide answers for beginning, intermediate, and advanced AIR developers.

AIR 1.5

This book introduces the newest version of the runtime, AIR 1.5. This is the fourth production release of AIR. This new version adds some great tools to the developer's toolset. In addition to many bug fixes, this version includes several new features:

- Support for Flash Player 10: The biggest addition to AIR 1.5 is the support for the new functionality in Flash Player 10 including 3D support, a new type engine, Pixel Bender filter integration, new Sound APIs, and much more.

- SquirrelFish JavaScript interpreter: The new SquirrelFish JavaScript interpreter from the WebKit project provides extremely fast JavaScript execution within AIR.

 For more information on the SquirrelFish JavaScript interpreter, visit the WebKit blog here: *http://webkit.org/blog/189/announcing -squirrelfish/*.

- Encrypted SQLite database support: Previously the only way to store encrypted data within the AIR API was to utilize the encrypted local store. Now AIR allows you to store structured relational data inside a SQLite database with AES encryption.
- Extended language support: In addition to the languages that were supported in AIR 1.1, the new release of AIR supports Swedish, Dutch, Czech, Turkish, and Polish.

In this book, you will learn about many of the new features that are included with AIR 1.5.

Flash Player 10 Support

Although we cover the new areas of the AIR API, many of the features within Flash Player 10 are specific to a certain development environment. If you are interested in learning more about 3D support, the new type engine, or the new Sound APIs, be sure to check out the documentation for your development environment (whether Flex or Flash).

Bonus Chapter Online: Developing Mashup AIR Applications

We wanted to strike a balance between providing single solutions for problems and also helping developers build AIR applications for the first time. Because of this, we have provided an additional chapter online that will walk you through the process of creating four different mashup applications with Adobe AIR utilizing the solutions found in this book. This chapter should assist anyone new to AIR in developing a complete application. Go to *http://www.oreilly.com/catalog/9780596522506* to read the bonus chapter.

Who This Book Is For

The *Adobe AIR 1.5 Cookbook* is for intermediate developers who already have an understanding of their specific development environment. That means Flash and Flex developers need to already have a good understanding of ActionScript 3. It also means that JavaScript developers need to have a working knowledge of the language. We have tried to provide background information where it is needed, but without a core understanding of your development environment, many solutions may not make sense.

Every recipe in this book contains code for each development environment. This means that if we are presenting a solution for the File API, we'll provide both the ActionScript and JavaScript solutions. It also means that if we are discussing how to edit the application descriptor file, we will cover how to manually edit the XML file for Flex and JavaScript AIR applications as well as how to use the graphical tool provided in Flash.

Who This Book Is Not For

This book is not for developers who are new to ActionScript 3 or JavaScript. You will need to understand one of these languages. If you are new to Flex, you may want to read *Programming Flex 3* by Joey Lott and Chafic Kazoun (O'Reilly, 2008), and if you are new to ActionScript 3, you may want to check out *Learning ActionScript 3* by Rick Shupe and Zevan Rosser (O'Reilly, 2007). If you are new to JavaScript, you may want to read *Learning JavaScript* by Shelley Powers (O'Reilly, 2006). However, if you are familiar with ActionScript 3 or JavaScript but you have not worked with AIR previously, there is ample material to get you started developing your first application here within the book.

How This Book Is Organized

This book is a collection of recipes intended to be a reference that you can use in your AIR development. Each recipe in this book is a stand-alone solution. However, where needed, the recipe might reference other recipes in the book to provide additional information that may be needed to solve the problem. Our hope is that this book can be a valuable resource in your development by providing quick and easy-to-understand solutions to common problems you may encounter.

This book is essentially divided into four content groupings:

> **Chapter 1–Chapter 2** give you basic information about how to develop AIR applications in the different development environments as well as how to configure an AIR application's settings.
>
> **Chapter 3–Chapter 15** provide solutions for working with the APIs that are included with AIR. This includes the file system, a network monitoring framework, the embedded SQLite database, and much more.
>
> **Chapter 16–Chapter 17** give you the information needed to distribute and update your application. This includes using the AIR Update Framework and using the install badges.
>
> The **online chapter** provides information needed to create mashup applications utilizing popular public APIs available to developers.

As mentioned earlier, each chapter provides information for each of the development environments.

Conventions Used in This Book

The following typographical conventions are used in this book:

Menu options
> Menu options are shown using the → character, such as File→Open.

Italic

> Italic indicates new terms, URLs, email addresses, filenames, and file extensions.

`Constant width`

> This is used for program listings, as well as within paragraphs, to refer to program elements such as variable or function names, databases, data types, environment variables, statements, and keywords.

`Constant width bold`

> This shows commands or other text that should be typed literally by you.

`Constant width italic`

> This shows text that should be replaced with user-supplied values or by values determined by context.

This Book's Example Files

You can download the example files for this book from this location:

http://www.oreilly.com/catalog/9780596522506

Where necessary, multiple code samples are provided for each recipe to correspond with the different development environments. Each sample will be separated into a folder for the specific environment. Each application should include the needed code for your environment as well as an application descriptor file.

Using the Code Examples

This book is here to help you get your job done. In general, you may use the code in this book in your programs and documentation. You do not need to contact us for permission unless you're reproducing a significant portion of the code. For example, writing a program that uses several chunks of code from this book does not require permission. In addition, answering a question by citing this book and quoting example code does not require permission. However, selling or distributing a CD-ROM of examples from O'Reilly books does require permission. Incorporating a significant amount of example code from this book into your product's documentation does require permission.

We appreciate, but do not require, attribution. An attribution usually includes the title, author, publisher, and ISBN. For example: "*Adobe AIR 1.5 Cookbook* by David Tucker, Marco Casario, Koen De Weggheleire, and Rich Tretola. Copyright © 2009 David Tucker, Marco Casario, Koen DeWeggheleire, and Rich Tretola 978-0-596-522506."

If you think your use of code examples falls outside fair use or the permission given here, feel free to contact us at *permissions@oreilly.com*.

How to Use This Book

Development rarely happens in a vacuum. In today's world, email, Twitter, blog posts, co-workers, friends, and colleagues all play a vital role in helping you solve development problems. Consider this book yet another resource at your disposal to help you solve the development problems you will encounter. The content is arranged in such a way that solutions should be easy to find and easy to understand. However, this book does have a big advantage: it is available anytime of the day or night.

The Adobe AIR Cookbook Cook-Off

O'Reilly sponsored the Adobe AIR Cookbook Cook-Off, a chance for developers to submit recipes and win prizes. Many of the top entries have been included in this book, and the winning entry from Greg Jastrab can be found at Recipe 9-13. This contest was open to developers in the United States. Greg's entry was chosen by a group of experts in the RIA development community. Congratulations, Greg!

O'Reilly Cookbooks

Looking for the right ingredients to solve a programming problem? Look no further than O'Reilly Cookbooks. Each cookbook contains hundreds of programming recipes and includes hundreds of scripts, programs, and command sequences you can use to solve specific problems.

The recipes you'll find in an O'Reilly Cookbook follow a simple formula:

Problem
Each problem addressed in an O'Reilly Cookbook is clearly stated, specific, and practical.

Solution
The solution is easy to understand and implement.

Discussion
The discussion clarifies and explains the context for the problem and the solution. It also contains sample code to show you how to get the job done. Best of all, all the sample code you see in an O'Reilly Cookbook can be downloaded from the book's website: *http://www.oreilly.com/catalog/9780596522506*.

To learn more about the O'Reilly Cookbook series or to find other Cookbooks that are up your alley, visit *http://cookbooks.oreilly.com*.

Safari® Books Online

Safari When you see a Safari® Books Online icon on the cover of your favorite
technology book, that means the book is available online through the
O'Reilly Network Safari Bookshelf.

Safari offers a solution that's better than e-books. It's a virtual library that lets you easily
search thousands of top tech books, cut and paste code samples, download chapters,
and find quick answers when you need the most accurate, current information. Try it
for free at *http://safari.oreilly.com*.

How to Contact Us

Please address comments and questions concerning this book to the publisher:

O'Reilly Media, Inc
1005 Gravenstein Highway North
Sebastopol, CA 95472
800-998-9938 (in the United States or Canada)
707-829-0515 (international or local)
707-829-0104 (fax)

We have a web page for this book, where we list errata, examples, and any additional
information. You can access this page here:

http://www.oreilly.com/catalog/9780596517359

Acknowledgments

While four of us get to share the cover of the book, we all know that none of this would
have been possible if it had not been for the hard work of many people behind the
scenes.

I certainly would like to thank everyone at O'Reilly who made this book possible. Steve
Weiss gave each of us an opportunity on this book, and his input and guidance has
been essential. Dennis Fitzgerald guided most of the development of the book, and his
wisdom of this entire process was certainly needed. Also, special thanks are due to
Linda Laflamme, Molly Sharp, and Kim Wimpsett, who worked tirelessly to be sure
the book was ready on time and in good form. Their work in coordinating the editing
effort with authors across two continents and multiple time zones is a testament to
their organization, hard work, and skill. In addition, I want to thank Michael Koch,
Amy Wong, and Ed Sullivan at Adobe for making the collaboration so easy.

While the authors have contributed some great solutions in this book, the technical
editors contributed a great deal of insight and knowledge into making the recipes easy
to understand and follow. The work of Ikezi Kamanu, Aaron Brownlee, and Peter Elst

was essential in developing the final recipes. They provided insight into every aspect of the recipes including the code content, the code structure, the wording of solutions, and the structure of the chapters. This book is significantly better because of their input.

From David

This book was truly a collaborative effort between Marco, Rich, Koen, and me. I have learned something from each of them, and I am extremely grateful to have such a great group of coauthors for this book.

I want to thank Steve Weiss for giving me the opportunity to write this book. Steve has been someone who I learned a great deal from, and he has opened many doors for me that would have taken me decades to open by myself. In addition, I want to thank Michael Koch at Adobe for giving me many opportunities to contribute to the Adobe AIR Developer Center. Many highlights in my career were initially brought about by the opportunities he gave me to write. In addition, Rich Tretola has provided a great example to me of how to positively contribute to the developer community in many different ways. Also, I want to thank Jill Parks and Sam Skinner whose wisdom served me well during my time at Georgia Tech, when the book was just in its conceptual stage.

Finally, I have several people to thank in my family: Brian and Kevin for providing a great example to follow, Mom for always providing encouragement, Dad for exemplifying hard work and integrity, and Shannon for being an amazingly patient and supportive wife during the writing of this book. Most of all, to Jesus, who blesses Shannon and me beyond what we deserve, even with suffering, so we could learn to love Him more.

From Marco

My contribution to this book wouldn't be possible without David Tucker, who gave me the possibility to collaborate with him on this awesome book, and of course without the support of the O'Reilly team, specifically, Steve Weiss and Dennis Fitzgerald. I'm amazed by the hard work done by the reviewers of this book. Thanks.

Finally, I would like to thank my girlfriend, Katia, for her patience with all the weekend hours spent on this book in the past months.

I dedicate this book to my mother who taught me to constantly challenge myself yet remain balanced.

From Koen

I really want to thank the dedicated people at O'Reilly for their professional help and guidance. I also want to thank my coauthors—David, Marco, and Rich—for the incredible amount of work they have put into this book to make it the best.

Of course, I also want to thank my colleagues, friends, and family for being supportive and for understanding why I sometimes didn't have enough time for them.

I learned a lot from the community, and I still do, but I am very happy that I can give something back. You know…it's all about giving back to the community!

Happy coding!

From Rich

Special thanks for the hard work of my coauthors—David, Marco, and Koen—and also Steve Weiss for asking me to be part of this book.

I would also like to thank my wife and best friend, Kim, and my daughters, Skye and Coral.

CHAPTER 1

AIR Basics

AIR is a runtime that can be installed on computers that are running Windows, Mac, or Linux (at the time of writing, Linux support is currently in beta).

After installing AIR (free from *http://get.adobe.com/air/*), users can install and run AIR applications, which are packaged as files with the extension *.air*. What this means to you, the developer, is that you can deploy a single *.air* file to any operating system that has AIR installed without making any changes—one of the greatest benefits of AIR. You can truly *write code once* and then deploy your application across multiple operating systems.

AIR provides multiple development pathways for you to create AIR applications. The free Adobe AIR software development kit (SDK) contains command-line tools and code templates for creating an AIR application and is downloadable from *http://www.adobe .com/products/air/*. With the AIR SDK, you can create Hypertext Markup Language (HTML)/JavaScript AIR applications or create an application with a precompiled Flash or Flex SWF file. In addition, Adobe provides integrated support for developing AIR applications in Adobe Flash, Flex, and Dreamweaver. A few other development environments also provide support for developing AIR applications including Aptana Studio, which provides comprehensive support for developing JavaScript AIR applications.

Although multiple development pathways exist for an AIR application, the following core concepts span each of these environments:

- Each application contains an *application descriptor file*, which is an Extensible Markup Language (XML) file containing the settings for the application.
- Each platform allows a developer to preview an application using the AIR Debug Launcher (**adl**) and also to package the AIR application as an installable *.air* file.
- Each AIR application must be signed with a *certificate*. This certificate can be a self-signed certificate or a commercial certificate. Applications are signed and packaged by using the AIR Developer Tool (**adt**). An unsigned AIR package file can also be exported. This file is referred to as an *intermediate file* and has an

extension of *.airi*. This allows the developer to pass the application along to someone else for signing.

This chapter discusses the key topics you will need for your platform: how to create a new AIR application, how to debug an application, and how to sign and package a completed AIR application for distribution.

1.1 Creating and Running an AIR Application with Flex Builder 3

Problem

You need to create an AIR application using Flex Builder 3.

Solution

Use the built-in support for AIR application development in Flex Builder 3.

Discussion

Flex Builder 3 has built-in support for creating AIR applications. In many ways, working with an AIR application is similar to working with a Flex application.

 Be sure that you have the latest updates for Flex Builder 3 before authoring AIR 1.5 applications. To check for updates, select Help→Search for Flex Builder Updates.

Creating a New AIR Application

To create a new AIR application project within Flex Builder, you first must create a new project. From the File menu, choose New→Flex Project. If you don't see this option, you may need to choose Other and then select Flex Project from the resulting list.

When the New Flex Project dialog box appears (Figure 1-1), you will notice an option to make this a Flex web application or a Flex-based AIR application. Be sure that the option for an AIR application is selected, and then click the Next button to proceed through the wizard-like interface.

As you proceed through the dialog box, you can set the application ID and default application MXML filename, as shown in Figure 1-2 (for more information on setting your application ID, see Recipe 2.1). The application ID will be prepopulated in the application descriptor file for your AIR application once you've created the project.

When you click Finish, Flex Builder creates a new project that includes the application MXML file as well the application descriptor XML file.

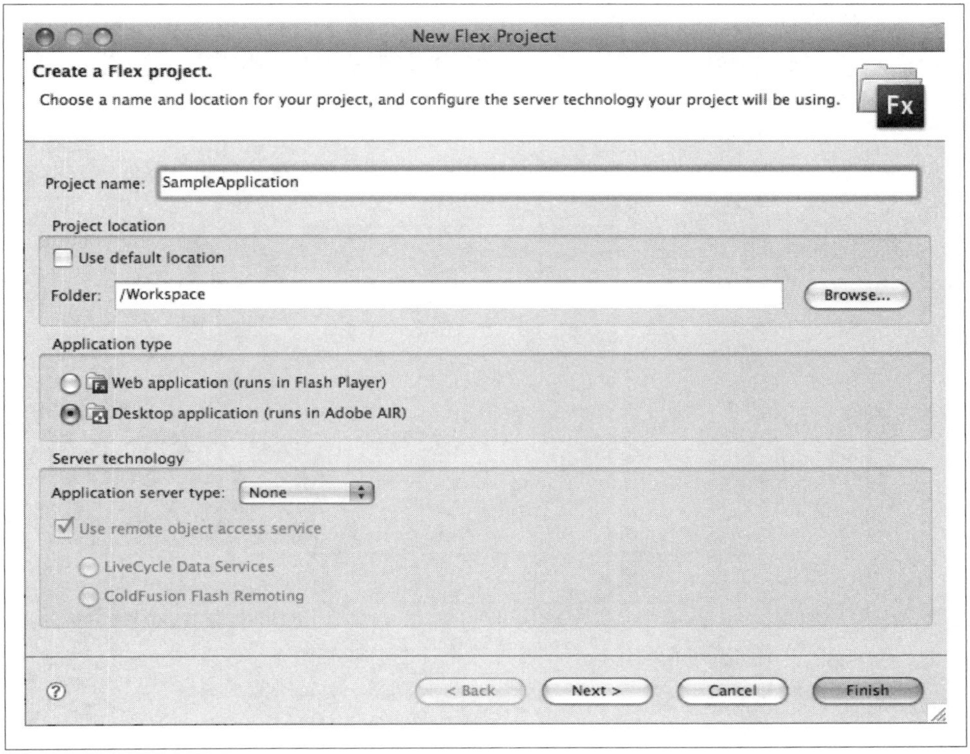

Figure 1-1. New Flex Project dialog box

Running and Debugging Your AIR Application

In Flex Builder, you can run an AIR application by selecting the application and clicking the Run button. Flex Builder takes care of calling `adl` and passing in your application descriptor file. Likewise, you can debug your application by clicking the Debug button. All the regular debugging tools are available to AIR applications.

Flex developers also have another advantage when it comes to AIR development. The profiler within Flex Builder also works seamlessly with AIR applications, so by selecting your AIR Application project and then clicking the Profiler button, you can determine what system resources are being used by your application.

1.2 Creating and Running an AIR Application with Flash

Problem

You need to create an AIR application using Flash.

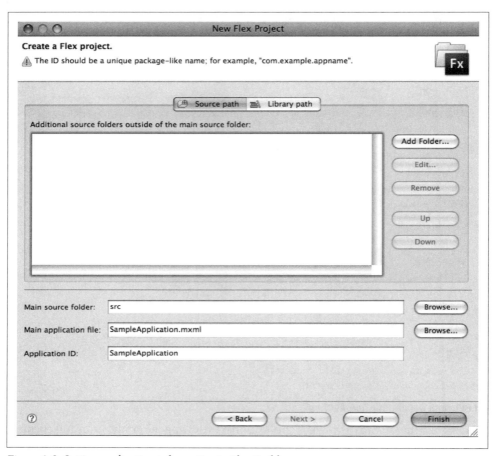

Figure 1-2. Setting application information in Flex Builder

Solution

Use the support for AIR application development in Flash CS3 or Flash CS4.

Discussion

Both Flash CS3 and CS4 will require an update to create AIR 1.5 applications. You will first need to ensure that you have the latest version of Flash. To check for updates, select Help→Updates.

> The updates for Flash CS3 and CS4 will be made available shortly after the release of AIR 1.5.

Figure 1-3. Flash opening screen with Adobe AIR support

Creating a New AIR Application

To create a new AIR application in Flash, select Flash File (Adobe AIR) under the Create New heading on the opening screen (Figure 1-3). This creates a new Flash file that is configured for Adobe AIR.

After you've created the file, save the Flash file. Next, you will be able to adjust the application settings, which will be reflected in the application's application descriptor file. You can find these settings in the Commands→AIR – Application and & Installer Settings menu in Flash CS3. In Flash CS4, you'll find this in the File→AIR Settings menu. Choosing either opens the AIR – Application & Installer Settings dialog box (Figure 1-4).

Running and Debugging Your AIR Application

After you create an AIR application in Flash, you can run your application just as you would run a Flash movie. If you choose Control→Test Movie, your AIR application should launch in a new window. Just as with normal Flash development, the Flash debugger is available to debug your AIR application. To debug your AIR application, choose Debug→Debug Movie.

1.3 Creating and Running an AIR Application with HTML and JavaScript

Problem

You need to create and run a new HTML/JavaScript-based AIR application.

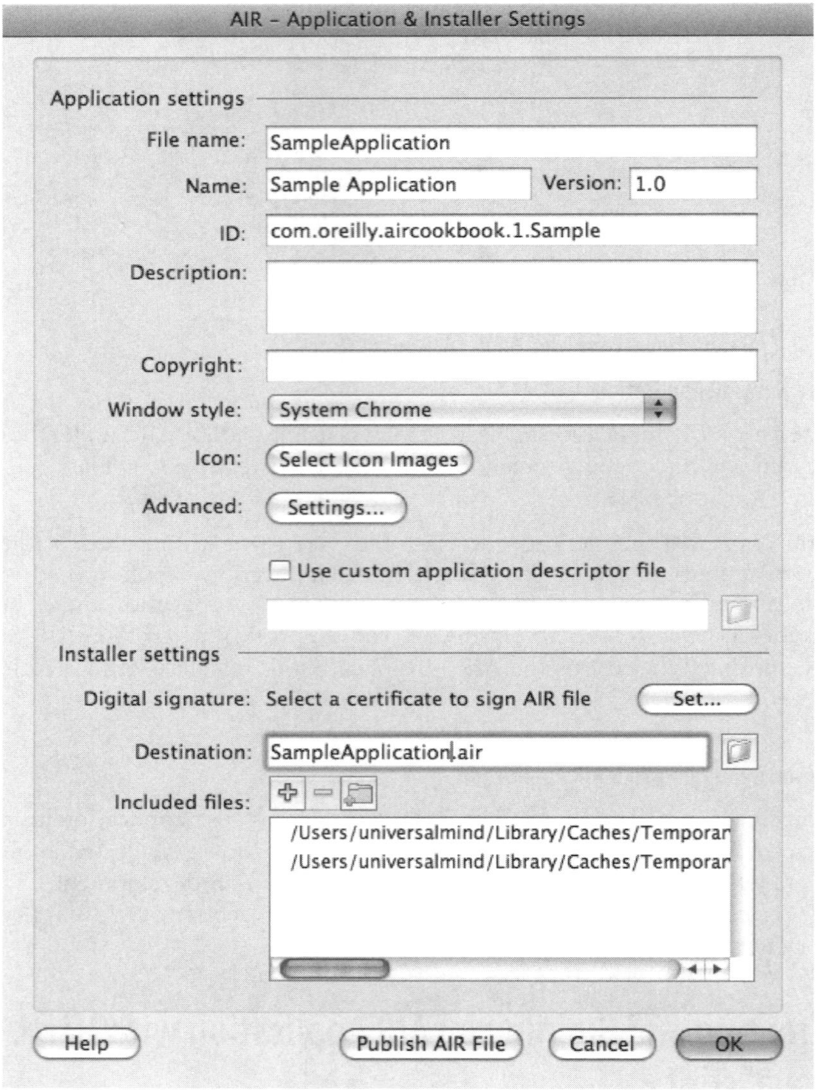

Figure 1-4. AIR application and installed settings in Flash

Solution

Use the application descriptor file template and the command-line tools included with the free Adobe AIR SDK to create and run an HTML/JavaScript AIR application.

Discussion

Several HTML/JavaScript development environments include built-in support for working with Adobe AIR applications including Adobe Dreamweaver and Aptana Studio. Regardless of your development environment, you can test and package AIR applications using the command-line tools included with the free Adobe AIR SDK. This lets you use any development environment that you are already comfortable using.

Creating a New AIR Application

A JavaScript AIR application consists of a minimum of two files: the application descriptor file, which defines the application settings, and a main HTML file that contains the content for the application. The AIR SDK contains a template for the application descriptor file, and you can copy this into the same directory as your main content HTML file. Chapter 2 in this book contains details on configuring this file for your application.

These two files are the only required files, but you will want to include a few additional files. *AIRAliases.js* provides aliases to the AIR APIs, and *AIRIntrospector.js* provides a debugging environment for your AIR application. You can find both of these files in the frameworks directory of the AIR SDK. You can copy both of these files into the same directory as your main content HTML file. They will also need to be included in the head of your HTML file:

```
<script type="text/javascript" src="AIRAliases.js"></script>
<script type="text/javascript" src="AIRIntrospector.js"></script>
```

Be sure to include the *AIRAliases.js* file before any code that uses the AIR APIs. If you do not, you will need to use the fully qualified name of the API names. For example, if you do not include the *AIRAliases.js* file, you must type `window.runtime.flash.display.NativeWindow` instead of `air.NativeWindow`.

Running Your AIR Application

To run your newly created AIR application, you can use the `adl` command-line tool from the AIR SDK; you can find this file in the bin directory of the AIR SDK. This doesn't create a distributable *.air* file, but it lets you run the application in your development environment. To run the application, you need to pass your application descriptor file as an argument of `adl`:

```
adl application.xml
```

This assumes the application files are in the same directory as your application descriptor file. If you entered it correctly, you should see your application open in a new window. Although it is easy to use the `adl` command, the developer environments mentioned earlier can make this process even easier.

1.4 Debugging an AIR Application with JavaScript

Problem

You need to debug a JavaScript AIR application.

Solution

Use the AIR application Introspector that is included with the Adobe AIR SDK.

Discussion

Many JavaScript developers are used to debugging their applications with tools such as the live code environment in Dreamweaver CS4 or browser-based tools such as Firebug during their development process. Because AIR exists outside the browser, these traditional tools for debugging JavaScript applications are not available. As an alternative, Adobe includes the Adobe AIR Introspector for JavaScript applications in the Adobe AIR SDK. The Introspector provides a debugging experience similar to traditional JavaScript debugging tools.

To include the AIR Introspector in an application, you first need to include the *AIRIntrospector.js* file in your project. You can find this file in the frameworks folder in the Adobe AIR SDK. You then need to include this file in your root document file:

```
<script type="text/javascript" src="AIRIntrospector.js"></script>
```

You now have access to the full features of the AIR Introspector within your application, and while running your application, you can press F12 to launch the debugging window (Figure 1-5). In addition, the methods for writing to the Introspector console are now available in the `air.Introspector` object.

Logging to the Introspector Console

The Console tab within the Introspector gives you the ability to trace both simple and complex objects. It has five main methods for writing data to the console: `log`, `warn`, `info`, `error`, and `dump` (Figure 1-6).

The methods `log`, `warn`, `info`, and `error` all work the same, but they display a different icon depending on the method. These methods let you view and edit complex data, because the console receives a reference to the actual object you pass into it.

The console displays an object with all its properties, and you can click each property and edit its value.

The `dump` method provides similar functionality, but it provides a copy of the data. Because of this, the data is not editable, but rather it gives you a snapshot of the state of the data at a given point.

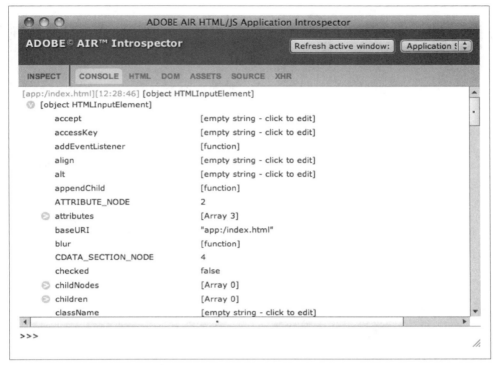

Figure 1-5. AIR JavaScript application Introspector

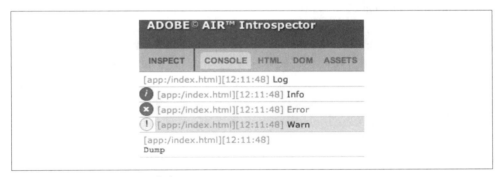

Figure 1-6. Introspector console logging types

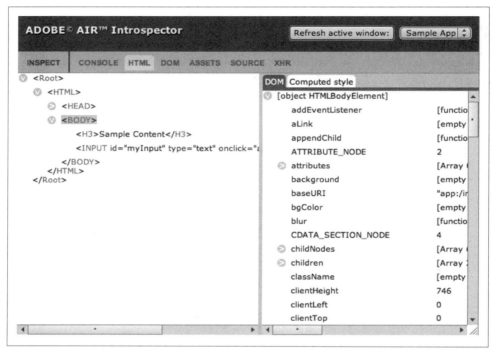

Figure 1-7. HTML tab in the Introspector

Viewing the DOM and Application Source

Three of the tabs within the Introspector let you view Document Object Model (DOM) and source information. The HTML tab lets you view the DOM in a tree (Figure 1-7). Click an item within the tree to see all its properties in the pane on the right.

The DOM tab lists all the DOM properties (Figure 1-8). To edit them, click a property, and change its value.

The Source tab lets you view both the actual and parsed source for your application as well as the source of your application files (Figure 1-9).

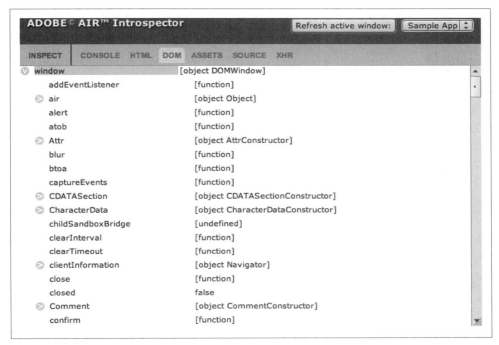

Figure 1-8. DOM tab in the Introspector

Visually Inspecting Application Elements

The Introspector also lets you visually inspect application elements. You can enter Inspect mode by clicking the Inspect button in Introspector. While in Inspect mode, you can mouse over an application element. The elements will appear with a yellow background and outline. In this mode, when you click an element, it is selected in HTML view, and you can interact with the element's properties.

Monitoring Network Communication

If you use XMLHTTPRequest within your application, you can monitor each of these requests on the XHR tab. This tab works in a similar manner to traditional debugging tools that let you view responseText and responseXML from your requests.

 In addition to the AIR Application Introspector, AIR 1.5 allows for step-debugging of HTML/JavaScript applications. For more information see the Adobe AIR 1.5 SDK.

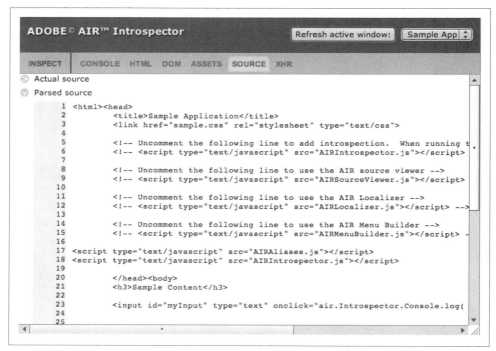

Figure 1-9. Source tab in the Application Introspector

1.5 Signing and Exporting an AIR Application

Problem

You need to create an installable packaged AIR application.

Solution

Sign your AIR application with a self-signed certificate with your AIR development tool, and then export the application as an *.air* file.

Discussion

AIR applications must be signed to be installable. This provides a level of security that is needed for desktop applications. For developers coming from web applications, using certificates may seem scary. However, AIR makes the certificate process easy, and the development environments for AIR provide easy ways to generate certificates and sign applications.

No matter which development environment you are using, the certificate process requires two steps: creating a certificate and signing your application with that certificate. You can use a single certificate multiple times with multiple applications, but you have

Figure 1-10. Installation dialog box with self-signed certificate

to sign the application each time it is packaged into an installable AIR application. Figure 1-10 illustrates the installation dialog box with a self-signed certificate.

When signing with a self-signed certificate, the publisher listed in the installer is not verified. To have the publisher value verified, you will need to use a trusted certificate authority (you can find a list of supported certificates in Recipe 1.6).

Signing and Exporting in Flex Builder

When you attempt to package and export your AIR application in Flex Builder, you will be asked which certificate you will be using to sign your application. Also, an alternate option lets you export an AIR application as an unsigned package. This type of packaged file has the extension *.airi*, and this type of package is not installable. To export an installable application, you need to select the first option: "Export and sign an AIR file with a digital certificate" (Figure 1-11).

The Export Release Build dialog box also gives you the option to create a certificate if you do not already have one. If you click the Create button, you will be presented with a new dialog box that enables you to create a new certificate (Figure 1-12). This dialog box requires you to enter a publisher name, a password, and the location where you want to save your certificate. You can enter a unique identifying piece of information for the publisher name. You need to remember the password that is entered when creating your certificate, because you must enter this value each time you sign an

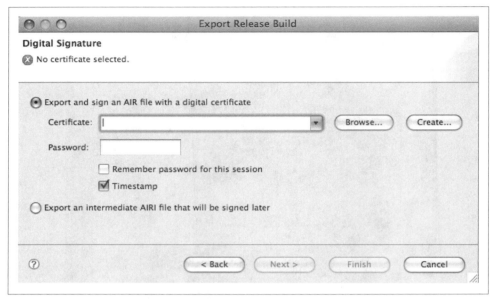

Figure 1-11. Export Release Build dialog box

application. Be sure to remember where you save your certificate, because you can use it to sign all your AIR applications. Be sure to also back up your certificate.

Once you click the OK button, you will be taken to the Export Release Build dialog box, and the information for your certificate will be populated in the Certificate field. You will need to enter your password in the Password entry field. You can also click the "Remember password for this session" check box so you will not have to enter the password each time you export this AIR application. Once Flex Builder is closed and reopened, you will have to reenter the password. Once the password has been entered, you can proceed through the dialog box and export your AIR application as an installable AIR file.

Signing and Exporting in Flash

You can find the certificate settings for a Flash AIR application in the AIR – Application & Installer Settings dialog box (Figure 1-13), which you can launch by selecting File→AIR Settings in your AIR application. If you are using Flash CS3, you can select Command →AIR Application & Installer Settings.

Before you export your AIR application, you must select a certificate. Click the button next to the Digital Signature field to set the digital certificate for your application.

Next, you are prompted either to select a certificate for the application or to prepare the application as an unsigned *.airi* file, which can be signed later (Figure 1-14). In this

Figure 1-12. Create Self-Signed Digital Certificate dialog box

case, be sure the first option is selected. If you do not already have a certificate, click the Create button.

You are now prompted to enter the information for your new certificate. You need to fill in every field in the Create Self-Signed Digital Certificate dialog box (Figure 1-15). You need to remember where you store the certificate as well as the password associated with this certificate. The password needs to be entered each time the certificate is used to sign an AIR application.

After the certificate is created and selected, you need to enter your password. After this is complete, you are returned to the AIR – Application & Installer Settings dialog box. At this point, you are able to export your application as an AIR installable package by clicking the Publish AIR File button.

Signing and Exporting with the AIR SDK

You can use the Adobe AIR SDK command-line tools to generate a certificate, sign an AIR application, and export the application as an installable *.air* file. These

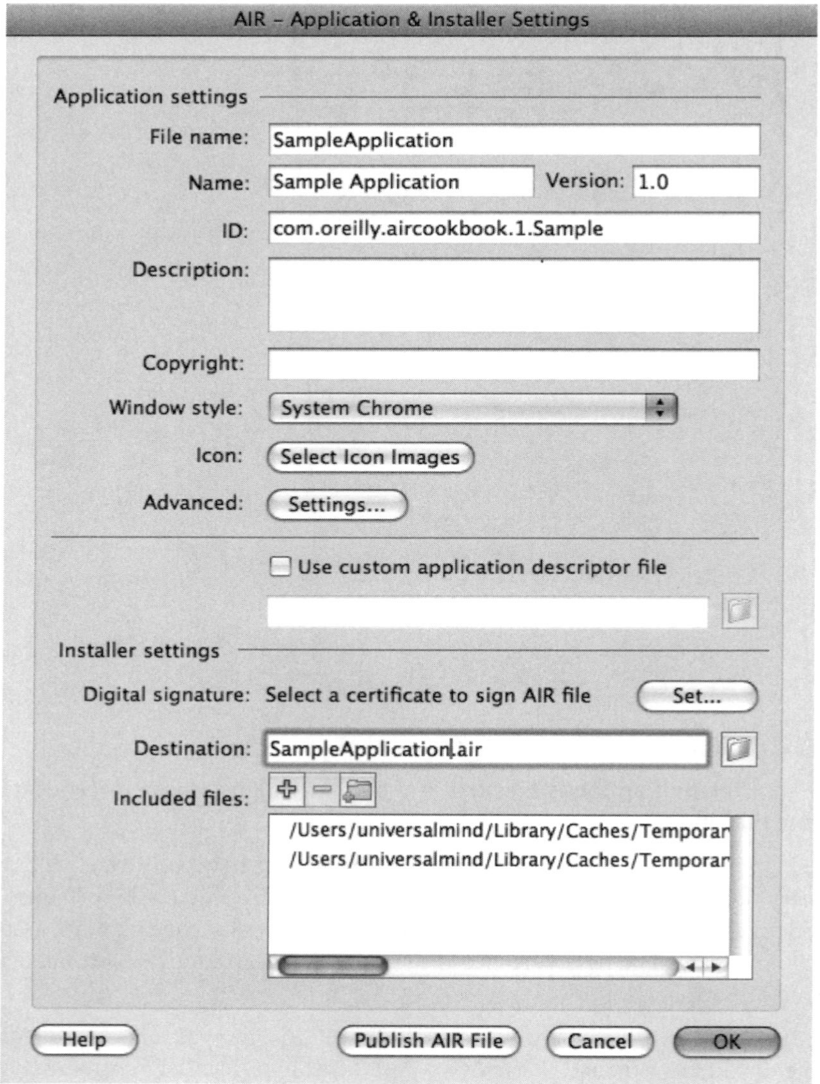

Figure 1-13. AIR – Application & Installer Settings dialog box in Flash

command-line tools are actually what power these features in Flash and Flex Builder. You can find the command-line utilities in the bin directory of the AIR SDK.

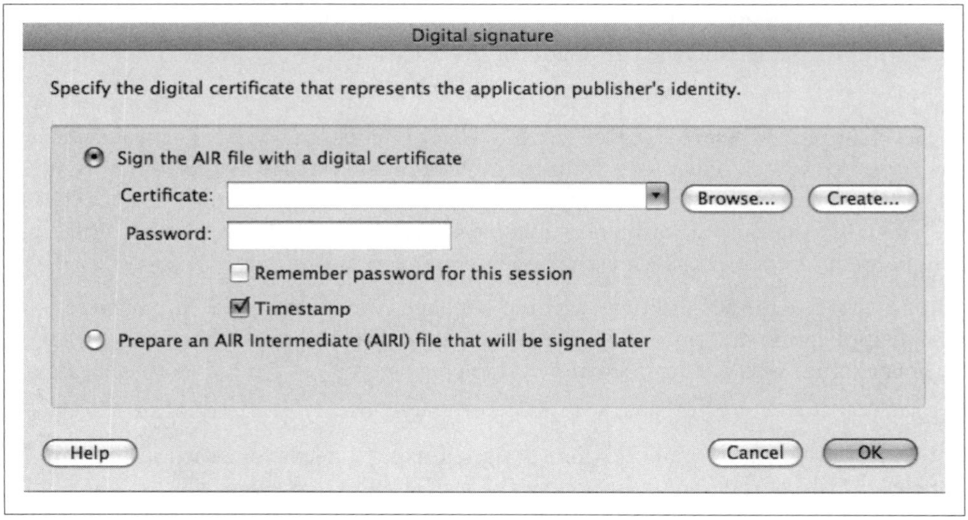

Figure 1-14. Digital signature dialog box in Flash

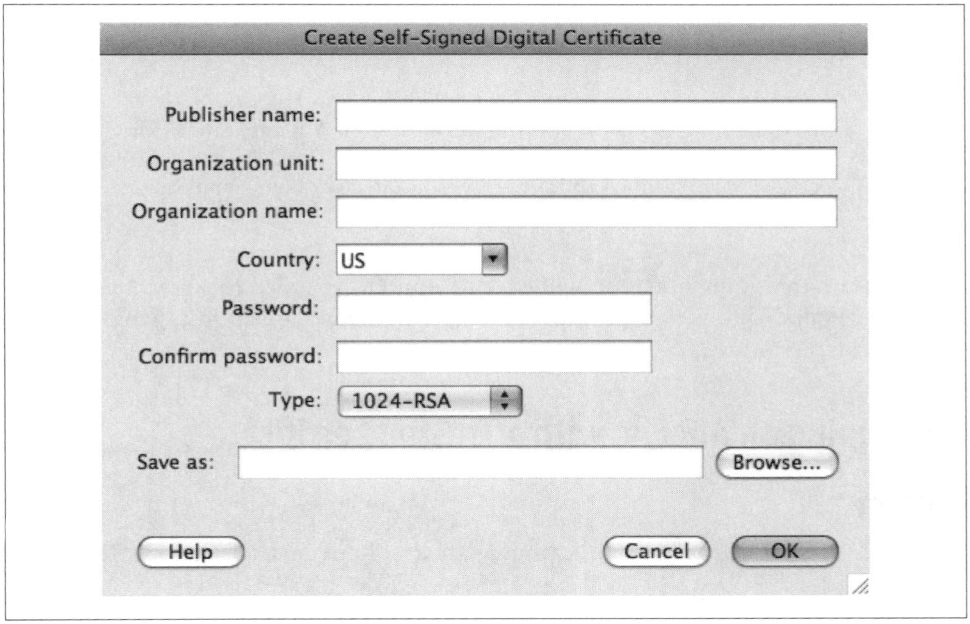

Figure 1-15. Create Self-Signed Digital Signature dialog box in Flash

The first step in exporting your application is to create a new self-signed certificate if you do not already possess one. You accomplish this by using the adt command-line utility. If you use this command with the -certificate option, you can generate certificates. You also need to pass in the certificate name, the key type for the certificate, the output filename, and the password for the certificate. For example:

```
adt -certificate -cn SampleCertificate 2048-RSA sampleCert.p12 password
```

In this example, the `-certificate` switch tells `adt` you want to create a new certificate. Next, the `-cn` switch tells it you want to use `SampleCertificate` as the common name for the certificate. Next, the key type is set to `2048-RSA`, but you could use `1024-RSA` as well. Finally, the output pathname and password are passed in. After you run this command, a *sampleCert.p12* file appears in your current directory.

You can also use the `adt` utility to sign and package your application. You need to pass in your application descriptor XML file as well as your certificate to generate a packaged and installable *.air* file. Consider this example:

```
adt -package -storetype pcks12 -keystore ../sampleCert.p12 sampleApp.air application.xml .
```

In this example, the AIR application is signed using a certificate with a filename of *sampleCert.p12* in the parent directory. The `storetype` is defined as `pcks12`. The application will be exported as *sampleApp.air* in the current directory. Next, the application descriptor file, *application.xml*, from the current directory is passed into `adt`. The last items that are passed into `adt` are the files that need to be compiled with the application. In this case, a period signifies that everything in the current directory and its subdirectories are included. Individual files could also be listed and separated with a space.

 Be sure not to include your certificate file in your AIR application. The can result in security concerns and is an unsafe practice. To avoid this, be sure to not store a certificate in the same directory as your application files.

After you run this command, you will have in your current directory a *sampleApp.air* file that is signed with the certificate you created. This will be an installable AIR file that you can distribute.

1.6 Signing an AIR File with a Trusted Certificate

Problem

You need to sign your AIR application with a commercial trusted certificate for deployment.

Solution

Obtain a trusted certificate from one of the vendors selling code-signing certificates for AIR applications.

Discussion

Signing an AIR application with a commercial certificate is the same process as signing an AIR application with a self-signed certificate. The only difference is the certificate used. The two companies that currently offer trusted certificates that can be used with AIR are VeriSign and Thawte.

It is important to note that the certificates used with AIR are code-signing certificates. These certificates are different from certificates used with secure web servers. Currently, the following types of certificates are supported for signing AIR applications:

- VeriSign
  - Microsoft Authenticode Digital ID
  - Sun Java Signing Digital ID
- Thawte
  - AIR Developer Certificate
  - Apple Developer Certificate
  - JavaSoft Developer Certificate
  - Microsoft Authenticode Certificate

 Additional certificate options will be available for AIR 1.5. At the time this book went to press, this list had not been finalized.

You can use one of these certificates to sign your AIR application. This causes the installer to appear differently, demonstrating that the publisher of the application has been verified. The name of the publisher will also be displayed (Figure 1-16).

You can read more about code-signing certificates for AIR at these addresses:

- VeriSign: *http://www.verisign.com/products-services/security-services/code-signing/*
- Thawte: *http://www.thawte.com/code-signing/*

1.7 Understanding Synchronous and Asynchronous Programming in AIR

Problem

You need to determine which programming method is appropriate for working with the local database and the file system in your AIR application.

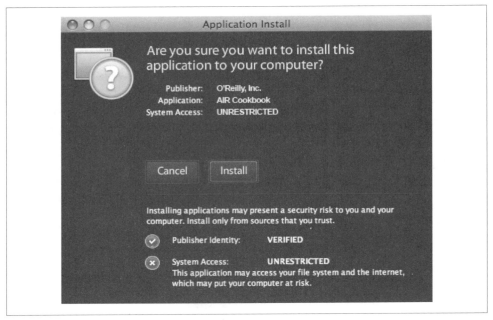

Figure 1-16. Installation dialog box with a commercial certificate

Solution

Weigh the benefits of both synchronous and asynchronous programming for your specific situation.

Discussion

Most developers who have worked in Flash or JavaScript are used to a synchronous programming model. This just means that each line of code is executed and completed before moving to the next line. In most situations, this works fine; however, in some circumstances, this is not ideal.

Both the file system API and the API for the SQLite embedded database have synchronous and asynchronous methods for many pieces of functionality. The following examples specifically highlight the benefits of each model in relation to the file system API. (The file system API is covered in Chapter 9.)

Advantages of Synchronous Programming

One main advantage to synchronous programming is having less code that is less complex. This can be a big advantage when working with a prototype or wireframe application. Consider this ActionScript example:

```
var myFile:File = File.documentsDirectory.resolvePath("textFile.txt");
var fileStream:FileStream = new FileStream();
```

```
fileStream.open(myFile, FileMode.READ);
var fileData:String = fileStream.readUTFBytes(fileStream.bytesAvailable);
fileStream.close();
```

In this example, the open method of the FileStream class is completed before moving on to the next line. In most cases, this is not a problem, but what if the file is a very large file? With synchronous programming, the application is frozen while this open method is executing, so no user interaction is possible until this method has finished executing.

Advantages of Asynchronous Programming

Asynchronous programming provides the best experience for the user. You have more code and have to respond to specific events, but the user can still interact with the application. The following code block has the same functionality as the code in the synchronous sample, but in this case it uses the asynchronous versions of the File Stream class's open method, openAsync:

```
var myFile:File = File.documentsDirectory.resolvePath("textFile.txt");
var fileStream:FileStream = new FileStream();
fileStream.addEventListener(Event.COMPLETE,handleComplete);
fileStream.openAsync(myFile,FileMode.READ);

function handleComplete(event:Event):void {
    var data:String = fileStream.readUTFBytes(fileStream.bytesAvailable);
    fileStream.close();
}
```

In this case, the code continues to execute after the openAsync method, but an event listener needed to be added to the instance of the FileStream class. This let the application know when the method had finished executing. Although this may seem like only a little extra code, the amount of extra code needed can increase exponentially when asynchronous method calls are chained together.

> Throughout this book, you will see that a majority of the examples are asynchronous. This has been done on purpose. First, as mentioned earlier, it provides the best experience for the end user. Second, if a developer can program asynchronously, transitioning to synchronous programming is easy. However, the reverse is not true. All the examples could be easily converted to synchronous programming if needed.

CHAPTER 2

Application Settings

Because AIR moves beyond the browser, your development environment is no longer fixed. Now you can control many different facets of the application including its appearance, positioning, size, and transparency. All these settings as well as information about the application's identity are contained in a single XML file called the *application descriptor file*.

Each AIR application is required to have an application descriptor file. The way you work with this information is different depending on which platform you are using to develop your AIR applications. In most situations, developers building Flex- or JavaScript-based AIR applications edit the application descriptor file's XML directly, while Flash developers use the GUI tool included with Flash CS3 and CS4. However, Flash developers who want to develop multilingual AIR applications or interact with the browser API need to forego the GUI and manually edit the application descriptor file.

Mastering the application descriptor file is essential to AIR development. These recipes will help you position and configure your application windows, set application identification information, and set the installation location.

2.1 Targeting a Specific Version of AIR

Problem

You need to ensure that your application is targeting version 1.5 of AIR.

Solution

Specify the version of the runtime in the XML namespace within the application descriptor file.

Discussion

The XML namespace that is referenced in the `application` node of the application descriptor file is what tells the compiler which version of AIR you are targeting. Because AIR 1.5 is the latest release of AIR, you will want to be sure that your opening `application` tag has the XML namespace defined as follows:

```
<?xml version="1.0" encoding="UTF-8"?>
<application xmlns="http://ns.adobe.com/air/application/1.5">
...
</application>
```

For example, if you were targeting the previous version of AIR, you could change the `1.5` in the XML namespace to `1.1`.

2.2 Setting the Application ID

Problem

You need to enable the runtime to distinguish your AIR application from other AIR applications.

Solution

Set the application ID in the application descriptor file; this required ID serves as a unique identifier for each AIR application.

Discussion

The most important setting in the application descriptor file, the application ID, is a piece of the unique identification signature for each AIR application. Because of the importance of this setting, you should set this value immediately upon creating your application. Also, you should avoid changing this value once you've set it.

The end user of your application will not see the application ID while installing or using your application. In most cases, developers use *reverse domain notation* for the application ID. For example, if you owned the domain *http://oreilly.com* and you wanted to create an application named AIR Cookbook, you could reverse the order of the domain and then add the name of your application. This would result in an application ID of `com.oreilly.aircookbook`. If you choose a domain you own or control, it will help ensure that your application ID is unique.

In reality, the application ID is one piece of the identification puzzle. In addition to the application ID, your application also has a publisher ID. The publisher ID is derived from the signing certificate used to create the AIR application file. The runtime uses the combination of these two items to identify your AIR application.

If a user has your application installed, it can be updated only by an application that has the same application ID and publisher ID. The only exception to this rule is if you create an AIR package with the migrate option, which lets you migrate the application from one certificate to another.

If you do need to migrate your application from one certificate to another, you can use the adt command-line tool that is included with the AIR SDK. This tool allows your application to work with two signing certificates: the old certificate and the new updated certificate. If you fail to use this tool, AIR tries to install multiple versions of your application, or in some cases it won't install your application at all.

Flex/JavaScript

In both Flex and HTML/JavaScript AIR applications, you set the application ID by manually editing the application descriptor file. You use the id node to set the application ID:

```xml
<?xml version="1.0" encoding="utf-8" ?>
<application xmlns="http://ns.adobe.com/air/application/1.5">

    <id>com.oreilly.aircookbook</id>
    ...

</application>
```

Flash

In Flash, you set the application ID using the Application & Installer Settings dialog box (Figure 2-1), which you can find in the Command menu. The application ID of the current application is in the ID field in the dialog box. (When you create a new AIR application in Flash, you first have to save the Flash file before you can launch the Application & Installer Settings dialog box.)

2.3 Setting the Application Name and Filename

Problem

You need to give your AIR application a name for the installer as well as a name for the executable file on the end user's computer.

Solution

Set the name and filename of your AIR application in the application descriptor file.

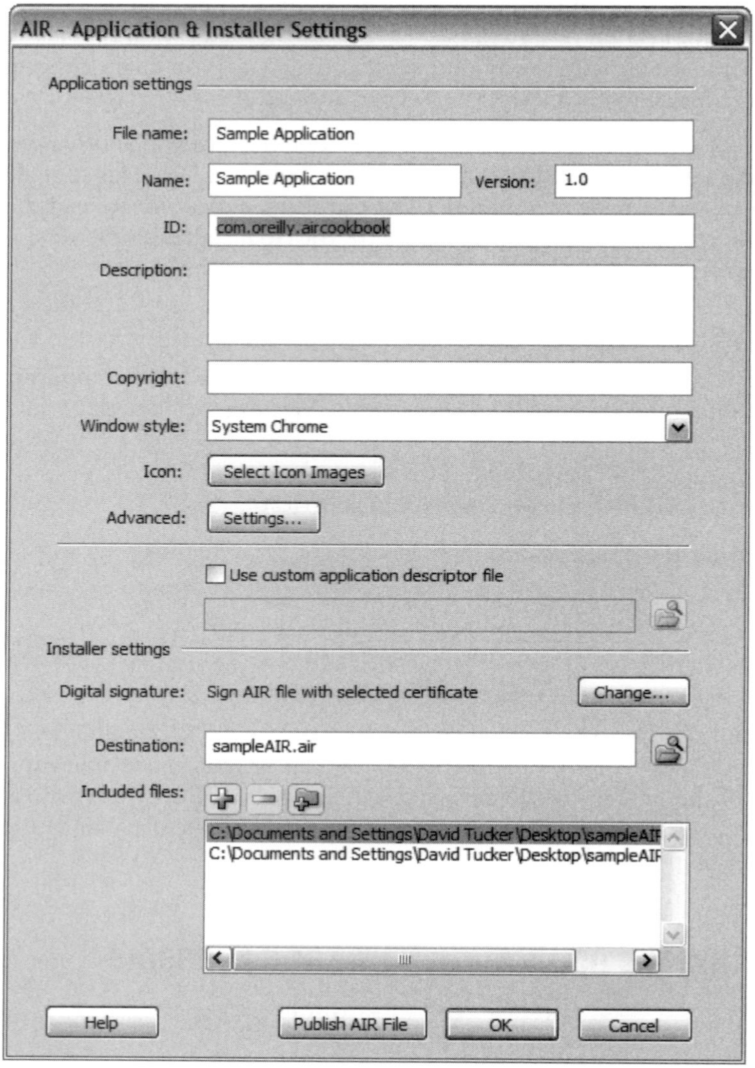

Figure 2-1. Setting the application ID in Flash

Discussion

Two additional items in the application descriptor file let you customize identification information about your application: the name and the filename. Unlike the application ID, the name and filename are visible to the end user and are not part of the way the runtime identifies applications.

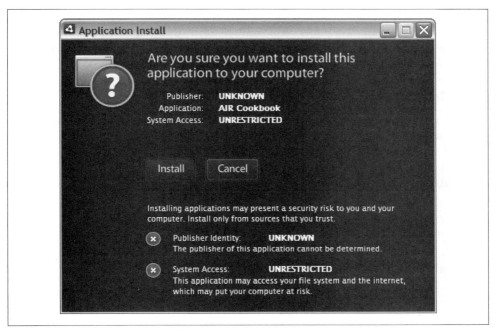

Figure 2-2. Initial application installation screen

Figure 2-3. Final application installation screen

The application name appears in multiple locations. The user first encounters it on the application installer's initial screens (Figure 2-2 and Figure 2-3). The application name also appears in the taskbar (Windows) or Dock (Mac) for your application.

The filename determines the name of the executable file for your application as well as the name of the installation folder. For example, if the filename of your application is *AIRCookbook* and it is installed in the default location on a Windows computer, the path to the executable file will be *C:\Program Files\AIRCookbook\AIRCookbook.exe*.

Flex/JavaScript

In Flex and HTML/JavaScript AIR applications, you set the name and filename settings by manually editing the application descriptor file. In the default template, these values immediately follow the application ID, as shown here:

```
<?xml version="1.0" encoding="utf-8" ?>
<application xmlns="http://ns.adobe.com/air/application/1.5">

    <id>com.oreilly.aircookbook</id>
    <filename>AIRCookbook</filename>
    <name>AIR Cookbook</name>
    ...

</application>
```

Flash

In Flash, you set the name and filename settings in the Application & Installer Settings dialog box, as shown in Figure 2-4.

2.4 Setting the Application Version

Problem

You need to distinguish between different versions of your application.

Solution

Designate a version string for your AIR application as required by the application descriptor file.

Discussion

The version setting in the application descriptor file is not required to be a number. For example, you could set your application version to be `Alpha 2` or simply `2.0.1`. In addition, it's not required that your version string be sequential. This is because the version number is parsed as a string and not a number. In many ways, you decide how you will define the versioning of your application.

The version string is crucial, however, when it comes to updating your application. The updating process requires you know both the current version string and the new version string.

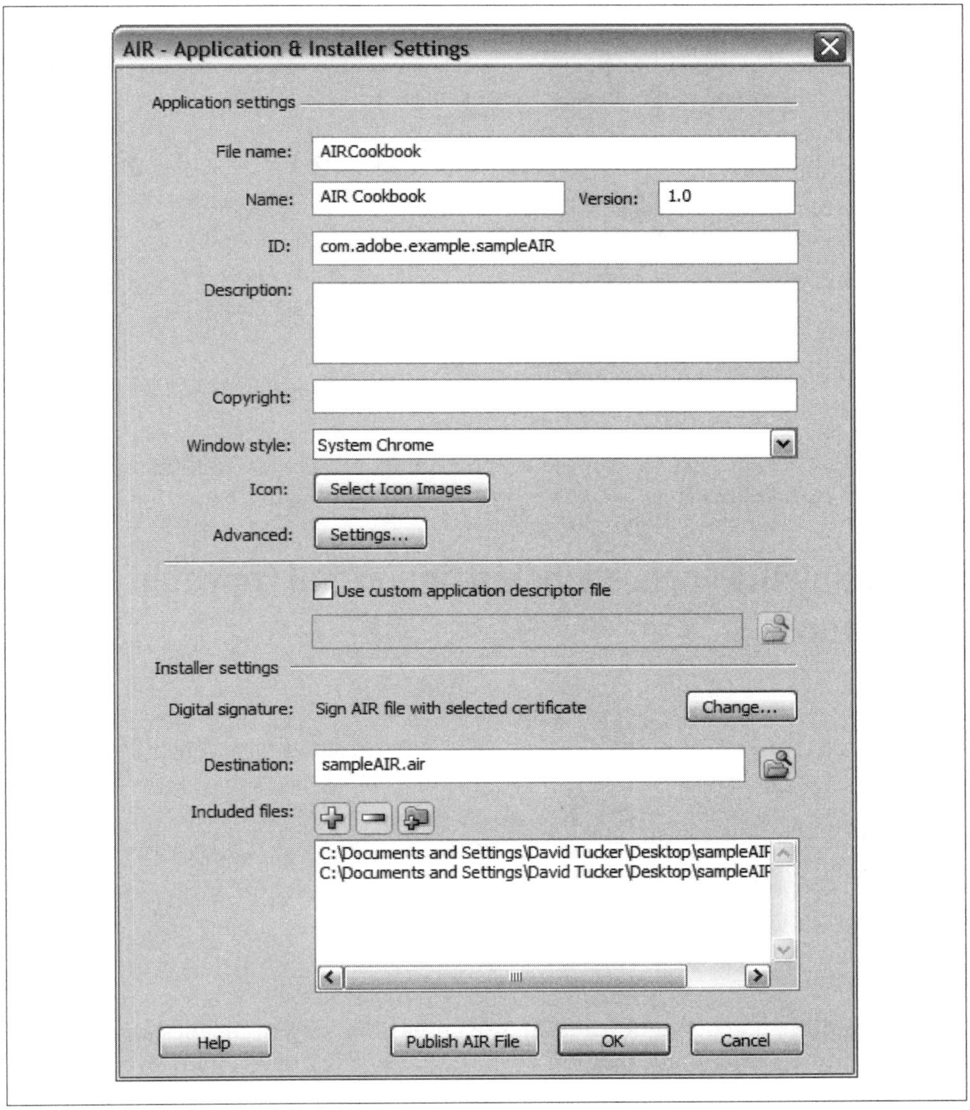

Figure 2-4. Setting the name and filename settings in Flash

Another important point to understand is that although the runtime can distinguish between two different versions of an application even if they both have the same version number, end users as well as developers can easily become confused if a consistent versioning string is not in place.

Flex/JavaScript

In Flex and HTML/JavaScript AIR applications, you set the version string by modifying the application descriptor file directly. For example:

```
<?xml version="1.0" encoding="utf-8" ?>
<application xmlns="http://ns.adobe.com/air/application/1.5">

    <id>com.oreilly.aircookbook</id>
    <filename>AIRCookbook</filename>
    <name>AIR Cookbook</name>
    <version>1.1</version>
    ...

</application>
```

Flash

In Flash AIR applications, you set the version number in the Version field of the Application & Installer Settings dialog box (shown earlier in Figure 2-4).

2.5 Editing the Application Description and Copyright Information

Problem

You want to give the end user more information about your application and your company, both during the installation process and after the application is installed.

Solution

Specify a description and copyright information for your AIR application in the application descriptor file.

Discussion

The description and copyright values in the application descriptor files are both optional but provide useful information to the end user. Any description you specify is displayed in the application installer (Figure 2-5). Your users will see this dialog box after they download your application file and start the installation progress.

Mac OS displays any copyright information and filename you provide in the About dialog box for your application (Figure 2-6). Currently, this information is not displayed for the Windows version of your application. On a Mac, the About dialog box also displays filename and version information.

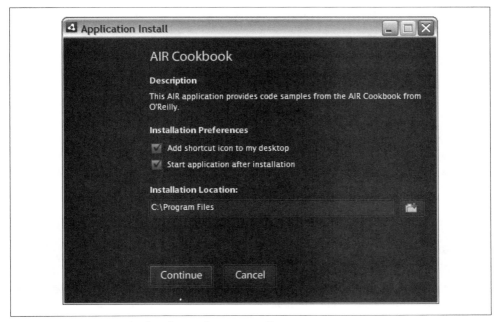

Figure 2-5. Description displayed in application installer

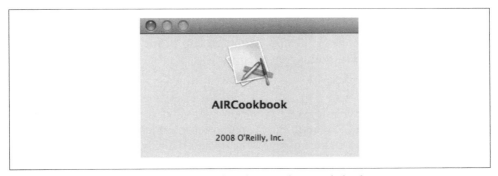

Figure 2-6. Copyright information displayed in about application dialog box

Flex/JavaScript

In Flex and HTML/JavaScript AIR applications, you specify the copyright and description settings by modifying the application descriptor file directly, as shown here:

```xml
<?xml version="1.0" encoding="utf-8" ?>
<application xmlns="http://ns.adobe.com/air/application/1.5">

    <id>com.oreilly.aircookbook</id>
    <filename>AIRCookbook</filename>
    <name>AIR Cookbook</name>
    <version>1.1</version>
```

```
<description>This AIR application provides code samples from the AIR Cookbook
from O'Reilly.</description>
    <copyright>2008 O'Reilly, Inc.</copyright>

    ...

</application>
```

Flash

In Flash AIR applications, you enter the description and copyright information in the
corresponding fields of the Application & Installer Settings dialog box (shown earlier
in Figure 2-4).

2.6 Editing the Initial Window Settings

Problem

You need to create an initial window that is 640 × 480 pixels with a minimum size of
320 × 240 and a maximum size of 800 × 600. In addition, the window needs to be
maximizable, minimizable, resizable, and visible when the application launches. The
initial window will be positioned 10 pixels below the top of the desktop and 10 pixels
from the left edge of the desktop.

Solution

Use the `initialWindow` node in the application descriptor file to configure the initial
window that is launched by your application.

Discussion

The `initialWindow` node enables you to configure virtually every aspect of the window
your application launches. In addition to setting these values in the application descriptor file, you can also change many of these values at runtime within your application by editing the window's properties. The many child nodes that set the values of
different properties for the initial window are as follows:

- `content`: The `content` node is required, and it sets the content for the window. In
  an HTML/JavaScript application, this is the name of the HTML file for the initial
  window. In Flex Builder and Flash, this value is populated for you automatically.

- `title`: You use the optional `title` node to designate the title of the initial window.
  If this value is not defined, the name of the application is used for the title.

- `systemChrome`: AIR applications can either use the default operating system look
  and feel for an application or use a custom look and feel. You can set this node to
  either `standard` for the default look or `none` if you plan to add a custom look. Unlike
  many of the other properties, this value cannot be changed at runtime.

- transparent: AIR application can have transparent windows. This requires extra system resources but can enhance the visual experience of an application. This node can be set to true or false.

- visible: In some situations you may want the initial window to be hidden until some task has been completed. In these cases, you can set the visible property to false and make it visible again from within the application.

- minimizable, maximizable, and resizable: In situations where you need to control how the user interacts with the initial window, you can set whether the user can maximize, minimize, and resize your application. Each of the corresponding nodes can be set to true or false, and they all are true by default.

- width and height: Using these nodes, you can set the width and height of the initial window. In the case of Flash and Flex, the initial window's width and height are set by the SWF if these values are undefined.

- x and y: x and y nodes correspond to the x and y pixel coordinates at which the application will be placed on the desktop.

- minSize and maxSize: If the resizable value is set to true, you can control to what extent the user can resize the application. If you set a pixel value for these nodes, the user will be able to resize the application no larger than the maxSize and no smaller than the minSize.

Flex/JavaScript

In Flex and HTML/JavaScript applications, you set the initial window settings by modifying the application descriptor file directly, as in the following example:

```
<?xml version="1.0" encoding="utf-8" ?>
<application xmlns="http://ns.adobe.com/air/application/1.5">

    <id>com.oreilly.aircookbook</id>
    <filename>AIRCookbook</filename>
    <name>AIR Cookbook</name>
    <version>1.1</version>
    <description>This AIR application provides code samples from the AIR Cookbook
from O'Reilly.</description>
    <copyright>2008 O'Reilly, Inc.</copyright>

    <initialWindow>
        <content>AIRCookbook.swf</content>
        <systemChrome>standard</systemChrome>
        <transparent>false</transparent>
        <visible>true</visible>
        <width>640</width>
        <height>480</height>
        <x>10</x>
        <y>10</y>
        <minSize>320 240</minSize>
        <maxSize>800 600</maxSize>
        <maximizable>true</maximizable>
```

```
            <minimizable>true</minimizable>
            <resizable>true</resizable>
        </initialWindow>

    </application>
```

Flash

In Flash, you use the Advanced Settings dialog box (Figure 2-7) to set the initial window
settings. You access this dialog box by clicking the Settings button in the Application
& Installer Settings dialog box (shown earlier in Figure 2-4).

2.7 Setting the Installation Folder for an Application

Problem

You want your AIR application to have a different default value for the installation
folder.

Solution

Define a different default folder name in the `installFolder` node of the application
descriptor.

Discussion

On each platform that AIR supports, the base path for AIR applications is the default
location for programs on the specific operating system. Ordinarily, AIR installs your
application in this default directory, but if you specify a folder in the `installFolder`
node, AIR installs your application in that folder.

This can be especially useful if you want to install a set of specific applications in a
single folder. For example, if the AIR Cookbook application provided a set of utilities,
the `installFolder` name could be set to `OReilly`, and then each application would be
installed in that folder. On Windows, this directory will be a subdirectory of the Program Files directory. On a Mac, this directory will be a subdirectory of the Applications
directory.

Flex/JavaScript

To set the `installFolder` value in a Flex or HTML/JavaScript application, you must
edit the application descriptor file directly, as shown here:

```
    <?xml version="1.0" encoding="utf-8" ?>
    <application xmlns="http://ns.adobe.com/air/application/1.5">

        <id>com.oreilly.aircookbook</id>
        <filename>AIRCookbook</filename>
```

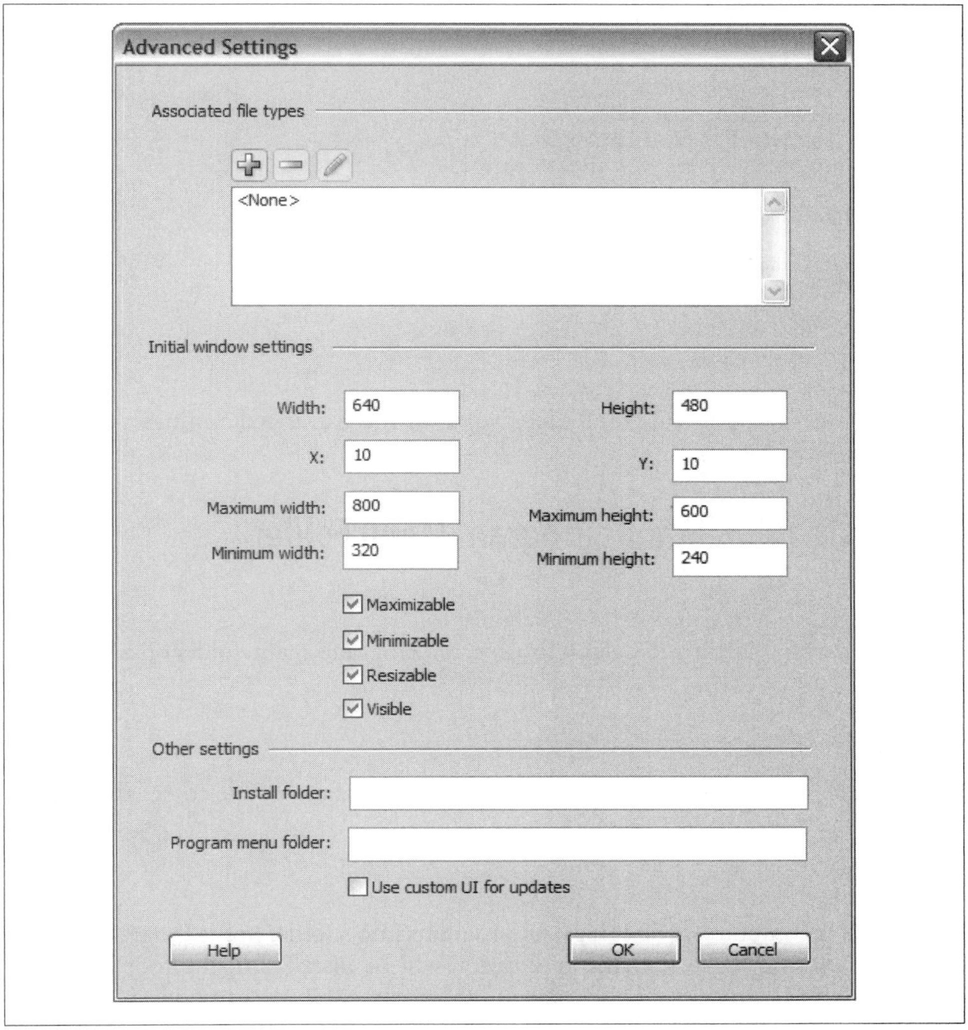

Figure 2-7. Advanced Settings dialog box in Flash

```
<name>AIR Cookbook</name>
<version>1.1</version>
<description>This AIR application provides code samples from the AIR Cookbook
from O'Reilly.</description>
<copyright>2008 O'Reilly, Inc.</copyright>

<initialWindow>
    <content>AIRCookbook.swf</content>
    <systemChrome>standard</systemChrome>
    <transparent>false</transparent>
    <visible>true</visible>
    <width>640</width>
```

```
        <height>480</height>
        <x>10</x>
        <y>10</y>
        <minSize>320 240</minSize>
        <maxSize>800 600</maxSize>
        <maximizable>true</maximizable>
        <minimizable>true</minimizable>
        <resizable>true</resizable>
    </initialWindow>

    <installFolder>OReilly</installFolder>

</application>
```

Flash

In Flash, you specify the `installFolder` value in the Advanced Settings dialog box (shown earlier in Figure 2-7).

2.8 Setting the Default Program Menu Folder

Problem

You want your application to default to a specific Programs menu folder on a Windows computer.

Solution

Use the `programMenuFolder` node of the application descriptor file to set the default Programs menu folder.

Discussion

On Windows computers, you can group programs into a folder in the Programs menu. By default, a shortcut to the AIR application will be installed in the root Programs folder, but you can specify a folder name in the `programMenuFolder` node.

For example, if you had a group of AIR applications that all were related to AIR Cookbook, you could set the `programMenuFolder` value to `AIR Cookbook`. When that application was installed on a Windows machine, a program folder named AIR Cookbook would be created with a shortcut to your application in it.

This setting has no effect if the application is installed on a Mac.

Flex/JavaScript

To set `programMenuFolder` for a Flex or HTML/JavaScript application, you edit the application descriptor file directly. For example:

```
<?xml version="1.0" encoding="utf-8" ?>
<application xmlns="http://ns.adobe.com/air/application/1.5">

    <id>com.oreilly.aircookbook</id>
    <filename>AIRCookbook</filename>
    <name>AIR Cookbook</name>
    <version>1.1</version>
    <description>This AIR application provides code samples from the AIR Cookbook
from O'Reilly.</description>
    <copyright>2008 O'Reilly, Inc.</copyright>

    <initialWindow>
        <content>AIRCookbook.swf</content>
        <systemChrome>standard</systemChrome>
        <transparent>false</transparent>
        <visible>true</visible>
        <width>640</width>
        <height>480</height>
        <x>10</x>
        <y>10</y>
        <minSize>320 240</minSize>
        <maxSize>800 600</maxSize>
        <maximizable>true</maximizable>
        <minimizable>true</minimizable>
        <resizable>true</resizable>
    </initialWindow>

    <installFolder>OReilly</installFolder>
    <programMenuFolder>AIR Cookbook</programMenuFolder>

</application>
```

Flash

In Flash, specify the `programMenuFolder` setting in the Other Settings section of the Advanced Settings dialog box (shown earlier in Figure 2-7), which you access via the Application & Installer Settings dialog box.

2.9 Setting a Custom Application Icon

Problem

You need to brand your application with a specific icon.

Solution

Set the custom icon in the application descriptor file for your application.

Discussion

A default set of application icons comes with the AIR SDK. In addition, both Mac and Windows provide a default icon for applications that do not have a predefined icon. In most cases, however, you will want to define an application icon that is specific to your application.

In both Windows and Mac, the application icon is used in multiple locations at different sizes. For example, in Windows the application icon appears on the desktop and also next to the title of the application's initial window in the taskbar. In the application descriptor file, AIR lets you define up to four different icons for these sizes and uses.

When you add icon files to your AIR application, the images must be in PNG format. AIR converts these images to the necessary format for each operating system. In addition, if you provide only the largest size of the icon, AIR will resize that image for the smaller icons, but in most cases resizing the image yourself will result in better quality.

Flex/JavaScript

In Flex and HTML/JavaScript applications, you can add a custom icon to your application by editing the application descriptor file directly. These settings exist in the `icon` node. The four child nodes of the `icon` node are `image16x16`, `image32x32`, `image48x48`, and `image128x128`, which relate to the sizes of each needed icon.

The following example assumes you have a folder named icon with the referenced images in it:

```xml
<?xml version="1.0" encoding="utf-8" ?>
<application xmlns="http://ns.adobe.com/air/application/1.5">

    <id>com.oreilly.aircookbook</id>
    <filename>AIRCookbook</filename>
    <name>AIR Cookbook</name>
    <version>1.1</version>
    <description>This AIR application provides code samples from the AIR Cookbook
from O'Reilly.</description>
    <copyright>2008 O'Reilly, Inc.</copyright>

    <initialWindow>
        <content>AIRCookbook.swf</content>
        <systemChrome>standard</systemChrome>
        <transparent>false</transparent>
        <visible>true</visible>
        <width>640</width>
        <height>480</height>
        <x>10</x>
        <y>10</y>
        <minSize>320 240</minSize>
        <maxSize>800 600</maxSize>
        <maximizable>true</maximizable>
        <minimizable>true</minimizable>
        <resizable>true</resizable>
```

```
    </initialWindow>

    <installFolder>OReilly</installFolder>
    <programMenuFolder>AIR Cookbook</programMenuFolder>

    <icon>
        <image16x16>icon/icon-16.png</image16x16>
        <image32x32>icon/icon-32.png</image32x32>
        <image48x48>icon/icon-48.png</image48x48>
        <image128x128>icon/icon-128.png</image128x128>
    </icon>

</application>
```

Flash

In Flash, you set the application icon in the Icon Images dialog box (Figure 2-8), which you can launch by clicking the Select Icon Images button in the Application & Installer Settings dialog box.

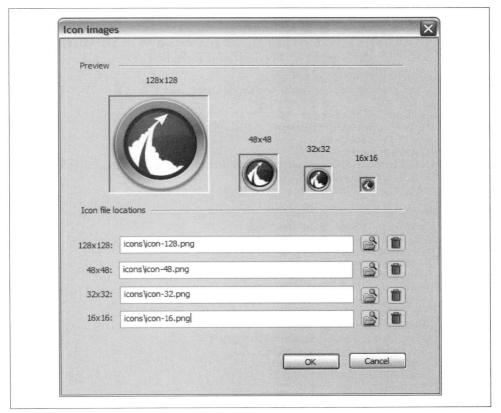

Figure 2-8. Setting the custom application icon in Flash

2.10 Allowing an AIR Application to Interact with the Browser

Problem

You need your application to be able to be launched from the browser.

Solution

Enable the application to interact with the AIR Browser API by setting the `allowBrowserInvocation` option in the application descriptor file to `true`.

Discussion

The Browser API allows an AIR application to interact with the browser through a SWF file. This gives the application the ability to be launched from the browser. By default, the `allowBrowserInvocation` setting is set to `false`, so you will need to enable it to take advantage of this functionality.

Flex/JavaScript

To enable your Flex or HTML/JavaScript AIR application to be launched from the browser, you modify the application descriptor file directly. For example:

```
<?xml version="1.0" encoding="utf-8" ?>
<application xmlns="http://ns.adobe.com/air/application/1.5">

    <id>com.oreilly.aircookbook</id>
    <filename>AIRCookbook</filename>
    <name>AIR Cookbook</name>
    <version>1.1</version>
    <description>This AIR application provides code samples from the AIR Cookbook
from O'Reilly.</description>
    <copyright>2008 O'Reilly, Inc.</copyright>

    <initialWindow>
        <content>AIRCookbook.swf</content>
        <systemChrome>standard</systemChrome>
        <transparent>false</transparent>
        <visible>true</visible>
        <width>640</width>
        <height>480</height>
        <x>10</x>
        <y>10</y>
        <minSize>320 240</minSize>
        <maxSize>800 600</maxSize>
        <maximizable>true</maximizable>
        <minimizable>true</minimizable>
        <resizable>true</resizable>
    </initialWindow>

    <installFolder>OReilly</installFolder>
    <programMenuFolder>AIR Cookbook</programMenuFolder>
```

```
<icon>
    <image16x16>icon/icon-16.png</image16x16>
    <image32x32>icon/icon-32.png</image32x32>
    <image48x48>icon/icon-48.png</image48x48>
    <image128x128>icon/icon-128.png</image128x128>
</icon>

<allowBrowserInvocation>true</allowBrowserInvocation>

</application>
```

Flash

Flash does not currently let you change the `allowBrowserInvocation` setting in the Application & Installer Settings dialog box. Because of this, you will need to tell Flash to include another application descriptor file.

Your application will already have an application descriptor file in the same directory as the Flash file. You can simply copy the values from this original file and paste them a new text file. Next, manually set the `allowBrowserInvocation` property of the new file to `true`. Finally, launch the Application & Installer Settings dialog box, select the "Use custom application descriptor file" option, and then browse to the file you just created.

2.11 Setting the Application to Handle All Updates

Problem

You need to ensure that users of your application always update to the newest version even though you previously distributed older versions of that application.

Solution

Set the `customUpdateUI` property of the application descriptor file to `true`.

Discussion

In many cases, it is advantageous to ensure users do not accidentally downgrade their application to an old version. In addition, you might need to take certain steps before an application is updated, such as backing up application data. In these cases, the `customUpdateUI` setting can be very useful.

When this property is set to `true`, AIR prevents the normal update process when a user clicks a packaged AIR file for an application that is already installed. Instead, AIR launches the existing application and dispatches an `InvokeEvent` to which it can respond. If the application is properly configured, it can ensure that the version the user clicked is the newest version and also check to see whether any last-minute maintenance is needed before the update process proceeds.

This setting does not change the install process for an application that is not yet installed on the user's computer.

Flex/JavaScript

To allow a Flex or HTML/JavaScript application to intercept the usual update process, you need to edit the application descriptor file directly. For example:

```
<?xml version="1.0" encoding="utf-8" ?>
<application xmlns="http://ns.adobe.com/air/application/1.5">

    <id>com.oreilly.aircookbook</id>
    <filename>AIRCookbook</filename>
    <name>AIR Cookbook</name>
    <version>1.1</version>
    <description>This AIR application provides code samples from the AIR Cookbook
from O'Reilly.</description>
    <copyright>2008 O'Reilly, Inc.</copyright>

    <initialWindow>
        <content>AIRCookbook.swf</content>
        <systemChrome>standard</systemChrome>
        <transparent>false</transparent>
        <visible>true</visible>
        <width>640</width>
        <height>480</height>
        <x>10</x>
        <y>10</y>
        <minSize>320 240</minSize>
        <maxSize>800 600</maxSize>
        <maximizable>true</maximizable>
        <minimizable>true</minimizable>
        <resizable>true</resizable>
    </initialWindow>

    <installFolder>OReilly</installFolder>
    <programMenuFolder>AIR Cookbook</programMenuFolder>

    <icon>
      <image16x16>icon/icon-16.png</image16x16>
      <image32x32>icon/icon-32.png</image32x32>
      <image48x48>icon/icon-48.png</image48x48>
      <image128x128>icon/icon-128.png</image128x128>
    </icon>

    <allowBrowserInvocation>true</allowBrowserInvocation>
    <customUpdateUI>true</customUpdateUI>

</application>
```

Flash

In Flash, you can configure your application to intercept the usual update process by selecting the "Use custom UI for updates" option in the Advanced Settings dialog box, which you launch from the Application & Installer Settings dialog box.

2.12 Determining the Application Version at Runtime

Problem

You need to determine the version of an application at runtime.

Solution

Extract the version number for the application's descriptor file at runtime.

Discussion

Often you may need to know the version number of an application. For AIR applications, the application version is not exposed in a variable; rather, you must extract it from the application's application descriptor file.

ActionScript

In ActionScript, the application descriptor file is exposed in the `NativeApplica` `tion.nativeApplication.applicationDescriptor` property. To extract the version number from your AIR application, you will need to first define the namespace in which the data is located. In this case, you can just use the first XML namespace and then extract the `version` property, as shown here:

```
private var airApplicationVersion:String = "";

private function getVersion():void
{
    // Get the Application Descriptor File
    var appXML:XML = NativeApplication.nativeApplication.applicationDescriptor;
    // Define the Default AIR Namespace
    var air:Namespace = appXML.namespaceDeclarations()[0];
    // Use E4X to Extract the Application Version
    this.airApplicationVersion = appXML.air::version;
}
```

JavaScript

In JavaScript, the application descriptor file is exposed in `air.NativeApplication.nati` `veApplication.applicationDescriptor`. By using a `DOMParser`, you can extract the data as XML and navigate through it to retrieve the application version:

```
var airApplicationVersion = "";
```

```
function getVersion()
{
    // Get Application Descriptor File
    var appXML = air.NativeApplication.nativeApplication.applicationDescriptor;
    // Parse the Application Descriptor File as XML
    var xmlObject = (new DOMParser()).parseFromString(appXML, "text/xml");
    // Get the Needed Values from the XML
    airApplicationVersion =
        xmlObject.getElementsByTagName('version')[0].firstChild.nodeValue;
}
```

2.13 Creating Multilingual AIR Installations

Problem

You need to display language-specific text in the installation dialog box.

Solution

Add language-specific text in the application descriptor file for the appropriate basic text property used in the installation dialog box.

Discussion

Within the application descriptor file, you can define multiple translations for the name and description nodes. In these cases, you can define child nodes that will include the locale-specific text.

 AIR supports these languages: Brazilian, Czech, Dutch, English, French, German, Italian, Japanese, Korean, Polish, Portuguese, Russian, Simplified Chinese, Spanish, Swedish, Traditional Chinese, and Turkish.

In the following example, the name and description are wrapped in a text tag. In addition, the language for that text is defined with the xml:lang="en" attribute. You could expand this to additional languages by including another text tag with a different standard country code and then the needed text in that tag.

```
<?xml version="1.0" encoding="utf-8" ?>
<application xmlns="http://ns.adobe.com/air/application/1.5">

    <id>com.oreilly.aircookbook</id>
    <filename>AIRCookbook</filename>
    <name>
        <text xml:lang="en">AIR Cookbook</text>
    </name>
    <version>1.1</version>
    <description>
        <text xml:lang="en"> This AIR application provides code samples from the
```

```
AIR Cookbook from O'Reilly.</text>
    </description>
    <copyright>2008 O'Reilly, Inc.</copyright>

    <initialWindow>
        <content>AIRCookbook.swf</content>
        <systemChrome>standard</systemChrome>
        <transparent>false</transparent>
        <visible>true</visible>
        <width>640</width>
        <height>480</height>
        <x>10</x>
        <y>10</y>
        <minSize>320 240</minSize>
        <maxSize>800 600</maxSize>
        <maximizable>true</maximizable>
        <minimizable>true</minimizable>
        <resizable>true</resizable>
    </initialWindow>

    <installFolder>OReilly</installFolder>
    <programMenuFolder>AIR Cookbook</programMenuFolder>

    <icon>
        <image16x16>icon/icon-16.png</image16x16>
        <image32x32>icon/icon-32.png</image32x32>
        <image48x48>icon/icon-48.png</image48x48>
        <image128x128>icon/icon-128.png</image128x128>
    </icon>

    <allowBrowserInvocation>true</allowBrowserInvocation>
    <customUpdateUI>true</customUpdateUI>

</application>
```

Flex/JavaScript

To add localization information in a Flex or HTML/JavaScript AIR application, you will need to edit your application descriptor file as demonstrated previously.

Flash

Flash does not let you add localization information in the Application & Installer Settings dialog box, so you need to tell Flash to include another application descriptor file.

Your application will already have an application descriptor file in the same directory as the Flash file. You can simply copy the values from this original file and paste them into a second, newly created file. Next, you can manually add your localization text in the new application descriptor file as demonstrated previously. Finally, launch the Application & Installer Settings dialog box, select the "Use custom application descriptor file" option, and then browse to the file you just created.

CHAPTER 3

Application Windows

The recipes in this chapter will demonstrate all the possibilities for using windows in your AIR application. In fact, when you run an AIR application, the first thing you see is the main application window. That first window is automatically created for you by AIR. You specify the properties and content of that first application window in the application descriptor file (the XML file that ends with -*app.xml*). You can also set some of the properties (such as `title`) in the application descriptor file using code (MXML, ActionScript, or JavaScript). Recipe 3.1 discusses setting the properties for the main application window.

In addition, when you are developing your AIR application with Flex, you can use the Flex chrome that is provided by the Flex Framework. Recipe 3.3 shows you that chrome while discussing how to launch an application window from within your AIR application.

Apart from the standard Flex chrome, one of the cool features of Adobe AIR is that you can create your own chrome. Recipe 3.9 will go into depth about creating windows with custom chrome, and you'll learn how to cast a drop shadow on the desktop around the borders of a custom chrome window in Recipe 3.15.

Apart from your initial main window, of course it is also possible to create other windows in your AIR application. Imagine, for example, that you want to make a multi-window application like a typical Internet browser or a panel-based application like Adobe Photoshop.

When working with windows in your AIR application, you will use the `NativeWindow` class. As you will see in Recipe 3.3, Flex does much of the hard work automatically, but ActionScript (Recipe 3.2) and JavaScript (Recipe 3.4) require more hand coding.

3.1 Changing the Main Application Window

Problem

You want to change the properties of the initial application window.

Solution

Change the values in the `initialWindow` node of the application descriptor file.

Discussion

In that application descriptor file, you'll see a node called `initialWindow`. This is how a typical empty `initialWindow` node looks:

```
<!-- Settings for the application's initial window. Required. -->
    <initialWindow>
        <!-- The main SWF or HTML file of the application. Required. -->
        <!-- Note: In Flex Builder, the SWF reference is set automatically. -->
        <content>[This value will be overwritten by Flex Builder in the output
app.xml]</content>

        <!-- The title of the main window. Optional. -->
        <!-- <title></title> -->

        <!-- The type of system chrome to use (either "standard" or "none").
Optional. Default standard. -->
        <!-- <systemChrome></systemChrome> -->

        <!-- Whether the window is transparent. Only applicable when systemChrome
is false. Optional. Default false. -->
        <!-- <transparent></transparent> -->

        <!-- Whether the window is initially visible. Optional. Default false. -->
        <!-- <visible></visible> -->

        <!-- Whether the user can minimize the window. Optional. Default true. -->
        <!-- <minimizable></minimizable> -->

        <!-- Whether the user can maximize the window. Optional. Default true. -->
        <!-- <maximizable></maximizable> -->

        <!-- Whether the user can resize the window. Optional. Default true. -->
        <!-- <resizable></resizable> -->

        <!-- The window's initial width. Optional. -->
        <!-- <width></width> -->

        <!-- The window's initial height. Optional. -->
        <!-- <height></height> -->

        <!-- The window's initial x position. Optional. -->
        <!-- <x></x> -->

        <!-- The window's initial y position. Optional. -->
        <!-- <y></y> -->

        <!-- The window's minimum size, specified as a width/height pair, such as
"400 200". Optional. -->
        <!-- <minSize></minSize> -->
```

```
        <!-- The window's initial maximum size, specified as a width/height pair,
    such as "1600 1200". Optional. -->
        <!-- <maxSize></maxSize> -->
    </initialWindow>
```

The content that can be loaded in a window is a SWF or HTML file. The path to that
SWF or HTML file is also the only attribute required in the initialWindow node. This
value is automatically filled in when you make a release build of your application using
Flex, Flash, or Dreamweaver.

Many configuration options for your initial window are not too complicated to understand: title, visible, maximizable, minimizable, resizable, width, height, x (the initial
x position), y (the initial y position), minSize, and maxSize. But two values require some
more clarification: systemChrome is the type of system chrome to use (standard or
none), and transparent specifies whether the window is transparent.

Window *chrome* is a set of controls for the window: title bar, title bar buttons, status
bar, resize gripper, and so on. To use custom chrome for your initial window, you first
have to set none as value for the systemChrome node. Then you can add your own chrome
controls to handle the interactions between a user and the window. You are also free
to make transparent (set the transparent node value to true) or even circular windows
if you like. Only windows that are not using the system chrome can be transparent.
When you have a transparent window, you can even click through to what is
"underneath."

3.2 Launching a New Window in ActionScript

Problem

You want to launch a new window from within your AIR application.

Solution

Use the NativeWindow class for creating native operating system windows with
ActionScript.

Discussion

When you want to launch a new window by using ActionScript (in the Flash authoring
environment or in an <mx:Script> block), first you have to create an instance of the
NativeWindow class. You then pass to the NativeWindow constructor a NativeWindowInit
Options object, which defines how your new window will look.

You can set the following options for NativeWindowInitOptions:

- maximizable: This specifies whether your new window can be maximized.
- minimizable: This specifies whether your new window can be minimized.

- `resizable`: This specifies whether your new window can be resized.
- `systemChrome`: This specifies the chrome your new window will have (`standard` or `none`).
- `transparent`: This specifies whether your new window supports transparency. This is available only if `systemChrome` is set to `none`.
- `type`: This specifies your window's type (`normal`, `utility`, or `lightweight`).

As mentioned in the previous recipe, window *chrome* is a set of controls for the window: title bar, title bar buttons, status bar, resize gripper, and so on. Application windows on Windows computers feature a different chrome than application windows on Mac and Linux. If you use the value `standard` for `systemChrome`, your AIR application will have the default chrome of the user's operating system.

AIR's three window types combine chrome and visibility attributes to create three functional types of windows: normal, utility, and lightweight (Figure 3-1).

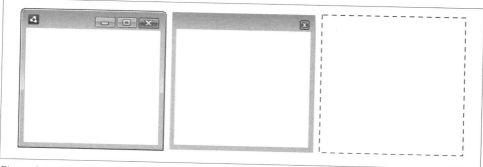

Figure 3-1. Overview of the different types of windows in AIR

Normal Window	Utility Window	Lightweight Window
Appears on the Windows taskbar or the Mac window menu	Does not appear on the Windows taskbar or the Mac window menu	Does not appear on the Windows taskbar or the Mac window menu
Chrome is fully available	Uses a slimmer version of the system chrome	Uses no system chrome

You can create lightweight windows only when `systemChrome` is set to `false`. This recipe and the next concentrates on creating normal windows, while Recipe 3.5 and Recipe 3.6 demonstrate how to create utility and lightweight windows.

The following example creates and launches a normal `NativeWindow` object (with the `standard` system chrome applied) and sets `NativeWindowInitOptions`. When the application starts, a second window is automatically instantiated and positioned on the right side of the initial application window.

```
<?xml version="1.0" encoding="utf-8"?>
<mx:WindowedApplication xmlns:mx="http://www.adobe.com/2006/mxml"
```

```
    applicationComplete="launchWindow()"
    title="First Window"
    layout="absolute">

    <mx:Script >
        <![CDATA[
            private function launchWindow():void{

                //define the init options
                var options:NativeWindowInitOptions =
new NativeWindowInitOptions();
                options.maximizable = true;
                options.minimizable = true;
                options.resizable = true;
                options.systemChrome = NativeWindowSystemChrome.STANDARD;
                options.transparent = false;
                options.type = NativeWindowType.NORMAL;

                //define a new window
                var window:NativeWindow = new NativeWindow(options);
                window.title="Second Window";
                window.width = 200;
                window.height = this.nativeWindow.height;
                window.x = this.nativeWindow.x + this.nativeWindow.width;
                window.y = this.nativeWindow.y;

                //show the window
                window.activate();
            }
        ]]>
    </mx:Script>
</mx:WindowedApplication>
```

As you can see in the code, launching a new native window involves three steps:

1. Define the initialization options by creating a new `NativeWindowInitOptions` object and setting the properties you want.

2. Define a window by creating a new `NativeWindow` object and passing the `Native WindowInitOptions` object to the constructor.

3. Show the newly created window by calling the **activate** method of the `Native Window` object. Activating a window will make the window visible, bring the window to the front, and give the keyboard and mouse focus. If you prefer, you can also show a window by setting the **visible** property to **true** (the default is **false**).

To add content, such as a SWF file in the newly created window, you add it to the display list of the **stage** property.

The following example loads a SWF file in the newly created window, and when the content is fully loaded, it displays the new window. Make sure you add the content to the **stage** property and not to the `NativeWindow` instance:

```
<?xml version="1.0" encoding="utf-8"?>
<mx:WindowedApplication xmlns:mx="http://www.adobe.com/2006/mxml"
```

```
            applicationComplete="launchWindow()"
            title="First Window"
            layout="absolute">

    <mx:Script >
        <![CDATA[

            private var window:NativeWindow ;

            private function launchWindow():void{
                //define the init options
                var options:NativeWindowInitOptions =
new NativeWindowInitOptions();
                options.maximizable = true;
                options.minimizable = true;
                options.resizable = true;
                options.systemChrome = NativeWindowSystemChrome.STANDARD;
                options.transparent = false;
                options.type = NativeWindowType.NORMAL;

                //define a new window
                window = new NativeWindow(options);
                window.title="Second Window";
                window.width = 200;
                window.height = this.nativeWindow.height;
                window.x = this.nativeWindow.x + this.nativeWindow.width;
                window.y = this.nativeWindow.y;
                var ldr:Loader = new Loader()
                ldr.load(new URLRequest("assets/Content.swf"));
                ldr.contentLoaderInfo.addEventListener(Event.COMPLETE,showWindow);
            }
            private function showWindow(event:Event):void{
                //set stage properties of new window
                window.stage.scaleMode = StageScaleMode.NO_SCALE;
                window.stage.align = StageAlign.TOP_LEFT;

                //add loaded content to the stage of the window
                window.stage.addChild(event.target.loader);

                //show the window
                window.activate();
            }
        ]]>
    </mx:Script>
</mx:WindowedApplication>
```

3.3 Launching a New Window (Flex)

Problem

You want to launch a new window from within your AIR application.

Solution

Use the `<mx:Window>` component (available in the Flex Framework).

Discussion

If you are using Flex to create your AIR application, you can create application windows by creating an MXML component based on one of the `<mx:WindowedApplication>` or `<mx:Window>` classes of the Flex Framework.

The `WindowedApplication` component defines the application container you use to create Flex-based AIR applications. Because this is a container object (it can contain only other Flex components), it defines the layout of the initial window of the AIR application. All the content you add in the `WindowedApplication` will become the content that is shown in the initial window loaded by the AIR application.

The `Window` component is a container for any additional window that you want to show in your AIR application. It has own window controls. Keep in mind that this component cannot be nested inside any other component; it's a *top-level layout container*.

The best way to use a `Window` component in your AIR application is to make a custom component that uses the `Window` component as the root tag for your MXML component. You can then add all your visual controls like you do inside another container. Finally, you can create an instance of your custom `Window` class in your AIR application and launch the window.

It is essential to understand that the `WindowedApplication` and `Window` components both have an underlying `NativeWindow` object that they use for creating and controlling the native operating system windows. The `NativeWindow` class is used in ActionScript to trigger a new window (Recipe 3.2). You can access a reference to that `NativeWindow` object by using the `stage.nativeWindow` property of any display object on that `Native Window`'s or `Window`'s stage. The example that follows adds Flex components as children to the `NativeWindow` component or custom `Window` component.

The example shows how to create a new instance of the `Window` class and set the properties the window needs. The code launches two windows.

```
<?xml version="1.0" encoding="utf-8"?>
<mx:WindowedApplication xmlns:mx="http://www.adobe.com/2006/mxml"
    applicationComplete="init()"
    layout="absolute"
    title="First Window"
    >

    <mx:Script >
        <![CDATA[

            private function init():void{
                secondWindow.open(true);
            }
        ]]>
```

```
        </mx:Script>

        <mx:Window id="secondWindow"  title="Second Window"
            width="400" height="400"
            layout="vertical"
            systemChrome="standard"
            showFlexChrome="false"
            transparent="false"
            >
            <mx:Label text="This is my second window"/>

        </mx:Window>
    </mx:WindowedApplication>
```

First, the example sets the systemChrome node in the application descriptor file to none and the transparent value to true for the initial application window. You have to set following node values in the –app.xml file:

```
        <systemChrome>none</systemChrome>
        <transparent>true</transparent>
```

When you create windows in Flex with the <mx:WindowedApplication> or <mx:Window> components and set the systemChrome property to none, the Flex chrome (the set of controls for the window) is used automatically (see Figure 3-2).

Figure 3-2. The Flex chrome

The second window has the standard chrome (the default controls for the user's operating system) applied because the showFlexChrome property is set to false.

You can easily add child elements to the window MXML component to build the content for your newly created window. The best practice when creating application windows in Flex with <mx:Window> is to create a separate MXML file using the <mx:Window> tag as the root tag (custom Window component). The moment you want to launch your window, you can then activate your custom Window component by using ActionScript or by writing the MXML tag of your custom component.

The following code (*BrowserWindow.mxml*) shows you how to create a `Browser Window` component that extends the `Window` component:

```xml
<?xml version="1.0" encoding="utf-8"?>
<mx:Window xmlns:mx="http://www.adobe.com/2006/mxml"
    width="800" height="600" layout="vertical"
    title="BrowserWindow"
    >
    <mx:Script >
        <![CDATA[
            private  var url:String;
            public function set theUrl(url:String):void{
                this.url = url;
                browser.location = url;
            }
            public function get theUrl():String{
                return (this.url);
            }

        ]]>
    </mx:Script>
    <mx:Label text="MY BROWSERWINDOW" fontWeight="bold" fontSize="17"
        textAlign="center" width="100%" height="50"/>
    <mx:HTML id="browser" width="100%" height="100%"/>
</mx:Window>
```

To use this component in your main AIR application, you just need to instantiate and open it. In the following example, the `BrowserWindow` component is automatically launched when the application is completely loaded:

```xml
<?xml version="1.0" encoding="utf-8"?>
<mx:WindowedApplication xmlns:mx="http://www.adobe.com/2006/mxml"
    applicationComplete="init()"
    layout="absolute"
    >
    <mx:Script>
        <![CDATA[
            import components.BrowserWindow;

            private function init():void{
                var browser:BrowserWindow = new BrowserWindow();
                browser.open(true);
                browser.theUrl = "http://www.newmovieclip.com";
            }
        ]]>
    </mx:Script>
</mx:WindowedApplication>
```

You can, of course, also use the `BrowserWindow` component as a Flex MXML tag instead of using ActionScript to instantiate it:

```xml
<?xml version="1.0" encoding="utf-8"?>
<mx:WindowedApplication xmlns:mx="http://www.adobe.com/2006/mxml"
    xmlns:browser="components.*"
    layout="absolute"
    >
```

```
<browser:BrowserWindow theUrl="http://www.newmovieclip.com" />

</mx:WindowedApplication>
```

This system of custom `Window` component development is the easiest way to work with a multiwindow application.

3.4 Launching a New Window (JavaScript)

Problem

You want to launch a new application window from within JavaScript and show HTML content that is in any security sandbox.

Solution

Make an instance of the `air.NativeWindow` instance, or use the standard JavaScript `Window.open` method to load HTML content.

Discussion

As you did with ActionScript (see Recipe 3.2), you can also launch a `NativeWindow` instance when developing with HTML and JavaScript.

The following example shows you how to launch a native window from within JavaScript:

```
<!DOCTYPE html PUBLIC "-//W3C//DTD XHTML 1.0 Transitional//EN"
"http://www.w3.org/TR/xhtml1/DTD/xhtml1-transitional.dtd">
<html xmlns="http://www.w3.org/1999/xhtml">
<head>
<meta http-equiv="Content-Type" content="text/html; charset=utf-8" />

<script src="AIRAliases.js" type="text/javascript"></script>
<script type="text/javascript">

function launchWindow(){
    nativeWindow.title = "First window";
    nativeWindow.width = 400;
    nativeWindow.height = 400;
    //create the init options
    var options = new air.NativeWindowInitOptions();
    options.transparent=false;
    options.systemChrome=air.NativeWindowSystemChrome.STANDARD;
    options.type=air.NativeWindowType.NORMAL;
    //create the window
    var window = new air.NativeWindow(options);
    window.title = "Second window";
    window.width = 200;
    window.height = nativeWindow.height;
    window.x = nativeWindow.x + nativeWindow.width;
    window.y = nativeWindow.y;
```

```
    //activate and show the new window
    window.activate();
    }

</script>
<title>Launch a new window</title>
</head>
<body onload="launchWindow()">
</body>
</html>
```

Another way to launch a new window is by using the `Window.open` method, but when launching windows from within JavaScript to create HTML windows, you always have to keep in mind where your HTML content originates. That's where the application sandbox comes in. Content inside the application sandbox is content that is installed with your AIR application. No user interaction to initiate the loading is needed when you load an HTML document that is located in your application sandbox. If your content is running outside the application sandbox, the `Window.open` method can be called only in response to user interaction, such as a button click to start the loading process.

The following example shows how to open a new window and load the *form.html* page. The *form.html* page is located in the application sandbox. The *form.html* page looks like this:

```
<html>
<head>
<title>Sign up form</title>
</head>
<body leftmargin="20">
<FORM action="http://somesite.com/prog/adduser" method="post">
    First name: <INPUT type="text" name="firstname"><BR>
    Last name: <INPUT type="text" name="lastname"><BR>
    email: <INPUT type="text" name="email"><BR>
</FORM>
</body>
</html>
```

The example loads this form in a new window that is created by using the standard JavaScript `Window.open` method:

```
<html>
<head>
<meta http-equiv="Content-Type" content="text/html; charset=utf-8" />
<title>Window.open()method</title>

<script type="text/javascript">
    function init(){
        window.open("form.html","SignUpWindow","height=400,width=300");
    }
</script>
</head>
<body onload="init()">
```

```
    </body>
    </html>
```

 Note that the example is a simple HTML and JavaScript example and can also be run completely independently of AIR.

When you use the `Window.open` method, you have to pass the URL of the HTML content to load, a window name, and a string with all the window attributes you want to adjust (`width`, `height`, `top`, `left`, and so on). By default, this method creates a window with system chrome.

If you want to specify more options when creating an HTML window, use the `HTMLLoader.createRootWindow` method, which lets you specify the same creation options as you can with `NativeWindowInitOptions` in ActionScript. The method actually creates a `NativeWindow` object that contains an `HTMLLoader` object. The parameters you have to pass to the method are as follows:

- `visible`: Specifies whether the window is visible
- `windowInitOptions`: Specifies an object that holds the initialization options
- `scrollBarsVisible`: Specifies whether the window displays scroll bars
- `bounds`: Lets you set the window bounds as a `Rectangle` object (x, y, `width`, `height`)

The following example creates two windows once again but this time uses the `HTMLLoader.createRootWindow` method to specify many more creation options:

```html
<html>
<head>
<meta http-equiv="Content-Type" content="text/html; charset=utf-8" />
<title>Window.open()method</title>
<script src="AIRAliases.js" type="text/javascript"></script>
<script type="text/javascript">
    function init(){
        var options = new air.NativeWindowInitOptions();
        options.systemChrome = air.NativeWindowSystemChrome.STANDARD;
        options.type = air.NativeWindowType.NORMAL;
        options.maximizable = false;
        options.minimizable = false;
        options.resizable = false;

        var bounds = new air.Rectangle(200,250,250,150);
        newHTMLLoader = air.HTMLLoader.createRootWindow(true, options, true, bounds);
        newHTMLLoader.load(new air.URLRequest("form.html"));
    }
</script>
</head>
<body onLoad="init()">
</body>
</html>
```

Figure 3-3. The look of a typical utility window (shown in Windows Vista)

3.5 Creating Utility Windows

Problem

You want to create a utility window.

Solution

Use the `NativeWindowInitOptions.type` or `Window.type` (in the Flex Framework) property to set your window type to `utility`.

Discussion

Utility and lightweight (see Recipe 3.6) windows are two types of window that combine chrome and visibility attributes to make them look different from the normal system windows.

Utility windows (Figure 3-3) are different from a typical application window because they use a slimmer version of the system chrome. Also, they do not appear on the Windows taskbar or the Mac OS window menu.

To create a new utility window, you have to specify only the type of your newly created window.

ActionScript

When using ActionScript, you can set the `NativeWindowInitOptions.type` property to define a utility window:

```
var options:NativeWindowInitOptions = new NativeWindowInitOptions();
options.type = NativeWindowType.UTILITY;
//...
//...set other options
var window:NativeWindow = new NativeWindow(options);
window.activate();
```

JavaScript

With JavaScript, you can set the `air.NativeWindowInitOptions.type` property to define a utility window:

```
var options = new air.NativeWindowInitOptions();
options.type = air.NativeWindowType.UTILITY;
//...
//...set other options var bounds = new air.Rectangle(200,250,250,150);
newHTMLLoader = air.HTMLLoader.createRootWindow(true, options, true, bounds);
newHTMLLoader.load(new air.URLRequest("form.html"));
```

This example loads an HTML file in the utility window and defines the initialization options by passing the `NativeWindowInitOptions` object to the `createRootWindow` method of the `HTMLLoader`.

Flex

This example shows how easy it is to create a simple utility window and also adds a way to communicate between your utility window and your main application window. In the Flex Framework, you can extend the `<mx:Window>` component to create a simple options panel. In the options panel, you can define a `TextInput` field that lets you set the title of the main application window.

The custom `<example root>/components/OptionsPanel.mxml` component, which extends `<mx:Window>`, looks like this:

```
<?xml version="1.0" encoding="utf-8"?>
<mx:Window xmlns:mx="http://www.adobe.com/2006/mxml"
    layout="vertical"
    title="options"
        width="180" height="101" paddingLeft="10"
        paddingRight="10" paddingTop="10" paddingBottom="10">
        <mx:Script >
            <![CDATA[

                private function sendToMain():void{
                    var evt:Event = new Event("valueReceived");
                    dispatchEvent(evt);
                }
            ]]>
        </mx:Script>
        <mx:Label text="Change main window title :"/>
        <mx:TextInput id="titleTextInput" keyUp="sendToMain()"/>
        <mx:Button label="Close" textAlign="right" width="160"
    click="this.nativeWindow.close()"/>
</mx:Window>
```

When a user types in the text input field, a function `sendToMain` is called that dispatches a `valueReceived` event to notify the main application of the entry.

The main AIR application creates a new instance of the custom window type called `OptionsPanel` when the application is completely loaded and sets `type` to `NativeWindowType.UTILITY`.

The main application code is as follows:

```
<?xml version="1.0" encoding="utf-8"?>
<mx:WindowedApplication xmlns:mx="http://www.adobe.com/2006/mxml"
    layout="absolute" cornerRadius="0"
    applicationComplete="init()"
     fontSize="14">

    <mx:Script >
        <![CDATA[
            import components.OptionsPanel;

            private var optionsPanel:OptionsPanel

            private function init():void{
                optionsPanel  = new OptionsPanel();

                optionsPanel.type = NativeWindowType.UTILITY;

                //show the panel
                optionsPanel.open(true);

                //align the panel
                optionsPanel.nativeWindow.x = this.nativeWindow.x+
                  this.nativeWindow.width;
                optionsPanel.nativeWindow.y = this.nativeWindow.y;
                optionsPanel.addEventListener("valueReceived",showValue);
            }
            private function showValue(evt:Event):void{
                this.title = optionsPanel.titleTextInput.text;
            }
        ]]>
    </mx:Script>
</mx:WindowedApplication>
```

As you can see, the utility window (`optionsPanel`) is positioned next to the main application window. You also added an event listener to the `optionsPanel` object because you want to know when the user types something in the options window so you can set the title according to that value.

3.6 Creating Lightweight Windows

Problem

You want to create a lightweight window.

Figure 3-4. A lightweight window has no chrome.

Solution

Use the `NativeWindowInitOptions.type` or `Window.type` (in the Flex Framework) property to set your window type to `lightweight`.

Discussion

Lightweight and utility (see Recipe 3.5) windows are two types of window that combine chrome and visibility attributes to make them look different from the normal system windows.

A lightweight window is different from a typical application window because it has no system chrome; despite the dashed outline for illustrative purposes in Figure 3-4, there is actually nothing to see when you create a new lightweight window because no chrome is applied at all.

Lightweight windows do not appear on the Windows taskbar or in the Mac OS window menu; instead, they are typically used to create notification windows or applications that need a nonrectangular chrome. To create a lightweight window, make sure `systemChrome` is set to `none`, and then set the type of your window to the `NativeWindow Type.LIGHTWEIGHT` constant.

This recipe uses the same approach as you used with utility windows, but now you explicitly set `systemChrome` to `none` and set the window type to `NativeWindowType.LIGHT WEIGHT`. Because a lightweight window has no chrome applied, you will need to program your own window controls by using the techniques explained in Recipe 3.10, Recipe 3.11, and Recipe 3.12.

ActionScript/Flex

The `OptionsPanel` component for a lightweight window is similar to the one in Recipe 3.5. This time, however, you set the `showFlexChrome` property to `false` to apply the default Flex chrome to your windows. In addition, the elements reside in a `VBox` control

---

with a `backgroundColor` applied, so you can clearly see the lightweight window. The updated code for the `OptionsPanel` component is as follows:

```xml
<?xml version="1.0" encoding="utf-8"?>
<mx:Window xmlns:mx="http://www.adobe.com/2006/mxml"
    layout="vertical"
    title="options"
      width="180" height="101" paddingLeft="0" paddingRight="0"
      paddingTop="0" paddingBottom="0"
      showFlexChrome="false"> ><!-- show no default flex chrome -->
      <mx:Script >
          <![CDATA[

              private function sendToMain():void{
                  var evt:Event = new Event("valueReceived");
                  this.dispatchEvent(evt);
              }
          ]]>
      </mx:Script>
      <mx:VBox  width="100%" height="100%" backgroundColor="#7A7979"
          paddingBottom="10" paddingLeft="10"
          paddingRight="10" paddingTop="10">
      <mx:Label text="Change main window title :" color="#FFFFFF"/>
      <mx:TextInput id="titleTextInput" keyUp="sendToMain()"/>
      <mx:Button label="Close" textAlign="right" width="160"
          click="this.nativeWindow.close()"/>
      </mx:VBox>
</mx:Window>
```

In the main application file, you just have to set `systemChrome` to `none` and create a new instance of the `OptionsPanel` component. When the `systemChrome` is set to `none`, you can set the window type to `NativeWindowType.LIGHTWEIGHT`:

```xml
<?xml version="1.0" encoding="utf-8"?>
<mx:WindowedApplication xmlns:mx="http://www.adobe.com/2006/mxml"
    layout="absolute" cornerRadius="0"
    applicationComplete="init()"

    fontSize="14">

<mx:Script >
    <![CDATA[
        import components.OptionsPanel;

        private var optionsPanel:OptionsPanel

        private function init():void{
            optionsPanel  = new OptionsPanel();

            //lightweight works only when systemChrome="none"
            optionsPanel.systemChrome = "none"
            optionsPanel.type = NativeWindowType.LIGHTWEIGHT;

            //show the panel
            optionsPanel.open(true);
```

```
            //align the panel
            optionsPanel.nativeWindow.x = this.nativeWindow.x +
              this.nativeWindow.width;
            optionsPanel.nativeWindow.y = this.nativeWindow.y;
            optionsPanel.addEventListener("valueReceived",showValue);
          }
        private function showValue(evt:Event):void{
            this.title = optionsPanel.titleTextInput.text;
          }
      ]]>
    </mx:Script>
  </mx:WindowedApplication>
```

JavaScript

To create a lightweight HTML window using JavaScript, you use the same code as you did for a utility window in Recipe 3.5. Simply set the `NativeWindowInitOptions.type` property to define a lightweight window:

```
var options = new air.NativeWindowInitOptions();
options.systemChrome = "none";
options.type = air.NativeWindowType.LIGHTWEIGHT;
//...
//...set other options
var bounds = new air.Rectangle(200,250,250,150);
newHTMLLoader = air.HTMLLoader.createRootWindow(true, options, true, bounds);
newHTMLLoader.load(new air.URLRequest("form.html"));
```

The example loads an HTML file in the lightweight window and defines the initialization options by passing the `NativeWindowInitOptions` object to the `createRootWindow` method of the `HTMLLoader`:

```
setting systemChrome = "none" is required to set NativeWindowType.LIGHTWEIGHT
```

3.7 Creating a Full-Screen Window

Problem

You want to create an AIR application window that runs in full-screen mode.

Solution

Use the different modes of the `stage.displayState` property. By setting that property, you can create an interactive or noninteractive full-screen experience for your user.

Discussion

Before you go full-screen with your application window, you need to decide whether to offer user interaction capabilities. By default when your window is in full-screen mode, users do not see the window chrome anymore; to leave the full-screen mode, they must press the Esc key.

If you want your application to stay fully interactive, you have to set the window's `stage.displayState` property to `StageDisplayState.FULL_SCREEN_INTERACTIVE`.

ActionScript

In ActionScript, the code to create an interactive, full-screen window is as follows:

```
<?xml version="1.0" encoding="utf-8"?>
<mx:WindowedApplication xmlns:mx="http://www.adobe.com/2006/mxml"
    applicationComplete="init()"
    layout="absolute">

    <mx:Script >
        <![CDATA[

            private function init():void{
                this.stage.displayState =
                    StageDisplayState.FULL_SCREEN_INTERACTIVE;
            }

        ]]>
    </mx:Script>

    <mx:Label x="10" y="40" text="The application is still interactive"/>
    <mx:TextArea x="10" y="66" width="260" height="66"/>
    <mx:Label x="10" y="14" text="PRESS THE ESC key to leave full-screen mode"/>
</mx:WindowedApplication>
```

JavaScript

In JavaScript, the code to create an interactive, full-screen window is as follows:

```
<html>
<head>
<meta http-equiv="Content-Type" content="text/html; charset=utf-8" />
<title>FULL SCREEN WINDOW</title>
<script type="text/javascript">
function init(){
    window.nativeWindow.stage.displayState=
        runtime.flash.display.StageDisplayState.FULL_SCREEN_INTERACTIVE;
    }
</script>
</head>

<body onLoad="init()">
<FORM method="post">
    First name: <INPUT type="text" name="firstname"><BR>
    Last name: <INPUT type="text" name="lastname"><BR>
    email: <INPUT type="text" name="email"><BR>
</FORM>
</body>
</html>
```

Noninteractive, Full-Screen Windows

Sometimes, such as when you are building a full-screen video player application, you do not want your window to allow interaction. To set up this behavior, you need to set the `stage.displayState` property of your window to `StageDisplayState.FULL_SCREEN`.

The following example creates a new window that plays a video file. The window also contains a button that enables the user to play the video in full-screen mode. The full MXML/ActionScript code is as follows:

```
<?xml version="1.0" encoding="utf-8"?>
<mx:WindowedApplication xmlns:mx="http://www.adobe.com/2006/mxml"
    layout="absolute"
    applicationComplete="playVideo()"
    >
    <mx:Script >
        <![CDATA[
            import mx.controls.Button;
            import mx.core.Window;
            import mx.core.ContainerLayout;
            import mx.controls.VideoDisplay;

            private var window:Window;
            private function playVideo():void{

                window = new Window();
                window.layout =  ContainerLayout.VERTICAL;
                window.width = 320;
                window.height = 300;

                //create the video component
                var video:VideoDisplay = new VideoDisplay();
                video.source = "assets/trailer.flv";
                var btn:Button = new Button();
                btn.label = "Go Full-Screen";
                btn.addEventListener(MouseEvent.CLICK,doFullScreen);
                window.addChild(video);
                window.addChild(btn);
                window.open(true);

                //play the video
                video.play();
            }

        ]]>
    </mx:Script>
</mx:WindowedApplication>
```

The example uses a `VideoDisplay` component to play the video in the `Window` instance. When the user clicks the Go Full-Screen button, the following `doFullScreen` method is executed:

```
private function doFullScreen(evt:Event):void{
    window.stage.fullScreenSourceRect =  new Rectangle(0,0,320,240);
    window.nativeWindow.stage.displayState =
```

```
        StageDisplayState.FULL_SCREEN;
}
```

The method uses the hardware-scaled full-screen mode that was first introduced in Flash Player 9.0.115. By assigning a value to `stage.fullScreenSourceRect` before going into full-screen mode, you can trigger a hardware-scaled view of your video that plays back your video with better performance. In the example, the rectangular region is made of the video boundaries.

When you are in full-screen mode playing a video, AIR automatically disables the system screen saver and any power-saving options.

3.8 Managing Multiple Windows

Problem

You want to manage the display order of your application's desktop windows, as well as hide and show specific windows.

Solution

Use the `orderToFront`, `orderInFrontOf`, `orderToBack`, and `orderBehind` methods of the `NativeWindow` class, as well as the `visible` property of that specific window.

Discussion

When working with multiple instances in an AIR application and especially when windows are dynamically created in your application, you want to have control over how the different windows are presented to the user. For example, you can order a window in front of or in back of another window or just send the window directly behind or in front of any other visible windows. When you call the `orderToBack` or `orderToFront` method of the `NativeWindow` class, AIR looks to all open windows on your operating system and places your window in front or in the back of all those windows.

In this recipe's examples, all open windows must be closed before you can fully close the application. Recipe 3.14 describes a way to close all window instances when the main application window is closed.

ActionScript

The following example demonstrates various reordering methods and uses a custom component called `BrowserWindow` that was developed in Recipe 3.3. When one of the buttons is clicked, the different windows are rearranged accordingly.

```
<?xml version="1.0" encoding="utf-8"?>
<mx:WindowedApplication xmlns:mx="http://www.adobe.com/2006/mxml"
    applicationComplete="init()"
    layout="vertical">

    <mx:Script >
        <![CDATA[
            import components.BrowserWindow;

            private var firstWindow:BrowserWindow ;
            private var secondWindow:BrowserWindow;
            private function init():void{
                firstWindow= new BrowserWindow();
                firstWindow.open(true);
                firstWindow.theUrl="http://www.oreilly.com";
                firstWindow.title = "FIRST WINDOW";
                secondWindow = new BrowserWindow();
                secondWindow.open(true);
                secondWindow.theUrl="http://www.adobe.com";
                secondWindow.title = "SECOND WINDOW";
            }
        ]]>
    </mx:Script>
    <mx:Button  label="Order to FRONT"
click="firstWindow.nativeWindow.orderToFront()"/>
    <mx:Button  label="Order to BACK"
click="firstWindow.nativeWindow.orderToBack()"/>
    <mx:Button  label="Second window in FRONT of first window"
        click="secondWindow.nativeWindow.orderInFrontOf((firstWindow.nativeWindow))"/>
    <mx:Button  label="FirstWindow BEHIND mainWindow"
        click="firstWindow.nativeWindow.orderInBackOf(this.nativeWindow)"/>
</mx:WindowedApplication>
```

JavaScript

The following example demonstrates various reordering methods. When one of the buttons is clicked, the different windows are rearranged accordingly.

```
<html>
<head>
<title>Close all windows</title>
<script src="AIRAliases.js" type="text/javascript"></script>
<script type="text/javascript">
var firstWindow;
var secondWindow;
function init(){
    window.nativeWindow.title = "Main window";
    window.nativeWindow.width = 400;
    window.nativeWindow.height = 400;
    //extra window
    var options = new air.NativeWindowInitOptions();
    options.transparent=false;
    options.systemChrome=air.NativeWindowSystemChrome.STANDARD;
    options.type=air.NativeWindowType.NORMAL;
    //create the window
```

```
    firstWindow = new air.NativeWindow(options);
    firstWindow.title = "First window";
    firstWindow.width = 200;
    firstWindow.height = nativeWindow.height;
    firstWindow.x = 300;
    firstWindow.y = nativeWindow.y;
    //activate and show the new window
    firstWindow.activate();

    secondWindow = new air.NativeWindow(options);
    secondWindow.title = "Second window";
    secondWindow.width = 200;
    secondWindow.height = nativeWindow.height;
    secondWindow.x = 200;
    secondWindow.y = nativeWindow.y;
    //activate and show the new window
    secondWindow.activate();
    //
    window.nativeWindow.activate();
}
function toFront(){
    firstWindow.orderToFront();
}
function inFrontOf(){
    secondWindow.orderInFrontOf(firstWindow);
}
function toBack(){
    firstWindow.orderToBack();
}
function inBackOf(){
    firstWindow.orderInBackOf(window.nativeWindow)
}

</script>
</head>
<body onLoad="init()">
<div align="center">
<form>
    <input type="button" value="ORDER TO FRONT"  onclick="toFront()"/>
    <input type="button" value="ORDER TO BACK"   onclick="toBack()"/>
    <input type="button" value="Second window in front of first window"
onclick="inFrontOf()"/>
    <input type="button" value="First window behind main window"
onclick="inBackOf()"/>
</form>
</div>
</body>
</html>
```

Window Focus

Keep in mind that the focus is not automatically given to a window when you call any of the ordering methods. To give a specific window the focus, you must call the **activate** method of that NativeWindow object:

```
firstWindow.activate();
```

If you want to display a window on top of the other windows, you can also set the `alwaysInFront` property. But when any of the reordering functions is called, this always-in-front behavior is gone.

```
firstWindow.alwaysInFront = true;
```

If at a given moment you want to hide a certain window instance, you can simply set the `visibility` property of that window to `false`. When you later make the window visible again, keep in mind that the window does not automatically get the focus. You need to call the `activate` method again to give the window the focus.

3.9 Creating Windows with Custom Chrome

Problem

You want to create a custom user interface for your window with customized buttons that minimize, maximize, restore, and close the window.

Solution

Set the `systemChrome` attribute to `none`. Call the `minimize`, `maximize`, `restore`, and `close` methods of the `Window` object to implement your window controls.

Discussion

By using custom chrome, you can completely control the look of your application. If you like, you can even design your layout in a design program such as Adobe Photoshop and use the graphics in HTML, Flash, or Flex Builder.

Once you have the graphics, you also need to add such typical window functionality as minimize, maximize, restore, and close buttons. You can easily do this by calling four `NativeWindow` methods: `NativeWindow.minimize`, `NativeWindow.maximize`, `Native Window.restore`, and `NativeWindow.close`.

Next you set the `systemChrome` attribute to `none` in the application descriptor file:

```
<systemChrome>none</systemChrome>
```

If you want your window to be transparent (for example, if you have special shapes as shown in Recipe 3.15), you also have to set the `transparent` attribute in the application descriptor file:

```
<transparent>true</transparent>
```

Depending on the API you use to create AIR applications, you create a custom chrome window in a slight different way.

Figure 3-5. Window with custom chrome built in Flash

Always use a custom chrome wisely, however, and only when it adds value for your users. Most users are used to system chrome, and they can get confused when window controls are completely removed or given a new appearance or position. It's best to think about this issue in the planning stage of your AIR project, of course.

Also, rendering transparent windows can take your application performance down, so also consider using transparent windows only when there is an extra value for your application.

ActionScript/Flash

When working with Adobe Flash, you can easily design your chrome in the Flash IDE. You can draw any shapes, convert them to a `MovieClip`, and you are ready to go, or you can import bitmap graphics from Photoshop in your Flash IDE and use those bitmaps.

This recipe's example builds the basic custom chrome window shown in Figure 3-5.

The window is a fixed width; it can be minimized or closed but cannot be resized. The buttons and background image were designed directly in Flash, given instance names, and placed on the stage of the AIR application.

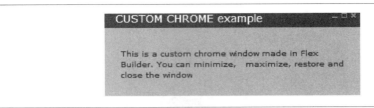

Figure 3-6. Window with custom chrome built in Flex Builder

Adding the following code on the first frame of the timeline gives the application some window control:

```
myCustomWindow.addEventListener(MouseEvent.MOUSE_DOWN,mouseDownHandler);
myCustomWindow.closeBTN.addEventListener(MouseEvent.MOUSE_DOWN,closeHandler);
myCustomWindow.minBTN.addEventListener(MouseEvent.MOUSE_DOWN,minimizeHandler);

function closeHandler(event:Event):void{
    this.stage.nativeWindow.close();
}
function minimizeHandler(event:Event):void{
    this.stage.nativeWindow.minimize();
}
function maximizeHandler(event:Event):void{
    this.stage.nativeWindow.maximize();
}
function mouseDownHandler(event:MouseEvent):void{
    this.stage.nativeWindow.startMove();
}
```

The myCustomWindow instance is the MovieClip that contains the rectangular background shape and the window controls to minimize and close the application. (See Recipe 3.10 for more details on how to minimize and maximize a native window.)

ActionScript/Flex/MXML

In Flex Builder you can easily develop a window that uses custom chrome. You can use the standard Flex Framework components and style them as you want. Of course, you can also use graphics for the styling, or you can import artwork from Flash as you can do in normal Flex web development. The following example builds the custom window shown in Figure 3-6.

When starting to build a custom chrome window, set the systemChrome attribute (and transparent if needed) to none in the application descriptor file. Because you're working in Flex Builder, flexChrome appears. You need to manually disable this by setting the showFlexChrome property of your window instance to false. In the example, this happens in the WindowedApplication component.

The MXML code is as follows:

```
<?xml version="1.0" encoding="utf-8"?>
<mx:WindowedApplication xmlns:mx="http://www.adobe.com/2006/mxml"
    layout="absolute" xmlns:comp="components.*"
```

```
            showFlexChrome="false"
            opaqueBackground="0xCECECE"
            >
            <comp:WindowControls/>
            <mx:TextArea x="19" y="49" backgroundAlpha="0.0" width="300" height="100%"
        borderThickness="0">
                <mx:text><![CDATA[This is a custom chrome window made in Flex Builder. You
        can minimize, maximize, restore and close the window]]></mx:text>
            </mx:TextArea>
        </mx:WindowedApplication>
```

As you can see in the previous code, a `comp:WindowControls` component is added to the application; this is a custom component that extends a normal `Canvas` component. The `WindowControls` component defines the title bar and contains the traditional window buttons to minimize, maximize, restore, and close the window. This custom component, based on a `Canvas`, looks like this:

```
<?xml version="1.0" encoding="utf-8"?>
<mx:Canvas xmlns:mx="http://www.adobe.com/2006/mxml" width="100%"
    backgroundColor="0x555555"
    creationComplete="init()"
    >
    <mx:Style >
        .appMinimizeButton
            {
                up-skin: Embed("/assets/icon_minimize_up.png");
                over-skin: Embed("/assets/icon_minimize_over.png");
                down-skin: Embed("/assets/icon_minimize_down.png");
            }
        .appMaximizeButton
            {
                up-skin: Embed("/assets/icon_expand_up.png");
                over-skin: Embed("/assets/icon_expand_over.png");
                down-skin: Embed("/assets/icon_expand_down.png");
            }

        .appCloseButton
            {
                up-skin: Embed("/assets/icon_close_up.png");
                over-skin: Embed("/assets/icon_close_over.png");
                down-skin: Embed("/assets/icon_close_down.png");
            }
        .titleText{
            color: #FFFFFF;
                font-family: "Verdana";
                font-size:14;
                left:12;

        }

    </mx:Style>
    <mx:Script>
        <![CDATA[
            private function maxRestore():void{
                if(stage.nativeWindow.displayState ==
```

```
NativeWindowDisplayState.MAXIMIZED){
                    stage.nativeWindow.restore();
            }else{
                    stage.nativeWindow.maximize();
            }

        }
        private function init():void{
            this.addEventListener(MouseEvent.MOUSE_DOWN,mouseDownHandler)
        }
        private function mouseDownHandler(event:MouseEvent):void{
            stage.nativeWindow.startMove();
        }
    ]]>
</mx:Script>
<mx:Label styleName="titleText" text="CUSTOM CHROME example" />

<mx:HBox y="4" verticalAlign="top" width="100%" horizontalAlign="right"
horizontalGap="0">
    <mx:Button styleName="appMinimizeButton"
click="stage.nativeWindow.minimize()"
        tabEnabled="false" toolTip="Minimize" />
        <mx:Spacer width="5"/>
    <mx:Button styleName="appMaximizeButton" click="maxRestore()"
        tabEnabled="false" toolTip="Maximize" />
        <mx:Spacer width="5"/>
    <mx:Button styleName="appCloseButton"
click="NativeApplication.nativeApplication.exit()"
        tabEnabled="false" toolTip="Close" />
        <mx:Spacer width="5"/>
</mx:HBox>
</mx:Canvas>
```

The style declaration block defines the styles for the three buttons that form the window controls. One button closes, the second minimizes, and a third maximizes and restores the application. The restore functionality is in the maxRestore method:

```
private function maxRestore():void{
  if(stage.nativeWindow.displayState == NativeWindowDisplayState.MAXIMIZED){
    stage.nativeWindow.restore();
  }else{
    stage.nativeWindow.maximize();
  }
}
```

You can ask the NativeWindow instance of the application what the displayState is. The displayState is set automatically when the state of your application changes. For example, when the user has minimized the application by clicking the minimize button, the state of your application can be either NativeWindowDisplayState.NORMAL, Native WindowDisplayState.MINIMIZED, or NativeWindowDisplayState.MAXIMIZED. In the previous maxRestore method, when the state is maximized, then you need to restore the window. Otherwise, the window can be maximized.

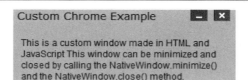

Figure 3-7. Window with custom chrome built with HTML/CSS and JavaScript

JavaScript/HTML

To develop a custom chrome window in HTML and JavaScript, just use normal CSS to make it look and feel as you want, such as the example shown in Figure 3-7.

In the example, CSS styling is added for the navigation, the content pane, and the program title. When the application loads, you define a mouse down handler so that you can move the window around on the screen.

The HTML/CSS/JavaScript code looks like this:

```
<html>
<head>
<script src="AIRAliases.js" type="text/javascript"> </script>
<script type="text/javascript">

function init(){
    document.body.onmousedown = mouseDownHandler;
}
function mouseDownHandler(){
    window.nativeWindow.startMove();
}
</script>

<title>Custom Chrome Example HTML/JavaScript</title>
<style >
#nav {
      text-align:right;
      padding-right:5px;
      position:absolute;
      right:0;
      top:-4px;
}
#nav button {
    color:#999;
    background-color:#555;
    border:1px inset #777;
    border-width:0 1px 1px;
    padding:6px 6px 3px;
    line-height:1;
    cursor:pointer;
}
#contentPane{
    background-color:#CCC;
    font-family:Arial, Helvetica, sans-serif;
    font-size:12px;
```

```
        padding-left:10;
        padding-right:10;
        padding-top:20;
        position:absolute;

    }
    #title{
        font-weight:400;
        font-family:Verdana,    Geneva, sans-serif;
        font-size:14px;
        padding-left:5px;
        top:0;
        }
    </style>

    </head>
    <body bgcolor="#CECECE" onLoad="init()">
    <div id="title">
    Custom Chrome Example
    </div>
    <div id="nav">
        <button id="btnmin" onClick="window.nativeWindow.minimize()">
            <img src="assets/minimize_icon.png" /></button>
        <button id="btnclose" onClick="window.nativeWindow.close()">
            <img src="assets/close_icon.png" /></button>
    </div>
    <div id="contentPane">
    This is a custom window made in HTML and JavaScript
    This window can be minimized and closed by
    calling the NativeWindow.minimize() and the
    NativeWindow.close() method.
    </div>
    </body>
    </html>
```

3.10 Minimizing and Maximizing a Window

Problem

You are using no system chrome in your application and want to enhance your window by providing minimize and maximize window controls.

Solution

Use the NativeWindow.minimize or NativeWindow.maximize method. When your window is maximized, use the NativeWindow.restore method to restore the window to its initial scale and position.

Discussion

When you are using custom chrome for your AIR application windows, you also have to make sure you have some standard window controls available for the user, such as those for minimizing and maximizing a window.

The base class for all windows created in AIR, the `NativeWindow` class, has two methods defined to minimize and maximize a native application window: `NativeWindow.mini mize` and `NativeWindow.maximize`. When your window is maximized and you want to restore it to the previous scale, you can use the `NativeWindow.restore` method.

ActionScript

The following example shows how to build your own minimize, maximize, and restore window controls:

```
<?xml version="1.0" encoding="utf-8"?>

<mx:WindowedApplication
    xmlns:mx="http://www.adobe.com/2006/mxml"
    layout="vertical">
    <mx:Script>
    <![CDATA[
    private function minimizeWindow():void
    {
        this.stage.nativeWindow.minimize();
    }

    private function maximizeWindow():void
    {
        this.stage.nativeWindow.maximize();
    }

    private function restoreWindow():void
    {
        this.stage.nativeWindow.restore();
    }
    ]]>
    </mx:Script>

    <mx:VBox>
        <mx:Button label="Minimize" click="minimizeWindow()"/>
        <mx:Button label="Maximize" click="maximizeWindow()"/>
        <mx:Button label="Restore" click="restoreWindow()"/>
    </mx:VBox>
</mx:WindowedApplication>
```

JavaScript

The following example shows how to build your own minimize, maximize, and restore window controls:

```html
<html>
<head>
<meta http-equiv="Content-Type" content="text/html; charset=utf-8" />
<title>MiniMize - Maximize - Restore a window</title>
<script src="AIRAliases.js" type="text/javascript"></script>
<script type="text/javascript">
    function minizeWindow(){
        nativeWindow.minimize();
    }
    function maximizeWindow(){
        nativeWindow.maximize();
    }
    function restoreWindow(){
        nativeWindow.restore();
    }
</script>
</head>
<body>
<form>
    <input type="button" value="Minimize"  onclick="minizeWindow()"/>
    <input type="button" value="Maximize" onclick="maximizeWindow()"/>
    <input type="button" value="Restore" onclick="restoreWindow()"/>
</form>
</body>
</html>
```

3.11 Resizing a Window

Problem

You want resizing functionality in your custom chrome AIR application.

Solution

Listen for a `mouseDown` event on a given object in your application, and call the `Native Window.startResize` method. The resize operation is driven by the mouse and will take as long as the mouse is down. You must define which edge or corner of the window to resize.

Discussion

The `NativeWindow.startResize` method starts a resize operation of a window. When you call this method, you have to pass an `edgeCorner` value, which is a constant defined in the `NativeWindowResize` class. This constant defines the edge or corner of your window to resize. Its value can be `BOTTOM`, `BOTTOM_LEFT`, `BOTTOM_RIGHT`, `LEFT`, `RIGHT`, `TOP`, `TOP_LEFT`, or `TOP_RIGHT`.

In your application, you will listen to the mouseDown event; then, on receiving it, you will define the corner the user wants to resize and call the startResize method.

ActionScript

The following example shows how to implement resizing of an application window. When the user moves the mouse pointer near a window's edge and presses the mouse button, the window can be resized.

```
<?xml version="1.0" encoding="utf-8"?>
<mx:WindowedApplication xmlns:mx="http://www.adobe.com/2006/mxml"

    applicationComplete="init()"
    showFlexChrome="false"

    layout="absolute">
    <mx:Script >
        <![CDATA[

            private function init():void{
                this.stage.addEventListener(MouseEvent.MOUSE_DOWN,
                    mousedownHandler);
            }
            private function mousedownHandler(event:MouseEvent):void{
                    var resizeFrom:String = "";

                    if(event.localY < this.height * .33){
                            resizeFrom = NativeWindowResize.TOP;
                    }
                    else if(event.localY > this.height * .66){
                            resizeFrom = NativeWindowResize.BOTTOM;
                    }

                    if(event.localX < this.width * .33){
                        resizeFrom += NativeWindowResize.LEFT;
                    }
                    else if(event.localX > this.width * .66){
                        resizeFrom += NativeWindowResize.RIGHT;
                    }
                    //resize the window
                    this.startResize(resizeFrom);
            }
        ]]>
    </mx:Script>
    <mx:Button label="CLOSE THIS WINDOW" horizontalCenter="0"
        verticalCenter="0" click="this.nativeWindow.close()"/>
</mx:WindowedApplication>
```

In the example, you determine the corner the user wants to resize. For example, if the y position value is less than one third the height of the window (this.height * 0.33), you know to resize from the top. Then you look to the x position; if the x position value is, for example, greater than two thirds the width of the window (this.width * 0.66), you know the user wants to resize from the right side of the window. The x and y positions' combined resizing will happen from the top right. This calculation is done for every corner of the window to determine the corner the user wants to resize.

JavaScript

The following example shows how to implement resizing of an application window. When the user moves the mouse pointer near a window's edge and presses the mouse button, the window can be resized.

```html
<html>
<head>
<script src="AIRAliases.js" type="text/javascript"></script>
<script type="text/javascript">

    function init(){
        window.onmousedown = mousedownHandler;
    }
    function mousedownHandler(e){

        var resizeFrom = "";

        if(e.clientY < nativeWindow.height * .33){
          resizeFrom = air.NativeWindowResize.TOP;
        }
        else if(e.clientY > nativeWindow.height * .66){
          resizeFrom = air.NativeWindowResize.BOTTOM;
        }
        if(e.clientX < nativeWindow.width * .33){
          resizeFrom += air.NativeWindowResize.LEFT;
        }
        else if(e.clientX > nativeWindow.width * .66){
          resizeFrom += air.NativeWindowResize.RIGHT;
        }
        //resize the window
        nativeWindow.startResize(resizeFrom);
    }
</script>
<title>Custom resize controls</title>

<body onLoad="init()" >
<div align="center">
<form>
    <input type="button" value="CLOSE"  onclick="nativeWindow.close()"/>
</form>
</div>
</body>
</html>
```

3.12 Closing a Window

Problem

You have created a window with custom chrome and want to give the user the ability to close the window.

Solution

Call the `NativeWindow.close` method. If the window is the initial application window, the application will also close.

Discussion

To close a window, you just have to call the `close` method of the `NativeWindow` class:

```
NativeWindow.close();
```

3.13 Displaying a Prompt Before Closing a Window

Problem

You want to display a prompt when a window is about to close.

Solution

Listen for the closing event (`Event.CLOSING`), and set a handler to display the prompt before the window closes.

Discussion

In many cases, you want to prompt the user for something, such as saving their changes when a window or your application is about to close. In a multiwindow application, you might want to display a prompt when the main application window is about to close asking whether the user also wants to close all the other windows that are open. At the moment, AIR doesn't have any built-in way to do this automatically, but you can easily implement it yourself by letting your main window listen for the `Event.CLOSING` event. When this event is dispatched, you close all the open windows using the `NativeWindow.close` method.

The `Event.CLOSING` event is dispatched automatically only when the system chrome close button is pressed or, on a Mac, when the Quit command is invoked. If no listeners cancel the closing event, the window closes, and the `Event.CLOSE` event is dispatched to any listeners. So if you are using custom chrome, you will have to construct a closing event yourself and dispatch it using the window's `dispatchEvent` method when the user clicks the close button of your custom chrome.

The example in this chapter is not addressing the custom chrome situation, but the following logic implements a cancelable event handler for a custom chrome window's close button:

```
public function onCloseCommand(event:MouseEvent):void{
    var closing:Event = new Event(Event.CLOSING,true,true);
    dispatchEvent(closing);
    if(!closing.isDefaultPrevented()){
        win.close();
    }
}
```

ActionScript

The following example demonstrates how to prompt the user to save their changes when the main application is closed. Notice that the preventDefault method of the Event class is called in the listener of the Event.CLOSING event. This way you cancel the default behavior of the Event.CLOSING event so the window does not automatically close.

```
<?xml version="1.0" encoding="utf-8"?>
<mx:WindowedApplication xmlns:mx="http://www.adobe.com/2006/mxml"
    layout="absolute"

    closing="closingHandler(event)"

>
<mx:Script >
    <![CDATA[
        import mx.events.CloseEvent;
        import mx.controls.Alert;

        private function closingHandler(event:Event):void{
            //cancel the event
            event.preventDefault();
            //show modal Alert box
    Alert.show("Save Changes", "Save Alert", Alert.YES | Alert.NO, null, closeHandler);

        }
        private function closeHandler(event:CloseEvent):void{
            if(event.detail ==Alert.NO){
                trace("NOT SAVING");
                this.nativeWindow.close();
            }else{
                trace("SAVING");
                //implement logic to save changes here
                //...
            }
        }
    ]]>
</mx:Script>
<mx:Label x="203" y="234" verticalCenter="0" horizontalCenter="0"
    text="When you close this window, you will be prompted
```

```
                    to save your changes"/>
    </mx:WindowedApplication>
```

JavaScript

The following example demonstrates how to prompt the user to save their changes when the main application is closed. Notice that the `preventDefault` method of the `Event` class is called in the listener of the `Event.CLOSING` event. This way, you cancel the default behavior of the `Event.CLOSING` event so the window does not automatically close.

```
<html>
<head>
<title>Prompt For Closing</title>
<script src="AIRAliases.js" type="text/javascript"></script>
<script type="text/javascript">

function init(){
    window.nativeWindow.addEventListener(air.Event.CLOSING, closingHandler);
}
function closingHandler(event){
    var toclose = confirm("Do you want to save your changes?");
    event.preventDefault();

    if(toclose){
        //saving
        //implement logic to save changes here
    }else{
        window.nativeWindow.close();
    }
}
</script>
</head>
<body onload="init()">
When you close this window, you will be prompted to save your changes.
</body>
</html>
```

3.14 Closing All Open Windows at Once

Problem

You want to close all the open windows when the main application window is closed.

Solution

Listen for the closing event (`Event.CLOSING`), cancel the close operation, and loop through all the open windows to close them manually.

Discussion

When building a multiwindow application, you may need to provide the ability to close all open windows when the main application window is closed.

In the example, the close operation from the main window is stopped by calling the `preventDefault` method of the `Event` class. This way, you cancel the default behavior of the closing event so the main window is not automatically closed. Then, any opened windows are closed first in the opposite order in which they were opened (more recent windows first). In this way, you are sure your application is fully exited when the user clicks the close button.

ActionScript

The ActionScript code you need is as follows:

```
<?xml version="1.0" encoding="utf-8"?>
<mx:WindowedApplication xmlns:mx="http://www.adobe.com/2006/mxml"
    closing="closeAllWindows(event)"
    applicationComplete="init()"
    title="Main window"
    layout="absolute">

    <mx:Script >
        <![CDATA[
            import mx.core.Window;

            private function init():void{
                var firstWindow:Window = new Window();
                firstWindow.title = "First Window"
                firstWindow.width = 400;
                firstWindow.height = 200;
                firstWindow.open(true);
                //
                var secondWindow:Window = new Window();
                secondWindow.title = "Second Window"
                secondWindow.width = 400;
                secondWindow.height = 200;
                secondWindow.open(true);
            }
            private function closeAllWindows(event:Event):void{
                event.preventDefault();
                //loop through all windows and close them
                 for (var i:int =
                 NativeApplication.nativeApplication.openedWindows.length - 1;
                 i >= 0; --i) {

                var closeWin:NativeWindow =
NativeApplication.nativeApplication.openedWindows[i] as NativeWindow;
closeWin.close();
                }
            }
        ]]>
```

```
        </mx:Script>
    </mx:WindowedApplication>
```

JavaScript

The JavaScript code you need is as follows:

```
<html>
<head>
<title>Close all windows</title>
<script src="AIRAliases.js" type="text/javascript"></script>
<script type="text/javascript">

function init(){
    window.nativeWindow.title = "Main window";
    window.nativeWindow.width = 400;
    window.nativeWindow.height = 400;
    //extra window
    var options = new air.NativeWindowInitOptions();
    options.transparent=false;
    options.systemChrome=air.NativeWindowSystemChrome.STANDARD;
    options.type=air.NativeWindowType.NORMAL;
    //create the window
    var firstWindow = new air.NativeWindow(options);
    firstWindow.title = "Second window";
    firstWindow.width = 200;
    firstWindow.height = nativeWindow.height;
    firstWindow.x = nativeWindow.x + nativeWindow.width;
    firstWindow.y = nativeWindow.y;
    //activate and show the new window
    firstWindow.activate();
    var secondWindow = new air.NativeWindow(options);
    secondWindow.title = "Second window";
    secondWindow.width = 200;
    secondWindow.height = nativeWindow.height;
    secondWindow.x = nativeWindow.x + nativeWindow.width + firstWindow.width;
    secondWindow.y = nativeWindow.y;
    //activate and show the new window
    secondWindow.activate();

    //
    window.nativeWindow.addEventListener(air.Event.CLOSING, closeAllWindows);
}
function closeAllWindows(event){
    event.preventDefault();
    for(var i = air.NativeApplication.nativeApplication.openedWindows.length-
1;i>=0;i--){

air.NativeWindow(air.NativeApplication.nativeApplication.openedWindows[i]).close()
    }
}
</script>
</head>
<body onload="init()">
When you close this window, all open windows will be also closed.
```

```
    </body>
    </html>
```

3.15 Adding a Drop Shadow to a Custom Chrome Window in ActionScript

Problem

You want to add a drop shadow to the border of a window that has custom chrome applied.

Solution

Pass a `DropShadowFilter` instance to the `filters Array` of the `NativeWindow` instance, or set the `dropShadowEnabled` and `dropShadowColor` styles.

Discussion

A window that has custom chrome applied can have a drop shadow around the borders of the window. The native window can be your main application window or any other window you have in your application. When you want to add a shadow around your main application window, make sure to set the `systemChrome` and `transparent` attributes in the application descriptor file:

```
<systemChrome>none</systemChrome>
<transparent>true</transparent>
```

You can add a drop shadow to your window in two ways. In the first way, you instantiate a `DropShadowFilter` (a subclass of the `BitmapFilter` class) object and set the properties for the drop shadow you want. Every `DisplayObject` has a `filters Array` property where you can store `BitmapFilter` instances you want to use on that `DisplayObject`. For the `DropShadowFilter`, you can define many properties such as `color`, `alpha`, `blurX`, `blurY`, `distance`, and `angle` to customize the look and feel of your drop shadow.

The following example is a basic AIR application with custom chrome applied (Figure 3-8). Actually, the chrome consists of just three `Canvas` components from the Flex Framework.

The drop shadow is configured as follows:

```
shadowFilter = new DropShadowFilter();
shadowFilter.color = 0xFF0000;
shadowFilter.alpha = 0.75;
shadowFilter.blurX = 5;
shadowFilter.blurY = 5;
shadowFilter.distance = 5;
shadowFilter.angle = 90;
```

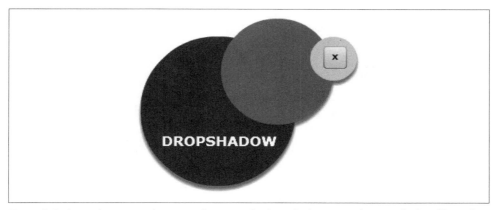

Figure 3-8. An application with custom chrome and a drop shadow using the **DropShadowFilter** *class*

To use the drop shadow for the window, assign the `shadowFilter` instance to the `filters` `Array` of the `WindowedApplication` instance. In this example, the `this` keyword refers to the `WindowedApplication` instance:

```
this.filters = [shadowFilter];
```

Here is the complete MXML code for the example:

```
<?xml version="1.0" encoding="utf-8"?>
<mx:WindowedApplication xmlns:mx="http://www.adobe.com/2006/mxml"
    applicationComplete="init()"

    showFlexChrome="false"
    layout="absolute" >

    <mx:Style>
        Canvas{
            border-style:solid;
            border-thickness:0;
            corner-radius:150;
        }
        WindowedApplication{

            drop-shadow-enabled:"true";
            drop-shadow-color:"0xFF0000";

        }
    </mx:Style>
    <mx:Script >
        <![CDATA[
            import mx.core.Window;

            private var shadowFilter:DropShadowFilter;
            private var newWindow:Window;

            private function init():void{
                shadowFilter = new DropShadowFilter();
                shadowFilter.color = 0xFF0000;
```

```
                    shadowFilter.alpha = 0.75;
                    shadowFilter.blurX = 5;
                    shadowFilter.blurY = 5;
                    shadowFilter.distance = 5;
                    shadowFilter.angle = 90;
                    //attach the dropshadow to the NativeWindow

                    this.filters = [shadowFilter];
                    this.stage.addEventListener(MouseEvent.MOUSE_DOWN,onMouseDown);

                }
                private function closeWindow(event:MouseEvent):void{
                    this.nativeWindow.close();
                }
                private function onMouseDown(event:MouseEvent):void{
                    this.nativeWindow.startMove();
                }
            ]]>
        </mx:Script>
        <mx:Canvas x="29" y="34" width="200" height="200" backgroundColor="#343434">
            <mx:Label x="25" y="127" text="DROPSHADOW"
                fontSize="18" color="#FFFFFF" fontWeight="bold"/>
        </mx:Canvas>
        <mx:Canvas x="132.7" y="10" width="145 " height="142" backgroundColor="#7A7C7E" >
        </mx:Canvas>
        <mx:Canvas x="248" y="34" width="60" height="59" backgroundColor="#D7D7D7" >
            <mx:Button label="X" width="30" paddingLeft="0" paddingRight="0"
                paddingTop="0" paddingBottom="0" height="30" color="#000000" right="12"
                top="13" themeColor="#949698" click="closeWindow(event)"/>
        </mx:Canvas>
    </mx:WindowedApplication>
```

The second way to show a drop shadow is by setting the drop-shadow-color and drop-shadow-enabled style properties of the displayObject you are using as the background of your application. In a basic AIR application with a Canvas component as a background container, set the style properties for the Canvas component as follows:

```
Canvas.BgCanvas {
            background-color:"0xE6E6E6";
            border-style:solid;
            border-color:"0xFFFFFF";
            border-thickness:10;
            corner-radius:20;

            drop-shadow-color:"0x000000";
            drop-shadow-enabled:true;

            shadow-direction:top;
            shadow-distance:5;

    }
```

You can also set shadow-distance as you like; of course, you can also set shadow-direction to be centered, left, or right.

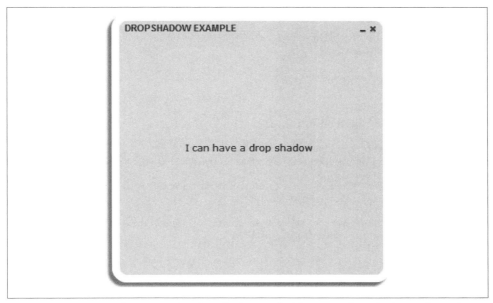

Figure 3-9. An AIR application with a drop shadow applied by setting drop shadow style attributes

Make sure the `systemChrome` attribute is set to `none` and the `transparent` attribute is set to `true`; otherwise, you will not see the shadow. Figure 3-9 shows the application.

Here is the full MXML code for the example:

```
<?xml version="1.0" encoding="utf-8"?>
<mx:WindowedApplication xmlns:mx="http://www.adobe.com/2006/mxml"
    xmlns:comp="*"
    applicationComplete="init()"
    layout="absolute"

  xmlns:ns1="*">
<mx:Style >

    WindowedApplication{
        padding-right:"5";
        padding-left:"5";
        padding-top:"5";
        padding-bottom:"5";
        show-flex-chrome:false;

    }
    Canvas.BgCanvas {
        background-color:"0xE6E6E6";
        border-style:solid;
        border-color:"0xFFFFFF";
        border-thickness:10;
        corner-radius:20;

        drop-shadow-color:"0x000000";
```

```
                    drop-shadow-enabled:true;

                    shadow-direction:left;
                    shadow-distance:5;

            }
        </mx:Style>
        <mx:Script >
            <![CDATA[
                import mx.core.Window;

                private function init():void{
                    stage.addEventListener(MouseEvent.MOUSE_DOWN,onMouseDown)
                }
                private function closeWindow(event:MouseEvent):void{
                    this.nativeWindow.close();
                }
                private function onMouseDown(event:MouseEvent):void{
                    this.nativeWindow.startMove();
                }
            ]]>
        </mx:Script>
        <mx:Canvas styleName="BgCanvas" right="20" bottom="20" top="20" left="20"    >
            <comp:WindowControls y="0"  right="5" left="5">
            </comp:WindowControls>
            <mx:Label text="I can have a drop shadow " horizontalCenter="0"
    verticalCenter="0" fontSize="12"/>
        </mx:Canvas>
    </mx:WindowedApplication>
```

Finally, when adding drop shadows to your application dynamically, you should know that this can be very CPU intensive, so in some circumstances it is better to create graphics and apply effects such as drop shadows to your chrome graphics instead of applying them as filters in ActionScript.

3.16 Applying a Pixel Bender Filter to a Custom Chrome Window in ActionScript

Problem

You need to apply a custom filter developed with the Pixel Bender Toolkit from Adobe to your custom chrome application window. In addition, you need to interact with the filter's variable settings.

Solution

Use the built-in support for Pixel Bender filters inside AIR 1.5 to load and interact with the filter inside your AIR application.

Discussion

The Pixel Bender Toolkit (formerly codename Hydra) provides a powerful way to create custom filters for graphics. It uses the Pixel Bender language to create algorithms that manipulate images in a uniform manner across a wide variety of graphics architectures. Although the process of creating these filters is beyond the scope of this book, once the filters are compiled for use with Flash Player, they can be used in an AIR application.

 The Pixel Bender Toolkit is currently available from Adobe Labs. The download includes the application for creating and compiling filters as well as some sample filters, such as the pixelate filter used in this example. Download the Pixel Bender Toolkit from *http://labs.adobe.com/wiki/index.php/Pixel_Bender_Toolkit*.

Once a filter has been compiled for use with Flash Player, it will have a `pbj` extension. Files with a `pbk` extension can be loaded into the Pixel Bender Toolkit but must be compiled before they can be used in a Flash, Flex, or AIR application.

The process of loading a Pixel Bender filter into an AIR application consists of a series of steps:

1. Create a `File` instance that points to the Pixel Bender filter file.
2. Create an instance of the `FileStream` class and an instance of the `ByteArray` class. Use the `FileStream` instance to read the binary contents of the Pixel Bender filter file into the `ByteArray`.
3. Create a new instance of the `flash.display.Shader` class, and pass in the `ByteArray` instance to the constructor.
4. Create a new instance of the `flash.filters.ShaderFilter` class, and pass in the instance of the `Shader` class to the constructor.
5. Add the instance of the `ShaderFilter` class to the `filters` array for a given `DisplayObject`.

Filters created within the Pixel Bender Toolkit can have parameters that affect the filter. In this example, the pixelate filter will be used. Included with the Pixel Bender Toolkit download, this filter has a single parameter, `dimension`, which can have a value from 1 to 100. Parameters can be accessed from the `data` property of the `Shader` class. In this case, it is expecting an array with the integer in it. To set this parameter, use this format:

```
myShader.data.dimension.value = [ 20 ];
```

When setting properties on an instance of the `Shader` class, you must create a new instance of the `ShaderFilter` class, add the `Shader` to the `ShaderFilter`, and finally add it to the filters array for the `DisplayObject`.

In this example, the pixelate filter's `dimension` property is linked to the `NativeWindow`'s x position. When the `NativeWindow` is all the way to the left, the `dimension` parameter is set to 1. When it is all the way to the right, it is at 20. This is accomplished by listening to the NativeWindowBoundsEvent.MOVE event. The handleWindowMove method then calculates the window's relative position and calls the setPixelateValue method, which assigns the parameter value, creates a new ShaderFilter, and adds it to the array of filters for the WindowedApplication.

```xml
<?xml version="1.0" encoding="utf-8"?>
<mx:WindowedApplication xmlns:mx=http://www.adobe.com/2006/mxml
    layout="vertical" verticalAlign="middle"
    backgroundColor="#ffffff"
    creationComplete="handleCreationComplete()">

    <mx:Script>
        <![CDATA[
            import flash.filters.ShaderFilter;
            import flash.display.Shader;
            import flash.utils.ByteArray;
            import flash.filesystem.*;

            private var shader:Shader;
            private var pixelator:File =
File.applicationDirectory.resolvePath('pixelate.pbj');
            private var filterData:ByteArray = new ByteArray();

            private function handleCreationComplete():void {
                this.nativeWindow.addEventListener(
NativeWindowBoundsEvent.MOVE, handleWindowMove );
                var stream:FileStream = new FileStream();
                stream.open( pixelator, FileMode.READ );
                stream.readBytes( filterData );
                shader = new Shader( filterData );
                var shaderFilter:ShaderFilter = new ShaderFilter( shader );
                this.filters = [ shaderFilter ];
            }

            private function handleWindowMove(event:NativeWindowBoundsEvent):void {
                if( shader ) {
                    setPixelateValue( event.afterBounds.x /
Screen.mainScreen.bounds.width );
                }
            }

            private function setPixelateValue( percent:Number ):void {
                var maxValue:int = 20;
                shader.data.dimension.value = [ int( percent * maxValue ) + 1 ];
                var shaderFilter:ShaderFilter = new ShaderFilter( shader );
                this.filters = [ shaderFilter ];
            }
        ]]>
    </mx:Script>

    <mx:Image source="http://www.davidtucker.net/cookbook.jpg" />

</mx:WindowedApplication>
```

CHAPTER 4

Screens

Breaking out of the browser provides you with additional challenges when developing applications. In addition to positioning elements within your application, you now have control over where the application itself is positioned. In addition, you now have to expand your thinking beyond a browser window to a user's desktop, which consists of one or more monitors.

The Screen class in Adobe AIR provides you with information about the current user's monitor setup. This allows you to take advantage of the full capability of the user's desktop, including multiple monitor configurations. By using the data contained in this class, you can get explicit information about the number of monitors, the positioning of these monitors, and even the capabilities of the monitors themselves.

4.1 Positioning Windows on the Desktop

Problem

You want to center your application on the user's primary monitor.

Solution

Use the Screen class to determine the width and height of the primary monitor on the user's computer. Using this information, you can position your application in the center of the screen.

Discussion

The Screen class has properties that reflect characteristics of the user's primary monitor and provides an instance of itself in the static variable Screen.mainScreen. Included in these properties are two variables that define the width and height of the monitor: bounds and visibleBounds.

- **bounds**: The **bounds** property of the **Screen** class is an instance of the **Rectangle** class, which provides the properties for the entire space on a screen that is available to the operating system.

- **visibleBounds**: The **visibleBounds** property is an instance of the **Rectangle** class, which provides the properties for the available space on the screen. On a Windows system, this is the full size of the screen without the taskbar. On a Mac, this could be the full size of the screen without the menu bar. Also, note that, depending on system preferences, this could include or not include the Dock on a Mac.

Both the **bounds** and **visibleBounds** variables are instances of the **Rectangle** class, which provides the width, height, x, and y values for the screen as well as additional positioning values. With these variables, you can determine the center point of the screen as well as the application's relative positioning.

After you have determined the center point, you can then calculate where the window will need to be positioned to be in the center. To accomplish this, you can adjust the x and y positions of the current **NativeWindow** instance in your application. To find these values, you subtract half the application's width and half the application's height from the center point and then position the **NativeWindow** instance at that point.

ActionScript

Within ActionScript, you first need to import the **flash.display.Screen** class. You then can determine the center x and y values by dividing the **Screen.main Screen.bounds.width** and **Screen.mainScreen.bounds.height** values by 2. Finally, you can position the **nativeWindow** instance's x and y values by subtracting half the window's width and height from the center points.

```
<?xml version="1.0" encoding="utf-8"?>
<mx:WindowedApplication
    xmlns:mx="http://www.adobe.com/2006/mxml"
    horizontalAlign="center" verticalAlign="middle">

<mx:Script>
    <![CDATA[

        import flash.display.Screen;

        private function handleClick(event:MouseEvent):void {
            var centerX:Number = Screen.mainScreen.bounds.width / 2;
            var centerY:Number = Screen.mainScreen.bounds.height / 2
            nativeWindow.x = centerX - (nativeWindow.width / 2);
            nativeWindow.y = centerY - (nativeWindow.height / 2);
        }

    ]]>
</mx:Script>

<mx:Button id="centerButton"
    click="handleClick(event)"
```

```
                label="Center Window" />

    </mx:WindowedApplication>
```

JavaScript

Within JavaScript, you can access the `Screen` class with `air.Screen`. To determine the width and height of the primary monitor, you use `air.Screen.main` `Screen.bounds.width` and `air.Screen.mainScreen.bounds.height`. By dividing these two values in half, you have the center point of the user's primary monitor.

Next, subtract half the application's width and height from these center values to determine the point at which the application should be positioned to center it on the screen. The `nativeWindow` instance that refers to the current application window is located in `window.nativeWindow`. Set its x and y values to the predetermined point to center the window on the user's screen.

```
<html>
<head>
    <title>Entry 4.1 - Center a Window</title>

    <script type="text/javascript" src="AIRAliases.js"></script>
    <script type="text/javascript">
        function handleClick(){
            var centerX = air.Screen.mainScreen.bounds.width / 2;
            var centerY = air.Screen.mainScreen.bounds.height / 2;
            window.nativeWindow.x = centerX - (window.nativeWindow.width / 2);
            window.nativeWindow.y = centerY - (window.nativeWindow.height / 2);
        }
    </script>
</head>

<body>
    <input id="centerButton" type="button" value="Center Window"
onclick="handleClick()" />
</body>
</html>
```

4.2 Positioning Windows Across Multiple Monitors

Problem

You want to be able to center your application on any of the available monitors for the user's current desktop.

Solution

Use the static `Screen.screens` array, which contains the properties of the available monitors.

Discussion

The process of centering the application on any available monitor is twofold. First, you need to loop through the array of screens to determine the monitors that are available. Second, you must calculate the center point of the monitor that is selected.

Looping through the available monitors requires looping through the `Screen.screens` array. To center your application in Recipe 4.1, you used the `Screen.mainScreen` property, which held a reference to an instance of the `Screen` class. Each element in the `Screen.screens` array is an instance of the `Screen` class as well. Each of these instances corresponds to one of the user's available screens. You can use the bounds rectangle of each `Screen` defined in the array to determine the width, height, x, and y values of the available monitors.

Calculating the center point now requires an additional step. In AIR, the primary monitor is always positioned at 0,0, and other monitors are positioned relative to their positioning on the user's desktop. For example, if the user had a monitor above the primary monitor, its x and y values would be negative. If you are trying to center a window on a specific monitor, the starting point will be that window's x and y positions as defined in its instance of the `Screen` class. From that point, you can add half the width and height to determine the center.

ActionScript

In this example, the `handleCreationComplete` method loops through each of the available monitors and populates a group of radio buttons. Each radio button is given a value that corresponds to the index of the screen in the `Screen.screens` array with which you can retrieve a reference to each screen instance and its properties.

When the `centerButton` is clicked, the `handleClick` method determines the monitor that the user selected with the radio buttons and calculates that screen's center point. Finally, the application window is positioned at the center point of the selected monitor. If a screen is not selected, an `Alert` window is shown.

```
<?xml version="1.0" encoding="utf-8"?>
<mx:WindowedApplication
    xmlns:mx="http://www.adobe.com/2006/mxml"
    layout="vertical"
    creationComplete="handleCreationComplete()">

    <mx:Script>
        <![CDATA[
            import mx.controls.Alert;
            import flash.display.Screen;
            import mx.collections.ArrayCollection;

            [Bindable]
            private var screens:ArrayCollection;

            private function handleCreationComplete():void {
```

```
                  screens = new ArrayCollection();
                  var output:String = "";
                  var screen:Screen;
                  for(var i:uint = 0; i < Screen.screens.length; i++) {
                      screen = Screen.screens[i];
                      output = "Screen " + i + " - ";
                      output += "Width: " + screen.bounds.width;
                      output += " Height: " + screen.bounds.height;
                      screens.addItem({ label: output });
                  }
              }

              private function handleClick(event:MouseEvent):void {
                  if(monitorButtonGroup.selectedValue != null) {
                      var selectedVal:Object = monitorButtonGroup.selectedValue;

                      var screen:Screen = Screen.screens[selectedVal] as Screen;
                      var centerX:Number = screen.bounds.x + screen.bounds.width / 2;
                      var centerY:Number = screen.bounds.y + screen.bounds.height / 2;
                      nativeWindow.x = centerX - (nativeWindow.width / 2);
                      nativeWindow.y = centerY - (nativeWindow.height / 2);
                  } else {
                      mx.controls.Alert.show("Please Select a Monitor","");
                  }
              }

          ]]>
      </mx:Script>

      <mx:RadioButtonGroup id="monitorButtonGroup" />

      <mx:Repeater id="screensRepeater" dataProvider="{screens}">
          <mx:RadioButton
              id="monitorsButton"
              group="{monitorButtonGroup}"
              value="{screensRepeater.currentIndex}"
              width="100%"
              label="{screensRepeater.currentItem.label}" />
      </mx:Repeater>

      <mx:Button id="centerButton"
          click="handleClick(event)"
          label="Center on Selected Monitor" />

  </mx:WindowedApplication>
```

JavaScript

In this example, the function populateScreens is called in response to the onload event. This method loops through each of the screens available on the user's computer. It adds a radio button for each of these screens along with a label for each button that gives the screen's index in the Screen.screens array as well as its width and height. It is important to note that if you have only one monitor, you will see only one option here.

The page also contains a button that triggers the `handleClick` function when clicked. This method determines which radio button is selected and then calculates the center point of the referenced screen. The application window is positioned at this center point. If no screen is selected, an alert window is launched.

```
<html>
<head>
    <title>Entry 4.2 - Multiple Monitors</title>

    <script type="text/javascript" src="AIRAliases.js"></script>
    <script type="text/javascript">
      function populateScreens() {
            var form = document.getElementById('radioButtons');
            for(i=0; I < air.Screen.screens.length; i++) {
                var screen = air.Screen.screens[i];
                var rb = document.createElement('input');
                rb.type='radio';
                rb.name='screens';
                rb.value=i;
                form.appendChild(rb);
                form.innerHTML += 'Screen ' + i + ' - '
                form.innerHTML += 'Width: ' + screen.bounds.width;
                form.innerHTML += ' Height: ' + screen.bounds.height;
                form.innerHTML += '<br />';
            }
        }
        function handleClick() {
            var buttons = document.forms['screensForm'].elements['screens'];
            var selectedValue;
            for( i=0; i<buttons.length;i++) {
                if( buttons[i].checked) {
                    selectedValue = buttons[i].value;
                }
            }
            if (selectedValue) {
                var screen = air.Screen.screens[selectedValue];
                var centerX = screen.bounds.x + screen.bounds.width / 2;
                var centerY = screen.bounds.y + screen.bounds.height / 2;
                window.nativeWindow.x = centerX - (window.nativeWindow.width / 2);
                window.nativeWindow.y = centerY - (window.nativeWindow.height / 2);
            } else {
                alert('Please Select a Screen');
            }
        }
    </script>
</head>

<body onload="populateScreens()" style="text-align:center;">
    <form id="radioButtons" name="screensForm"></form>
    <br />
    <input type="button" value="Center on Selected Screen" onclick="handleClick()" />
</body>
</html>
```

4.3 Determining the Monitors on Which an Application Is Currently Displayed

Problem

You need to determine which screens currently display your AIR application.

Solution

Use the getScreensForRectangle, which is a static method of the Screen class, to determine which screens are being used to display a given region as defined by the given rectangle instance.

Discussion

In situations where the current screen needs to be calculated, you can use the get ScreensForRectangle. This static method of the Screen class takes one argument: a rectangle. When you pass in an instance of the Rectangle class, it returns an array of the screens the rectangle occupies.

In this case, the bounds property of the NativeWindow class provides the instance of the Rectangle class that is needed for the getScreensForRectangle method. By passing this value into the method, you can determine which screens the referenced window occupies.

In the following examples, an event listener is attached to the native window's moving event. This means that each time the application window is moved, the event listener method will be called. In the handleMove method, the currently occupied screens are calculated and then displayed in the application.

ActionScript

In this example, the list of the currently occupied screens is stored in an ArrayCollection, which is bound to a List and updated in the handleMove listener method for the moving event when the window is moved. This listener method is also added as a listener to the creationComplete event to ensure it is executed when the application is launched and rendered.

```
<?xml version="1.0" encoding="utf-8"?>
<mx:WindowedApplication
    xmlns:mx="http://www.adobe.com/2006/mxml"
    layout="vertical"
    moving="handleMove(event)"
    creationComplete="handleMove(event)">
    width="320" height="240">

    <mx:Script>
        <![CDATA[
```

```
import mx.collections.ArrayCollection;

[Bindable]
private var monitors:ArrayCollection = new ArrayCollection();

private function handleMove(event:Event):void {
    monitors.removeAll();
    var windowBounds:Rectangle = this.nativeWindow.bounds;
    var screens:Array = Screen.getScreensForRectangle(windowBounds);

    var output:String = "";
    var screen:Screen;
    for( var i:uint = 0; i < screens.length; i++ ) {
        screen = screens[i];
        output = "Screen " + i + " - ";
        output += "Width: " + screen.bounds.width;
        output += " Height: " + screen.bounds.height;
        monitors.addItem({ label: output });
    }
}
    ]]>
</mx:Script>

<mx:Label text="Occupied Screens" fontWeight="bold" />
<mx:List id="monitorsList" dataProvider="{monitors}" width="100%" height="100%" />


</mx:WindowedApplication>
```

JavaScript

In this example, the event listener, handleMove, is registered for the AIR moving event and also for the JavaScript onload event of the page body. The method is called any time the window is moved and also when the page is loaded. It determines the currently occupied screens before adding a new div to the main listing div for each of the screens that is returned from the call to getScreensForRectangle.

```
<html>
<head>
    <title>Entry 4.3 - Get Current Application Screens</title>

    <script type="text/javascript" src="AIRAliases.js"></script>
    <script type="text/javascript">
        window.nativeWindow.addEventListener(air.NativeWindowBoundsEvent.MOVING,
handleMove);

        function handleMove(event) {
            var listing = document.getElementById('listing');
            while(listing.hasChildNodes()) {
                listing.removeChild(listing.firstChild);
            }
            var screens =
air.Screen.getScreensForRectangle(window.nativeWindow.bounds);
            for(i=0;i < screens.length;i++) {
```

```
                    var newDiv = document.createElement('div');
                    newDiv.innerHTML += "Screen " + i;
                    newDiv.innerHTML += " WIDTH: " + screens[i].bounds.width;
                    newDiv.innerHTML += " HEIGHT: " + screens[i].bounds.height;
                    listing.appendChild(newDiv);
                }
            }
        </script>
    </head>

    <body onload="handleMove(event)" style="text-align:center;">
        <strong>Occupied Screens</strong>
        <div id="listing"></div>
    </body>
</html>
```

CHAPTER 5

HTML Content

Adobe AIR allows a strong integration with HTML content and JavaScript. Thanks to the WebKit open source browser engine embedded in the Adobe runtime, AIR offers a complete and robust HTML renderer and JavaScript interpreter to re-create a browser-like experience. Through the WebKit framework (*http://webkit.org/*), developers can create an AIR application completely in HTML, JavaScript, DOM, and CSS. In AIR 1.5, the new SquirrelFish JavaScript interpreter from the WebKit project was added. This makes JavaScript code execution extremely fast within AIR.

The core of the HTML and JavaScript environment is represented by the `HTMLLoader` class, which enables you to specify the HTML content to display in an AIR application. `HTMLLoader` is part of the `flash.html` package and is a subclass of the `Sprite` class that does not implement the `UIComponent` interface. If you want to use the class in AIR applications created with Flex, you have to extend the `UIComponent` interface and include an `HTMLLoader` object.

The `HTMLLoader` object can also be accessed via JavaScript by using the `htmlLoader` property of the `window` object. In HTML windows, the `HTMLLoader` object contains all the HTML content that is, in turn, contained in a `NativeWindow` object. Furthermore, the `HTMLLoader` object provides properties, methods, and events to control how content is loaded and rendered within the AIR application.

When you use HTML content in an application, you need to understand how to interact with the AIR environment by using JavaScript as well as ActionScript. In this chapter, you will learn how to access JavaScript from ActionScript, as well as how to access ActionScript from JavaScript in an HTML container.

5.1 Displaying HTML Content

Problem

You need to display HTML content in an AIR application.

Solution

Use the HTMLLoader class to directly load HTML content via a URL or assign the content as an HTML string. The HTML content will be rendered through the HTML WebKit engine, embedded in AIR.

Discussion

The HTMLLoader class enables you to load and view HTML content from a desktop application in several ways. Part of the flash.html package, HTMLLoader is a Sprite subclass and inherits all the display properties, methods, and events of a Sprite object: click, mouseMove, rotation, and so on. No matter which method you choose for loading HTML content, you must make an HTMLLoader object visible onscreen by changing its default height and width properties (0 × 0 pixels) to your preferred size. Remember that the maximum width allowed is 2880 pixels. So if you set the dimension to more than 2880 pixels, an ArgumentError exception will be thrown.

The first method is to load HTML content from a URL in an HTMLLoader class. To do so, create an instance of the HTMLLoader class, set its width and height, and then launch its load method. The load method accepts a URLRequest object as a parameter, which specifies the URL to load. For example:

```
var html:HTMLLoader = new HTMLLoader();
html.width = 320;
html.height = 240;
var urlReq:URLRequest = new URLRequest("http://www.comtaste.com/en");
html.load(urlReq);
```

After the load method has been launched, several are dispatched, as listed in Table 5-1.

Table 5-1. ActionScript Events Dispatched by the HTMLLoader Class

ActionScript Event	Description
htmlDOMInitialize	Before any script or DOM is parsed, this event is dispatched when the HTML document is created.
complete	Immediately after the onload event of the HTML page, this event is dispatched when the load method is launched and the HTML DOM is created.
htmlBoundsChanged	This event is dispatched if the contentWidth and contentHeight properties change.
locationChange	This event is dispatched when the location property of the HTMLLoader changes.
scroll	This event is dispatched when the HTML engine changes the scroll position of an HTML element (also using the toScroll JavaScript method).
uncaughtScriptException	This event is dispatched when a JavaScript exception occurs in the HTMLLoader and the exception is not caught in JavaScript code.
htmlRender	This event is dispatched when the rendering of content is fully up-to-date in the HTMLLoader object.

The second method of loading content is to assign an HTML string, instead of a URL, to the HTMLLoader class, as in loadString(htmlContent:String):void.

This method loads and renders the HTML string, which is passed as a parameter to loadString:

```
var html:HTMLLoader = new HTMLLoader();
html.width = 320;
html.height = 240;
var htmlCode:String = "<html><body><h1>Hello World!</h1></b>.</body></html>";

html.loadString(htmlCode);
```

It is also possible to use the HTMLLoader class to load an HTML page instead of an HTML string. In this scenario, the syntax doesn't change and entails the creation of a Native WindowInit object, where the HTMLLoader object will be hosted.

ActionScript/Flash

To demonstrate how loading HTML could fit into a larger application, the following ActionScript 3 class uses the SimpleButton and TextField classes to build an application's visual elements dynamically and then triggers the load method of the HTMLLoader upon the click event of the button. You can easily implement this snippet in a SWF-based application for loading into HTML content from a URL.

```
package com.oreilly.aircookbook.ch5
{
    import flash.display.NativeWindowInitOptions;
    import flash.display.SimpleButton;
    import flash.display.Sprite;
    import flash.display.StageAlign;
    import flash.display.StageScaleMode;
    import flash.events.MouseEvent;
    import flash.geom.Rectangle;

    import flash.html.HTMLLoader;

    import flash.net.URLRequest;
    import flash.text.TextField;
    import flash.text.TextFieldAutoSize;
    import flash.text.TextFieldType;
    import flash.text.TextFormat;
    import flash.text.TextFormatAlign;

    public class DisplayHTMLContent extends Sprite
    {
        private var _html:HTMLLoader;
        private var _field:TextField;
        private var _loadBtn:SimpleButton;

        public function DisplayHTMLContent()
        {
            this.stage.scaleMode = StageScaleMode.NO_SCALE;
            this.stage.align = StageAlign.TOP_LEFT;
```

```
        drawLayout();
    }

    private function drawLayout():void
    {
        // draw URL input bar
        _field = new TextField();
        _field.type = TextFieldType.INPUT;
        _field.multiline = false;
        _field.width = 300;
        _field.height = 50;
        _field.border = true;
        _field.borderColor = 0x999999;
        _field.x = 50;
        _field.y = 10;
        _field.textColor = 0x666666;
        _field.text = "http://www.comtaste.com/en";
        this.addChild(_field);

        createButton();
    }

    private function createButton():void
    {
        var upState:Sprite = new Sprite();
        upState.graphics.lineStyle( 1, 0x330000 );
        upState.graphics.beginFill( 0x999999 );
        upState.graphics.drawRect( 0,0,40,30 );
        upState.graphics.endFill();
        var upLabel:TextField = new TextField();
        upLabel.width = 50;
        upLabel.height = 30;
        upLabel.autoSize = TextFieldAutoSize.NONE;
        var upFo:TextFormat = new TextFormat();
        upFo.size = 12;
        upFo.color = 0x330000;
        upFo.align = TextFormatAlign.CENTER;
        upLabel.defaultTextFormat = upFo;
        upLabel.text = "LOAD";
        upState.addChild( upLabel );

        var downState:Sprite = new Sprite();
        downState.graphics.lineStyle( 1, 0x000033 );
        downState.graphics.beginFill( 0xcc0000 );
        downState.graphics.drawRect( 0,0,40,30 );
        downState.graphics.endFill();
        var downLabel:TextField = new TextField();
        downLabel.width = 50;
        downLabel.height = 30;
        downLabel.autoSize = TextFieldAutoSize.NONE;
        var downFo:TextFormat = new TextFormat();
        downFo.size = 12;
        downFo.color = 0x000000;
        downFo.align = TextFormatAlign.CENTER;
```

```
        downLabel.defaultTextFormat = downFo;
        downLabel.text = "LOAD";
        downState.addChild( downLabel );

        _loadBtn = new SimpleButton( upState, downState, downState, downState );
        _loadBtn.x = _field.x + _field.width + 10;
        _loadBtn.y = _field.y;

        _loadBtn.addEventListener(MouseEvent.CLICK, onClickLoad);

        addChild( _loadBtn );
    }

    private function onClickLoad( evt:MouseEvent ):void
    {
        if( _field.text == "" )
        trace ( "Button clicked but none URL to load has been specified !" );

        var initOptions:NativeWindowInitOptions = new NativeWindowInitOptions();
        var bounds:Rectangle = new Rectangle(50, 30, 500, 400);

        _html = HTMLLoader.createRootWindow(false, initOptions, true, bounds);
        _html.stage.nativeWindow.activate();

        var urlReq:URLRequest = new URLRequest( _field.text );
        _html.load( urlReq );
    }
  }
 }
}
```

The core of the class is in the private onClickLoad method, which is an event handler that is triggered by the click event dispatched from the SimpleButton instance. In this event handler, the load method is launched, and the text contained in the _field text field is assigned as a URL.

ActionScript/Flex

In Flex, only classes that extend the UIComponent class can be added as children of the Flex container. Because the HTMLLoader class is a Sprite subclass, you cannot add an HTMLLoader object as a child of a container. If you try, you'll get an error. You can avoid this minor inconvenience in two ways. The first is to use the Flex component <mx:HTML>, whereas the second is to create an ActionScript class that extends the UIComponent class and that contains an HTMLLoader class, making it a child of this UIComponent instance.

To use the <mx:HTML> control in Flex, simply call it as you do with any other control on a page:

```
<?xml version="1.0" encoding="utf-8"?>
<mx:WindowedApplication xmlns:mx="http://www.adobe.com/2006/mxml">

    <mx:HTML id="content" location="http://www.comtaste.com/en"/>
```

```
    </mx:WindowedApplication>
```

Within the control tag definition, you assign the location property to specify the URL of an HTML page whose content is displayed in the control, or you can set the htmlText property to specify a String containing HTML-formatted text that is rendered in the control.

On the other hand, you can create an ActionScript 3 class that extends the UIComponent class, and then you can use the class within a Flex container. To do so, use code similar to this:

```
package com.oreilly.aircookbook.ch5
{
    import mx.core.UIComponent;


    import flash.events.Event;
    import flash.html.HTMLLoader;
    import flash.net.URLRequest;

    [Event(name="complete")]
    public class DisplayHTMLContentFromFlex extends UIComponent
    {
        private var _html:HTMLLoader;

        public function DisplayHTMLContentFromFlex()
        {
          super();
        }


        override protected function createChildren():void
        {
            _html = new HTMLLoader();
            _html.width = 800;
            _html.height = 600;
            addChild(_html);

            _html.addEventListener( Event.COMPLETE, onComplete );
        }


        override protected function measure():void
        {
            measuredWidth = 800;
            measuredHeight= 600;
        }

        override protected function updateDisplayList(unscaledWidth:Number,
                                               unscaledHeight:Number):void
        {
            super.updateDisplayList(unscaledWidth, unscaledHeight);

            _html.width = unscaledWidth;
```

```
        _html.height= unscaledHeight;
    }

    private function onComplete( event:Event ) : void
    {
        var newEvent:Event = new Event(Event.COMPLETE);
        dispatchEvent( newEvent );
    }

    public function load( url:String ) : void
    {
        var request:URLRequest = new URLRequest(url);
        _html.load(request);
    }
}
}
```

Before the declaration of the class, the [Event] metadata has been used. The [Event] metadata tag defines events dispatched by a component. In this way, the Flex compiler can recognize them as MXML tag attributes in an MXML file.

Then an instance of the HTMLLoader class is created with the createChildren method, which creates child objects for the component. Next, the methods to assign a default dimension of the UIComponent class are overridden, first measure and then updateDisplay List(unscaledWidth:Number, unscaledHeight:Number). Finally, the complete event of the HTMLLoader is registered with the addEventListener method. Within the onComplete event handler, a new complete event is dispatched because this event does not bubble:

```
private function onComplete(event:Event):void
{
    var newEvent:Event = new Event(Event.COMPLETE);
    dispatchEvent( newEvent );
}
```

To implement this class in an AIR application created with Flex Builder, import the class as a custom component by creating a custom namespace:

```
<?xml version="1.0" encoding="utf-8"?>
<mx:WindowedApplication xmlns:mx="http://www.adobe.com/2006/mxml"
layout="vertical"
xmlns:comp="com.oreilly.aircookbook.ch5.*">

    <mx:Script>
    <![CDATA[

        private function loadHTML():void
        {
            htmlComp.load("http://www.comtaste.com");
        }

    ]]>
    </mx:Script>
```

```
    <comp:DisplayHTMLContentFromFlex id="htmlComp" />

    <mx:Button click="loadHTML()" label="Load HTML page" >

    </mx:Button>

  </mx:WindowedApplication>
```

JavaScript/HTML

The JavaScript environment of AIR is represented by the `HTMLLoader` class. The environment provides an HTML renderer, DOM, and JavaScript interpreter.

Figure 5-1 illustrates the relationship between the JavaScript environment and AIR in a bit more detail.

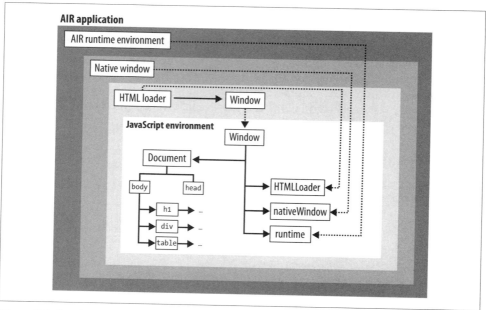

Figure 5-1. JavaScript environment in the AIR architecture

In Figure 5-1 notice that the JavaScript environment has its `Document` and `Window` objects. As you can see, the JavaScript environment can communicate with AIR through the following properties:

- `runtime` (allows access to AIR API classes)
- `nativeWindow`
- `htmlLoader`

The ActionScript code can access and communicate with the JavaScript environment through the following:

- The `window` property
- The `HTMLLoader` object (referenced to the JavaScript `Window` object)

In JavaScript, you use the `createRootWindow` method, which returns an `HTMLLoader` object and accepts the following values as parameters:

- `visible: Boolean`
- `windowInitOptions: NativeWindowInitOptions`
- `scrollBarsVisible: Boolean`
- `bounds: Rectangle`

Before invoking the `createRootWindow` method, you must create an instance of the `air.NativeWindowInitOptions` class, as well as a `Rectangle` object, which is an area defined by its position, as indicated by its top-left corner point (x, y) and by its width and its height.

This example implements an `HTMLLoader` in JavaScript and uses the `activate` method to bring the window to the front and give it focus:

```
var _initOptions = new air.NativeWindowInitOptions();
var _bounds = new air.Rectangle(50, 50, 320, 240);

var html = air.HTMLLoader.createRootWindow(false, _initOptions, true, _bounds);

var urlReq = new air.URLRequest( 'http://www.comtaste.com/en' );
html.load( urlReq );

html.stage.nativeWindow.activate();
```

5.2 Accessing JavaScript from ActionScript in an HTML Container

Problem

You need to access JavaScript functions from ActionScript in an HTML container.

Solution

Use the global `window` property of the `HTMLLoader` class.

Discussion

AIR applications that use the `HTMLLoader` class to load and view HTML content frequently must also contain a means of communication between the JavaScript code and ActionScript properties, methods, or objects. For example, you may need to pass

ActionScript data to HTML content or launch JavaScript functions from the application's ActionScript classes.

The HTML content loaded within an HTMLLoader object can easily access ActionScript objects through JavaScript by using the window property of the HTMLLoader class in the ActionScript class. The window property, typed as a generic Object, represents the global JavaScript object for the content loaded into the HTML control, and therefore it lets you make ActionScript properties, methods, and objects available to JavaScript. When you type something as a generic Object, you are implying that there is no type checking on the properties you add on that object.

After creating the instance of the HTMLLoader object, you can make ActionScript objects and functions available to JavaScript code by creating references within the JavaScript execution context.

The following ActionScript class, saved as *AccessJavaScript.as*, creates an instance of the HTMLLoader object and loads the *htmlcontent.html* page as HTML content. Then it adds the HTMLStringFromAS property and the linkedToAS function referencing ActionScript objects to the window object of an HTML page:

```
package com.oreilly.aircookbook.ch5
{

    import flash.display.Sprite;
    import flash.display.StageAlign;
    import flash.display.StageScaleMode;
    import flash.events.Event;
    import flash.html.HTMLLoader;
    import flash.net.URLRequest;

    public class AccessJavaScript extends Sprite
    {
        private var _html:HTMLLoader;

        public function AccessJavaScript ()
        {
            this.stage.scaleMode = StageScaleMode.NO_SCALE;
            this.stage.align = StageAlign.TOP_LEFT;

            var urlReq:URLRequest = new URLRequest( "htmlcontent.html" );
            _html.load( urlReq );

            initLayout();
        }

        protected function initLayout():void
        {
            _html = new HTMLLoader();
            _html.width = stage.stageWidth;
            _html.height = stage.stageHeight;
            _html.addEventListener(Event.COMPLETE, onComplete);
            this.addChild( _html );
        }
```

```
private function onComplete(e:Event):void
{
    _html.window.HTMLStringFromAS = "<div style= ' overflow:hidden;
            height:20px' id= ' fromAS ' ><strong>This is an HTML
            string generated by ActionScript</strong></div>"
    _html.window.linkedToJS = linkedToAS;
}

private function linkedToAS( messageFromJS:String ):void
{
    trace( "From JavaScript: ", messageFromJS );
}

    }
}
```

Take a closer look at what's happening in the class. The HTMLLoader object, which has the name instance_html assigned, registers the onComplete event handler upon the COMPLETE event. In this event handler, the HTMLStringFromAS property is assigned a value, and the linkedToAS ActionScript function is mapped to the linkedToJS JavaScript function.

 If you use the COMPLETE event, only scripts in the page that run after the page load event can access the added objects.

An HTML string that includes a div tag is assigned as a value to the HTMLStringFromAS property, which contains simple bold text:

```
<div style='overflow:hidden; height:20px' id='fromAS'>
<strong>This is an HTML string generated by ActionScript</strong></div>
```

The linkedToAS function is an ActionScript function that accepts a simple String as a parameter. This function will be invoked by the JavaScript code declared in the *htmlcon tent.html* page and loaded in the HTMLLoader class. This function executes a simple trace command:

```
private function linkedToAS( messageFromJS:String ):void
{
    trace( "From JavaScript: ", messageFromJS );
}
```

The *htmlcontent.html* page, loaded in the HTMLLoader object, uses the HTMLStringFromAS ActionScript property and invokes the linkedToAS ActionScript function:

```
<!DOCTYPE html PUBLIC "-//W3C//DTD XHTML 1.0
 Transitional//EN" "http://www.w3.org/TR/xhtml1/DTD/xhtml1-transitional.dtd">
<html xmlns="http://www.w3.org/1999/xhtml">
<head>
```

```
<meta http-equiv="Content-Type" content="text/html; charset=UTF-8">
<title>Solution 15.2: Accessing JavaScript from ActionScript in an HTML
Container</title>

<script type="text/javascript" src="frameworks/AIRAliases.js"></script>
<script type="text/javascript" src="frameworks/AIRIntrospector.js" ></script>

<script type="text/javascript">

    var messageFromAir = null;

    function showMessageFromAir()
    {
        document.getElementById("contentData").innerHTML = HTMLStringFromAS;
    }

</script>

</head>

<body>

    <h2>Display the HTMLStringFromAS ActionScript-generated strings</h2>
    <p>
        <button onclick="showMessageFromAir()">
            Access to ActionScript property from JavaScript
        </button>
    </p>

        <h2>Send a trace action into Adobe AIR output console from JavaScript</h2>
        <p>

        <button onclick="linkedToAS('This is a JavaScript generated string.')">
            Access to ActionScript function from JavaScript
        </button>
    </p>

    <div id="contentData" style="overflow:auto; width:100%; height:100%"></div>

</body>

</html>
```

The HTML page defines the showMessageFromAir JavaScript function, which has the task of adding the HTMLStringFromAS HTML string, declared in the ActionScript class, in the contentData div.

The ActionScript property from the innerHTML is consumed in the body of the HTML page, and the ActionScript function is invoked and is passed on a String directly from JavaScript.

The first button launches the showMessageFromAir JavaScript function upon the click event, which loads the content of the ActionScript property HTMLStringFromAS within the `contentData` `div` tag. The second button invokes the ActionScript function `linkedToAS`, to which it assigns a `String` as a parameter.

AIR also lets you make an ActionScript class definition available to JavaScript. With this possibility, you can create an instance of an ActionScript object by inheriting all its properties directly from JavaScript. To make an ActionScript class available, you need to set the `runtimeApplicationDomain` property of the `HTMLLoader` class to `ApplicationDomain.currentDomain` or to the application domain containing the class definitions. `runtimeApplicationDomain` is a property of the `HTMLLoader` class that specifies the application domain to use for the `window.runtime` object in JavaScript in the HTML page:

```
html.runtimeApplicationDomain = ApplicationDomain.currentDomain;
```

Once you specify the `runtimeApplicationDomain`, you can create an instance of a class in JavaScript by referring to the `window.runtime` property:

```
var customClassObject = new window.runtime.CustomClass();
```

But be careful of the security domain of the HTML content. If you are actually loading a remote HTML content from the Internet, you cannot set the `runtimeApplication Domain` property to the `ApplicationDomain.currentDomain` value.

5.3 Accessing ActionScript from JavaScript in an HTML Container

Problem

You need to access ActionScript functions, properties, and methods from JavaScript in an HTML container.

Solution

The `window` property of the `HTMLLoader` class is typed as `Object` to represent the global JavaScript object for the content loaded into the HTML control. By mapping the elements you want to refer to from ActionScript to JavaScript, you can then call the objects themselves with the JavaScript code specified in the HTML content.

Discussion

When you load HTML content by using the `HTMLLoader` class, that content is able to communicate with and access its parent. This means an AIR application can call ActionScript functions or use properties declared in an ActionScript class through JavaScript code contained in a loaded HTML page.

The window property of the HTMLLoader class allows AIR developers to map any Action-Script object so as to make it available to the HTML content. For example:

```
private var ASProperty:String = new String("Hello JavaScript !");

private var _html:HTMLLoader = new HTMLLoader();
private var _urlReq:URLRequest = new URLRequest("myPage.html");

private function init():void
{
   _html.load(_urlReq);
   _html.addEventListener(Event.COMPLETE, onComplete);
}

private function onComplete (e:Event):void
{
   _html.window.JSfunction = ASfunction;
   _html.window.JSproperty = ASProperty;
}

private function ASfunction ( evt:MouseEvent ):void
{
   trace( "JavaScript calls !" );
}
```

The complete event of the HTMLLoader class corresponds to the load event of the body of the HTML page. The previous example creates a listener for this COMPLETE event to execute the mapping of the ActionScript objects. The onComplete event handler is executed only after the whole page is loaded.

Inside the onComplete event handler, you need to link JSFunction, which was declared in the HTML page, to ASfunction, which is defined in the ActionScript code. Next, you map the JSproperty property, which was created in the JavaScript code of the HTML page, to ASProperty, which is declared via ActionScript.

The following example creates an ActionScript class that extends the Sprite class and that exposes a method and a property to JavaScript:

```
package com.oreilly.aircookbook.ch5
{

   import flash.display.Sprite;
   import flash.display.StageAlign;
   import flash.display.StageScaleMode;
   import flash.events.Event;
   import flash.events.MouseEvent;
   import flash.html.HTMLLoader;
   import flash.net.URLRequest;


   public class AccessingActionScript extends Sprite
   {

      private var _html:HTMLLoader;
```

```
        private var ASProperty:String = new String("Hello JavaScript !");

        public function AccessingActionScript()
        {
            this.stage.scaleMode = StageScaleMode.NO_SCALE;
            this.stage.align = StageAlign.TOP_LEFT;

            _html = new HTMLLoader();

            var urlReq:URLRequest = new URLRequest( "myHTMLContent.html" );
            _html.load( urlReq );

            _html.width = stage.stageWidth;
            _html.height = stage.stageHeight;
            _html.addEventListener(Event.COMPLETE, onComplete);

            this.addChild( _html );

        }

        private function onComplete (e:Event):void
        {
            _html.window.JSfunction = ASfunction;
            _html.window.JSproperty = ASProperty;
        }

        // Pass the trace string to the Adobe AIR output console
        private function ASfunction( evt:MouseEvent=null ):void
        {
            trace( "JavaScript calls !" );
        }
    }
}
```

The previous example maps the ActionScript method and property to the JavaScript property and method on the event handler registered for the COMPLETE event, which is dispatched by HTMLLoader when the content of the page has been loaded.

In the *myHTMLContent.html* page, which is loaded in the HTMLLoader class instance, you can access the ASfunction ActionScript function and the ASProperty property through JavaScript.

This is the code of the *myHTMLContent.html* page, loaded by the HTMLLoader class:

```
<!DOCTYPE html PUBLIC "-//W3C//DTD XHTML 1.0 Transitional//EN"
"http://www.w3.org/TR/xhtml1/DTD/xhtml1-transitional.dtd">
<html xmlns="http://www.w3.org/1999/xhtml">
<head>

<meta http-equiv="Content-Type" content="text/html; charset=UTF-8">
<title>Solution 15.3: Accessing ActionScript  from JavaScript  in an HTML
Container</title>

<script type="text/javascript" src="frameworks/AIRAliases.js"></script>
<script type="text/javascript" src="frameworks/AIRIntrospector.js"></script>
```

```
<script type="text/javascript">

    function accessingASProperty()
    {
        document.getElementById("contentData").innerText = JSproperty;
    }

</script>

</head>

<body>

<p>
    <button onClick="accessingASProperty()">
        Access to ActionScript property from JavaScript
    </button>
</p>

<h2>Send a trace action into Adobe AIR output console from JavaScript</h2>
<p>

    <button onClick="JSfunction()">
        Access to ActionScript function from JavaScript
    </button>

</p>

<div id="contentData" style="overflow:auto; width:100%; height:100%"></div>

</body>

</html>
```

The JavaScript code accesses the ActionScript function when the user clicks the button. It is precisely on the onclick event that Jsfunction, a function that is mapped in the ActionScript code to ASfunction, is called.

The HTML page, on the other hand, accesses the ASProperty ActionScript property, when the JavaScript accessingASProperty event handler is invoked.

The accessingASProperty JavaScript function accesses the contentData div element and sets the innerText property to the value assigned to the ASProperty ActionScript property.

With this same approach, you can access practically any element of the HTML page loaded in the HTMLLoader and interact with the HTML DOM. In the next recipe, you will access the HTML DOM of the HTML page that is loaded in an instance of the HTMLLoader class through ActionScript.

5.4 Scripting the DOM from ActionScript

Problem

You need to access and manipulate the elements in the HTML DOM for the page loaded within the `HTMLLoader` class.

Solution

Use the `getElementById` and `getElementsByTagName` methods, as well as `innerText` and `innerHTML`, to access DOM elements in AIR.

Discussion

The term *DOM* refers to an object model to represent XML and related formats. By using the DOM, you can dynamically edit any element in an HTML page through ActionScript, as well as create new pages programmatically. To do so, you use some methods and properties of the DOM. The DOM methods and properties you need to use are as follows:

`getElementsByTagName` (*in* `DOMString tagname`)

This method enables you to access a DOM element of the document by referring to the name of the tag. This method is very useful when you want to number and access all the elements of the same kind. The following code iterates the entire document of the HTML document node tree and returns the nodes that have been passed onto the function in an `Array`:

```
function listElements(whichTag, whichAttr, whichValue)
{

    var startElement;
    var listElement_arr= new Array();

    if (whichTag) {
        startElement = document.getElementsByTagName(whichTag);
    } else {
        startElement = (document.all) ? document.all :
            document.getElementsByTagName("*");
    }
    if (whichAttr) {
        for (var i = 0; i < startElement.length; i++) {
            if (startElement[i].getAttribute(whichAttr)) {
                if (whichValue) {
                    if (startElement[i].getAttribute(whichAttr) == whichValue) {
                        listElement_arr[listElement_arr.length] = startElement[i];
                    }
                } else {
                    listElement_arr[listElement_arr.length] = startElement[i];
                }
            }
        }
    }
```

```
        } else {

            listElement_arr= startElement;
        }
        return listElement_arr;
    }
```

This function can be invoked by ActionScript by using the name of the instance of the HTMLLoader object and its window property:

```
var myElementArray:Array = _html.window.listElements("a","class", "trainingLink");
```

By launching the JavaScript function with these parameters, an Array will be returned with all the a type nodes that will have the attribute class set to the value trainingLink.

getElementById *(in* DOMString elementId*)*

This method enables you to access an element by referring to its ID attribute, specified in the tag node. You have already seen an example that uses this method in Recipe 5.3:

```
function accessingASProperty()
{
    document.getElementById("contentData").innerText = "Hello World" ;
}
```

innerText

This DOM property sets or retrieves the text between the start and end tags of the object.

innerHTML

This DOM property returns or sets all the content of the specified element in the html tag of the page. This property also enables you to set the content for one or more of the DOM's elements.

> To see which DOM classes are contained in the WebKit engine, visit
> *http://developer.apple.com/documentation/AppleApplications/Reference/*
> *WebKitDOMRef/index.html.*

After you create an HTMLLoader object, you can navigate the DOM tree of the elements contained in the HTML contents. The following example of ActionScript code creates an HTMLLoader object that loads the page *http://www.comtaste.com/en/training.htm*:

```
var initOptions:NativeWindowInitOptions = new NativeWindowInitOptions();
var bounds:Rectangle = new Rectangle(50, 30, 800, 600);
var _html = HTMLLoader.createRootWindow(false, initOptions, true, bounds);
_html.stage.nativeWindow.activate();
var _urlReq:URLRequest = new URLRequest( "http://www.comtaste.com/en/training.htm" );
_html.load( _urlReq );
_html.addEventListener( Event.COMPLETE, onComplete );
```

Be aware that before the COMPLETE event is dispatched, the DOM elements may not have been parsed or created. As best practice, wait for this event before accessing any HTML DOM elements.

Upon the COMPLETE event, the onComplete event handler is invoked. Within the event handler, you'll write the code to access the HTML DOM. The following example accesses the DOM element with the same ID of the container and returns the HTML content of that node.

The hmtlCode variable contains the following HTML content:

```
<ul class="primary-links">
<li><a href="company.htm">COMPANY</a></li>
  <li><a href="solutions.htm">SOLUTIONS</a></li>
  <li><a href="consulting.htm">CONSULTING</a></li>
  <li><a href="training.htm" class="active">TRAINING</a></li>
  <li><a href="clients.htm">CLIENTS</a></li>
  <li><a href="casestudieslist.htm">CASE STUDIES</a></li>
</ul>
```

This content corresponds precisely with the HTML code contained in the div with ID="menu" of the *http://www.comtaste.com/en/training.htm* page.

In addition to accessing the DOM elements, you can change their properties. For example, you could change the src attributes of the img tag, add the alt attribute to all the a links, or even dynamically add elements to the page with ActionScript. The following example adds a portion of HTML code that creates a div element with a text value to the onComplete event handler:

```
private function onComplete( event:Event ) : void
{
    var htmlCode:String = _html.window.document.getElementById("menu").innerHTML;
    _html.window.document.getElementById("menu").innerHTML =
                        "<div style=\"overflow:hidden; height:20px\"
                        id=\"fromAS\"><strong>This is an HTML string
                        generated by ActionScript</strong></div>"
}
```

In the previous example, you programmatically changed the elements of an HTML page accessing the DOM directly. Accessing HTML DOM directly from ActionScript offers many possibilities for creating highly interactive AIR applications. For example, you could create applications that exploit HTML and JavaScript by programming directly from ActionScript and by leveraging the more advanced functions of the programming language of Flash and Flex.

ActionScript/Flex

The following ActionScript class accesses and manipulates the HTML DOM to dynamically change the elements of the HTML content that is loaded in an HTMLLoader object.

The class is a subclass of the Flex Framework's UIComponent class and can, therefore, also be used in this environment:

```
package com.oreilly.aircookbook.ch5
{
    import flash.events.Event;
    import flash.html.HTMLLoader;
    import flash.net.URLRequest;

    import mx.core.UIComponent;


    [Event(name="complete")]
    public class AccessDOMElements extends UIComponent
    {

        private var _html:HTMLLoader;


        public function AccessDOMElements()
        {
            super();
        }

        override protected function createChildren():void
        {
            _html = new HTMLLoader();
            _html.width = 800;
            _html.height = 600;
            addChild(_html);

            _html.addEventListener( Event.COMPLETE, onComplete );
        }


        override protected function measure():void
        {
            measuredWidth = 800;
            measuredHeight= 600;
        }


        override protected function updateDisplayList(unscaledWidth:Number,
                                            unscaledHeight:Number):void
        {
            super.updateDisplayList(unscaledWidth, unscaledHeight);

            _html.width = unscaledWidth;
            _html.height= unscaledHeight;
        }


        private function onComplete( event:Event ) : void
        {
            var newEvent:Event = new Event(Event.COMPLETE);
```

```
            dispatchEvent( newEvent );

        }


        public function load( url:String ) : void
        {
            var request:URLRequest = new URLRequest(url);
            _html.load(request);

        }


        public function htmlCodebyID():String
        {

            var htmlCode:String = _html.window.document.getElementById("container").innerHTML;

            return htmlCode;
        }

        public function htmlCodebyTag():String
        {

            var htmlCode:Object = _html.window.document.getElementsByTagName("img");
            var htmlStr:String;

            if (htmlCode != null)

            for (var i:Number = 0; i < htmlCode.length; i++)
            {
                if (htmlCode[i].getAttribute("class") == "logo")
                {
                    htmlCode[i].src =
"http://livedocs.adobe.com/air/1/devappsflash/images/adobe.png";
                    htmlStr += htmlCode[i].src +"\n";
                    htmlStr += htmlCode[i].width +"\n";
                    htmlStr += htmlCode[i].height +"\n";
                }
            }

        return htmlStr;
        }

        private  function listElements(whichTag:String,
                                       whichAttr:String="",
                                       whichValue:String=""):Object
        {

            var startElement:Object = new Object();
            var listElement_arr:Object= new Object();

            if (whichTag) {
                startElement =
_html.window.document.getElementsByTagName(whichTag);
```

```
            } else {
                startElement = (_html.window.document.all) ?
_html.window.document.all :
                    _html.window.document.getElementsByTagName("*");
            }
            if (whichAttr) {
                for (var i:Number = 0; i < startElement.length; i++) {
                    if (startElement[i].getAttribute(whichAttr)) {
                        if (whichValue) {
                            if (startElement[i].getAttribute(whichAttr) ==
whichValue) {
                                listElement_arr[listElement_arr.length] =
startElement[i];
                            }
                        } else {
                            listElement_arr[listElement_arr.length] =
startElement[i];
                        }
                    }
                }
            } else {

                listElement_arr= startElement;
            }

            return listElement_arr;
        }

        public function walkingTree(tagName:String):String
        {
            var DOMList:Object = listElements(tagName);
            var walkingTreeList:String;

            if (DOMList != null)

            for (var i:Number = 0; i < DOMList.length; i++)
            {
             walkingTreeList += DOMList[i].innerHTML +"\n";
            }

        return walkingTreeList;

        }

    }
}
```

The `AccessDOMElements` class navigates through the DOM elements of the HTML page loaded into the `HTMLLoader` instance looking for an explicit image within the HTML code. Upon finding the image, the code switches to the new one.

The `AccessDOMElements` class has three public methods. The first, `htmlCodebyID`, is a public method and returns a `String` that contains HTML code in the tag that is specified by using the `getElementById` method.

The second public method, htmlCodebyTag, returns the HTML code contained in a certain HTML tag that is specified with the getElementsByTagName method. Furthermore, this method uses the DOM getAttribute method, which allows access to certain attributes of the selected node. That way, you are able to act on the single HTML element and change any of its values. With a loop, this function looks in all the img tags of the content, and when it verifies a condition on the attribute class of that tag, it changes its src attribute, loading a new image from a new pathway:

```
public function htmlCodebyTag():String
{

    var htmlCode:Object = _html.window.document.getElementsByTagName("img");
    var htmlStr:String;

    if (htmlCode != null)

    for (var i:Number = 0; i < htmlCode.length; i++)
    {
        if (htmlCode[i].getAttribute("class") == "logo")
        {
        htmlCode[i].src =
"http://livedocs.adobe.com/air/1/devappsflash/images/adobe.png";
        htmlStr += htmlCode[i].src +"\n";
        htmlStr += htmlCode[i].width +"\n";
        htmlStr += htmlCode[i].height +"\n";
        }
    }

    return htmlStr;
}
```

The third public function, walkingTree, returns the content of the HTML DOM elements that correspond to the search criteria; it returns the content with the innerHTML property. This criteria is specified in another method that is launched by the walking Tree: the private listElements method. The listElements method accepts three parameters: whichTag (the name of the tag to point to), whichAttr (the attribute of the specified tag to use), and whichValue (the value of the attribute to compare). This method returns a collection of elements that verify the conditions of the parameters sent to it.

The property that is returned by the method is called listElement_arr. Even if in theory this property contains an array of elements and if you assign them as data type Array, the application will raise a Type coercion error:

Error #1034: Type Coercion failed: cannot convert __HTMLScriptObject@fb55b1 in Array.

Instead, you must type the properties as Object classes that return the elements by using the getElementsByTagName method.

You can use the AccessDOMElements class in a simple MXML application that will then be packaged in AIR. You can use Flex Builder 3 as an environment to write the following code, or you can write it with any text editor and then compile it with the AIR `adl` command-line compiler (which you can find in the AIR SDK):

```
<?xml version="1.0" encoding="utf-8"?>
<mx:WindowedApplication xmlns:mx="http://www.adobe.com/2006/mxml"
layout="vertical">

    <mx:Script>
    <![CDATA[

        private var list_arr:Array;

        private function loadHTML():void
        {
            htmlComp.load("http://www.comtaste.com/en/training.htm");

        }

    ]]>
    </mx:Script>

    <mx:TextArea width="800" height="300" id="myTA" />
    <mx:HBox>

        <mx:Button label="Show HTML Code"  click="myTA.text =
        htmlComp.htmlCodebyID()" />

        <mx:Button label="Change Image"  click="myTA.text =
        htmlComp.htmlCodebyTag()" />

        <mx:Label text="Insert the name of the Tag: " />
        <mx:TextInput id="tagName" text="*" />
        <mx:Button label="Navigate The DOM Tree by Tag"
        click="myTA.text = htmlComp.walkingTree(tagName.text)" />

    </mx:HBox>

    <comp:AccessDOMElements xmlns:comp="com.oreilly.aircookbook.ch5.*"
    id="htmlComp"
     initialize="loadHTML()" />

</mx:WindowedApplication>
```

It is the `AccessDOMElements` component that creates the instance of the `AccessDOMElements` ActionScript class, created in the `com.oreilly.aircookbook.ch5` package and associated to the namespace `comp`.

Once the AIR application has been compiled, it will load the content of the page *http://www.comtaste.com/en/training.htm* in the `HTMLLoader` object and will expose three buttons (Figure 5-2), which will launch the previously mentioned three public methods of the ActionScript class.

```
<title>Training | Comtaste</title>
<meta http-equiv="Content-Type" content="text/html; charset=iso-8859-1">
<style type="text/css" media="all">
@import "img/style.css";
.Stile1 {
    color: #FF6600;
    font-weight: bold;
}
</style>
</head><body>
<div id="header"><a href="index.php"> <img src="img/logoComtaste.gif" alt="Comtaste" title="Comtaste" class="logo"></a>
  <div id="alpha">
    <ul>
     <li><a href="http://blog.comtaste.com/">Blog</a></li>
     <li><a href="contact.htm">Contact</a></li>
     <li><a href="working-with-us.htm">Work with us</a></li>
              <li class="language"><a href="../index.php">Italiano</a></li>
    </ul>
  </div>
</div>
<div id="container">
```

Figure 5-2. *The AIR example shows the HTML content within the* HTMLLoader *class and iterates through the HTML DOM in search of nodes meeting set criteria.*

When the user inserts the name of an HTML tag in the TexInput, the walkingTree method will be called by clicking the Navigate button, and all the elements on the page that have been declared with that tag will be returned.

By clicking the Change Image button, the image of the Comtaste logo will be replaced with an image loaded from a remote source at the following URL: *http://livedocs.adobe .com/air/1/devappsflash/images/adobe.png*.

This exchange of images is made possible thanks to the htmlCodebyID method that accesses the DOM element with the img tag and verifies the following condition with the DOM getAttribute:

```
htmlCode[i].getAttribute("class") == "logo"
```

The ActionScript class created in this solution is tied to the Flex SDK. If, on the other hand, you want to use it in the Flash applications, you have to extend the `Sprite` class and delete all references to the Flex Framework (such as, for example, the [`Event`] or [`Bindable`] metatags).

5.5 Accessing and Editing an HTML Style Sheet from ActionScript

Problem

You want to access and manipulate CSS styles in a page from ActionScript.

Solution

Edit the CSS styles using the `cssRules` property, which contains an array of the `window.document.styleSheets` elements.

Discussion

To access the attributes that regulate the CSS styles of an element in an HTML page, you can use the `getElementById` and `getElementsByTagName` methods to access the HTML element and then edit its `style` property:

```
_html.window.document.getElementById("contentID").style.color = "#FF6600";
_html.window.document.getElementById("contentID").style.size = 2;
```

For accessing and editing HTML style sheets, however, you can use the `cssRules` property of the `window.document` object that contains an array of the styles declared on the page. This is a better approach.

Consider this example of HTML, which specifies a style sheet with two CSS classes:

```
<html>
<style>
    .button1{
    background-color: #ffff00;
    font-size: 12px;
    }
    .button2{
    color: #ff0000;
    }
</style>
```

To access and edit these style sheets, use the following ActionScript code:

```
var myStyle:Object = _html.window.document.styleSheets[0];

myStyle.cssRules[0].style.backgroundColor = "#00ff00";
myStyle.cssRules[0].style.fontSize = "20px";
```

The myStyle object provides access to the HTML code's CSS style declaration. You edit its existing settings through the backgroundColor and fontSize properties.

If you like, you can even add new properties that weren't previously specified in the element's style sheet:

```
myStyle.cssRules[1].style.textDecoration = "underline";
```

5.6 Accessing the HTML Container History List

Problem

You want to access the HTML history list and move forward or backward throughout the HTML pages loaded within the HTML container.

Solution

Use the historyLength, historyPosition, historyAt, historyBack, historyForward, and historyGo methods of the HTMLLoader class to interact with the HTML history.

Discussion

When you navigate and load new pages in the HTMLLoader object, you will need to access a list that contains the pages loaded so far. AIR automatically maintains a history list for the pages.

AIR provides plenty of flexibility for working with the HTML history list, as you can see in Table 5-2.

Table 5-2. Methods and Properties for Working with the HTML History List

Methods	Description
historyLength	This returns the length of the history list, including back and forward entries.
historyPosition	This returns the current position in the history list. You use this position for back navigation and forward navigation.
historyAt	This returns the object corresponding to the history entry at the specified position in the history list typed as URLRequest.
historyBack	This navigates back in the history list.
historyForward	This navigates forward in the history list.
historyGo	This navigates the indicated number of steps in the browser history (forward if positive; backward if negative). When set to zero, it reloads the page.

The items maintained by the runtime are typed as HistoryListItem objects. The HistoryListItem contains the properties shown in Table 5-3.

Table 5-3. HistoryListItem Class Properties

Property	Description
isPost	Set to true if the HTML page includes POST data
originalUrl	The original URL of the HTML page, before any redirects
title	The title of the HTML page
url	The URL of the HTML page

Items in the history list are stored as objects of type HistoryListItem. To be able to access the properties that contain the URL and the title of the HTML pages loaded in the HTML container, for example, you have to first create a variable, typed as History ListItem, and from this instance access the url property and title:

```
var tempHistoryItem:HTMLHistoryItem = _html.getHistoryAt(index);
myDataProvider.addItem({label:tempHistoryItem.title,data:tempHistoryItem.url});
```

In this recipe, you will work with some of the methods of the HTML history list.

ActionScript/Flex

To access the history list from your Flex project, you need to create a custom Action-Script call that uses the HTMLLoader class and extends the UIComponent class. The code for this class, named HandleHistory, is shown later in this section.

As you examine it, focus your attention on the onComplete event handler of the COMPLETE event; here you need to register a listener for the LOCATION_CHANGE event:

```
_html.addEventListener(Event.LOCATION_CHANGE, showHistoryHTMLContent);
```

This event defines the value of the type property of a locationChange event object and is triggered every time the HTML content changes within the HTMLLoader object. This event is therefore used to monitor all navigation of a user in an HTML page. In the showHistoryHTMLContent event handler, an instance of the HTMLHistoryItem is created, from which the URL properties and titles of the HTML content are taken. This information is added to an ArrayCollection, which will contain the navigation history.

If you want to use the UIComponent class in a Flash project, all you have to do is change the parent class from UIComponent to Sprite and replace the ArrayCollection class with the DataProvider class. (For more information, see the Flash documentation at *http://livedocs.adobe.com/flash/ 9.0/main/wwhelp/wwhimpl/common/html/wwhelp.htm?context=Live Docs_Parts&file=00000410.html*.)

```
package com.oreilly.aircookbook.ch5
{
    import flash.events.Event;
    import flash.html.HTMLHistoryItem;
    import flash.html.HTMLLoader;
```

```
import flash.net.URLRequest;

import mx.collections.ArrayCollection;
import mx.core.UIComponent;

public class HandleHistory extends UIComponent
{

    private var _html:HTMLLoader;
    private var _historyDP:ArrayCollection = new ArrayCollection();

    public function get html():HTMLLoader
    {
    return _html;
    }

    public function get historyDP():ArrayCollection
    {
    return _historyDP;
    }


    public function HandleHistory()
    {
    super();
    }

    override protected function createChildren():void
    {
        _html = new HTMLLoader();
        _html.width = 800;
        _html.height = 600;
        addChild(_html);

        _html.addEventListener( Event.COMPLETE, onComplete );
    }

    override protected function measure():void
    {
        measuredWidth = 800;
        measuredHeight= 600;
    }

    override protected function updateDisplayList(unscaledWidth:Number,
                                        unscaledHeight:Number):void
    {
        super.updateDisplayList(unscaledWidth, unscaledHeight);

        _html.width = unscaledWidth;
        _html.height= unscaledHeight;
    }

    private function onComplete( event:Event ) : void
    {
        _html.addEventListener(Event.LOCATION_CHANGE, showHistoryHTMLContent);
```

```
                    }

                    public function loadURL( url:String ) : void
                    {
                        var request:URLRequest = new URLRequest(url);
                        _html.load(request);
                    }

                    public function showHistoryHTMLContent(evt:Event):void
                    {
                        _historyDP.removeAll();

                        for (var i:int = 0; i< _html.historyLength ; i++)
                        {
                            var tempHistoryItem:HTMLHistoryItem = _html.getHistoryAt(i);

                            _historyDP.addItem({label:tempHistoryItem.title,data:tempHistoryItem.url});
                        }
                    }

                    public function gotToURL(selIndex:int):void
                    {
                        loadURL(historyDP.getItemAt(selIndex).data as String);
                    }
                }
            }
```

You now have access to the history list. To move backward and forward in the list,
you'll add the code for management of the Back and Forward buttons to your class. To
do so, simply use the HTMLLoader class's historyBack, historyForward, and historyGo
methods as event handlers for the click event of the button instances. The history
Back and historyForward methods navigate back and forward through the history list,
respectively. The historyGo method navigates forward and backward by passing a positive or negative number as a parameter (a positive number will make the historyGo
method navigate forward).

You can use the HandleHistory class you created in a Flex project by creating an MXML
file with three buttons to manage the historyGo, historyForward, and historyBack
functions, as well as a list that contains the history list of the HTMLLoader object. To
create the list, simply load the ArrayCollection instance of the HandleHistory class with
a binding.

Here is the complete MXML file:

```
<?xml version="1.0" encoding="utf-8"?>
<mx:WindowedApplication
xmlns:mx="http://www.adobe.com/2006/mxml" layout="vertical"
xmlns:comp="com.oreilly.aircookbook.ch5.*">

    <mx:Script>
    <![CDATA[
        import mx.events.ListEvent;
```

```
            import mx.collections.ArrayCollection;
            import mx.events.CollectionEvent;

            private var list_arr:Array;
            [Bindable]
            private var myAC:ArrayCollection;

            private function loadHTML():void
            {
                htmlComp.loadURL("http://www.comtaste.com/");


                htmlComp.historyDP.addEventListener(CollectionEvent.COLLECTION_CHANGE,
                                            onACChange);
                gotorul.addEventListener(MouseEvent.CLICK, onGotourl);

                myAC = htmlComp.historyDP;
            }

            private function onShowHistoryClick(evt:MouseEvent):void
            {
                hisList.dataProvider =  htmlComp.historyDP;
            }

            private function onGotourl(evt:MouseEvent):void
            {
                htmlComp.gotToURL(hisList.selectedIndex);
            }

            private function onACChange(evt:CollectionEvent):void
            {
                hisList.selectedIndex = htmlComp.html.historyPosition;
            }

        ]]>
        </mx:Script>
        <mx:HBox>
            <mx:Button label="Back" id="backBtn" click="htmlComp.html.historyGo(-1)" />
            <mx:Button label="Next" id="ffBtn" click="htmlComp.html.historyGo(1)" />
            <mx:Button label="Go to URL" id="gotorul" />
        </mx:HBox>

        <mx:List id="hisList" dataProvider="{myAC}" />

        <comp:HandleHistory id="htmlComp" initialize="loadHTML()" />

    </mx:WindowedApplication>
```

In JavaScript, the implementation of the history list is identical to the one used in ActionScript. The methods shown by the HTMLLoader class are the same, and the history list corresponds to the window.history object in the HTML page.

5.7 Bridging Content from Different Security Sandboxes

Contributed by MarinTodorov (http://www.underplot.com) with an introduction by Marco Casario

Problem

You may want to run content, exchange data, and use functionality from the application sandbox and a nonapplication sandbox at the same time. You may even want to do all this between different nonapplication sandboxes.

Solution

Use the provided bridging interface to expose variables or methods between the sandboxes. For communication between nonapplication sandboxes, use the application sandbox as a proxy between them.

Discussion

The security of a desktop application is fundamentally important. AIR applications run directly on the desktop, and the security model for HTML content running in AIR is more stringent than the security model of a typical web browser.

AIR follows a series of rules to guarantee the security of the applications and the users.

When the application has to do with HTML content, it exposes itself to a series of potential attacks that are launched following malicious code execution. One of these techniques is known as *cross-site scripting*.

A malicious developer could, for example, use the `eval` method of JavaScript, the JavaScript pattern in the `a` tag, or the DOM properties `innerHTML` and `innerText` to execute malicious code. The following is a classic example of malicious code that can create serious security problems:

```
<a href="#" onclick="var myFile=new air.File('c:\\windows\myFile.dll');
myFile.deleteFile();">Click here to read the file. </a>
```

When users are unaware of the code behind the link, they will click the text, thinking they are reading something, and instead they will be able to delete a system file.

To avoid this and many other problems linked to security, Adobe AIR allows you to define the permits for each file (internally as well as externally) in an application. Using *sandboxes*, AIR establishes access protocols to data and operations by using two concepts of sandboxes: an *application sandbox* and a *nonapplication sandbox*. According to the sandbox that is specified, different rules apply.

Code in an application sandbox context has access to AIR APIs, has a limited ability to generate code dynamically after a page loads, and cannot load content via a `script` tag. In this sandbox, the possibility of executing JavaScript code is disabled after a page has been loaded. This stops malicious code from being created, for example, on the eval method or by interacting with DOM properties. The developers specify the trusted directories to work on by using the app:/ schema. All files and data are installed and copied in app:/, and the ones that are outside this folder are treated as if they were in the web browser.

Code in nonapplication sandboxes essentially imitates typical browser restrictions and behaviors for local trusted HTML. This is the sandbox that is automatically assigned to all content that is loaded from an Internet location (or from a network). The content specified in this sandbox can access the JavaScript code and interact with DOM.

The AIR sandbox bridge model enables broader functionality and less risk than is associated with typical browser-based applications.

Application Sandbox from Nonapplication Content

The application sandbox can set up a bridge interface inside the nonapplication box called parentSandboxBridge that can be accessed by the nonapplication sandbox code. Consider the following example:

```
var parentBridge = {
    sayHello = function (msg) {
        alert("Hello from the application sandbox! "+msg);
};

function setupBridge(){
    document.getElementById("sandbox").contentWindow.parentSandbox
Bridge = parentBridge;
}
```

This example creates the bridge between the different sandboxes. Specifically, the following code includes the nonapplication sandbox content in the application:

```
<iframe id="sandbox" src="http://www.site_abc.com/sandbox.html"
    documentRoot="app:/"
    sandboxRoot="http://www.site_abc.com/"
    ondominitialize="setupBridge ()">
</iframe>
```

In this way, the nonapplication sandbox code (in *sandbox.html*) can invoke the method sayHello from the application sandbox:

```
window.parentSandboxBridge.sayHello("and from non-app sandbox");
```

Communicate Between Different Nonapplication Sandboxes

The nonapplication code can access the parent via the parentSandboxBridge and can expose data and methods via the childSandboxBridge. You might immediately suppose that in this case it is possible to expose directly the childSandboxBridge of nonapplication sandbox 1 to nonapplication sandbox 2 (using the application sandbox's parentSandboxBridge), but this setup does not work (for security reasons). The access to the bridges is very restricted. From outside the sandbox, the bridges are defined and are read-only. In addition, if you try to read an exposed method's body in order to peek at the nonexposed objects, you will find out `alert(childSandboxBridge.exposedMe thod)` will give you an empty function.

To exchange data between nonapplication sandboxes, you should set up a bridge proxy in the application sandbox code. The following example is an application that loads two different websites: one that has a database with clients and another where the user wants to copy some of those clients (of course, the two sites must implement the appropriate code, as described in a moment, for this setup to work).

The parent code (running on AIR) is as follows:

```html
<html>
<head>
<script type="text/javascript">

    var bridgeProxy = {
        broadcast: function (method, args, sandbox) {
            document.getElementById(sandbox).contentWindow.childSandboxBridge.
callMethod(method, args)
            }
    }

    function setupBridge(sandbox){
        sandbox.contentWindow.parentSandboxBridge = bridgeProxy;
    }

</script>
</head>
<body>

<!-- that's the first non-app sandbox www.abc.com -->
<iframe id="site_abc" src="http://www.abc.com/site_abc.html" documentRoot="app:/"
sandboxRoot="http://www.abc.com/" ondominitialize="setupBridge(this)"></iframe>

<!-- that's the second non-app sandbox www.xyz.com -->
<iframe id="site_xyz" src="http://www.xyz.com/site_xyz.html" documentRoot="app:/"
sandboxRoot="http://www.xyz.com/" ondominitialize="setupBridge(this)"></iframe>

</body>
</html>
```

Note that each `iframe` calls the `setupBridge` function to create the `parentSandbox Bridge` in its `window` object. This is the code of the view customer page on the website ABC (your first nonapplication sandbox):

```html
<html>
<head>
<script type="text/javascript">

    function copyInfo() {
        // call the parent bridge with arguments : method name, data, iframe id
        window.parentSandboxBridge.broadcast('copyInfo1',
        {
```

```
            firstName: document.getElementById('firstName').value,
            lastName : document.getElementById('lastName').value,
            street : document.getElementById('street').value,
            city : document.getElementById('city').value
        },
      'site_xyz');
    }

</script>
</head>
<body>

<b>Web site ABC</b><br />
View Client information:<br /><br />

First name: <input type="text" id="firstName" value="Ford" /> <br />
Last name: <input type="text" id="lastName" value="Prefect" /> <br />
Street: <input type="text" id="street" value="42, East side drive" /> <br />
City: <input type="text" id="city" value="Manchester" /> <br />

<input type="button" value="Copy information" onClick="copyInfo()" />

</body>
</html>
```

When the user clicks the Copy Information button, the form information is gathered and sent to the parent bridge proxy, and the data is addressed to the sandbox with the ID site_xyz. Here is the code in the other website, which has to receive the customer information:

```
<html>
<head>

<script type="text/javascript">
    function copyInfo (args)
    {
        document.getElementById('name').value = args.firstName +" "+ args.lastName;
        document.getElementById('address').value = args.street +", "+ args.city;
    }

    var childBridge = {

        callMethod : function(name, args) {
            if (window[name]) window[name](args);
            else alert("No "+name+" defined!");
        }
    }

    window.childSandboxBridge = childBridge;

</script>
</head>
<body>
<b>Web site XYZ</b><br />
Create new customer:<br /><br />
```

```
Name: <input type="text" id="name" value="" /> <br />
Address: <input type="text" id="address" value="" /> <br />

<input type="button" value="Create customer" onClick="alert('New
  customer created!')" />

</body>
</html>
```

The bridge interface of site_xyz just calls the required method and passes the data—in this case, the method copyInfo, which reformats the customer data and fills in the form. The user now has to just click Create Customer, and you're done.

This example shows how far you can go by exposing the window's methods via the bridge. In most cases, it would have been better to encapsulate the exposed methods in the bridge object.

 For more details on AIR security, see the "Adobe AIR Security" white paper at *http://www.adobe.com/go/learn_air_security_wp_en*.

5.8 Creating JavaScript Functions from ActionScript

Problem

You need to define JavaScript functions and properties that ActionScript can then access.

Solution

Use the loadString method of the HTMLLoader class to load HTML code passed in as a simple string. Create a complex HTML code snippet that also includes JavaScript using only the ActionScript language.

Discussion

By passing an HTML string to the loadString method, you can load HTML content. The syntax of the method is as follows:

```
public function loadString(htmlContent:String):void
```

where the htmlContent parameter is the HTML string that will be loaded in the HTMLLoader class.

Using this technique, you can assign a whole HTML page with JavaScript code to the loadString method.

When you call the loadString method, any pending load operation initiated with this method or with the load method is canceled. This means that the complete event for the previous load operation will never be delivered.

ActionScript/Flex

The following example creates HTML content directly in an ActionScript class. The htmlToLoad property, typed as XML, is set with HTML content, which loads a text message into a div:

```
package com.oreilly.aircookbook.ch5
{

    import flash.display.Sprite;
    import flash.display.StageAlign;
    import flash.display.StageScaleMode;
    import flash.events.Event;
    import flash.html.HTMLLoader;
    import flash.net.URLRequest;


    public class CreateJSfromAS extends Sprite
    {

        private var _html:HTMLLoader;
        private var htmlToLoad:XML = new XML();


        public function CreateJSfromAS()
        {
            this.stage.scaleMode = StageScaleMode.NO_SCALE;
            this.stage.align = StageAlign.TOP_LEFT;

            _html = new HTMLLoader();

            _html.width = stage.stageWidth;
            _html.height = stage.stageHeight;

            loadHTMLcontent();

            _html.addEventListener(Event.COMPLETE, onComplete);

            this.addChild( _html );

        }


        private function onComplete (e:Event):void
        {
            // The window.document object includes the contentData element
            // that we access using the getElementById method.
            // It returns the text into the contentData div
```

```
        trace(html.window.document.getElementById("contentData").innerText);

}


private function loadHTMLcontent( ):void
{

    // Define the HTML string to pass to the
    // loadString() method of the _html istance

    _htmlToLoad = <![CDATA[
    <html xmlns="http://www.w3.org/1999/xhtml">
    <head>

    <title>Solution 15.X: Creating a JavaScript function from
        ActionScript</title>

    <script type="text/javascript">

    function showMessage(message)
    {
    document.getElementById("contentData").innerHTML = message;
    }

    </script>

    <body onload=" showMessage ('This is a JavaScript function created
        within an ActionScript class')">

    <p>

    <div id="contentData" style="overflow:auto; width:100%; height:100%">
    </div>

    </p>

    <p>


    </p>

    </body>
    </html> ]]>;

    // Loads the htmlToLoad string within the
    // HTMLLoader class

    _html.loadString(htmlToLoad.toString());


    }
    }
}
```

The long HTML string contained in the `htmlToLoad` property is assigned to the `load String` method. The `onComplete` event handler provides access to the `resultDiv` element through ActionScript, specifically with the `getElementById` method specified in the HTML string:

```
private function onComplete (e:Event):void
{
    // The window.document object includes the contentData element
    // that we access using the getElementById method.
    // It returns the text into the contentData div

    trace(html.window.document.getElementById("contentData").innerText);

}
```

Only after the page has been completely loaded, when the `HTMLLoader` object dispatches the `complete` event, can you access the HTML DOM through the ActionScript code.

5.9 Scrolling HTML Content in ActionScript

Problem

You need to create a window with scrolling HTML content or simply want to scroll HTML content.

Solution

Scroll HTML content by setting the `scrollBarsVisible` parameter of the `HTMLLoader` `createRootWindow` method to `true`.

Discussion

By default, the `HTMLLoader` class does not provide scroll bars for the HTML content it displays. By specifying a parameter in the `createRootWindow` method, however, you can force the `HTMLLoader` window to use the horizontal and vertical scroll bars.

The static `createRootWindow` method of the `HTMLLoader` class has the following syntax:

```
createRootWindow(visible:Boolean = true, windowInitOptions:NativeWindowInitOptions
= null, scrollBarsVisible:Boolean = true, bounds:Rectangle = null):HTMLLoader
```

This method lets you create a new `NativeWindow` object that contains an `HTMLLoader` object for which a URL can be specified to be loaded. The third parameter of this method, `scrollBarsVisible`, enables you to specify whether the window with HTML content uses scroll bars. To turn on scroll bars, set `scrollBarsVisible` to `true`, as shown here:

```
var _initOptions = new air.NativeWindowInitOptions();
var _bounds = new air.Rectangle(50, 50, 320, 240);

var html = air.HTMLLoader.createRootWindow(false, _initOptions, true, _bounds);
```

```
var urlReq = new air.URLRequest( "http://www.comtaste.com/en " );
html.load( urlReq );

html.stage.nativeWindow.activate();
```

The `HTMLLoader` class has the following properties to control the scrolling of the HTML content:

- `contentHeight`: Specifies the height of the HTML content
- `contentWidth`: Specifies the width of the HTML content
- `scrollH`: Represents the horizontal scroll position of the HTML content
- `scrollV`: Represents the vertical scroll position of the HTML content

To check the scrolling of the HTML content, you use the properties `contentHeight`, `contentWidth`, `scrollH`, and `scrollV`.

The following example creates an event handler on the `htmlBoundsChange` event, which is triggered every time the `contentHeight` or `contentWidth` property changes. This event handler always places the vertical scroll of the HTML content in the top position:

```
var html:HTMLLoader = new HTMLLoader();
html.width = 640;
html.height = 480;
var urlReq:URLRequest = new URLRequest("http://www.comtaste.com/en");
html.load(urlReq);

html.addEventListener(Event.HTML_BOUNDS_CHANGE, onContentChange);

this.addChild(html);

private function onContentChange(event:Event):void
{
    // Scroll to the top
    html.scrollV = 1;
}
```

5.10 Using ActionScript Libraries Within an HTML Page

Problem

You need to import and use an ActionScript library within an HTML page.

Solution

Use the HTML `script` tag to import and use ActionScript classes within an HTML page. To ensure the ActionScript class is imported properly, specify the `script` tag's `type` attribute as `type="application/x-shockwave-flash"`.

Discussion

AIR can import ActionScript classes in a compiled SWF file within an HTML page.

To import an ActionScript library in an HTML page, you must first compile the library as a SWF file with the acompc compiler.

The acompc tool is a command-line compiler included in the AIR SDK (*http://www .adobe.com/products/air/tools/sdk/*). It is launched by a terminal window and requires the classes to be specified within the code base to include the library or component and, if necessary, a configuration file.

In this example, you will be working with a simple ActionScript class that has one public property. You will learn how to access that public property from within JavaScript. Here is the class you will be working with:

```
package com.oreilly.aircookbook.ch5 {

    public class CreateJSfromAS
    {

        public var resultValue:String = "A Variable from ActionScript";

        public function CreateJSfromAS(){
        }

    }
}
```

The configuration file is a simple XML-based file that contains the information regarding the classes to include in the compiled file and their packages.

The following code is an example of a configuration:

```
<air-config>
    <compiler>
        <source-path>
            <path-element>source</path-element>
        </source-path>
    </compiler>
    <include-classes>
        <class>com.oreilly.aircookbook.ch5.CreateJSfromAS</class>
    </include-classes>
</air-config>
```

It is even possible to specify more than one ActionScript class in the include-classes node by declaring more than one class node:

```
<include-classes>
    <class>com.oreilly.aircookbook.ch5.CreateJSfromAS</class>
    <class>com.oreilly.aircookbook.ch5.myClass2</class>
    <class>com.oreilly.aircookbook.ch5.myClass3</class>
</include-classes>
```

This file is assigned to the command-line compiler by using the `load-config` attribute and by specifying the name and the folder in which the compiled file will be placed. For example, in the following command line, the compiler loads the configuration file *air-config.xml* and creates the *asLib.swf* file in the lib folder:

```
acompc -load-config air-config.xml -output lib/asLib.swf
```

After you create the ActionScript library, you can import it into the HTML page and therefore use it in your JavaScript code. The example of HTML page that follows imports the class with the `script` tag and creates an instance upon the `onload` event. In addition, it takes the value of the `resultValue` public variable from the ActionScript class and populates the `innerHTML` property of the result `div`:

```
<!DOCTYPE html PUBLIC "-//W3C//DTD XHTML 1.0 Transitional//EN"
"http://www.w3.org/TR/xhtml1/DTD/xhtml1-transitional.dtd">
<html xmlns="http://www.w3.org/1999/xhtml">
<head>

<meta http-equiv="Content-Type" content="text/html; charset=UTF-8">
<title>5.9 Using ActionScript libraries within an HTML page</title>

<script type="text/javascript" src="frameworks/AIRAliases.js"></script>
<script type="text/javascript" src="frameworks/AIRIntrospector.js"></script>

<script src="lib/asLib.swc" type="application/x-shockwave-flash"></script>

<script type="text/javascript">

    var libIstance = null;


    function loadASClass()
    {
        var libIstance = new
window.runtime.com.oreilly.aircookbook.ch5.CreateJSfromAS;
        var result = document.getElementById('result');
        result.innerHTML = libInstance.resultValue;
    }

</script>

</head>

<body onload="loadASClass()">

    <div id="result"> </div>

</body>
</html>
```

To import the library properly, be sure to set the `type` attribute of the `script` tag to `application/x-shockwave-flash`:

```
<script src="lib/asLib.swc" type="application/x-shockwave-flash"></script>
```

To access the imported library (`asLib.swc`), you have to create a reference through the `runtime` property of the JavaScript `window` object (including the package name for which the classes are organized), as shown below. Since you have created the reference to the ActionScript class, you can then access its public methods and properties:

```
function loadASClass()
{
    var libIstance = new window.runtime.com.oreilly.aircookbook.ch5.CreateJSfromAS;
    var result = document.getElementById('result');
    result.innerHTML = libIstance.resultValue;
}
```

CHAPTER 6

PDF Support

6.1 Detecting Whether PDF Support Is Available

Problem

You want to detect whether the user is able to display PDF content in your AIR application.

Solution

Read the value of the HTMLLoader.pdfCapability property to check that the user has a version of Adobe Reader or Adobe Acrobat 8.1 (or newer) installed.

Discussion

The HTMLLoader.pdfCapability property is set to one of the following constants of the HTMLPDFCapability class:

- HTMLPDFCapability.STATUS_OK
- HTMLPDFCapability.ERROR_INSTALLED_READER_NOT_FOUND
- HTMLPDFCapability.ERROR_INSTALLED_READER_TOO_OLD
- HTMLPDFCapability.ERROR_PREFERRED_READER_TOO_OLD

If the property has the value of the constant HTMLPDFCapability.STATUS_OK, then you are sure that PDF content can be loaded into the HTMLLoader object. It also can happen that the user does not have the right version of Adobe Reader installed. If the installed Adobe Reader version is too old, then the constant ERROR_INSTALLED_READER_TOO_OLD is returned when you call the HTMLLoader.pdfCapability property. If the user has different versions of Adobe Reader installed but the one that is set up to handle PDF content is older than Adobe Reader 8.1, the constant ERROR_PREFERRED_READER_TOO_OLD is returned. If the user has no version of Adobe Reader installed at all, then the HTMLLoader object will not be able to display any PDF content.

Working with PDF content on Windows involves one other important caveat. If Adobe Acrobat or Adobe Reader version 7.*x* (or newer) is opened on the user's system, AIR references that specific opened version even if another version (8.1 or newer, for example) is installed on that system also. In this case, your PDF content will not load in your AIR application. When your PDF content is not loading within an acceptable time frame, it's a best practice to inform the user that Adobe Acrobat must be closed while running your application.

ActionScript/Flex/Flash

The following code detects whether a user can display PDF content in an AIR application. If the STATUS_OK code is returned, then the application can display the content; if it isn't, then you must trace the error code that corresponds to the HTMLPDFCapability error object.

```
if(HTMLLoader.pdfCapability == HTMLPDFCapability.STATUS_OK)
{
    trace("The user is able to display PDF content !");
}
else
{
    trace("PDF cannot be displayed. Error code:", HTMLLoader.pdfCapability);
}
```

JavaScript

The following code detects whether a user can display PDF content in an AIR application. If the STATUS_OK code is returned, then the application can display the content; if it isn't, then you need to trace the error code that corresponds to the HTMLPDFCapability error object.

```
if(air.HTMLLoader.pdfCapability == air.HTMLPDFCapability.STATUS_OK)
{
    air.trace("The user is able to display PDF content ");
}
else
{
    air.trace("PDF cannot be displayed. Error code:", HTMLLoader.pdfCapability);
}
```

6.2 Loading a PDF Document

Problem

You want to load a PDF document in an AIR application.

Solution

Create an HTMLLoader instance, set the dimensions, and load the path of a PDF.

Discussion

Loading and rendering PDF content in your AIR application are identical to loading and rendering HTML. All you need to do is specify the path to the actual PDF when requesting the content to load into the `HTMLLoader` instance.

ActionScript/Flex

The following code snippet loads a PDF document using the `HTMLLoader` class. The `HTMLLoader` class loads a `URLRequest` object that points to the actual PDF document.

```
<?xml version="1.0" encoding="utf-8"?>
<mx:WindowedApplication xmlns:mx="http://www.adobe.com/2006/mxml"
    height="900" width="700" horizontalAlign="left">
    <mx:Script>
        <![CDATA[
            private function loadPDF():void
            {
                var request:URLRequest = new URLRequest("test.pdf");
                var pdf:HTMLLoader = new HTMLLoader();

                //set the dimensions
                pdf.height = 800;
                pdf.width = 600;

                //call the load method
                pdf.load(request);

                //add the HTMLLoader object to the display list to make it visible
                container.addChild(pdf);
            }
        ]]>
    </mx:Script>

    <mx:VBox>
        <mx:Label text="Dipsplay 'test.pdf'" />
        <mx:Button label="Load" click="loadPDF()" />
    </mx:VBox>
    <mx:Spacer id="container" />
</mx:WindowedApplication>
```

JavaScript/HTML

If you want to load a PDF in your AIR application using HTML, you follow similar steps for loading a PDF document into a browser. For example, you can load a PDF into the top-level HTML content of a window, into an **object** tag, into a frame, or into an `iframe`.

This is the HTML code for loading a PDF into an `iframe`:

```
<html>
    <body>
        <h1>PDF test</h1>
        <iframe id="pdfFrame"
```

```
                width="100%"
                height="100%"
                src="test.pdf"/>
        </body>
    </html>
```

This is the HTML code for loading a PDF into an `object` tag:

```
<object id="PDFObj" data="test.pdf" type="application/pdf" width="100%"
height="100%"/>
```

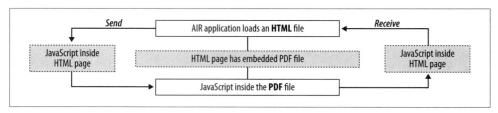

Figure 6-1. Communication flow between an AIR application and PDF

6.3 Communicating from AIR to PDF

Problem

You want to communicate with a PDF in your AIR application.

Solution

In your AIR application, load an HTML file (wrapper) that holds your PDF. Use Java-Script in your wrapper to communicate in both directions with the embedded JavaScript in your PDF file.

Discussion

Communicating with the PDF has many advantages. If a PDF document has, for example, a form, you can simply execute a JavaScript function when a user clicks a button in the form. You also can control page navigation with custom buttons in your PDF or can control the magnification of the document, to name only a few possibilities.

JavaScript handles the communication between your AIR application and the PDF document. Your AIR application loads an HTML file, and that HTML file loads the PDF file. In this way, you can easily send messages to the PDF or receive messages from the PDF in an AIR application. Figure 6-1 diagrams a simple communication flow.

As you can see, the AIR application first loads an HTML file (as you did in Recipe 6.2), and that HTML file loads the actual PDF document. If you want to communicate with the loaded PDF, however, you need to set up some JavaScript in the PDF document. This is possible through the JavaScript extensions for Adobe Acrobat. (You can find full details on the JavaScript extensions for Adobe Acrobat in the Acrobat Developer Center at *http://www.adobe.com/devnet/acrobat/javascript.html*.)

If you want to send messages to the PDF (for example, "Next Page"), then you have to make sure the PDF can react to these messages. You need Adobe Acrobat Professional to add JavaScript to the PDF that can react to the messages you send. This kind of JavaScript is called *document-level JavaScript*.

Every PDF document has a HostContainer object. This object manages the communication between a PDF document and a corresponding host container that the document is contained within, such as an HTML page. You specify the host container for a document using the document's hostContainer property.

The HostContainer object has a messageHandler property that is invoked when JavaScript in the host container calls the postMessage method. This property should reference a notification object that has three methods:

- onMessage: A method that is called in response to postMessage
- onError: A method that is called in response to an error
- onDisclose: A method that is called to determine whether the host application is permitted to send messages to the document

The following code is a typical host container message handler:

```
this.hostContainer.messageHandler =
{
    onMessage: function(aMessage)
    {
        for(var i = 0; i < aMessage.length; i++)
        console.println(aMessage[i]);
    },
    onError: function(error, aMessage){ } ,

    onDisclose: function (cURL,cDocumentURL){return true;}
};
```

The this keyword in the first line of the code points to the Doc object of the document. The Doc object provides the interface between a PDF document and the JavaScript interpreter. It provides methods and properties for accessing a PDF document. For this example, use the pageNum property of the Doc object to jump from one page to another.

To add the JavaScript to the PDF, you need Adobe Acrobat. Create a new PDF document, and choose Advanced→Document Processing→Document JavaScripts. In the JavaScript Functions dialog box, type **onMessage** as the script name, and then click the Add button.

In the JavaScript Editor window, type the following code:

```
function myOnMessage(aMessage)
{
    if (aMessage.length==1) {
        switch(aMessage[0])
```

```
        {
            case "PageUp":
                pageNum--;
                break;
            case "PageDn":
                pageNum++;
                break;
            default:
                app.alert("Unknown message: " + aMessage[0]);
        }
    }
    else
    {
        app.alert("Message from hostContainer: \n" + aMessage);
    }
}

function myOnDisclose(cURL,cDocumentURL)
{
    return true;
}

function myOnError(error, aMessage)
{
    app.alert(error);
}

var msgHandlerObject = new Object();
msgHandlerObject.onMessage = myOnMessage;
msgHandlerObject.onError = myOnError;
msgHandlerObject.onDisclose = myOnDisclose;

this.hostContainer.messageHandler = msgHandlerObject;
```

When you save the PDF file, be sure to hide the menu bar, toolbars, and window controls. By doing so, you restrict the user's navigation options to the controls in your Flex interface. You can set these values in the Document Properties dialog box.

Now you are ready to load the PDF in an AIR application. Because AIR applications can show HTML pages, embed the PDF in an HTML wrapper:

```
<html>
    <body>
        <object id="PDFObj"
            data="PDF_COM_with_AIR.pdf"
            type="application/pdf"
            width="100%"
            height="100%"/>
    </body>
</html>
```

You can now load the HTML file with the Flex HTML component:

```
<?xml version="1.0" encoding="utf-8"?>
<mx:WindowedApplication xmlns:mx="http://www.adobe.com/2006/mxml"
 width="900" height="700" layout="vertical">
```

```
    <mx:HTML id="pdfHtml" location="PDF_COM_with_AIR.html" width="100%"
height="100%" />
```

```
</mx:WindowedApplication>
```

If you run your application now, you will see your PDF document rendered in the AIR application.

If you add, for example, two buttons in the application, you can control the paging by sending the right message `String` to the PDF document:

```
<mx:Button id="btn3" label="&lt;" click="sendMessage('PageUp')" width="35"
enabled="false" />
```

```
<mx:Button id="btn4" label="&gt;" click="sendMessage('PageDn')" width="35"
enabled="false" />
```

When the user clicks the buttons, the `sendMessage` function sends commands to the PDF object using the `postMessage` method of the PDF object. The `sendMessage` function in your script block looks like this:

```
private function sendMessage(message:String):void
{
    var pdfObj:Object =
pdfHtml.htmlLoader.window.document.getElementById("PDFObj");

    pdfObj.postMessage([message]);

}
```

The document-level JavaScript in the PDF file has a `hostContainer.messageHandler` object defined, and that object knows how to handle the incoming messages. In this way, you can communicate with a PDF document from inside an AIR application.

You'll now learn how you can communicate from inside the PDF to the AIR application. It is actually a similar technique, as you will see in the next example.

6.4 Communicating from PDF to AIR

Problem

You want to communicate from a loaded PDF document to your AIR application.

Solution

In your AIR application, load an HTML file (wrapper) that holds your PDF. Use JavaScript in your wrapper to communicate in both directions with the embedded JavaScript in your PDF file.

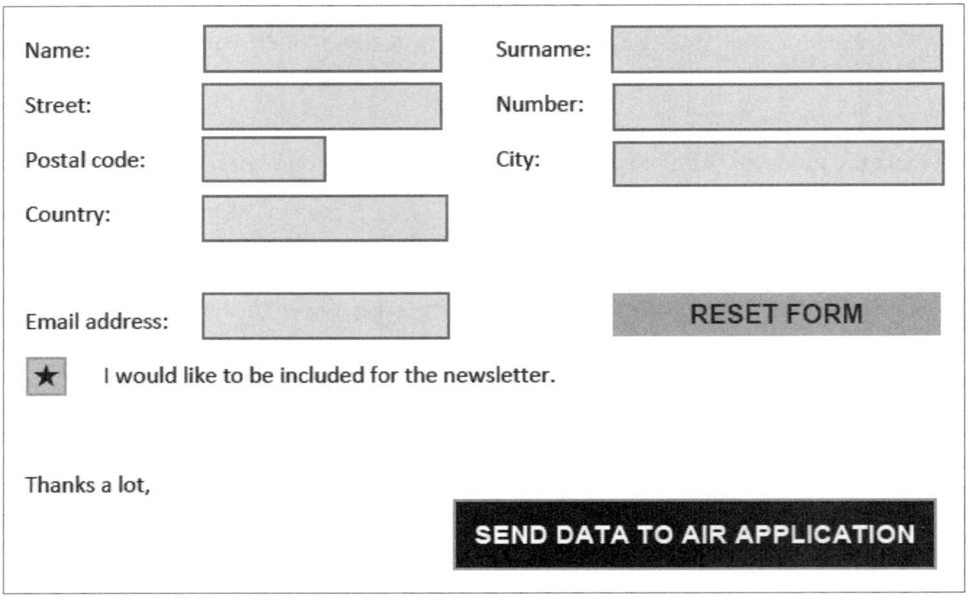

Figure 6-2. A PDF contact form

Discussion

A simple form-processing example demonstrates communication from a PDF document to its hosting AIR environment. This example loads a PDF document, which includes a form and a submit button, into an AIR application. When the user fills in the form and clicks the submit button, the form data is sent to the hosting AIR application, and a customized "thank you" message is displayed to the user.

ActionScript code in an AIR application cannot directly communicate with JavaScript in the PDF. ActionScript can communicate with the JavaScript in the HTML page, however, and that JavaScript code can communicate with the JavaScript in the loaded PDF file.

Figure 6-2 shows the simple PDF contact form.

When the user clicks the button, the JavaScript code gets the values from the respective fields in the PDF form and stores them in an **Array** called **arrMsg**. By calling the **post Message** method, the data is sent to the **hostContainer**, which is the JavaScript in the HTML page that loads the PDF:

```
this.hostContainer.postMessage(arrMsg);
```

The complete JavaScript code on the **click** action of the submit button in the PDF looks like this:

```
var strName = this.getField("nameField").value.toString();

    var strSurname = this.getField("surnameField").value.toString();
```

```
var strNumber = this.getField("numberField").value.toString();
var strStreet = this.getField("streetField").value.toString();
var strCity = this.getField("cityField").value.toString();
var strPostalcode = this.getField("postalcodeField").value.toString();
var strCountry = this.getField("countryField").value.toString();
var strEmailAddress = this.getField("EmailAddressField").value.toString();
var boNewsLetter = this.getField("newsletterCheck").value;


var arrMsg = null;
try{
  arrMsg = new Array();
  arrMsg=[strName,strSurname,strNumber,strStreet,strCity,strPostalcode,strCountry,str
EmailAddress,boNewsLetter];

}catch(e){
  arrMsg = ["Error"];
}
console.println("Msg: " + arrMsg.length + " : " + arrMsg);

try{
  this.hostContainer.postMessage(arrMsg);
}catch(e){

}
```

To receive the data in the HTML page, use the same messageHandler system as you did in Recipe 6.3. The complete HTML page code looks like this:

```
<html>
    <head>
        <title>Communicate from PDF to AIR</title>
        <script type="text/javascript" >

            function initialize()
            {
                var PDFObject = document.getElementById("PDF");
                PDFObject.messageHandler =
                {
                  onMessage: function(aMessage)
                  {
                      alert(aMessage);
                      return true;
                  },
                  onError: function(error, aMessage)
                  {
                    alert("!error!");
                  }
                };
            }
        </script>
    </head>
    <body onLoad="initialize()">
        <object id="PDF" height=90% width=90% type="application/pdf"
data="ContactForm.pdf"></object>
```

```
        </div>
        </body>
    </html>
```

When you are developing AIR applications with HTML and JavaScript/Ajax, you are done with the communication. In the previous JavaScript block, the aMessage parameter passed to the methods in the messageHandler is an Array containing all the data from the PDF form you might need to access.

If you are developing with Flex (ActionScript), you need to go one step further. Figure 6-3 shows the application's layout.

When the user clicks the Load PDF button, the HTML page is loaded into the HTML control; this happens by executing the following function:

```
private function loadPdf(path:String):void{
    var url:URLRequest = new URLRequest(path);
    pdfContainer.addEventListener(Event.COMPLETE,completeHandler);
    pdfContainer.htmlLoader.load(url);
}
```

In the previous code, the pdfContainer is a reference to the HTML control hosting the PDF document, and the completeHandler is where the application will talk with the global JavaScript object for the content loaded into the HTML control. You can get a reference to that JavaScript object by using the htmlLoader.window property of the HTML control (here called pdf). When you have the reference, you have a good level of control; for example, you can create a new function at runtime in the JavaScript of your HTML page and set that function to "point to" a function defined in ActionScript. So, the completeHandler looks like this:

```
private function completeHandler(event:Event):void{
    pdf.htmlLoader.window.storeValues = storeValues;
}
```

Because you couple the storeValues JavaScript function to the storeValues Action-Script function, when you define a function call for the storeValues function in the JavaScript of the HTML page, the ActionScript version of the function will be used.

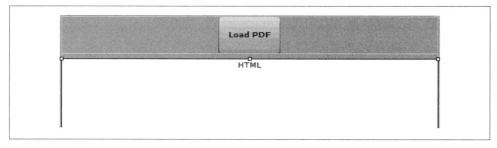

Figure 6-3. The application layout of the example

The final JavaScript function in the HTML page looks like this:

```
<script type="text/javascript" >

        function initialize()
        {
            var PDFObject = document.getElementById("PDF");
            PDFObject.messageHandler =
            {
              onMessage: function(aMessage)
              {
                  storeValues(aMessage);
                  return true;
              },
              onError: function(error, aMessage)
              {
                alert("!error!");
              }
            };
        }
    </script>
```

Now you can also write the **storeValues** function in ActionScript:

```
private function storeValues(fieldArray:Object):void{
    //get the values from the sent object
    var thanksStr:String = "THANKS FOR FILLING IN THE FORM " + fieldArray[0] +", "
+fieldArray[1];
    currentState='thanks';
    thanksLabel.text = thanksStr;
}
```

This function switches application states and shows a customized "thank you" message to the user. The **fieldArray** contains all the data from the contact form. As you can see, the **fieldArray** is typed as a simple **Object**. This is done because the **fieldArray** has a special type that you can easily check as follows:

```
trace(flash.utils.getQualifiedClassName(fieldArray));
```

This **trace** statement returns the following result:

```
flash.html::__HTMLScriptArray
```

In ActionScript you are not able to define this type, so you must type the incoming **Array** as an **Object** or eventually type it as an asterisk (**fieldArray: ***).

The complete Flex code for this example looks like this:

```
<?xml version="1.0" encoding="utf-8"?>
<mx:WindowedApplication xmlns:mx="http://www.adobe.com/2006/mxml"

    layout="absolute"

    >
<mx:states>
    <mx:State name="thanks">
        <mx:RemoveChild target="{pdf}"/>
```

```
            <mx:RemoveChild target="{hbox1}"/>
            <mx:RemoveChild target="{vbox1}"/>
            <mx:AddChild position="lastChild">
                <mx:Label textAlign="center" id="thanksLabel" fontSize="18"
width="100%" x="0" y="233"/>
            </mx:AddChild>
        </mx:State>
    </mx:states>
    <mx:Script>
        <![CDATA[

            private function loadPdf(path:String):void{
                var url:URLRequest = new URLRequest(path);
                pdfContainer.addEventListener(Event.COMPLETE,completeHandler);
                pdfContainer.htmlLoader.load(url);
            }
            private function completeHandler(event:Event):void{
                pdfContainer.htmlLoader.window.storeValues = storeValues;
            }
            private function storeValues(fieldArray:Object):void{
                //get the values from the sent object
                var thanksStr:String = "THANKS FOR FILLING IN THE FORM " +
fieldArray[0] +", " +fieldArray[1];
                currentState='thanks';
                thanksLabel.text = thanksStr;
            }
        ]]>
    </mx:Script>
        <mx:VBox width="100%" height="100%" id="vbox1">
        <mx:HBox width="100%" height="50" id="hbox1" horizontalAlign="center">
            <mx:Button label="Load PDF" click="loadPdf('DocRight.htm')" width="80"
height="50"/>
        </mx:HBox>
        <mx:HTML id="pdfContainer" width="100%" height="75%" />
    </mx:VBox>
</mx:WindowedApplication>
```

CHAPTER 7

Clipboard Support

Because support for the clipboard is essential in any desktop application, AIR allows for access to the operating system clipboard in several data formats. AIR also provides support for many operations beyond the standard copying, cutting, and pasting of text within an application. The standard data formats within AIR let you work with many types of text data, bitmap data, and even file references. Another great feature of the clipboard support within AIR is that you can extend it and create your own custom clipboard data format to fit your AIR application.

7.1 Working with the Clipboard Data Types

Problem

You need to be able to see whether a specific type of data is present on the operating system clipboard.

Solution

Use the `hasFormat` method of the `ClipboardFormats` class to determine whether the desired format is defined by that class.

Discussion

The clipboard is designed to hold multiple types of data simultaneously. It is often prudent to store multiple formats of the same data when you store to the clipboard, because you may not know the preferred format of the application that may later use the clipboard data. AIR gives you the ability to work with the different data formats via many of the methods of the `Clipboard` class. To begin with, six default clipboard data formats are defined in AIR:

- `ClipboardFormats.TEXT_FORMAT`: This format contains simple text data within the clipboard.

- `ClipboardFormats.HTML_FORMAT`: This format contains formatted HTML data within the clipboard.

- `ClipboardFormats.RICH_TEXT_FORMAT`: This format contains a `ByteArray` of Rich Text Format (RTF) data. There are no components yet that let you directly display RTF data within AIR, and in addition, there are no methods in place for converting this data into another format.

- `ClipboardFormats.URL_FORMAT`: This format contains a URL within the clipboard.

- `ClipboardFormats.FILE_LIST_FORMAT`: This format contains an array of file references on the file system within the clipboard.

- `ClipboardFormats.BITMAP_FORMAT`: This format contains bitmap data within the clipboard.

Additionally, AIR lets you use custom formats defined by you, the developer, that are specific to your application. For example, you may have `DashboardClipboardFormats.CHART_DATA_FORMAT` to indicate you are copying and pasting chart data between application modules. When using custom formats, the data is retrieved as an object reference or serialized clone. See Recipe 7.6 for more on custom formats.

One of the methods that uses these values is the `hasFormat` method of the `Clipboard` class. The `hasFormat` method on a clipboard instance accepts one of these format constants as a parameter and returns a Boolean value indicating whether any data of that format exists on the clipboard.

ActionScript

In ActionScript, you can easily access the operating system clipboard with the `general Clipboard` property of the `Clipboard` class. In the following example, you can select a data format and click the Check Clipboard button to determine whether that data is present on the clipboard.

```
<mx:WindowedApplication
    xmlns:mx="http://www.adobe.com/2006/mxml"
    layout="vertical">

    <mx:Script>
        <![CDATA[
            import flash.desktop.ClipboardFormats;
            import flash.desktop.Clipboard;

            private function handleClick( event:MouseEvent ):void
            {
                var systemClipboard:ClipBoard = Clipboard.generalClipboard;
                if(systemClipboard.hasFormat( formatsBox.selectedItem.value ) ){
                    resultText.text = "There is " +
                formatsBox.selectedItem.label + " data on the clipboard.";
                } else {
                    resultText.text = "There is not " +
                formatsBox.selectedItem.label + " data on the clipboard.";
                }
```

```
                }
            ]]>
        </mx:Script>

        <mx:Array id="formats">
            <mx:Object value="{ClipboardFormats.TEXT_FORMAT}" label="Text" />
            <mx:Object value="{ClipboardFormats.URL_FORMAT}" label="URL" />
            <mx:Object value="{ClipboardFormats.HTML_FORMAT}" label="HTML" />
            <mx:Object value="{ClipboardFormats.RICH_TEXT_FORMAT}" label="Rich Text" />
            <mx:Object value="{ClipboardFormats.BITMAP_FORMAT}" label="Bitmap" />
            <mx:Object value="{ClipboardFormats.FILE_LIST_FORMAT}" label="File List" />
        </mx:Array>

        <mx:ComboBox id="formatsBox" dataProvider="{formats}" />
        <mx:Button label="Check Clipboard" click="handleClick(event)" />
        <mx:Text id="resultText" />

    </mx:WindowedApplication>
```

JavaScript

In the following JavaScript example, a select list is populated in a method that executes
when the application is loaded. This method populates the select list with the various
default clipboard data types. The user can click the Check Clipboard button, which
will call a method that executes the `air.Clipboard.generalClipboard.hasFormat` method to determine whether the data is present on the clipboard. This will then update the
result `div` with the result.

```
<html>
<head>
    <title>Entry 7.1 - JavaScript</title>

    <script type="text/javascript" src="AIRAliases.js"></script>
    <script type="text/javascript">
        function populateSelectOptions() {
            document.formatForm.formats.options[0] = new Option( "Text",
air.ClipboardFormats.TEXT_FORMAT );
            document.formatForm.formats.options[1] = new Option( "URL",
air.ClipboardFormats.URL_FORMAT );
            document.formatForm.formats.options[2] = new Option( "HTML",
air.ClipboardFormats.HTML_FORMAT );
            document.formatForm.formats.options[3] = new Option( "Rich Text",
air.ClipboardFormats.RICH_TEXT_FORMAT );
            document.formatForm.formats.options[4] = new Option( "Bitmap", //

air.ClipboardFormats.BITMAP_FORMAT );
            document.formatForm.formats.options[5] = new Option( "File List",
air.ClipboardFormats.FILE_LIST_FORMAT );
        }
        function handleClick( event ) {
            var resultDiv = document.getElementById( 'result' );
            var selectedOption =
document.formatForm.formats.options[document.formatForm.formats.selectedIndex];
            if( air.Clipboard.generalClipboard.hasFormat( selectedOption.value )
```

```
        ) {
                             resultDiv.innerHTML = "There is " +selectedOption.text + " data
        on the clipboard.";
                    } else {
                             resultDiv.innerHTML = "There is not " +selectedOption.text + "
        data on the clipboard.";
                    }
             }
        </script>
    </head>

    <body onload="populateSelectOptions()" style="text-align:center;">

        <form name="formatForm">
             <select name="formats"></select><br />
             <input type="button" value="Check Clipboard" onclick="handleClick(event)" />
        </form>
        <div id="result"></div>

    </body>
    </html>
```

7.2 Adding Data to the Operating System Clipboard

Problem

You need to add data to the operating system clipboard so that it can be accessed by other applications on the user's computer.

Solution

Use the Clipboard class, which contains a reference to the operating system clipboard in the generalClipboard property. In this reference, you can call the setData method to add data to the clipboard.

Discussion

The static property generalClipboard of the Clipboard class contains an instance of the Clipboard class that represents the operating system clipboard and lets you perform get and set operations, among others. To set data onto the operating system clipboard, you use the setData method of this instance.

The setData method takes three parameters: the format of the data, the actual data, and an optional Boolean that indicates whether the data is serializable (defaults to true).

ActionScript

To set data on the operating system clipboard in ActionScript, you need to call the Clipboard.generalClipboard.setData method and pass in both the data and the data format. For example:

```
Clipboard.generalClipboard.setData( ClipboardFormats.TEXT_FORMAT, "Sample Text" );
```

This would place the words *Sample Text* onto the clipboard so that it is accessible from other applications.

In an actual Flex application, you could retrieve this text dynamically from a control. In the following example, you are given a text input where you can enter text to copy. After you enter the text, you can click the Copy button, and the text will be added to the operating system clipboard in the TEXT_FORMAT clipboard data format.

```
<mx:WindowedApplication xmlns:mx="http://www.adobe.com/2006/mxml" layout="vertical">

    <mx:Script>
        <![CDATA[

            import flash.desktop.Clipboard;
            import flash.desktop.ClipboardFormats

            private function handleCopyClick(event:MouseEvent):void
            {
                Clipboard.generalClipboard.setData(ClipboardFormats.TEXT_FORMAT,
textInput.text);
            }

        ]]>
    </mx:Script>

    <mx:TextInput id="textInput" />
    <mx:Button id="copyButton" label="Copy" click="handleCopyClick(event)"/>

</mx:WindowedApplication>
```

JavaScript

To use the setData method of the Clipboard class within JavaScript, you need to pass in the data type as well as the actual data to be added to the clipboard. For example:

```
air.Clipboard.generalClipboard.setData( air.ClipboardFormats.TEXT_FORMAT, "Sample
Text" );
```

This would place the words *Sample Text* onto the clipboard so that it is accessible from other applications.

In an actual application, you can pull this information dynamically from a control. In this example, the user is given a text input where you can enter text to be copied to the clipboard. When you click the Copy button, this text will be added to the operating system clipboard in the TEXT_FORMAT clipboard data format.

```
<html>
    <head>
        <title>Copy to Clipboard</title>

        <script type="text/javascript" src="AIRAliases.js"></script>
        <script type="text/javascript">
```

```
                    function handleCopyClick(event) {
                        var textInput = document.getElementById('userInput');
                        air.Clipboard.generalClipboard.setData(air.ClipboardFormats.TEXT_FORMAT,
textInput.value);
                    }

            </script>
        </head>

        <body>
            <input id="userInput" type="text" />
            <input id="copyButton" type="submit" value="Copy"
onclick="handleCopyClick(event)" />
        </body>
    </html>
```

7.3 Retrieving Data from the Operating System Clipboard

Problem

You need to be able to access data from the operating system clipboard.

Solution

Use the static `getData` method of the `Clipboard` class to retrieve data from any `Clipboard` instance.

Discussion

The `getData` method takes two parameters: the data type of the data you are requesting and an optional parameter that defines the `ClipboardTransferMode` used to access that data, indicating whether the data comes back as a reference or as a serialized copy. The second parameter is not used with the default data formats that are defined in the `ClipboardFormats` class but is used only when accessing application-defined formats.

ActionScript

In ActionScript, you can retrieve data from the clipboard by calling the `getData` method on an instance of the `Clipboard` class. For example:

```
Clipboard.generalClipboard.getData( ClipboardFormats.FILE_LIST_FORMAT );
```

This example retrieves the clipboard data from the operating system clipboard that is in the file list format.

In this example, the user can click the Get Data button, and if there is `FILE_LIST_FORMAT` data present on the clipboard, it will be retrieved and used to populate the `List` control. The names of the files will also be traced to the console. Also, note in this example you want to work only with copies of the files, not the originals. Because of this, the transfer mode is set to CLONE_ONLY. For more information on transfer modes with the clipboard, see Recipe 7.6.

```
<mx:WindowedApplication xmlns:mx="http://www.adobe.com/2006/mxml" layout="vertical">

    <mx:Script>
        <![CDATA[
            import mx.collections.ArrayCollection;
            import flash.desktop.Clipboard;
            import flash.desktop.ClipboardFormats;
            import flash.desktop.ClipboardTransferMode;

            [Bindable]
            private var files:ArrayCollection = new ArrayCollection();

            private function handleGetDataClick(event:MouseEvent):void {
                if(Clipboard.generalClipboard.hasFormat(Clipboard
Formats.FILE_LIST_FORMAT)) {
                    var items:Array = Clipboard.generalClipboard.getData(
ClipboardFormats.FILE_LIST_FORMAT, ClipboardTransferMode.CLONE_ONLY) as Array;
                    files = new ArrayCollection( items );
                    for each (var aFile:File in items) {
                        trace( "[FILE REFERENCE]: " + aFile.name );
                    }
                }
            }

        ]]>
    </mx:Script>

    <mx:Button id="getData" label="Get Data" click="handleGetDataClick(event)" />
    <mx:Label text="File List on Clipboard" />
    <mx:List id="results" dataProvider="{files}" labelField="nativePath"/>

</mx:WindowedApplication>
```

JavaScript

In JavaScript, you can access data from the clipboard by calling the getData method of the Clipboard class. For example:

```
air.Clipboard.generalClipboard.getData( air.ClipboardFormats.FILE_LIST_FORMAT );
```

This example will return an array of file references that represents the files that have been added to the operating system clipboard.

In the following example, the application has a single button. When the button is clicked, data in the FILE_LIST_FORMAT is retrieved from the clipboard if it is present. There is a div with an id of result. The native paths of the referenced files will be added to this div. In addition, the names of the files will be traced to the console. Also, note in this example you want to work with copies of the files only, not the originals. Because of this, the transfer mode is set to CLONE_ONLY. For more information on transfer modes with the clipboard, see Recipe 7.6.

```
<html>
    <head>
        <title>Retrieve Data from Clipboard</title>
        <link href="sample.css" rel="stylesheet" type="text/css"/>

        <script type="text/javascript" src="AIRAliases.js"></script>
        <script type="text/javascript">
            function handleGetDataClick(event) {
                    result.innerHTML = "";
                    if(air.Clipboard.generalClipboard.hasFormat
(air.ClipboardFormats.FILE_LIST_FORMAT)) {
                        var items = new Array();
                        items =
air.Clipboard.generalClipboard.getData(air.ClipboardFormats.FILE_LIST_FORMAT,air.Cl
ipboardTransferMode.CLONE_ONLY);
                        for (index = 0; index < items.length; index++) {
                            var aFile = items[index];
                            result.innerHTML += aFile.nativePath + " <br/> ";
                             air.trace("[FILE REFERENCE]:" + aFile.name);
                        }
                    } else {
                        result.innerHTML = "No File References on Clipboard"
;
                    }
                }
        </script>
    </head>

    <body>
        <input type="button" value="Get Data" onclick="handleGetDataClick(event)" />
        <div id="result"></div>
    </body>
</html>
```

7.4 Clearing Data from a Clipboard

Problem

You need to be able to clear a certain type of data from the operating system clipboard.

Solution

Use the clearData method to clear a specific type of data from an instance of the Clipboard class, or use the clear method to remove data of all types from an instance of the Clipboard class.

Discussion

In many cases you may need to clear a specific type of data from the operating system clipboard. In those cases you can rely on the two methods provided by the Clipboard class: clear and clearData.

ActionScript

You can clear all the data from a clipboard with ActionScript by calling the `clear` method. For example:

```
Clipboard.generalClipboard.clear();
```

This would clear all the data on the operating system clipboard from your AIR application. If you need to clear only a specific data type, you can use the `clearData` method. For example:

```
Clipboard.generalClipboard.clearData( ClipboardFormats.BITMAP_FORMAT );
```

In the following example, you are able to select a specific clipboard data format and clear the selected format from the operating system clipboard by using the `clearData` method:

```
<mx:WindowedApplication xmlns:mx="http://www.adobe.com/2006/mxml" layout="vertical">

    <mx:Script>
        <![CDATA[

            import flash.desktop.Clipboard;
            import flash.desktop.ClipboardFormats;

            private function handleClearFormatClick(event:MouseEvent):void {
                Clipboard.generalClipboard.clearData(format.selectedItem.value
as String);
            }

        ]]>
    </mx:Script>

    <mx:ComboBox id="format">
        <mx:dataProvider>
            <mx:Array>
                <mx:Object value="{ClipboardFormats.TEXT_FORMAT}" label="Text" />
                <mx:Object value="{ClipboardFormats.URL_FORMAT}" label="URL" />
                <mx:Object value="{ClipboardFormats.HTML_FORMAT}" label="HTML" />
                <mx:Object value="{ClipboardFormats.RICH_TEXT_FORMAT}"
label="Rich Text" />
                <mx:Object value="{ClipboardFormats.BITMAP_FORMAT}"
label="Bitmap" />
                <mx:Object value="{ClipboardFormats.FILE_LIST_FORMAT}"
label="File List" />
            </mx:Array>
        </mx:dataProvider>
    </mx:ComboBox>

    <mx:Button label="Clear Format Data" click="handleClearFormatClick(event)" />

</mx:WindowedApplication>
```

JavaScript

To clear all the data from an instance of the Clipboard class within JavaScript, you need to call the clear method. For example:

```
air.Clipboard.generalClipboard.clear()
```

This would clear all the data on the operating system clipboard from your AIR application. Likewise, if you need to clear only a specific format, you can use the clear Data method and pass in the format you want removed:

```
air.Clipboard.generalClipboard.clearData( air.ClipboardFormats.BITMAP_FORMAT );
```

In the following example, you are able to select a specific clipboard data format and clear the selected format from the operating system clipboard by using the clearData method:

```
<html>
    <head>
        <title>Entry 7.4 - Clear Data From Clipboard</title>
        <script type="text/javascript" src="AIRAliases.js"></script>
        <script type="text/javascript">
            function populateSelectOptions() {
                document.formatForm.formats.options[0] = new Option( "Text",
air.ClipboardFormats.TEXT_FORMAT );
                document.formatForm.formats.options[1] = new Option( "URL",
air.ClipboardFormats.URL_FORMAT );
                document.formatForm.formats.options[2] = new Option( "HTML",
air.ClipboardFormats.HTML_FORMAT );
                document.formatForm.formats.options[3] = new Option( "Rich
Text", air.ClipboardFormats.RICH_TEXT_FORMAT );
                document.formatForm.formats.options[4] = new Option( "Bitmap",
air.ClipboardFormats.BITMAP_FORMAT );
                document.formatForm.formats.options[5] = new Option( "File
List", air.ClipboardFormats.FILE_LIST_FORMAT );
            }

            function handleClearFormatClick(event) {
                var selectedOption = document.formatForm.formats.options[
document.formatForm.formats.selectedIndex];
                air.Clipboard.generalClipboard.clearData(selectedOption.value);
            }
        </script>
    </head>

    <body onload="populateSelectOptions()">
        <form name="formatForm">
            <select name="formats"></select><br />
            <input type="button" value="Clear Format"
onclick="handleClearFormatClick(event)" />
        </form>

    </body>
</html>
```

7.5 Using Deferred Rendering with Clipboard Data

Problem

You want clipboard data to be rendered (or created) when it is pasted instead of when it is copied.

Solution

Use the `setDataHandler` method, which doesn't store the actual data in the clipboard but rather references a method for rendering the data.

Discussion

In cases where rendering the clipboard data requires a large amount of system resources or where the data is changing on a regular basis, you may want the data to be rendered when it is pasted instead of when it is copied to the clipboard. To accomplish this in AIR, you can use the `setDataHandler` method.

This method works in a similar manner to the `setData` method, except instead of passing in the actual data, you pass in a function that will render the data. This function is called only when the data is needed. The first time the data is requested, the function is called, and the return value of the function populates the clipboard with the correct data. Subsequent calls to that data return that value. The function will not called again until the data is copied and requested again. It is important to remember this so as to not have undesired effects when working with stale data. Also noteworthy is that when data of a particular format is set using both the `setData` method and the `setDataHandler` method, `setData` takes priority. In this case, the handler function is never called when retrieving the data.

ActionScript

In this Flex example, there are three user interface elements: a Copy button, a Paste button, and a text element to contain the result text:

```
<mx:Button label="Copy" click="handleCopyClick(event)" />
<mx:Button label="Paste" click="handlePasteClick(event)" />
<mx:Text id="resultText" />
```

When the user clicks the Copy button, the current application time is stored, and the data is added to the clipboard with deferred rendering:

```
import flash.desktop.Clipboard;
import flash.desktop.ClipboardFormats;
import flash.utils.getTimer;

private var timeCopied:int;

private function handleCopyClick( event:MouseEvent ):void {
    timeCopied = getTimer();
```

```
    Clipboard.generalClipboard.setDataHandler( ClipboardFormats.TEXT_FORMAT,
dataHandler );
}

private function dataHandler():String {
    return "[Time Copied]: " + timeCopied + " [Time First Pasted]: " + getTimer();
}
```

When the user clicks the Paste button, the data is retrieved from the clipboard using deferred rendering. It lists both the time when the data was pasted as well as the time the data was pasted.

```
private function handlePasteClick( event:MouseEvent ):void {
    var data:String = Clipboard.generalClipboard.getData( Clipboard
Formats.TEXT_FORMAT ) as String;
    resultText.text = data;
}
```

If you click the Paste button twice, you will notice that the result stays the same. This is because the dataHandler method is called only the first time the data is requested. If you wanted the method to be called each time the Paste button was clicked, you would need to call the setDataHandler method again at the end of the handlePasteClick method.

JavaScript

In this example, there are three user interface elements: a Copy button, a Paste button, and a result div that will display the result text:

```
<input type="button" value="Copy" onclick="handleCopyClick(event)" /><br />
<input type="button" value="Paste" onclick="handlePasteClick(event)" />
<div id="result"></div>
```

When the application loads, the value of appStartTime is set to the current time. This value is used to calculate the number of milliseconds since the application launched. Another variable, timeClicked, is also created when the application launches.

```
var appStartTime = new Date();
var timeClicked;
```

When the user clicks the Copy button, the timeClicked variable is set to the current time and the data is added to the clipboard with deferred rendering.

```
function handleCopyClick(event) {
    timeClicked = new Date();
    air.Clipboard.generalClipboard.setDataHandler(
air.ClipboardFormats.TEXT_FORMAT, dataHandler );
}

function dataHandler() {
    var data =  "[TIME COPIED]: " + ( timeClicked.getTime() -
appStartTime.getTime() );
    data +=  " [TIME First PASTED]: " + ( new Date().getTime() -
appStartTime.getTime() );
```

```
        return data;
    }
```

When the user clicks the Paste button, the data is retrieved from the clipboard using deferred rendering, and the result from the clipboard is displayed in the result `div`. It lists both the time when the data was pasted as well as the time the data was pasted.

```
function handlePasteClick(event) {
    var result = document.getElementById( 'result' );
    result.innerHTML = air.Clipboard.generalClipboard.getData(
air.ClipboardFormats.TEXT_FORMAT );
}
```

If you click the Paste button twice, you will notice that the result stays the same, because the `dataHandler` method is called only the first time the data is requested. If you wanted the method to be called each time the Paste button is clicked, you need to call the `setDataHandler` method again at the end of the `handlePasteClick` method.

7.6 Creating Custom Clipboard Data Formats

Problem

You want to use a data format for the clipboard that is not one of the five default formats defined in `ClipboardFormats`.

Solution

Create a custom `Clipboard` data format using the built-in support for custom formats within AIR.

Discussion

In some situations, the standard clipboard data formats do not meet the needs of your application. For these situations, you can take advantage of the custom data formats of the `Clipboard` class.

To create a custom data format in AIR, you need a string that identifies your format. You will pass this to the `Clipboard` methods instead of a constant from the `Clipboard` `DataFormats` class. The only limitation on this string is that it cannot begin with *air:*. The AIR documentation suggests you use your application ID as the prefix for the format. For example:

```
com.oreilly.aircookbook.MyApplication:customdata
```

This helps to ensure your custom data format identifier will not match any other custom data formats from other AIR applications.

Transfer Modes

When you are dealing with custom data formats, you use the third parameter of the `setData` and `setDataHandler` methods to control how your data is placed on the clipboard. Essentially, there are two ways to place your data: as a copy and as a reference to the original object. Most any object can be added to the clipboard as a reference, but classes that are copied onto the clipboard must be serializable. If your class is serializable, you can pass `true` to the third parameter of these methods, and your data will be placed on the clipboard as a copy. If you pass `false`, it will be passed as a reference.

The transfer mode is not just important when pasting data, but it also plays a key role in retrieving data. `getData` has a third parameter that lets you indicate whether you want a copy of the data or a reference to the original data. The values for this parameter are defined as constants in the `ClipboardTransferMode` class.

- `ClipboardTransferMode.ORIGINAL_ONLY`: This mode takes only a reference of the data. If this is passed as the third parameter of the `getData` method, the method will take the original only. If only the copy of the data is available, no data will be returned.
- `ClipboardTransferMode.CLONE_ONLY`: This mode takes only a copy of the clipboard data. If only the reference to the original object is available, no data will be returned.
- `ClipboardTransferMode.ORIGINAL_PREFERRED`: In this mode, the `getData` method is requesting a reference to the original object, but if a copy is all that is available, the method will take that value.
- `ClipboardTransferMode.CLONE_PREFERRED`: In this mode, the `getData` method is requesting a copy of the original data. It will be returned if available. If only a reference to the original is available, the method will still use that value.

In some cases, it might not be apparent which transfer mode is appropriate. However, this value can become extremely important when working with clipboard data in the file list format. This could mean the difference between deleting a file and deleting a copy of a file. Unless you are performing actual file system operations, you will probably want to use `ClipboardTransferMode.CLONE_ONLY` when working with file list format data.

Sharing Data Between AIR Applications

If you want this custom data format to be available to other AIR applications, the data must be passed as a copy. When using a reference to the original data, you can paste the data only within the same AIR application.

ActionScript

The first step to creating a custom data format in ActionScript is to define your data. For your data class to be serializable, it must implement the `IExternalizable` interface. This requires that you define two methods, `readExternal` and `writeExternal`, which allow your data class to be broken down into binary data and copied onto the clipboard.

In the writeExternal method, you use the methods of the IDataOutput interface to write your data into binary form. Each standard ActionScript data type has a corresponding method that enables you to write the data. Be sure to pay attention to the order the data is written in this method. This order must be repeated in the readExternal method.

For the readExternal method, you use the read methods of the IDataInput interface to read your data back into your class. They do not need to be in the same order as they were written in the writeExternal method. For example:

```
package{

    import flash.utils.IExternalizable;
    import flash.utils.IDataInput;
    import flash.utils.IDataOutput;
    import flash.net.registerClassAlias;

    [Bindable]
    public class Person implements IExternalizable {

        public var firstName:String;
        public var lastName:String;
        public var age:int;

        public function Person() {
            registerClassAlias( "Person", Person );
        }

        public function readExternal(input:IDataInput):void {
            firstName = input.readUTF();
            lastName = input.readUTF();
            age = input.readInt();
        }

        public function writeExternal(output:IDataOutput):void {
            output.writeUTF(firstName);
            output.writeUTF(lastName);
            output.writeInt(age);
        }

    }
}
```

In this example, the custom data defines a person. It has the properties firstName, lastName, and age. Because the data has been defined, you can now add it to the clipboard as a custom data format. For this example, you will be using the following Flex user interface:

```
<mx:Label text="Input Data" fontSize="20" fontWeight="bold" />

<mx:Label text="First Name" />
<mx:TextInput id="firstName" />
<mx:Label text="Last Name" />
<mx:TextInput id="lastName" />
<mx:Label text="Age" />
```

```
<mx:TextInput id="age" />

<mx:HBox>
    <mx:Button label="Copy" click="handleCopyClick(event)" />
    <mx:Button label="Paste" click="handlePasteClick(event)" />
    <mx:Button label="Clear All Data" click="handleClearClick(event)" />
</mx:HBox>

<mx:Label text="Result" fontSize="20" fontWeight="bold" />

<mx:Label text="First Name" />
<mx:TextInput id="resultFirstName" enabled="false"/>
<mx:Label text="Last Name" />
<mx:TextInput id="resultLastName" enabled="false"/>
<mx:Label text="Age" />
<mx:TextInput id="resultAge" restrict="0-9" enabled="false"/>
```

The application should allow the user to fill in the fields on the top with the first name, last name, and age of the person. Then, if you click the Copy button, the data will be added to the clipboard through a custom data type identified by the string person. Next, if you click the Paste button, that data will be retrieved from the clipboard and used to populate the values in the lower form. The handleCopyClick method handles adding the data to the clipboard.

```
public function handleCopyClick( event:MouseEvent ):void {
    var data:Person = new Person();
    data.firstName = firstName.text;
    data.lastName = lastName.text;
    data.age = parseInt( age.text );
    var setResult:Boolean = Clipboard.generalClipboard.setData( "person", data,
true );
}
```

First, an instance of the data class Person is created. Then its properties are assigned the values of their respective text inputs. Finally, the data is added to the operating system clipboard with the setData method. The data is passing a copy of itself because the value true was passed as the third parameter indicating that the data is to be serialized.

```
public function handlePasteClick(event:MouseEvent):void {
    var result:Person = Clipboard.generalClipboard.getData
( "person", ClipboardTransferMode.CLONE_PREFERRED ) as Person;
    if (result) {
        resultFirstName.text = result.firstName;
        resultLastName.text = result.lastName;
        resultAge.text = result.age.toString();
    }
}
```

The handlePasteClick method gets the data from the clipboard using the same identifier that was used to set it on the clipboard. It also indicates that it wants a copy of the data if available as opposed to the original object. Finally, the values of the lower form are set. After using the Paste button, you can use the Clear All Data button to clear all the data from the form fields as well as the clipboard. Note that if you clear the clipboard, attempting to paste will cause the player to throw an "end of file" error, because there is no relevant data to be read. It is prudent to have error handling in place in the form of a `try...catch` block, because simply checking with `hasFormat` is not sufficient.

```
public function handleClearClick( event:MouseEvent ):void {
    firstName.text = "";
    lastName.text = "";
    age.text = "";
    resultFirstName.text = "";
    resultLastName.text = "";
    resultAge.text = "";
    Clipboard.generalClipboard.clearData( "person" );
}
```

JavaScript

The following user interface demonstrates the custom clipboard data formats within JavaScript. It consists of two forms, one to enter the data and one to display the data from the clipboard. In addition, it contains three buttons that enable you to copy, paste, and clear data.

```
<h2>Enter Data</h2>
<form name="dataForm">
    First Name: <input name="firstName" /><br />
    Last Name: <input name="lastName" /><br />
    Age: <input name="age" />
</form>
<input type="button" value="Copy" onclick="handleCopyClick(event)" />
<input type="button" value="Paste" onclick="handlePasteClick(event)" />
<input type="button" value="Clear All Data" onclick="handleClearClick(event)" />

<h2>Results</h2>
<form name="resultForm">
    First Name: <input name="firstName" disabled="true" /><br />
    Last Name: <input name="lastName" disabled="true" /><br />
    Age: <input name="age" disabled="true" />
</form>
```

The work of placing the custom data onto the clipboard is handled by the `handleCopy Click` method. This method creates a new object, `person`, and assigns the `firstName`, `lastName`, and `age` properties to it. Then, the data is placed on the operating system clipboard by using the `setData` method and the unique identifier of `person`.

```
function handleCopyClick( event ) {
    var person = {};
    person.firstName = document.dataForm.firstName.value;
    person.lastName = document.dataForm.lastName.value;
    person.age = document.dataForm.age.value;
    air.Clipboard.generalClipboard.setData( "person", person, true );
}
```

The `handlePasteClick` method handles the actual retrieving of the custom clipboard data. This method creates a new object to hold the results of the `getData` method. Then, the getData method is called while passing in the unique identifier used to place the date on the clipboard. Finally, the results are placed in their respective form fields.

```
function handlePasteClick( event ) {
    var result = {};
    if(air.Clipboard.generalClipboard.hasFormat( "person")) {
        result = air.Clipboard.generalClipboard.getData( "person",
air.ClipboardTransferMode.ORIGINAL_PREFERRED );
            document.resultForm.firstName.value = result.firstName;
            document.resultForm.lastName.value = result.lastName;
            document.resultForm.age.value = result.age;
    }
}
```

Finally, the Clear All Data button lets you clear all the form fields as well as the custom data from the clipboard.

```
function handleClearClick ( event ) {
    document.dataForm.firstName.value = "";
    document.dataForm.lastName.value = "";
    document.dataForm.age.value = "";
    document.resultForm.firstName.value = "";
    document.resultForm.lastName.value = "";
    document.resultForm.age.value = "";
    air.Clipboard.generalClipboard.clearData( "person" );
}
```

CHAPTER 8

Drag and Drop Support

Because almost every graphical operating system environment supports some level of drag and drop functionality, AIR provides an easy way to work with drag and drop gestures across multiple platforms. AIR supports both the dragging out and the dropping in of the standard data types; however, ActionScript and JavaScript deal with these gestures in very different ways.

8.1 Dragging Data Out of an Application in ActionScript

Problem

You need to drag a file reference from your application to the desktop.

Solution

Use the `NativeDragManager` class to control the drag-in gesture in your AIR application.

Discussion

In ActionScript, you manage drag and drop gestures with the `NativeDragManager` class. To support a drag-out gesture specifically, you use the `doDrag` static method of the `NativeDragManager` class. You can pass in five parameters; the first two are required: `dragInitiator` and `clipboard`.

The first required parameter, `dragInitiator`, is the object that initiated the drag action. It is required to be an `InteractiveObject` or a class that inherits from it. The second parameter, `clipboard`, is an instance of the `Clipboard` class or a class inheriting from the `Clipboard` class. In this case, you actually need to instantiate an instance of the `Clipboard` class and add the data that needs to be passed with the drag-out gesture.

In this example, the user interface consists of a label, a button, and a list:

```
<mx:Label id="directoryName"
    fontSize="20" fontWeight="bold" />
```

```
<mx:Button label="Select Directory"
    click="{file.browseForDirectory('Select Directory')}" />

<mx:List id="fileList" width="100%" height="100%"
    dataProvider="{files}" labelField="name"
    mouseDown="handleMouseDown(event)" />
```

When the button is clicked, it prompts the user to select a directory. When the user selects a directory, the list will be populated with all the files in the directory. The code you need is as follows:

```
<mx:WindowedApplication xmlns:mx="http://www.adobe.com/
2006/mxml" layout="vertical" preinitialize="init();">

<mx:Script>
    <![CDATA[

import mx.core.UIComponent;
import mx.collections.ArrayCollection;
import flash.filesystem.File;

[Bindable]
private var files:ArrayCollection = new ArrayCollection();
private var file:File = new File();


private function init():void {
    file.addEventListener( Event.SELECT, handleDirectorySelect );
}

private function handleDirectorySelect( event:Event ):void {
    files = new ArrayCollection( file.getDirectoryListing() );
    directoryName.text = file.name;
}
```

When the user performs a mouseDown gesture on the list, the handleMouseDown method is called. First, a new instance of the Clipboard class is created. The instance of the File class is passed into the instance of the Clipboard with the setData method. It is passed in as a one-element array because the ClipboardFormats.FILE_LIST_FORMAT is expecting an array. Next, a new instance of the BitmapData class is instantiated. This will contain the image that will be dragged. For the example, the BitmapData instance draws the list item that is being dragged. Finally, the doDrag method is called, and the list item, the instance of the Clipboard class, and the instance of the BitmapData class are passed in as parameters. The code for this is as follows:

```
private function handleMouseDown( event:MouseEvent ):void {
    if (fileList.selectedItem) {
        var data:Clipboard = new Clipboard();
        data.setData( ClipboardFormats.FILE_LIST_FORMAT, [ fileList.selectedItem ] );
        var bmd:BitmapData = new BitmapData( InteractiveObject( event.target
).width, InteractiveObject( event.target ).height );
        bmd.draw( InteractiveObject( event.target ) );
        NativeDragManager.doDrag( event.target as InteractiveObject, data, bmd );
```

```
        }
    }
```

Just as with the clipboard, you can add multiple types of data to a draggable object, enabling the receiving application to select the type of data that is most relevant.

8.2 Dragging Data Out of an Application in JavaScript

Problem

You need to drag a file reference from your application onto the desktop.

Solution

Listen to the `dragstart` event within the HTML in your AIR application.

Discussion

In JavaScript, dragging and dropping is handled by listening for specific events on an element. When dragging out, you listen specifically for the `dragstart` event. In the method that is listening for the event, you define the actual data that gets passed with the drag gesture.

To demonstrate the drag-out gesture in JavaScript, the following example provides a modest user interface that consists of three elements: a header `div`, a button that enables the user to select a directory, and a `div` that contains a list of the files in that directory.

```
<html>
<head>
    <title>Entry 8.2 - JavaScript</title>

    <script type="text/javascript" src="AIRAliases.js"></script>

    <style type="text/css">
        #files {width: 300px;height: 200px;overflow: auto;}
        #header{ font-weight: bold;font-size: 20px;}
        .listing {background-color: #efefef; padding: 3px;margin: 3px 0;-webkit-
user-drag: element;}
    </style>

</head>

<body onload="init()" style="margin: 10px;">
    <div id="header">Select a Directory</div>
    <input type="button" value="Select Directory" onclick="handleSelectButton()"/>
    <div id="files"></div>
</body>
</html>
```

Before the individual files can be dragged out of the application, the previously mentioned items need to be listed in the `div` named `files`. When clicked, the Select

Directory button launches the directory selection window, and when a directory is selected, the `directorySelected` method is called. This clears the `files` div and adds a new div for each file. The important item to notice here is that an event listener is being configured for each div that is listening for the `dragstart` event. This is the event that is dispatched when the user performs a `mouseDown` gesture on the object.

In addition, each new div that is created is assigned a property called `fileReference`. The actual instance of the `File` class for each file is assigned to this property. This assignment enables the instance to be passed with the object when dragged.

```
var file = new air.File();
var directoryFiles = {};

function init() {
    file.addEventListener(air.Event.SELECT, directorySelected);
}

function handleSelectButton() {
    file.browseForDirectory("Select a directory");
}

function directorySelected(event) {
    directoryFiles = file.getDirectoryListing();
    var header = document.getElementById( 'header' );
    header.innerHTML = file.name;
    var files = document.getElementById( 'files' );
    while( files.hasChildNodes() ) {
        files.removeChild( listing.firstChild );
    }
    for (i = 0; i < directoryFiles.length; i++) {
        var item = document.createElement( 'div' );
        item.innerHTML = directoryFiles[i].name;
        item.className = "listing";
        item.fileReference = directoryFiles[i];
        item.addEventListener( "dragstart", handleDragStart );
        files.appendChild( item );
    }
}
```

After each `file` div is configured to listen for the `dragstart` event, you can add data to the drag object. For this example, the data is copied, as you can see by the `String` value `copy` assigned to the `effectAllowed` property of the `dataTransfer` object in the event. Next, the data is added to the drag object with the `setData` method just as with the clipboard. The format and the actual data are both passed in.

Because the data format is `air.ClipboardFormats.FILE_LIST_FORMAT`, the data needs to be in an array variable. It will have only a single element, which is the `fileReference` property of the dragged object that was assigned earlier.

```
function handleDragStart(event) {
    event.dataTransfer.effectAllowed = "copy";
    event.dataTransfer.setData(air.ClipboardFormats.FILE_LIST_FORMAT,new Array(
```

```
event.target.fileReference ) );
}
```

With just these lines of code, the application now supports the drag-out gesture. In this case, if one of the file listings is dragged from the application to the desktop, a new copy of the file will appear on the desktop.

Working with other types of clipboard data is similar. You can add multiple types of data to the `dataTransfer` object, and an application that has been written to receive dragged-in content can be configured to handle the different data formats.

8.3 Dragging Data Into an Application in ActionScript

Problem

You want to be able to drag text into your AIR application from another application.

Solution

AIR provides the capability to support the drag-in gesture in both ActionScript and JavaScript.

Discussion

In ActionScript, the `NativeDragManager` class handles the drag-in gesture. Its static method `acceptDragDrop` enables you to define whether you will accept the dragged data based on its contents.

In this example, the user interface consists of a box that functions as the target area and a text area that will be used to display the text data from the drag-in gesture:

```
<mx:WindowedApplication xmlns="http://www.adobe.com/2006/mxml"
    layout="vertical" creationComplete="init()">

    <mx:Script>
    ...
    </mx:Script>

    <mx:Box id="target" width="200" height="200" backgroundColor="#efefef"
        nativeDragEnter="handleDragEnter(event)"
nativeDragDrop="handleDrop(event)"
        horizontalAlign="center" verticalAlign="middle">

        <mx:Label text="Target Area" fontSize="20" fontWeight="bold"
color="#666666" />

    </mx:Box>

    <mx:TextArea id="content" width="100%" height="100%"/>

</mx:WindowedApplication>
```

The target area box contains event listeners configured for the `nativeDragEnter` and `nativeDragDrop` events. The `nativeDragEnter` event is dispatched when dragged data is brought over an object. If you plan to accept only certain types of dropped data, you need to add logic to this method to check the data formats. The `NativeDragEvent` contains a property named `clipboard` that is an instance of the `Clipboard` class and that contains all the data for the dragged object. You can use the `hasFormat` method of this property to determine whether the needed data is present. Once you are sure that the needed data is present, you can call the `NativeDragManager.acceptDragDrop` method and pass in the target area as the parameter.

```
private function handleDragEnter( event:NativeDragEvent ):void {
    if( event.clipboard.hasFormat( ClipboardFormats.TEXT_FORMAT ) ) {
        NativeDragManager.acceptDragDrop( target );
    }
}
```

If the `acceptDragDrop` method is called, then the `nativeDragDrop` method is dispatched when the object is dropped onto the target area. In this case, once the data is dropped, any data in the `ClipboardFormats.TEXT_FORMAT` format is extracted and placed into the text area.

```
private function handleDrop( event:NativeDragEvent ):void {
    content.text = event.clipboard.getData( ClipboardFormats.TEXT_FORMAT ) as
String;
}
```

8.4 Dragging Data Into an Application in JavaScript

Problem

You want to be able to drag text into your AIR application from another application.

Solution

Listen to the `dragenter`, `dragover`, and `drop` events within the HTML of your AIR application.

Discussion

In JavaScript, the drag-in gesture is supported by listening for specific events. If you want to use a `div` as a target for the drag in, you need to listen for three specific events: `dragenter`, `dragover`, and `drop`. By default, you cannot use a noneditable region as a drop target, but if you listen for the `dragenter` and `dragover` events and call the `event.preventDefault` method, you can use noneditable regions as drop targets.

To perform the drop, you need to listen for the `drop` event. The `drop` event contains a `dataTransfer` object that works like the `Clipboard` class. You can call the `event.data`

`Transfer.getData` method and pass in the data type. It then returns the data from the drag-in gesture in that format.

In this example, the user interface consists of two `div` elements. The first `div` with an `id` of `targetArea` is used as the drop target. The second `div` with an `id` of `content` is updated with the value of the dropped text.

```
<html>
<head>
    <title>Entry 8.4 - JavaScript</title>

    <style type="text/css">
        #targetArea { width: 250px;height: 250px;background-color:
#efefef;border: 1px solid #cccccc; color: #cccccc;text-align: center;font-size:
20px; }
        #content { font-size: 11px; }
    </style>

</head>

<body onload="init()" style="margin: 10px;">
    <div id="targetArea">Drop Target</div>
    <div id="content"></div>
</body>
</html>
```

The event listeners that are needed for the drag-in gesture are added in the `init` method, which is called in response to the `onload` event. Also, the method `handleDefaultE vents` calls the `event.preventDefault` method to allow the `targetArea` to be used as a drop target.

```
function init() {
    var targetArea = document.getElementById( 'targetArea' );
    targetArea.addEventListener( "dragenter", handleDefaultEvents );
    targetArea.addEventListener( "dragover", handleDefaultEvents );
    targetArea.addEventListener( "drop", handleDrop );
}

function handleDefaultEvents( event ) {
    event.preventDefault();
}
```

The `handleDrop` method responds to the drop event. In this method, the text data is extracted from the event by calling the `event.dataTransfer.getData` method and passing in the `air.ClipboardFormats.TEXT_FORMAT` value. This text is then added to the `div` named `content`.

```
function handleDrop( event ) {
    var dragText = event.dataTransfer.getData( air.ClipboardFormats.TEXT_FORMAT );
    var content = document.getElementById( 'content' );
    content.innerHTML = dragText;
}
```

8.5 Dragging and Dropping Within an Application in ActionScript

Problem

You need to enable drag and drop gestures that work both within your application and outside your application.

Solution

Use the `NativeDragManager`'s static methods to enable both drag-in and drag-out gestures.

Discussion

In ActionScript, you can use both static methods of the `NativeDragManager` class to achieve drag and drop functionality within your application. In this example, the user interface consists of two `VBox` components that function as drop targets. Each `VBox` contains three labels that function as the drag objects. Each `Label` is configured with an event listener that listens for the `mouseDown` event. Each `VBox` is configured with an event handler for the `nativeDragEnter` and `nativeDragDrop` events.

```
<mx:Style>
    .target { backgroundColor: #ffffff; borderStyle: solid; borderColor: #666666; }
</mx:Style>

<mx:Label text="Drag and Drop" fontSize="20" fontWeight="bold" />

<mx:HBox>

    <mx:VBox id="target1" width="250" nativeDragEnter="handleDragEnter(event)"
nativeDragDrop="handleDrop(event)" styleName="target">
        <mx:Label text="One" mouseDown="handleMouseDown(event)" />
        <mx:Label text="Two" mouseDown="handleMouseDown(event)" />
        <mx:Label text="Three" mouseDown="handleMouseDown(event)" />
    </mx:VBox>

    <mx:VBox id="target2" width="250" nativeDragEnter="handleDragEnter(event)"
nativeDragDrop="handleDrop(event)" styleName="target">
        <mx:Label text="Four" mouseDown="handleMouseDown(event)" />
        <mx:Label text="Five" mouseDown="handleMouseDown(event)" />
        <mx:Label text="Six" mouseDown="handleMouseDown(event)" />
    </mx:VBox>

</mx:HBox>
```

The `handleMouseDown` method performs three specific functions:

- It creates a new instance of the `Clipboard` class and adds the `text` property of the `Label` as text data.

- An instance of the `BitmapData` class draws the `Label`.
- Calling the `acceptDragDrop` method of the `NativeDragManager` and passing it the `Label`, the instance of the `Clipboard` class, and the instance of the `BitmapData` class initiates the drag gesture.

The code you need is as follows:

```
private function handleMouseDown( event:MouseEvent ):void {
    var data:Clipboard = new Clipboard();
    var labelToDrag:Label = Label(event.currentTarget);
    data.setData( ClipboardFormats.TEXT_FORMAT, labelToDrag.text );
    var bmpProxy:BitmapData = new BitmapData(labelToDrag.width, labelToDrag.height );
    bmd.draw(labelToDrag);
    NativeDragManager.doDrag(labelToDrag, data, bmpProxy);
}
```

The `handleDragEnter` method that is triggered by the `VBox` components performs one specific function: accepting the drag-in gesture. The static `NativeDragManager.accept DragDrop` method must be called so the drag object knows the target is willing to accept its data. To ensure this text is plain-text data, the `hasFormat` method of the `Clipboard` class is called.

```
private function handleDragEnter( event:NativeDragEvent ):void {
    if( event.clipboard.hasFormat( ClipboardFormats.TEXT_FORMAT ) )
        NativeDragManager.acceptDragDrop(VBox(event.currentTarget));
}
```

The `handleDrop` method takes the data that was dropped and creates a new `Label` in the target `VBox` identical to the drag object:

```
private function handleDrop( event:NativeDragEvent ):void {
    var newLabel:Label = new Label();
    newLabel.text = event.clipboard.getData( ClipboardFormats.TEXT_FORMAT ) as
String;
    newLabel.addEventListener( MouseEvent.MOUSE_DOWN, handleMouseDown );
    VBox( event.target ).addChild( newLabel );
}
```

With this simple application, you now can drag the label to either target, and the application will be replicated. In addition, you can drag any of these drag objects outside the application to any application that supports plain-text data. The `VBox` drag targets will also accept text dragged in from outside the AIR application.

8.6 Dragging and Dropping Within an Application in JavaScript

Problem

You need to enable drag and drop gestures that work both within your application and outside your application.

Solution

Listen to the dragenter, dragover, dragstart, and drop events from the HTML within your AIR application.

Discussion

In JavaScript, you can perform drag and drop operations by listening to the dragenter, dragover, dragstart, and drop events. In this example, the user interface consists of two div elements that function as drop targets. Each div contains three div elements that function as drag objects. The target div elements have event listeners for the dragover, dragenter, and drop events. The drag objects have an event listener for the dragstart event. For example:

```
<html>
<head>
    <title>Entry 8.6 - JavaScript</title>

    <script type="text/javascript" src="AIRAliases.js"></script>
    <script type="text/javascript" src="AIRIntrospector.js"></script>
    <script type="text/javascript">
        function init() {
            var target1 = document.getElementById( 'target1' );
            target1.addEventListener( "dragenter", handleDefaultEvents );
            target1.addEventListener( "dragover", handleDefaultEvents );
            target1.addEventListener( "drop", handleDrop );
            var target2 = document.getElementById( 'target2' );
            target2.addEventListener( "dragenter", handleDefaultEvents );
            target2.addEventListener( "dragover", handleDefaultEvents );
            target2.addEventListener( "drop", handleDrop );
        }

    </script>

    <style type="text/css">
        .target {  width: 150px;height: 250px;border: 1px solid #cccccc;
color: #cccccc;text-align: center;font-size: 20px; margin: 5px; }
        #content { font-size: 11px; }
        #sourceArea { background-color: #efefef;-webkit-user-drag: element; }
        .listItem {background-color: #efefef;-webkit-user-drag: element; font-
size: 11px;margin: 3px;padding:3px;}
    </style>

</head>

<body onload="init()" style="margin: 10px;">
    <h1>Drag and Drop</h1>
    <div id="target1" class="target" style="float: left;">
        <div class="listItem" ondragstart="handleDragStart(event)">One</div>
        <div class="listItem" ondragstart="handleDragStart(event)">Two</div>
        <div class="listItem" ondragstart="handleDragStart(event)">Three</div>
    </div>
    <div id="target2" class="target" style="float: left;">
```

```
        <div class="listItem" ondragstart="handleDragStart(event)">Four</div>
        <div class="listItem" ondragstart="handleDragStart(event)">Five</div>
        <div class="listItem" ondragstart="handleDragStart(event)">Six</div>
    </div>
</body>
</html>
```

The handleDefaultEvents method that is triggered by the drop target div elements calls the event.preventDefault method to enable them to function as drop targets:

```
function handleDefaultEvents( event ) {
    event.preventDefault();
}
```

The handleDragStart method that is triggered when you drag one of the drag objects calls dataTransfer.setData, passing the innerHTML property of the object to be dragged as the drag data. This will be used to create a duplicate div when the drag object is dropped onto a drop target.

```
function handleDragStart( event ) {
    event.dataTransfer.setData( air.ClipboardFormats.TEXT_FORMAT,
event.target.innerHTML );
}
```

The handleDrop method creates a new div with the same innerHTML as the drag object and adds it to the drop target. An event listener is added for the dragstart event so the new div can function as a drag object as well.

```
function handleDrop( event ) {
    var newDiv = document.createElement( 'div' );
    newDiv.innerHTML = event.dataTransfer.getData( air.ClipboardFormats.TEXT_FORMAT );
    newDiv.className = 'listItem';
    newDiv.addEventListener( "dragstart", handleDragStart );
    event.currentTarget.appendChild( newDiv );
}
```

By using AIR's drag and drop support, you can drag objects within the application or outside the application to any application that supports plain text.

CHAPTER 9

File System Integration

One of the main benefits of developing applications for the Adobe AIR runtime rather than Flash Player through a browser is that the security sandbox restrictions placed on the browser-based Flash Player do not exist within AIR applications. AIR applications are installed on the desktop with full permissions to access the operating system's file system.

This means your applications have the ability to read, write, move, and delete files. With this ability comes additional responsibility, because it would be very easy to cause damage or even render a machine inoperable. Therefore, this chapter will show you how to safely work with the file system.

9.1 Accessing Directory Aliases in the File Class

Problem

You want to access a user's Documents directory but don't want to have to prompt the user to find out where the directory is located or which system the user has.

Solution

Read the `userDirectory` property within the `File` class to determine the path to the Documents directory. AIR has already accounted for these differences between operating systems.

Discussion

AIR has several aliases as part of the `File` class that hold information about the user's system, including one called `userDirectory`, which is a reference to the user's home or Documents directory. Using these aliases is simple and also extremely powerful because it gives you an easy way to make your application work with many operating systems without having to specifically code for each.

In addition to userDirectory, four other directory aliases exist:

- applicationDirectory: The directory where the application is installed
- applicationStorageDirectory: A unique directory created for each AIR application where application-specific files (database, images, and so on) may be stored
- desktopDirectory: A reference to the user's desktop directory
- documentsDirectory: A reference to the user's Documents directory

Using these aliases is easy. You simply need to reference them from the File class.

ActionScript/Flex

To solve the needs of this recipe, you can simply reference the User directory with File.userDirectory. To see how these aliases work, refer to the following example, which shows the native paths of each of the five aliases.

 If you are working within any class file in your application other than the main WindowedApplication file, you need to import the flash.file System.File class.

```
<?xml version="1.0" encoding="utf-8"?>
<mx:WindowedApplication xmlns:mx="http://www.adobe.com/2006/mxml"
layout="vertical"
    creationComplete="showPaths()">
    <mx:Script>
    <![CDATA[

    private function showPaths():void{

path1.text = "applicationDirectory : " + File.applicationDirectory.nativePath;
path2.text = "applicationStorageDirectory : " + File.applicationStorage
Directory.nativePath;
path3.text = "desktopDirectory : " + File.desktopDirectory.nativePath;
path4.text = "documentsDirectory : " + File.documentsDirectory.nativePath;
path5.text = "userDirectory : " + File.userDirectory.nativePath;

    }
    ]]>
    </mx:Script>
    <mx:Label id="path1" />
    <mx:Label id="path2" />
    <mx:Label id="path3" />
    <mx:Label id="path4" />
    <mx:Label id="path5" />

</mx:WindowedApplication>
```

The following is one example of the results on a Mac:

```
applicationDirectory : /Users/rich/Desktop/Books/AIRCookbook/code/Chapter9_1/bin-debug
applicationStorageDirectory : /Users/rich/Library/Preferences/Chapter9-1/Local Store
desktopDirectory : /Users/rich/Desktop
documentsDirectory : /Users/rich/Documents
userDirectory : /Users/rich
```

JavaScript

To solve the needs of this recipe, you can simply reference the User directory with
`air.File.userDirectory`. To see how these aliases work, refer to the following example,
which shows the native paths of each.

 You need to include the `AIRAliases.js` file within your file.

```
<html>
    <head>
    <script src="AIRAliases.js" />
    <script>
    function showPaths(){
        paths.innerHTML = "applicationDirectory : " +
        air.File.applicationDirectory.nativePath + "<br/>" +
        "applicationStorageDirectory : " +
        air.File.applicationStorageDirectory.nativePath + "<br/>" +
        "desktopDirectory : " +
        air.File.desktopDirectory.nativePath + "<br/>" +
        "documentsDirectory : " +
        air.File.documentsDirectory.nativePath + "<br/>" +
        "userDirectory : " +
        air.File.userDirectory.nativePath;
    }
    </script>
    </head>
    <body onLoad="showPaths()">
        <div id="paths"></div>
    </body>
</html>
```

The following is one example of the results on a Mac:

```
applicationDirectory : /Users/rich/Desktop/Books/AIR Cookbook/code/Chapter9_1_JS
applicationStorageDirectory : /Users/rich/Library/Preferences/ch91JS/Local Store
desktopDirectory : /Users/rich/Desktop
documentsDirectory : /Users/rich/Documents
userDirectory : /Users/rich
```

9.2 Creating a New File or Directory

Problem

You want to create a new file called *MyFile.txt* on the user's desktop. You want this file to reside within a custom directory named test.

Solution

Use the `File` class, which is located within the `flash.fileSystem` package, to first create a directory; then create a file within the directory.

Discussion

AIR allows developers to build applications that can create directories and files on a user's file system. To create a new directory, you need to create a path to the new directory's desired location using the `resolvePath` method of the `File` class. You then call the `createDirectory` method, and the new directory will be created.

ActionScript/Flex

The following example shows how to create a new directory named test on the desktop as well as a reference to a new file called *MyFile.txt* within this directory:

```
private function createDirectory():void{
    var newDirectory:File = File.desktopDirectory.resolvePath("test");
    newDirectory.createDirectory();
    var newFile:File = newDirectory.resolvePath("MyFile.txt");
}
```

JavaScript

The following example demonstrates how to create a new directory named test on the desktop as well as a reference to a new file called *MyFile.txt* within this directory:

```
function createDirectory(){
    var newDirectory = air.File.desktopDirectory.resolvePath("test");
    newDirectory.createDirectory();
    var newFile = newDirectory.resolvePath("MyFile.txt");
}
```

 Although a reference to the new file *MyFile.txt* is created in the previous code, the file itself will not exist until something is written into the file. See Recipe 9.8 and Recipe 9.9 for information on reading and writing data to files via the `FileStream` class.

9.3 Deleting a File or Directory

Problem

You need to delete a file from the user's file system.

Solution

Use the `File` class methods `deleteFile`, `deleteDirectory`, `deleteFileAsync`, and `delete DirectoryAsync` to delete files and directories.

Discussion

To delete files and directories, you use the `deleteFile` and `deleteDirectory` methods, respectively. These methods perform a delete on the `File` object against which they are called. For example, you can create a reference to a directory using the `resolvePath` method as shown in Recipe 9.2 and then call the appropriate delete function.

However, this approach has two possible issues:

- The directory may not be empty, which would cause the delete to fail.
- The file or directory may be very large, which would cause a long wait period for the user while the delete is performed.

To deal with the first issue, the `deleteDirectory` method accepts a single argument of type `Boolean`, which, when set to `true`, will delete the directory and all of its contents. It is `false` by default.

The second issue is more of an architecture problem, but AIR has accounted for this. In addition to the `deleteDirectory` and `deleteFile` methods, AIR also provides the `deleteDirectoryAsync` and `deleteFileAsync` methods that will perform these actions asynchronously in the background. The following code will demonstrate both synchronous and asynchronous examples of deleting files and directories.

ActionScript/Flex

To delete a directory, use this code:

```
private function deleteDirectory():void{
    File.desktopDirectory.resolvePath("test").deleteDirectory();
}
```

To delete a nonempty directory, use this code:

```
private function deleteNonEmptyDirectory():void{
    File.desktopDirectory.resolvePath("test").deleteDirectory(true);
}
```

To delete a directory asynchronously with an event listener, use this code:

```
private function deleteDirectoryAsync():void{
    var temp:File = File.desktopDirectory.resolvePath("test")
    temp.addEventListener(Event.COMPLETE, deleteDirListener);
    temp.deleteDirectoryAsync();
}

private function deleteDirListener(event:Event):void{
    trace("directory deleted");
}
```

To delete a file, use this code:

```
private function deleteFile():void{
    File.desktopDirectory.resolvePath("test.txt").deleteFile();
}
```

To delete a file asynchronously with an event listener, use this code:

```
private function deleteFileAsync():void{
    var temp:File = File.desktopDirectory.resolvePath("test.txt")
    temp.addEventListener(Event.COMPLETE, deleteFileListener);
    temp.deleteFileAsync();
}

private function deleteFileListener(event:Event):void{
    trace("file deleted");
}
```

JavaScript

To delete a directory, use this code:

```
function deleteDirectory(){
    air.File.desktopDirectory.resolvePath("test").deleteDirectory();
}
```

To delete a nonempty directory, use this code:

```
function deleteNonEmptyDirectory(){
    air.File.desktopDirectory.resolvePath("test").deleteDirectory(true);
}
```

To delete a directory asynchronously with an event listener, use this code:

```
function deleteDirectoryAsync(){
    var temp = air.File.desktopDirectory.resolvePath("test");
    temp.addEventListener(air.Event.COMPLETE,deleteDirListener);
    temp.deleteDirectoryAsync();
}
function deleteDirListener(event){
    alert("directory deleted");
}
```

To delete a file, use this code:

```
function deleteFile(){
    air.File.desktopDirectory.resolvePath("test.txt").deleteFile();
}
```

To delete a file asynchronously with an event listener, use this code:

```
function deleteFileAsync(){
    var temp = air.File.desktopDirectory.resolvePath("test.txt");
    temp.addEventListener(air.Event.COMPLETE,deleteFileListener);
    temp.deleteFileAsync();
}
function deleteFileListener(event){
    alert("file deleted");
}
```

9.4 Copying a File or Directory

Problem

You want to copy a directory to a new location on the user's file system.

Solution

Use the `File` class methods `copyTo` and `copyToAsync` to copy files and directories.

Discussion

The `copyTo` method of the `File` class performs a copy on the `File` object against which it is called. For example, you could create a reference to a directory using the `resolve Path` method as shown in Recipe 9.2 and then call the `copyTo` function to pass in a reference to the destination.

This approach, however, has a possible issue in that the file or directory may be very large, which would cause a long wait period for the user while the copy is performed.

This issue is more of an architecture problem, but AIR has accounted for this. In addition to the `copyTo` method, AIR also provides a `copyToAsync` method, which will perform this action asynchronously in the background. The following code demonstrates both synchronous and asynchronous examples of copying files and directories.

ActionScript/Flex

To copy a directory, use this code:

```
private function copyDirectory():void{
    var origDirLoc:File = File.desktopDirectory.resolvePath("OrigDirectory");
    var newDirLoc:File = File.desktopDirectory.resolvePath("CopiedDirectory");
    origDirLoc.copyTo(newDirLoc);
}
```

To copy a directory asynchronously with an event listener, use this code:

```
private function copyDirectoryAscnc():void{
    var origDirLoc:File = File.desktopDirectory.resolvePath("OrigDirectory");
    origDirLoc.addEventListener(Event.COMPLETE,copyDirListener);
    var newDirLoc:File = File.desktopDirectory.resolvePath("CopiedDirectory");
    origDirLoc.copyToAsync(newDirLoc);
}

private function copyDirListener(event:Event):void{
    trace("directory copied");
}
```

To copy a file, use this code:

```
private function copyFile():void{
    var origFileLoc:File = File.desktopDirectory.resolvePath("OrigFile.txt");
    var newFileLoc:File = File.desktopDirectory.resolvePath("CopiedFile.txt");
    origFileLoc.copyTo(newFileLoc);
}
```

To copy a file asynchronously with an event listener, use this code:

```
private function copyFileAscnc():void{
    var origFileLoc:File = File.desktopDirectory.resolvePath("OrigFile.txt");
    origFileLoc.addEventListener(Event.COMPLETE,copyFileListener);
    var newFileLoc:File = File.desktopDirectory.resolvePath("CopiedFile.txt");
    origFileLoc.copyToAsync(newFileLoc);
}

private function copyFileListener(event:Event):void{
    trace("file copied");
}
```

JavaScript

To copy a directory, use this code:

```
function copyDirectory(){
    var origDirLoc = air.File.desktopDirectory.resolvePath("OrigDirectory");
    var newDirLoc = air.File.desktopDirectory.resolvePath("CopiedDirectory");
    origDirLoc.copyTo(newDirLoc);
}
```

To copy a directory asynchronously with an event listener, use this code:

```
function copyDirectoryAsync(){
    var origDirLoc = air.File.desktopDirectory.resolvePath("OrigDirectory");
    origDirLoc.addEventListener(air.Event.COMPLETE,copyDirListener);
    var newDirLoc = air.File.desktopDirectory.resolvePath("CopiedDirectory");
    origDirLoc.copyToAsync(newDirLoc);
}

function copyDirListener(event){
    alert("directory copied");
}
```

To copy a file, use this code:

```
function copyFile(){
    var origFileLoc = air.File.desktopDirectory.resolvePath("OrigFile.txt");
    var newFileLoc = air.File.desktopDirectory.resolvePath("CopiedFile.txt");
    origFileLoc.copyTo(newFileLoc);
}
```

To copy a file asynchronously with an event listener, use this code:

```
function copyFileAsync(){
    var origFileLoc = air.File.desktopDirectory.resolvePath("OrigFile.txt");
    origFileLoc.addEventListener(air.Event.COMPLETE,copyFileListener);
    var newFileLoc = air.File.desktopDirectory.resolvePath("CopiedFile.txt");
    origFileLoc.copyToAsync(newFileLoc);
}

function copyFileListener(event){
    alert("file copied");
}
```

9.5 Moving a File or Directory

Problem

You want to move a directory to a new location on the user's file system.

Solution

Use the moveTo and moveToAsync methods of the File class to move files and directories.

Discussion

The moveTo method performs a move on the File object against which it is called. For example, you could create a reference to a directory using the resolvePath method as shown in Recipe 9.2 and then call the moveTo function to pass in a reference to the destination.

This approach has a possible issue in that the file or directory may be very large, which would cause a long wait period for the user while the move is performed.

This issue is more of an architecture problem, but AIR has accounted for this. In addition to the moveTo method, AIR also provides a moveToAsync method, which will perform this action asynchronously in the background. The following code demonstrates both synchronous and asynchronous examples of moving files and directories.

ActionScript/Flex

To move a file, use this code:

```
private function moveDirectory():void{
    var origDirLoc:File = File.desktopDirectory.resolvePath("OrigDirectory");
```

```
    var newDirLoc:File = File.desktopDirectory.resolvePath("MovedDirectory");
    origDirLoc.moveTo(newDirLoc);
}
```

To move a directory asynchronously with an event listener, use this code:

```
private function moveDirectoryAsync():void{
    var origDirLoc:File = File.desktopDirectory.resolvePath("OrigDirectory");
    origDirLoc.addEventListener(Event.COMPLETE,moveDirListener);
    var newDirLoc:File = File.desktopDirectory.resolvePath("MovedDirectory");
    origDirLoc.moveToAsync(newDirLoc);
}

private function moveDirListener(event:Event):void{
    trace("directory moved");
}
```

To move a file, use this code:

```
private function moveFile():void{
    var origFileLoc:File = File.desktopDirectory.resolvePath("OrigFile.txt");
    var newFileLoc:File = File.desktopDirectory.resolvePath("MovedFile.txt");
    origFileLoc.moveTo(newFileLoc);
}
```

To move a file asynchronously with an event listener, use this code:

```
private function moveFileAsync():void{
    var origFileLoc:File = File.desktopDirectory.resolvePath("OrigFile.txt");
    origFileLoc.addEventListener(Event.COMPLETE,moveFileListener);
    var newFileLoc:File = File.desktopDirectory.resolvePath("MovedFile.txt");
    origFileLoc.moveToAsync(newFileLoc);
}

private function moveFileListener(event:Event):void{
    trace("file moved");
}
```

JavaScript

To move a directory, use this code:

```
function moveDirectory(){
    var origDirLoc = air.File.desktopDirectory.resolvePath("OrigDirectory");
    var newDirLoc = air.File.desktopDirectory.resolvePath("MovedDirectory");
    origDirLoc.moveTo(newDirLoc);
}
```

To move a directory asynchronously with an event listener, use this code:

```
function moveDirectoryAsync(){
    var origDirLoc = air.File.desktopDirectory.resolvePath("OrigDirectory");
    origDirLoc.addEventListener(air.Event.COMPLETE,
    function(event){moveDirListener(event)});
    var newDirLoc = air.File.desktopDirectory.resolvePath("MovedDirectory");
    origDirLoc.moveToAsync(newDirLoc);
}
```

```
function moveDirListener(event){
    alert("directory moved");
}
```

To move a file, use this code:

```
function moveFile(){
    var origFileLoc = air.File.desktopDirectory.resolvePath("OrigFile.txt");
    var newFileLoc = air.File.desktopDirectory.resolvePath("MovedFile.txt");
    origFileLoc.moveTo(newFileLoc);
}
```

To move a file asynchronously with an event listener, use this code:

```
function moveFileAsync(){
    var origFileLoc = air.File.desktopDirectory.resolvePath("OrigFile.txt");
    origFileLoc.addEventListener(air.Event.COMPLETE,moveFileListener);
    var newFileLoc = air.File.desktopDirectory.resolvePath("MovedFile.txt");
    origFileLoc.moveToAsync(newFileLoc);
}

function moveFileListener(event){
    alert("file moved");
}
```

9.6 Moving a File or Directory to the Trash

Problem

You want to delete a file by moving it to the trash rather than permanently deleting it.

Solution

Use the `moveToTrash` and `moveToTrashAsync` methods of the `File` class to move files and directories.

Discussion

The `moveToTrash` method performs a move on the `File` object against which it is called. For example, you could create a reference to a directory using the `resolvePath` method as shown in Recipe 9.2 and then call the `moveToTrash` function to pass in a reference to the destination.

This approach, however, has a possible issue in that the file or directory may be very large, which would cause a long wait period for the user while the move to the trash is performed.

This issue is more of an architecture problem, but AIR has accounted for this. In addition to the `moveToTrash` method, AIR also provides a `moveToTrashAsync` method, which performs the action asynchronously in the background. The following code demonstrates both synchronous and asynchronous examples of moving files and directories to the trash.

ActionScript/Flex

To move a directory, use this code:

```
private function moveDirectoryToTrash():void{
    var myDirLoc:File = File.desktopDirectory.resolvePath("MyDirectory");
    myDirLoc.moveToTrash();
}
```

To move a directory asynchronously with an event listener, use this code:

```
private function moveDirectoryToTrashAsync():void{
    var myDirLoc:File = File.desktopDirectory.resolvePath("MyDirectory");
    myDirLoc.addEventListener(Event.COMPLETE,moveDirToTrashListener);
    myDirLoc.moveToTrashAsync();
}

private function moveDirToTrashListener(event:Event):void{
    trace("directory moved to trash");
}
```

To move a file to the trash, use this code:

```
private function moveFileToTrash():void{
    var myFileLoc:File = File.desktopDirectory.resolvePath("MyFile.txt");
    myFileLoc.moveToTrash();
}
```

To move a file to the trash asynchronously with an event listener, use this code:

```
private function moveFileToTrashAsync():void{
    var myFileLoc:File = File.desktopDirectory.resolvePath("MyFile.txt");
    myFileLoc.addEventListener(Event.COMPLETE,moveFileToTrashListener);
    myFileLoc.moveToTrashAsync();
}

private function moveFileToTrashListener(event:Event):void{
    trace("file moved to trash");
}
```

JavaScript

To move a directory to the trash, use this code:

```
function moveDirectoryToTrash(){
    var myDirLoc = air.File.desktopDirectory.resolvePath("MyDirectory");
    myDirLoc.moveToTrash();
}
```

To move a directory to the trash asynchronously with an event listener, use this code:

```
function moveDirectoryToTrashAsync(){
    var myDirLoc = air.File.desktopDirectory.resolvePath("MyDirectory");
    myDirLoc.addEventListener(air.Event.COMPLETE,moveDirToTrashListener);
```

```
        myDirLoc.moveToTrashAsync();
    }

    function moveDirToTrashListener(event){
        alert("moved to trash");
    }
```

To move a file to the trash, use this code:

```
    function moveFileToTrash(){
        var myFileLoc = air.File.desktopDirectory.resolvePath("MyFile.txt");
        myFileLoc.moveToTrash();
    }
```

To move a file to the trash asynchronously with an event listener, use this code:

```
    function moveFileToTrashAsync(){
        var myFileLoc = air.File.desktopDirectory.resolvePath("MyFile.txt");
        myFileLoc.addEventListener(air.Event.COMPLETE,moveFileToTrashListener);
        myFileLoc.moveToTrashAsync();
    }

    function moveFileToTrashListener(event){
        alert("moved to trash");
    }
```

9.7 Prompting the User to Select a File or Directory

Problem

You want the user to be able to select a file or directory on their file system.

Solution

Use the browseForOpen and browseForDirectory methods of the File class.

Discussion

When called, the browseForOpen method opens the default file-browsing dialog box on the user's machine. This method requires an event listener to handle the user's selection. To browse for a directory, you use the browseForDirectory method, which also requires an event listener to handle the user's selection. Both methods accept a String as an argument, which will be displayed as directions to the user.

In the following sections, the first example shows a new File instance being created and an event listener being assigned to listen for the Event.SELECT event. The browseForOpen method is then called on the File instance, which launches the file-browsing dialog box. The event handler shows how to capture the nativePath from the selected file.

The second example shows a new `File` instance being created and an event listener being assigned to listen for the `Event.SELECT` event. The `browseForDirectory` method is then called on the `File` instance, which launches the file-browsing dialog box. The event handler shows how to capture the `nativePath` from the selected directory.

ActionScript/Flex

To browse for a file, use this code:

```
private function browseForFile():void{
    var file:File = new File();
    file.addEventListener(Event.SELECT,fileSelectHandler);
    file.browseForOpen("Select a File");
}
private function fileSelectHandler(event:Event):void{
    trace(event.target.nativePath);
}
```

To browse for a directory, use this code:

```
private function browseForDirectory():void{
    var file:File = new File();
    file.addEventListener(Event.SELECT,dirSelectHandler);
    file.browseForDirectory("Select a Directory");
}
private function dirSelectHandler(event:Event):void{
    trace(event.target.nativePath);
}
```

JavaScript

To browse for a file, use this code:

```
function browseForFile(){
    var file = new air.File();
    file.addEventListener(air.Event.SELECT,
    function(event){fileSelectHandler(event)});
    file.browseForOpen("Select a File");
}
function fileSelectHandler(event){
    alert(event.target.nativePath);
}
```

To browse for a directory, use this code:

```
function browseForDirectory(){
    var file = new air.File();
    file.addEventListener(air.Event.SELECT,
    function(event){dirSelectHandler(event)});
    file.browseForDirectory("Select a Directory");
}
function dirSelectHandler(event){
    alert(event.target.nativePath);
}
```

9.8 Reading Data from a File

Problem

You want to read data in from a file within the file system.

Solution

Use the `File` class to create a reference to the file to be opened, and then use the `FileStream` class located within the `flash.fileSystem` package to open the file.

Discussion

You can use the `FileStream` class to work with the contents of a file within the file system. This class can open a file with different levels of permissions, including the following:

- `FileMode.READ`: Setting the mode to `READ` opens the file with read-only permissions.
- `FileMode.WRITE`: Setting the mode to `WRITE` opens the file with full write permissions. If the file does not yet exist, it is created. If the file already exists, its contents are overwritten.
- `FileMode.APPEND`: Setting the mode to `APPEND` allows you to append data to an existing file. If the file does not exist, it is created. If the file does exist, any additions occur at the end of any existing contents, and existing data is not overwritten.
- `FileMode.UPDATE`: Setting the mode to `UPDATE` opens a file with both read and write permissions. If the file does not exist, it is created. If the file does exist, only data that is changed will be overwritten.

Because you simply want to read data from a file, you can use the `READ` level of permissions when opening the `FileStream`.

In the following example, an instance of the `File` class named `myFile` is created and resolved to a text file on the system's desktop named *MyFile.txt*.

Next, an instance of the `FileStream` class is created, and the `open` method is used to open the `myFile` `File` instance. Because the second argument passed into the open method is `FileMode.READ`, the `myFile` instance is opened as read-only.

The file is then read with the `FileStream`'s `readUTFBytes` method, which accepts a single argument that passes in the `FileStream`'s `byteAvailable` property. This ensures that the file is read completely. Lastly, the `FileStream` is closed.

Recipe 9.9 will demonstrate how to open the file with write permissions.

ActionScript/Flex

To read a file, use this code:

```
private function readFile():void{
    var myFile:File = File.desktopDirectory.resolvePath("MyFile.txt");
    var fileStream:FileStream = new FileStream();
    fileStream.open(myFile, FileMode.READ);
    trace(fileStream.readUTFBytes(fileStream.bytesAvailable));
    fileStream.close();
}
```

JavaScript

To read a file, use this code:

```
function readFile(){
    var myFile = air.File.desktopDirectory.resolvePath("MyFile.txt");
    var fileStream = new air.FileStream();
    fileStream.open(myFile, air.FileMode.READ);
    alert(fileStream.readUTFBytes(fileStream.bytesAvailable));
    fileStream.close();
}
```

9.9 Writing Data to a File

Problem

You want to write data to a file within the file system.

Solution

Use the File class to create a reference to the file to be opened, and then use the FileStream class located within the flash.fileSystem package to open the file.

Discussion

As discussed in Recipe 9.8, you can open FileStream with several levels of permissions. Because you want to write data in this case, you need to open the file with WRITE, APPEND, or UPDATE permission.

In the following example, an instance of the File class named myFile is created and resolved to a text file on the system's desktop named *MyFile.txt*.

Next, an instance of the FileStream class is created, and the open method is used to open the myFile File instance. Because the second argument passed into the open method is FileMode.WRITE, the myFile instance is opened and is writable.

The writeUTFBytes method is then called, and the "Hello World" String is passed in. Because this file was opened with the FileMode of WRITE, any existing contents will be overwritten. To edit an existing file, you need to open the file with either APPEND or UPDATE permission.

ActionScript/Flex

To write to a file, use this code:

```
private function writeToFile():void{
    var myFile:File = File.desktopDirectory.resolvePath("MyFile.txt");
    var fileStream:FileStream = new FileStream();
    fileStream.open(myFile, FileMode.WRITE);
    fileStream.writeUTFBytes("Hello World");
    fileStream.close();
}
```

JavaScript

To write to a file, use this code:

```
function writeToFile(){
    var myFile = air.File.desktopDirectory.resolvePath("MyFile.txt");
    var fileStream = new air.FileStream();
    fileStream.open(myFile, air.FileMode.WRITE);
    fileStream.writeUTFBytes("Hello World from JS");
    fileStream.close();
}
```

9.10 Creating a Temporary File or Directory

Problem

You want a temporary storage area for files and directories for your application.

Solution

Use the createTempFile and createTempDirectory methods of the File class.

Discussion

The createTempFile and createTempDirectory methods create temporary files and directories but do not automatically delete them, so if you want them only temporarily, you will need to manually delete them. For help with deleting a directory, please refer to Recipe 9.3.

ActionScript/Flex

To create a temporary directory, use this code:

```
private function createTempDirectory():void{
    var tempDirectory:File = File.createTempDirectory();
```

```
    trace(tempDirectory.nativePath);
}
```

To create a temporary file, use this code:

```
private function createTempFile():void{
    var tempFile:File = File.createTempFile();
    trace(tempFile.nativePath);
}
```

JavaScript

To create a temporary directory, use this code:

```
function createTempDirectory(){
    var tempDirectory = air.File.createTempDirectory();
    alert(tempDirectory.nativePath);
}
```

To create a temporary file, use this code:

```
function createTempFile(){
    var tempFile = air.File.createTempFile();
    alert(tempFile.nativePath);
}
```

9.11 Caching Images to Disk in ActionScript

Contributed by Jeff Tapper (http://blogs.digitalprimates.net/jefftapper)

Problem

You need to properly display remote images even when your AIR application is not connected to the Internet.

Solution

Use the File API in AIR to cache the remote images to the local hard drive while the application is connected to the Internet.

Discussion

In this example, the custom class, ImageCacheManager, checks whether the requested image is cached locally first, before trying to load it from the Internet. If the local version exists, it is used. If not, the remote version is loaded and cached. This class is a singleton, and the single instance of this class can be retrieved by calling the getInstance method.

 The application uses the as3corelib library for the MD5 hashing. You must add this library to your project for it to work. You can download the application here: *http://code.google.com/p/as3corelib/*.

The following is the custom class:

```
package managers{
    import flash.filesystem.File;
    import flash.net.URLRequest;
    import flash.net.URLLoader;
    import flash.events.Event;
    import flash.net.URLLoaderDataFormat;
    import flash.utils.Dictionary;
    import flash.filesystem.FileStream;
    import flash.filesystem.FileMode;
    import com.adobe.crypto.MD5;

    public class ImageCacheManager{
        private static const imageDir:File =
            File.applicationStorageDirectory.resolvePath("cachedimages/");
        private static var instance:ImageCacheManager;
        private var pendingDictionaryByLoader:Dictionary = new Dictionary();
        private var pendingDictionaryByURL:Dictionary = new Dictionary();


        public function ImageCacheManager(){
        }

        public static function getInstance():ImageCacheManager{
            if (instance == null){
                instance = new ImageCacheManager();
            }

            return instance;
        }

        public function getImageByURL(url:String):String{

            var cacheFile:File = new File(imageDir.nativePath +File.separator+
cleanURLString(url));
            if(cacheFile.exists){
                return cacheFile.url;
            } else {
                addImageToCache(url);
                return url;
            }

        }

        private  function addImageToCache(url:String):void{
            if(!pendingDictionaryByURL[url]){
                var req:URLRequest = new URLRequest(url);
                var loader:URLLoader = new URLLoader();
                loader.addEventListener(Event.COMPLETE,imageLoadComplete);
                loader.dataFormat = URLLoaderDataFormat.BINARY;
                loader.load(req);
                pendingDictionaryByLoader[loader] = url;
                pendingDictionaryByURL[url] = true;
            }
        }
```

```
private function imageLoadComplete(event:Event):void{
    var loader:URLLoader = event.target as URLLoader;
    var url:String = pendingDictionaryByLoader[loader];
    var cacheFile:File = new File(imageDir.nativePath +File.separator+
cleanURLString(url));
    var stream:FileStream = new FileStream();
    stream.open(cacheFile,FileMode.WRITE);
    stream.writeBytes(loader.data);
    stream.close();
    delete pendingDictionaryByLoader[loader]
    delete pendingDictionaryByURL[url];
}

private function cleanURLString(url:String):String{
    var hash:String = MD5.hash(url);
    return hash;
}

    }
}
```

To implement this in an application, you can call the getImageByURL method to return
either the cached filename (if it is present) or the remote URL:

```
<mx:Image    source="{ImageCacheManager.getInstance().getImageByURL('
http://image.weather.com/images/maps/current/cur_se_440x297.jpg')}"/>
```

9.12 Searching for Files of a Given Extension in a Directory in ActionScript

Contributed by Matt Poole (http://blog.barncar.com/)

Problem

You have a directory, and you need to retrieve all files of a certain type in all directories
below it.

Solution

By binding an asynchronously updated ArrayCollection to a DataGrid's dataProvider,
you can see all the files that are found as soon as the operating system returns them.
Each time you discover a directory, you asynchronously request a directory listing and
respond in its handler by iterating over the result and doing the same with each subsequent directory discovered down through the tree.

Discussion

This example allows users to select a start directory and up to three video file extensions
to search. To accomplish this, the application will need a basic user interface:

```
<mx:WindowedApplication
    xmlns:mx="http://www.adobe.com/2006/mxml"
    layout="absolute"
    height="450" width="500"
    creationComplete="init()">

    <mx:Label top="10" left="10" text="Search for files of type:"/>
    <mx:CheckBox x="10" y="36" label="AVI" id="avi_chk" />
    <mx:CheckBox x="66" y="36" label="MPG" id="mpg_chk" />
    <mx:CheckBox x="123" y="36" label="FLV" id="flv_chk" />

    <mx:Button id="browse_btn" right="10" y="36" label="Browse"
click="openDirectorySelection()" />
    <mx:Label left="180" y="10" text="Search Within:" width="240"/>
    <mx:TextInput id="directory_txt" right="90" left="180" y="36" />

    <mx:Button x="10" y="68" label="search" click="search()" enabled="false"
id="search_btn"  />
    <mx:Text y="70" left="90" right="10" id="searching_txt" />

    <mx:DataGrid top="110" left="10" bottom="40" right="10"
dataProvider="{filesFound}" >
        <mx:columns>
            <mx:DataGridColumn headerText="name" dataField="name"/>
            <mx:DataGridColumn headerText="location" dataField="nativePath"/>
            <mx:DataGridColumn headerText="type" dataField="extension"/>
            <mx:DataGridColumn headerText="size (bytes) " dataField="size"/>
        </mx:columns>
    </mx:DataGrid>

    <mx:ButtonBar id="controls_btnbar" right="10" bottom="10"
itemClick="onButtonBarItemClick( event )">
        <mx:dataProvider>
            <mx:String>stop</mx:String>
            <mx:String>pause</mx:String>
            <mx:String>play</mx:String>
        </mx:dataProvider>
    </mx:ButtonBar>

</mx:WindowedApplication>
```

This interface includes a check box for the extensions to search for, a Browse button, and a text field, the DataGrid in which to show the results, and a button bar with buttons to control the search process (Figure 9-1).

The user begins by selecting the file extensions to search for and then clicks the Browse button to select a start directory. Clicking the Search button now returns all the results to the DataGrid asynchronously when the OS returns.

The search method takes the start directory and asynchronously requests the directory listing from the operating system. The directoryListingHandler is fired when it comes back. The following process takes place with each iteration:

1. Remove the listing event listener from the target that has just triggered the event.

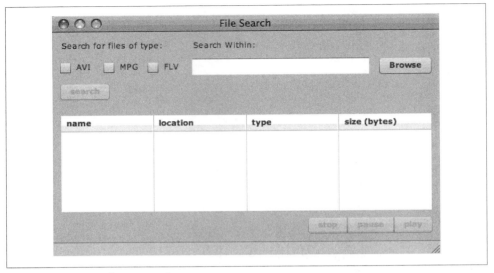

Figure 9-1. File search user interface

2. For each `File` object in the result set, execute the `checkExtensions` method.

3. If the `File` object is a directory, start the loop again by requesting the listing and handling the result in `directoryListingHandler`. If the result is a file, check its extension.

4. If the file is a match, add it to the `filesFound` `ArrayCollection`, which is bound to the `DataGrid`.

The following code shows this process:

```
import mx.collections.ArrayCollection;
import mx.events.ItemClickEvent;
import mx.controls.Alert;
import mx.controls.buttonBarClasses.ButtonBarButton;

private var extensions:Array = new Array;
private var startDirectory:File = new File;
private var pendingFileListings:ArrayCollection = new ArrayCollection;

[Bindable]
public var filesFound:ArrayCollection = new ArrayCollection;

public function init():void {
    avi_chk.addEventListener(Event.CHANGE, onExtensionsChange);
    mpg_chk.addEventListener(Event.CHANGE, onExtensionsChange);
    flv_chk.addEventListener(Event.CHANGE, onExtensionsChange);

    ButtonBarButton( controls_btnbar.getChildAt(0) ).enabled = false;
    ButtonBarButton( controls_btnbar.getChildAt(1) ).enabled = false;
    ButtonBarButton( controls_btnbar.getChildAt(2) ).enabled = false;
}
```

```actionscript
// Start the search
public function search():void {
    search_btn.enabled = false;
    try {
        if ( startDirectory.nativePath != directory_txt.text ) {
            startDirectory = startDirectory.resolvePath( directory_txt.text );
        }

        pendingFileListings.addItem( startDirectory );

        startDirectory.addEventListener( FileListEvent.DIRECTORY_LISTING,
directoryListingHandler );
        startDirectory.addEventListener( IOErrorEvent.IO_ERROR, onIOError );
        startDirectory.getDirectoryListingAsync();

        ButtonBarButton( controls_btnbar.getChildAt(0) ).enabled = true;
        ButtonBarButton( controls_btnbar.getChildAt(1) ).enabled = true;
    }
    catch ( e:Error ) {
        search_btn.enabled = true;
        Alert.show( e.message );
    }
}

// Opens a directory browsing window
private function openDirectorySelection():void {
    startDirectory.browseForDirectory("Choose a search directory:");
    startDirectory.addEventListener(Event.SELECT, onSelectStartDirectory );
}

// Fired when the users selects a directory to search within
private function onSelectStartDirectory(e:Event):void {
    startDirectory.removeEventListener(Event.SELECT, onSelectStartDirectory );
    directory_txt.text = startDirectory.nativePath;
}

// Fired when the result of an asynchronous directory listing is returned
private function directoryListingHandler(e:FileListEvent):void {
    pendingFileListings.removeItemAt( pendingFileListings.getItemIndex( e.target ) );
    e.target.removeEventListener( FileListEvent.DIRECTORY_LISTING,
directoryListingHandler );
    e.files.forEach( checkExtensions );
}

// The array iterator function for the listing of each directory found
private function checkExtensions(file:File, index:int, arr:Array):void {
    if ( file.isDirectory ) {
        pendingFileListings.addItem( file );
        file.addEventListener(FileListEvent.DIRECTORY_LISTING,
directoryListingHandler);
        file.getDirectoryListingAsync();
    } else {
        if ( file.exists ) {
            searching_txt.text = file.nativePath;
```

```
                    for ( var i:int=extensions.length; i--; ) {
                        if ( file.extension!=null && file.extension.toUpperCase() ==
        extensions[i] ) {
                            // add this one to the datagrid
                            filesFound.addItem( file )
                            break;
                        }
                    }
                }
            }
        }

        // Handles user input on the file extension check boxes
        private function onExtensionsChange(e:Event):void {
            if ( !e.target.selected ) {
                for ( var i:int=extensions.length; i--;) {
                    if ( extensions[i] == e.target.label ) {
                        extensions.splice( i, 1 );
                        break;
                    }
                }
            } else {
                if ( e.target.selected ) {
                    extensions.push( e.target.label );
                }
            }
            search_btn.enabled = extensions.length > 0;
        }

        // Fired when a IO Error occurs with the startDirectory File object
        private function onIOError (e:IOErrorEvent):void {
            search_btn.enabled = true;
            Alert.show( "Error: "+e.errorID );
        }

        // Called when the last pending asychornous file operation has completed;
        private function onListingComplete():void {
            searching_txt.text = "";
            search_btn.enabled = true;

            ButtonBarButton( controls_btnbar.getChildAt(0) ).enabled = false;
            ButtonBarButton( controls_btnbar.getChildAt(1) ).enabled = false;
            ButtonBarButton( controls_btnbar.getChildAt(2) ).enabled = false;
        }

        // Fired when one of the button bar items are clicked
        private function onButtonBarItemClick(e:ItemClickEvent):void {
            var i:int;
            switch ( e.label ) {
                case "stop":
                    for ( i=pendingFileListings.length; i--; ) {
                        pendingFileListings[i].removeEventListener(FileListEvent.DIRECTORY_LISTING,
        directoryListingHandler);
                        pendingFileListings[i].cancel();
                    }
```

```
            pendingFileListings.removeAll();
            onListingComplete();
            break;
        case "pause":
            for ( i=pendingFileListings.length; i--; )
pendingFileListings[i].cancel();

            ButtonBarButton( controls_btnbar.getChildAt(1) ).enabled = false;
            ButtonBarButton( controls_btnbar.getChildAt(2) ).enabled = true;
            break;
        case "play":
            for ( i=pendingFileListings.length; i--; )
pendingFileListings[i].getDirectoryListingAsync();

            ButtonBarButton( controls_btnbar.getChildAt(0) ).enabled = true;
            ButtonBarButton( controls_btnbar.getChildAt(1) ).enabled = true;
            ButtonBarButton( controls_btnbar.getChildAt(2) ).enabled = false;
            break;
    }
}
```

9.13 Migrating Serialization Changes in ActionScript

Contributed by Greg Jastrab (http://www.smartlogicsolutions.com)

This is the winning entry for the Adobe AIR Cookbook Cook-Off contest, sponsored by O'Reilly. The judges—a team of RIA experts—chose this entry because it shows how to accomplish a single task in a clear, concise, and clever manner. It was also selected because of its importance to AIR developers. As developers store instances of classes on the local file system or in the embedded SQLite database, this problem will become even more commonplace. Greg's solution provides a fix that will be easy for developers to implement. Great job, Greg!

Problem

Your AIR application stores an instance of a custom IExternalizable class to disk, and a later update to the application adds new variables to the class that would cause a runtime error in your readExternal method call if you try to read in the new variables.

Solution

Include a version marker in your serialization class so that you may parse the data according to the appropriate version that is stored.

Discussion

Consider an AIR application that stores historical weather data about a town. The data object is written as a class implementing IExternalizable so that reading and writing the data is as simple as calling `readObject` or `writeObject`. Assume the first version of the serialization class simply stores the date and a high temperature of that date.

```
public class WeatherData implements IExternalizable {
  public var date:Date;
  public var high:Number;
}
```

Poor Serialization Choice

Typically, the `readExternal` and `writeExternal` functions would be implemented in a straightforward manner:

```
function readExternal(input:IDataInput):void {
  date = input.readObject() as Date;
  high = input.readFloat();
}
function writeExternal(output:IDataOutput):void {
  output.writeObject(date);
  output.writeFloat(high);
}
```

This may seem fine, but what if you want to add the low temperature for the day in a later version? You could add `low = input.readFloat` to the `readExternal` function, but because the data was written to disk without the low data, it would cause a runtime error when a user who upgraded the application runs it again.

Migratable Serialization

To avoid this error, you should add a version marker to the beginning of the serialization so that it can be read first in order to determine how the data should be read:

```
public class WeatherData implements IExternalizable {
  namespace wd1_0 = "WD1.0";
  namespace wd1_1 = "WD1.1";

  protected var version:String;
  public var date:Date;
  public var low:Number;
  public var high:Number;

  public function WeatherData() {
    version = "WD1.1";
    date = new Date();
    low = high = 0;
  }
  public function readExternal(input:IDataInput):void {
    version = input.readUTF();
    var ns:Namespace = new Namespace(version);
    ns::parse(input);
  }
  public function writeExternal(output:IDataOutput):void {
    output.writeUTF(version);
    output.writeObject(date);
```

```
      output.writeFloat(low);
      output.writeFloat(high);
    }
    wd1_0 function parse(input:IDataInput):void {
      date = input.readObject() as Date;
      high = input.readFloat();
    }
    wd1_1 function parse(input:IDataInput):void {
      date = input.readObject() as Date;
      low = input.readFloat();
      high = input.readFloat();
    }
  }
}
```

This allows the class to be properly read if the user had run the initial version of the application that wrote the WD1.0 version of WeatherData and then ran an updated version for the first time with this as the WeatherData code.

Adding Members in Future Versions

Now whenever you need to add a field to the class, you need to do the following:

1. Add the variable to the class.
2. Modify the writeExternal method to include that variable in the serialization.
3. Increment the version string in the constructor.
4. Add a namespace for this new version.
5. Add a parse function scoped to the namespace you just added and implement readExternal to correspond to your updated writeExternal method.

CHAPTER 10

Embedded SQL Database Programming

Adobe AIR doesn't include only Flash Player to execute SWF content and only the WebKit engine to load HTML content and JavaScript. AIR also has an embedded version of the SQLite database engine that makes the runtime truly complete; SQLite gives developers the opportunity to store data locally offline and to do it via the same language they use to store data for web applications: SQL.

Widely used across platforms, SQLite is an open source, award-winning database engine that implements the SQL-92 specifications (*http://www.sqlite.org/omitted.html*).

SQLite in Adobe AIR gives applications the ability to persistently store data and easily manage it. This data can be stored locally in offline situations but then can be synchronized with network data store. With the 1.5 version of Adobe AIR, it isn't possible, however, to natively connect to remote databases.

To be able to access, store, and manipulate data in a SQLite database in Adobe AIR, you first must create the database as a local file. Each database needs its own local file. The AIR SDKs contain the APIs you need to work with SQLite via ActionScript or JavaScript. For ActionScript code, SQL database classes are in the `flash.data` package, whereas for JavaScript, the classes can be directly instanced by using AIR aliases (you just have to import the *AIRAliases.js* file into your HTML document).

10.1 Creating a Database

Problem

You need to create a local database using SQLite.

Solution

Create a local SQLite database in the same way you create a local file.

Discussion

The simple operation of creating the database file doesn't involve using any specific SQLite class. To create a database without creating a connection to it, you use the File class and its resolvePath method to create a file with a *.db* file extension:

```
var dbRef:File;
dbRef = File.applicationStorageDirectory.resolvePath("myDB.db");
```

You next have to connect to the database to start working with it. In the following solutions, you will see how to make a connection to the database.

ActionScript/Flex

To simply create a database file, you don't need any class from the flash.data package; all you have to do is work with the File class.

The following ActionScript class launches the createLocalDB method in the constructor, which points to applicationStorageDirectory, creates the db folder, and creates the *myDBFile.db* database file:

```
package com.oreilly.aircookbook.ch10
{
    import flash.filesystem.File;

    public class CreateDB
    {

        private var _myDB:File;

        public function get myDB():File
        {
          return _myDB;
        }

        public function CreateDB()
        {
          createLocalDB();
        }

        private function createLocalDB():void
        {
         var folder:File = File.applicationStorageDirectory.resolvePath( "db" );
          folder.createDirectory();
          _myDB = folder.resolvePath( "myDBFile.db" );
          _myDB.createDirectory();

        }

    }
}
```

The resolvePath method of the File object creates a new File object with a path relating to this File object's path, based on the path parameter. The folder is actually created with the `createDirectory` method. This method doesn't execute any operation if the directory already exists. The _myDB private variable uses the `getter` method to return the instances of the `File` object you created.

The following example implements the ActionScript class in an application file created with Flex Builder:

```
<?xml version="1.0" encoding="utf-8"?>
<mx:WindowedApplication
xmlns:mx="http://www.adobe.com/2006/mxml"
layout="absolute"
    initialize="init()">


<mx:Script>
<![CDATA[
    import com.oreilly.aircookbook.ch10.CreateDB;

    private var myDB:File;

    private function init():void
    {
      createBtn.addEventListener(MouseEvent.CLICK, onClick);
    }

    private function onClick(evt:MouseEvent):void
    {
      var myDBclass:CreateDB = new CreateDB();
      myDB = myDBclass.myDB;

      mx.controls.Alert.show("Database File Was Created : \n" + myDB.nativePath );
    }
]]>
</mx:Script>

<mx:Button id="createBtn" label="Create DB"  />


</mx:WindowedApplication>
```

At the click of the button, the `onClick` event handler creates an instance of the `CreateDB` class, which creates the database file on the constructor.

The path where the file was created is shown in an `Alert` window with the `show` method.

JavaScript

Even for JavaScript, you create a database file by creating a local file through the `File` class. To be able to use the AIR aliases, you have to import the JavaScript library *AIRAliases.js* into the HTML page.

The following code is created in an external JavaScript file saved as *CreateDB.js*:

```
// Constants
var DB_NAME = 'db/myDBFile.db';
```

```
var myDB;

function createDB()
{
myDB = air.File.applicationStorageDirectory.resolvePath(DB_NAME);

myDB.createDirectory();
air.Introspector.Console.log( "Database File was created: " + myDB.nativePath );

}
```

The following HTML page invokes the **createDB** method:

```
<!DOCTYPE html PUBLIC "-//W3C//DTD XHTML 1.0 Transitional//EN"
"http://www.w3.org/TR/xhtml1/DTD/xhtml1-transitional.dtd">
<html xmlns="http://www.w3.org/1999/xhtml">
<head>

<script type="text/javascript" src="frameworks/AIRAliases.js"></script>
<script type="text/javascript" src="frameworks/AIRIntrospector.js"></script>

<script type="text/javascript" src="CreateDB.js"></script>

<meta http-equiv="Content-Type" content="text/html; charset=utf-8" />

<title>AIR Cookbook: 10.1 Creating a Database (JavaScript)</title>
</head>

<body onload="createDB()">
<h1>AIR Cookbook: 10.1 Creating a Database (JavaScript)</h1>

<p> Open the AIR Introspector window to see the following message:</p>
<p><img src="images/Ch10_Sol1_1.jpg" width="641" height="480" /></p>
</body>
</html>
```

The **createDB** method is launched on the **onload** event of the **body** tag, which creates the *myDFFile.db* database file in applicationStorageFolder and sends a message to the AIR Introspector Console tab, as shown in Figure 10-1.

10.2 Connecting to a Database in Synchronous Mode

Problem

You need to open a database and create a synchronous connection to it.

Solution

Create a connection to an existing database file using the **SQLConnection** class.

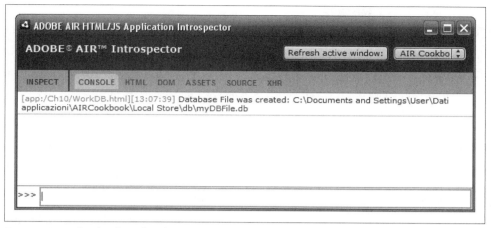

Figure 10-1. The database has been created, and the message is shown in the AIR Introspector Console tab.

Discussion

You can create a database by creating a simple local file. To carry out any operations on the database, however, you need to create and open a connection to the file.

With the `SQLConnection` class, you can do more than establish a connection to the database; you can use it for SQL statements, and it provides a mechanism to execute multiple statements in a transaction (via the `begin`, `commit`, and `rollback` methods).

A `SQLConnection` instance enables you to carry out operations in synchronous and asynchronous modes (see Recipe 10.3). The synchronous operation prevents users from interacting with the application until the database has been opened successfully or in the event of an error. To connect to the database in synchronous mode, use the `open` method of the `SQLConnection` class:

```
open(reference:Object = null, openMode:String = "create", autoCompact:Boolean =
false, pageSize:int = 1024, encryptionKey:ByteArray = null):void
```

The method can accept five parameters:

- `reference:Object` (the default is `null`): Contains the location of the database file you want to open. This is a `File` instance.
- `openMode:String` (the default is `create`): Specifies how the database is opened. Valid values are constants for the `SQLMode` class (`CREATE`, `READ`, `UPDATE`).
- `autoCompact:Boolean` (the default is `false`): Reclaims unused space if set to `true`. You can use this value only when creating a database or opening an empty database (with no tables). AIR ignores this parameter if `openMode` is set to `SQLMode.READ`.

Note that the `autoCompact` operation can decrease the performance of database access and can also cause the database data to become fragmented over time.

- `pageSize:int` (the default is `1024`): Indicates the page size for the database specified in bytes. You can use this value only when creating a database or opening an empty database (with no tables).
- `encryptionKey:ByteArray` (the default is `null`): The encryption key used to encrypt and decrypt the SQLite database file. For more information, see Recipe 10.5.

If you pass a `File` instance that refers to a nonexistent file location for the `reference` parameter (the first parameter), the `open` method creates a database file at that file location and opens a connection to the newly created database.

As for the other synchronous operations that AIR offers (such as for opening and reading a file), you don't need to register event listeners to determine when an operation completes or fails. To be able to manage the errors that occur when opening or creating a database using the `open` method, use the error handling statements in a `try...catch` block.

A crucial aspect of synchronous operations is that the entire application is frozen when the synchronous operations are being executed. In fact, because synchronous operations execute in the main execution thread, all application functionality is paused while the database operation or operations are performed. If the database file you are trying to open is large, the `open` method can cause a noticeable pause in the application.

To invoke the `open` method to open the database synchronously, you have to create an instance of the `SQLConnection` object. Only after having created an instance of this class will it be possible to execute the operations on the database, such as opening the SQLite file:

```
_myDB = File.applicationStorageDirectory.resolvePath( "db/myDBFile.db" );
_dbConn = new SQLConnection();
_dbConn.open( _myDB );
```

Being a synchronous execution, the error handling in the opening of the database is provided by using the error-throwing statements in a `try...catch` block (an example is given in the next section).

ActionScript/Flex

The following ActionScript class continues the class created in Recipe 10.1, and as well as creating a database file, it opens the file in synchronous mode with the `open` method of the `SQLConnection` class. An `_isOpen` private variable typed as a `Boolean` will tell the application that uses this class whether the database has been successfully opened. With the `isOpen` getter method, it will be possible to access the property.

Here is the complete code for the ActionScript *OpenDB.as* class:

```
package com.oreilly.aircookbook.ch10
{
    import flash.data.SQLConnection;
    import flash.errors.SQLError;
    import flash.events.SQLErrorEvent;
    import flash.events.SQLEvent;
    import flash.filesystem.File;

    import mx.controls.Alert;

    public class OpenDB
    {
        private var _myDB:File;
        private var _isOpen:Boolean = false;

        private var _dbConn:SQLConnection;

        public function get myDB():File
        {
          return _myDB;
        }

        public function get isOpen():Boolean
        {
          return _isOpen;
        }


        public function OpenDB()
        {
          createLocalDB();
        }

        private function createLocalDB():void
        {
            var folder:File= File.applicationStorageDirectory.resolvePath( "db" );
            folder.createDirectory();
            _myDB = folder.resolvePath( "myDBFile.db" );
        }

        public function openLocalDB(dbFile:File):void
        {
            _dbConn = new SQLConnection();

            try
            {
                _dbConn.open(dbFile);
                _isOpen = true;
                mx.controls.Alert.show("The Database File " +_myDB.nativePath + "
                                        was opened");
            }
            catch (error:SQLError)
            {
                mx.controls.Alert.show("Error message:", event.error.message);
                mx.controls.Alert.show("Details:", event.error.details);
```

```
                    }
                }
            }
        }
```

This class can be easily instanced in an AIR application that uses Flex SDK's MXML code such as this:

```
<?xml version="1.0" encoding="utf-8"?>
<mx:WindowedApplication
xmlns:mx="http://www.adobe.com/2006/mxml"
layout="vertical"
initialize="init()">

<mx:Script>
<![CDATA[

    import com.oreilly.aircookbook.ch10.OpenDB;

    private var myDB:File;
    private var myDBclass:OpenDB;

    private function init():void
    {
        createBtn.addEventListener(MouseEvent.CLICK, onClick);
        openBtn.addEventListener(MouseEvent.CLICK, onClickOpen);
    }

    private function onClick(evt:MouseEvent):void
    {
        myDBclass = new OpenDB();
        myDB = myDBclass.myDB;
        openBtn.enabled = true;

        mx.controls.Alert.show("Database File Was Created : \n" + myDB.nativePath );
    }

    private function onClickOpen(evt:MouseEvent):void
    {
      myDBclass.openLocalDB(myDB)

        if (myDBclass.isOpen)
        {
            mx.controls.Alert.show("Database File Was Opened" );
        }
    }
]]>
</mx:Script>

<mx:Button id="createBtn" label="Create DB"  />

<mx:Button label="Open DataBase" id="openBtn" enabled="false"  />

</mx:WindowedApplication>
```

The two buttons launch the methods of the `myDBclass` class to create and then connect to the database. By checking the value of the `isOpen` property, you check whether connecting to and opening the database file have been successful.

JavaScript/HTML

The following is the code of the external *OpenDB.js* JavaScript file that will be imported in the HTML page:

```
// Constants
var DB_NAME = 'db/myDBFile.db';

var myDB;
var dbConn;


function createDB()
{
myDB = air.File.desktopDirectory.resolvePath(DB_NAME);

var folder = air.File.applicationStorageDirectory.resolvePath("db");
folder.createDirectory();

myDB = folder.resolvePath(DB_NAME);

air.Introspector.Console.log( "Database File was created: " + myDB.nativePath );
}

function openDB()
{
    dbConn = new air.SQLConnection();

    try
    {
        dbConn.open(myDB);
        air.Introspector.Console.log("Database File Was Opened successfully with a
                                synchronous operation");
    }
    catch (error)
    {
        air.Introspector.Console.log("Error message:", error.message);
        air.Introspector.Console.log("Details:", error.details);
    }

}
```

The `openDB` method creates a `SQLConnection` instance, and then it uses a `try...catch` block to open the SQL database file contained in the `myDB File` instance with the `open` method. Possible error messages are passed to the AIR Introspector Console.

The following is the HTML page that uses the JavaScript file to make the call:

```
<!DOCTYPE html PUBLIC "-//W3C//DTD XHTML 1.0 Transitional//EN"
"http://www.w3.org/TR/xhtml1/DTD/xhtml1-transitional.dtd">
<html xmlns="http://www.w3.org/1999/xhtml">
```

```
<head>

<script type="text/javascript" src="frameworks/AIRAliases.js"></script>
<script type="text/javascript" src="frameworks/AIRIntrospector.js"></script>

<script type="text/javascript" src="OpenDB.js"></script>

<meta http-equiv="Content-Type" content="text/html; charset=utf-8" />

<title>AIR Cookbook: 10.2 Creating a Database (JavaScript)</title>
</head>

<body onload="createDB()">
<h1>AIR Cookbook: 10.2 Creating a Database (JavaScript)</h1>


<p>
<label>Open Database File

<input type="button" name="openDB" id="openDB" value="Open" accesskey="o"
 tabindex="1" onclick="openDB();document.getElementById('resultDiv').innerText =
'Database was opened successfully';" />

</label>
</p>
<p><div id="resultDiv"></div></p>
</body>
</html>
```

The database is created on the onload event of the body, which invokes the createDB method. When you click the button, the SQLConnection is created, and the database file is opened. Furthermore, the message "Database was opened successfully" is written in the resultDiv div using the innerText property:

```
<input type="button" name="openDB" id="openDB" value="Open" accesskey="o"
tabindex="1" onclick="openDB();document.getElementById('resultDiv').innerText =
'Database was opened successfully';" />
```

10.3 Connecting to a Database in Asynchronous Mode

Problem

You need to open a database and connect to it in asynchronous mode.

Solution

Use the openAsync method, which opens a database file at the specified location in the file system with an asynchronous execution.

Discussion

The openAsync method performs the opening operation asynchronously. When the operation completes successfully, openAsync dispatches an open event; when it fails, the method dispatches an error event. When the error event is fired, the connection to the database is closed automatically. These two events are part of the SQLEvent and SQLErrorEvent classes. When opening the database with the openAsync method, you have to manage the listeners for these two events:

```
private var _dbConn:SQLConnection = new SQLConnection();
_dbConn.openAsync(_myDB);
_dbConn.addEventListener(SQLEvent.OPEN, openHandler);
_dbConn.addEventListener(SQLErrorEvent.ERROR, errorHandler);
```

If you pass to the method a reference of a File instance of a file that doesn't exist, you'll automatically create the database file in the specified location.

A database that is connected using the openAsync method is automatically assigned the database name main; you can use this name to explicitly qualify table names in SQL statements using the format [database-name].[table-name].

ActionScript/Flex

The following class continues and modifies the class you created in Recipe 10.3 and adds the isAsync parameter typed as a Boolean to the openLocalDB method. This parameter tells the method whether the database has to be opened by using the synchronous open method or the openAsync asynchronous method:

```
package com.oreilly.aircookbook.ch10
{
    import flash.data.SQLConnection;
    import flash.errors.SQLError;
    import flash.events.SQLErrorEvent;
    import flash.events.SQLEvent;
    import flash.filesystem.File;

    import mx.controls.Alert;

    public class OpenDBAsync
    {
        private var _myDB:File;
        private var _isOpen:Boolean = false;

        private var _dbConn:SQLConnection;

        public function get myDB():File
        {
            return _myDB;
        }

        public function get isOpen():Boolean
        {
            return _isOpen
```

```
    }

    public function OpenDBAsync()
    {
        createLocalDB();
    }

    private function createLocalDB():void
    {
        var folder:File= File.applicationStorageDirectory.resolvePath( "db" );

        folder.createDirectory();

        _myDB = folder.resolvePath( "myDBFile.db" );

    }

    public function openLocalDB(dbFile:File,isAsync:Boolean=true):void
    {
        _dbConn = new SQLConnection();

        if(isAsync)
        {
            _dbConn.openAsync(dbFile);

            _dbConn.addEventListener(SQLEvent.OPEN, openHandler);
            _dbConn.addEventListener(SQLErrorEvent.ERROR, errorHandler);

        }else{

            try
            {
                _dbConn.open(dbFile);

            }
            catch (error:SQLError)
            {
                trace("Error message:", error.message);
                trace("Details:", error.details);
            }


        }
    }

    private function openHandler(event:SQLEvent):void
    {
        trace("The Database File " + _myDB.nativePath + " was opened");
        _isOpen = true;
    }

    private function errorHandler(event:SQLErrorEvent):void
    {
        mx.controls.Alert.show("Error message:", event.error.message);
```

```
        mx.controls.Alert.show("Details:", event.error.details);
        _isOpen = false;
    }

  }
}
```

The class checks whether the condition in the open method has occurred. If the
isAsync parameter is true, a connection is made, and the database file is opened in
asynchronous mode.

Two event handlers are created for the OPEN and ERROR events, which change the value
of the _isOpen property. The SQLConnection class has a connected public property that
returns a Boolean, which indicates whether the SQLConnection instance has an open
connection to a database file.

The following is the entire example in MXML that instances the *OpenDBAsync.as*
ActionScript class:

```
<?xml version="1.0" encoding="utf-8"?>
<mx:WindowedApplication
xmlns:mx="http://www.adobe.com/2006/mxml"
layout="vertical"
initialize="init()">


<mx:Script>
<![CDATA[
    import com.oreilly.aircookbook.ch10.OpenDBAsync;

    private var myDB:File;
    private var myDBclass:OpenDBAsync;

    private function init():void
    {
        createBtn.addEventListener(MouseEvent.CLICK, onClick);
        openBtn.addEventListener(MouseEvent.CLICK, onClickOpen);
    }

    private function onClick(evt:MouseEvent):void
    {
        myDBclass = new OpenDBAsync();
        myDB = myDBclass.myDB;

        openBtn.enabled = true;

        mx.controls.Alert.show("Database File Was Created : \n" + myDB.nativePath );
    }

    private function onClickOpen(evt:MouseEvent):void
    {
        myDBclass.openLocalDB(myDB)

        if (myDBclass.isOpen)
        {
```

```
                        mx.controls.Alert.show("Database File Was Opened" );
            }
        }
]]>
</mx:Script>

<mx:Button id="createBtn" label="Create DB"  />

<mx:Button label="Open DataBase" id="openBtn" enabled="false"  />


</mx:WindowedApplication>
```

JavaScript/HTML

To obtain the same result by using JavaScript, you modify the JavaScript file you created in Recipe 10.2 by adding the isAsync parameter to the openDB(isAsync) method, which indicates whether to use a synchronous or asynchronous connection:

```
// Constants
var DB_NAME = 'db/myDBFile.db';

var myDB;
var dbConn;

var isAsync;

function createDB()
{
    var folder = air.File.applicationStorageDirectory.resolvePath("db");
    folder.createDirectory();
    myDB = folder.resolvePath(DB_NAME);
    myDB = air.File.desktopDirectory.resolvePath(DB_NAME);

    air.Introspector.Console.log( "Database File was created: " + myDB.nativePath );

}

function openDB(isAsync)
{
    dbConn = new air.SQLConnection();

    if (isAsync)
    {

        dbConn.openAsync(myDB);
        dbConn.addEventListener(air.SQLEvent.OPEN, onOpenHandler);
        dbConn.addEventListener(air.SQLErrorEvent.ERROR, onErrorHandler);

    }
    else
    {
        try
        {
            dbConn.open(myDB);
```

```
            air.Introspector.Console.log("Database File Was Opened successfully with
                                   a synchronous operation");

        }
        catch (error)
        {
            air.Introspector.Console.log("Error message:", error.message);
            air.Introspector.Console.log("Details:", error.details);
        }
    }
}

function onOpenHandler(event)
{
    air.Introspector.Console.log("Database File Was Opened successfully");
}

function onErrorHandler(event)
{
    air.Introspector.Console.log("Error message:", event.error.message);
    air.Introspector.Console.log("Details:", event.error.details);
}
```

The following is the HTML page that uses this JavaScript file with the calls to the methods:

```
<!DOCTYPE html PUBLIC "-//W3C//DTD XHTML 1.0 Transitional//EN"
"http://www.w3.org/TR/xhtml1/DTD/xhtml1-transitional.dtd">
<html xmlns="http://www.w3.org/1999/xhtml">
<head>

<script type="text/javascript" src="frameworks/AIRAliases.js"></script>
<script type="text/javascript" src="frameworks/AIRIntrospector.js"></script>

<script type="text/javascript" src="OpenDB.js"></script>

<meta http-equiv="Content-Type" content="text/html; charset=utf-8" />

<title>AIR Cookbook: 10.2 Creating a Database (JavaScript)</title>
</head>

<body onload="createDB()">
<h1>AIR Cookbook: 10.3 Connecting to a Database Asynchronously (JavaScript)</h1>


<p>
  <label>Open Database File
  <input type="button" name="openDB" id="openDB" value="Open" accesskey="o"
tabindex="1" onclick="openDB(true);document.getElementById('resultDiv').innerText =
'Database was opened successfully';" />
  </label>
</p>
<div id="resultDiv"></div>
</body>
</html>
```

10.4 Creating an In-Memory Database

Problem

You need to create an in-memory database without creating a local file.

Solution

Set the `reference` parameter of the `open` and `openAsync` methods to `null` to create an in-memory database.

Discussion

For a desktop application, it is often useful to be able to manage the data structurally by using a powerful language such as SQL but without having to save the data locally.

You can create an in-memory database by passing a `null` value to the `reference` parameter of either the synchronous `open` method or the `openAsync` asynchronous method. The temporary database will exist while your application is open but is not saved to disk; instead, it's deleted when your application closes.

ActionScript

The `reference` parameter is an `Object` that specifies the location of the database file that is being opened. Set it to `null` to create an in-memory database:

```
var _dbConn:SQLConnection = new SQLConnection();
_dbConn.openAsync(null);
```

JavaScript

To create an in-memory database with JavaScript, use the following syntax:

```
var dbConn = new air.SQLConnection();
dbConn.openAsync(null);
```

10.5 Creating an Encrypted Database

Problem

You need to ensure that the sensitive information contained in the database for your AIR application cannot be accessed outside the application.

Solution

Encrypt the database with the Advanced Encryption Standard (AES) encryption inside AIR 1.5.

Discussion

AIR 1.5 introduced encrypted database support within the runtime. This enabled entire database files to be encrypted without using any tools outside AIR. It uses *Advanced Encryption Standard* (AES) encryption, which provides a tested algorithm to secure your data.

Normal database files within an AIR application can be accessed by any program that can read the SQLite database format. Because of this, sensitive data within an AIR database needs to be encrypted. When encryption is used, the entire database is secured with a 16-byte (128-bit) key. Without this key, the database data cannot be read.

Within AIR, encrypted databases and unencrypted databases are separate. There is no mechanism for encrypting only certain tables. In these cases, you can create multiple database files and set encryption as needed. Also, encryption can be set when the database is created only, and it cannot be removed from a database file.

 In this recipe's example, you will be using AS3Crypto, an open source cryptology library for ActionScript 3 that is released under the BSD license. You can find it at *http://code.google.com/p/as3crypto/*.

In this example, a single random key will be generated to secure all the databases within the application. To accomplish this, you can use the `Random` class within AS3Crypto. The key will then be stored in the encrypted local store with the `stronglyBound` parameter set to `true` (for more information on the `stronglyBound` parameter, see Recipe 11.4). This key will be retrieved when the application launches. With this method, the key is never exposed outside the application.

 Never store the key that will be used to encrypt the databases on the local file system. This could enable someone to view the contents of the encrypted database.

ActionScript/Flex

Because the AS3Crypto project will be used to generate the random encryption key in this exercise, you need to download the *as3crypto.swc* file from the previous URL. In addition, you must ensure that it is added to your project's build path.

When this application launches, it checks whether the encryption key is present inside the encrypted local store. If it is not present (and it will not be on the first launch), the `createRandomKey` method is called, a new key is generated as a binary 16-byte `ByteArray`, and this key is saved into the encrypted local store. The key generation process uses the `Random` class from the AS3Crypto library, as shown here:

```
public function createRandomKey():ByteArray {
    var encryptionKey:ByteArray = new ByteArray();
```

```
        var random:Random = new Random();
        random.nextBytes(encryptionKey, 16);
        return encryptionKey;
    }
```

When the user clicks the Connect button, the instances of the File class and the
SQLConnection class are created. Next, the needed event listeners are added to detect
whether the connection is successful. Finally, the openAsync method is called:

```
connection.openAsync(dbFile,SQLMode.CREATE,null,false,1024,storedKey);
```

The database encryption key is passed in as the last parameter in the open and
openAsync methods.

If the database does not already exist, a new encrypted database is created, and the
SQLEvent.OPEN event is dispatched when the connection is complete. If the database
exists and the encryption key is correct, the SQLEvent.OPEN event is dispatched when
the connection is complete. If the key is incorrect or if the referenced database file is
not encrypted, a SQLErrorEvent.ERROR event is dispatched.

```
<?xml version="1.0" encoding="utf-8"?>
<mx:WindowedApplication
    xmlns:mx="http://www.adobe.com/2006/mxml"
    layout="vertical" horizontalAlign="left"
    creationComplete="handleCreationComplete()">

    <mx:Script>
        <![CDATA[
            import flash.utils.ByteArray;
            import mx.collections.ArrayCollection;
            import com.hurlant.crypto.prng.Random;

            public static const ENCRYPTED_STORE_KEY_NAME:String = "databaseKey";
            public static const ENCRYPTED_DB_FILE:String = "encrypted.db";

            [Bindable]
            private var results:ArrayCollection = new ArrayCollection();

            private var connection:SQLConnection;
            private var dbFile:File;
            private var storedKey:ByteArray;

            private function handleCreationComplete():void {
                results.addItem("[ACTION]: Attempting to Retrieve Key from
ELS");
                storedKey =
EncryptedLocalStore.getItem(ENCRYPTED_STORE_KEY_NAME);
                if(!storedKey) {
                    results.addItem("[ACTION]: Key Not Retrieved - Creating New
Key");
                    storedKey = createRandomKey();
                    EncryptedLocalStore.setItem(ENCRYPTED_STORE_KEY_NAME,
storedKey, true);
                } else {
                    results.addItem("[ACTION]: Key Retrieved Successfully");
```

```
                }
            }

            private function createRandomKey():ByteArray {
                var encryptionKey:ByteArray = new ByteArray();
                var random:Random = new Random();
                random.nextBytes(encryptionKey, 16);
                results.addItem("[ACTION]: Creating New Key " +
encryptionKey.toString());
                return encryptionKey;
            }

            private function handleConnectClick(event:MouseEvent):void {
                results.addItem("[ACTION]: Attempting Database Connection");
                dbFile =
File.applicationStorageDirectory.resolvePath(ENCRYPTED_DB_FILE);
                connection = new SQLConnection();
                connection.addEventListener(SQLEvent.OPEN, handleDatabaseOpen);
                connection.addEventListener(SQLErrorEvent.ERROR,
handleDatabaseError);
                connection.openAsync(dbFile,SQLMode.CREATE,null,false,1024,storedKey);
            }

            private function handleDatabaseOpen(event:SQLEvent):void {
                results.addItem("[ACTION]: Database Connection Successful");
            }

            private function handleDatabaseError(event:SQLErrorEvent):void {
                results.addItem("[ACTION]: Could Not Connect to Database " +
event.error.detailArguments.toString() );
            }

        ]]>
    </mx:Script>

    <mx:Label text="Encrypted Database Connection" fontWeight="bold" fontSize="18"/>
    <mx:Button label="Connect" click="handleConnectClick(event)" />
    <mx:List width="100%" height="100%" dataProvider="{results}" />

</mx:WindowedApplication>
```

JavaScript

To properly access the AS3Crypto library with a JavaScript AIR application, you must download *as3crypto.swc* (*http://code.google.com/p/as3crypto/*) and rename the extension of the file to **zip**. Next, extract the *library.swf* file from the package. Rename the file *as3crypto.swf*, and place it into your project directory. Finally, place the following tag in your application to include the library:

```
<script type="application/x-shockwave-flash" src="as3crypto.swf"></script>
```

When the application launches, checks whether a value exists in the encrypted local store with the key **databaseKey**. If this value does not exist (and it will not on the first launch), a new key is created with the `createRandomKey` method. This function uses the `Random` class from the AS3Crypto library to generate a random 16-byte key:

```
function createRandomKey() {
    var encryptionKey = new air.ByteArray();
    var randomBytes = new window.runtime.com.hurlant.crypto.prng.Random();
    randomBytes.nextBytes(encryptionKey, 16);
    return encryptionKey;
}
```

This new key is then stored into the encrypted local store.

When the user clicks the Connect button, the instances of the `File` class and the `SQLConnection` class are created. Next, the needed event listeners are added to detect whether the connection is successful. Finally, the `openAsync` method is called:

```
connection.openAsync(dbFile,air.SQLMode.CREATE,null,false,1024,storedKey);
```

The final parameter is the actual 16-byte binary key used for the encryption. If the database file does not exist at this point, an encrypted database is created with the specified key. If the encrypted database already exists, the connection will be successful only if the key is correct. When the connection is complete, a `SQLEvent.OPEN` is dispatched. If the key is incorrect, it dispatches a `SQLErrorEvent.ERROR`. Additionally, if the database file exists but it is not encrypted, a `SQLErrorEvent.ERROR` is dispatched.

```
<html>
    <head>
        <title>Encrypted Database Sample</title>
        <script type="text/javascript" src="AIRAliases.js"></script>
          <script type="text/javascript" src="AIRIntrospector.js"></script>
           <script type="application/x-shockwave-flash" src="as3crypto.swf"></script>
        <script type="text/javascript">
                var ENCRYPTED_STORE_KEY_NAME = "databaseKey";
                var ENCRYPTED_DB_FILE = "encrypted.db";
                var storedKey;
                var dbFile;
                var conn;

                function retrieveStoredKey() {
                    logAction("Attempting to Retrieve Key from ELS");
                    storedKey = air.EncryptedLocalStore.getItem(ENCRYPTED_STORE_KEY_NAME);
                    if( !storedKey ) {
                        logAction("Key Not Retrieved - Creating New Key");
                        storedKey = createRandomKey();
                        air.EncryptedLocalStore.setItem(ENCRYPTED_STORE_KEY_NAME,
storedKey, true);
                    } else {
                        logAction("Key Was Retrieved from ELS Correctly");
                    }
                }

                function createRandomKey() {
                    var encryptionKey = new air.ByteArray();
                    var randomBytes = new
window.runtime.com.hurlant.crypto.prng.Random();
```

```
                    randomBytes.nextBytes(encryptionKey, 16);
                    logAction("Creating New Key " + encryptionKey.toString() );
                    return encryptionKey;
            }

            function connectToDatabase(event) {
                    logAction("Attempting to Connect to Database");
                    dbFile =
air.File.applicationStorageDirectory.resolvePath(ENCRYPTED_DB_FILE);
                    conn = new air.SQLConnection();
                    conn.addEventListener(air.SQLEvent.OPEN, handleDatabaseOpen);
                    conn.addEventListener(air.SQLErrorEvent.ERROR,
handleDatabaseError);
                    conn.openAsync(dbFile,air.SQLMode.CREATE,null,false,1024,storedKey);
            }

            function handleDatabaseOpen(event) {
                    logAction("Connection to Encrypted Database Successful");
            }

            function handleDatabaseError(event) {
                    logAction("Could Not Connect to Database "+
event.error.detailArguments.toString() );
            }

            function logAction(action) {
                    var resultsDiv = document.getElementById('results');
                    resultsDiv.innerHTML += "[ACTION]: " + action + "<br />";
            }

            window.onload = retrieveStoredKey;
        </script>
        <style type="text/css">
            body {font-family: Arial; font-size:12px;padding: 15px;}
            #results {padding: 5px;border: 1px solid #666;}
        </style>
    </head>
    <body>
        <h3>Encrypted Database Connection Test</h3>
        <input type="button" value="Connect" onclick="connectToDatabase(event)" />
        <div>Results:</div>
        <div>
            <div id="results"></div>
        </div>
    </body>
</html>
```

10.6 Encrypting a Database with a Password

Problem

You need to encrypt a database based on a user's password. In addition, you need to allow the user to change his password and update the encryption accordingly.

Solution

Use the user's password as the basis for the encryption key, and use the `reencrypt` method of the `SQLConnection` class to change the encryption key for a database.

Discussion

Although creating a random key may work for many situations, in some cases it is ideal to base the key off of user input. This is ideal in situations where you are downloading password-protected data from an online service. This allows the same password that secures the data online to secure the data in the AIR application.

Because the `open` and `openAsync` methods of the `SQLConnection` class are expecting a 16-byte binary key, you will be creating an MD5 hash of the user's password by utilizing the AS3Crypto library. This creates the needed 16-byte `ByteArray` that can then be passed into the `open` or `openAsync` methods.

When the user changes his password, the `reencrypt` method of the `SQLConnection` class will allow the application to change the encryption key for a specific database. This requires that the database connection was already opened with the old encryption key. Once the method has been called, the process runs inside a transaction-like process. If the process is interrupted before completion, the database retains the old encryption key. If the process is completed successfully, a `SQLEvent.REENCRYPT` event is dispatched, and if it fails, a `SQLError.ERROR` event is dispatched.

 Remember that a database that is not encrypted cannot be encrypted. To make an unencrypted database encrypted, the data must be imported into a new encrypted database.

In this example, the user must specify a password to connect to the database. If the database does not exist, a new database is created using the password hash as the encryption key. While the database is connected, the user can enter a new password and click the Change Password button. This triggers the `reencrypt` method, which changes the encryption key for the database.

You will need to include the AS3Crypto library for this project. See Recipe 10.5 for instructions on how to include it in your environment.

ActionScript/Flex

To create the encryption key, the `MD5` class from the AS3Crypto library is used along with the password entered by the user. The password, which is passed into the function as a string, is converted into a `ByteArray` by using the `writeUTFBytes` method. Next, the `MD5` class is instantiated, and the `hash` method is called on the `ByteArray`. This value is returned and used as the encryption key for the database.

```
private function createEncryptionKey(password:String):ByteArray {
    var ba:ByteArray = new ByteArray();
    ba.writeUTFBytes(password);
    var md5:MD5 = new MD5();
    var output:ByteArray = md5.hash(ba);
    return output;
}
```

To allow the changing of the password, the `reencrypt` method of the `SQLConnection` class is used. This method must be called while the `SQLConnection` is open.

```
connection.addEventListener(SQLEvent.REENCRYPT, handleDatabaseReencrypt);
connection.reencrypt( createEncryptionKey(newPassword.text) );
```

The completed example, shown here, integrates all this functionality into a single AIR application:

```
<?xml version="1.0" encoding="utf-8"?>
<mx:WindowedApplication
    xmlns:mx="http://www.adobe.com/2006/mxml"
    layout="vertical" horizontalAlign="left">

    <mx:Script>
        <![CDATA[
            import flash.utils.ByteArray;
            import mx.collections.ArrayCollection;
            import com.hurlant.crypto.hash.MD5;

            public static const ENCRYPTED_DB_FILE:String = "encrypted.db";

            [Bindable]
            private var results:ArrayCollection = new ArrayCollection();

            private var connection:SQLConnection;
            private var dbFile:File;

            private function createEncryptionKey(password:String):ByteArray {
                var ba:ByteArray = new ByteArray();
                ba.writeUTFBytes(password);
                var md5:MD5 = new MD5();
                var output:ByteArray = md5.hash(ba);
                results.addItem("[ACTION]: Hash Key Created " +
output.toString());
                return output;
            }

            private function handleConnectClick(event:MouseEvent):void {
                results.addItem("[ACTION]: Attempting Database Connection");
                dbFile =
File.applicationStorageDirectory.resolvePath(ENCRYPTED_DB_FILE);
                connection = new SQLConnection();
                connection.addEventListener(SQLEvent.OPEN, handleDatabaseOpen);
                connection.addEventListener(SQLErrorEvent.ERROR,
handleDatabaseError);
                connection.openAsync(dbFile,SQLMode.CREATE,null,false,1024,
createEncryptionKey(password.text));
```

```
                    }

                    private function handleDisconnectClick(event:MouseEvent):void {
                            connection.close();
                            disconnectButton.enabled = false;
                            password.enabled = true;
                            connectButton.enabled = true;
                            newPassword.enabled = false;
                            reencryptButton.enabled = false;
                    }

                    private function handleReencryptClick(event:MouseEvent):void {
                            connection.addEventListener(SQLEvent.REENCRYPT,
handleDatabaseReencrypt);
                            connection.reencrypt(createEncryptionKey(newPassword.text));
                    }

                    private function handleDatabaseOpen(event:SQLEvent):void {
                            results.addItem("[ACTION]: Database Connection Successful");
                            disconnectButton.enabled = true;
                            newPassword.enabled = true;
                            reencryptButton.enabled = true;
                            password.enabled = false;
                            connectButton.enabled = false;
                    }

                    private function handleDatabaseReencrypt(event:SQLEvent):void {
                            connection.removeEventListener(SQLEvent.REENCRYPT,
handleDatabaseReencrypt);
                            results.addItem("[ACTION]: Database Reencrypted");
                    }

                    private function handleDatabaseError(event:SQLErrorEvent):void {
                            results.addItem("[ERROR]: Database Error " +
event.error.detailArguments.toString() );
                    }

            ]]>
    </mx:Script>

    <mx:Label text="Encryption By Password" fontWeight="bold" fontSize="18" />

    <mx:Label text="Connect To Database" fontWeight="bold"/>
    <mx:HBox>
            <mx:Label text="Password" />
            <mx:TextInput id="password" />
            <mx:Button id="connectButton" label="Connect"
click="handleConnectClick(event)" />
            <mx:Button id="disconnectButton" label="Disconnect"
click="handleDisconnectClick(event)" enabled="false" />
    </mx:HBox>

    <mx:Label text="Change Password / ReEncrypt" fontWeight="bold"/>
    <mx:HBox>
            <mx:Label text="New Password" />
```

```
            <mx:TextInput id="newPassword" enabled="false" />
            <mx:Button id="reencryptButton" label="Change Password"
click="handleReencryptClick(event)" enabled="false" />
        </mx:HBox>

        <mx:List width="100%" height="100%" dataProvider="{results}" />

    </mx:WindowedApplication>
```

JavaScript

To create the encryption key, the MD5 class from the AS3Crypto library is used along with the password entered by the user. The password, which is passed into the function as a string, is converted into a ByteArray by using the writeUTFBytes method. Next, the MD5 class is instantiated, and the hash method is called on the ByteArray. This value is returned and used as the encryption key for the database.

```
function createEncryptionKey(password) {
    var ba = new air.ByteArray();
    ba.writeUTFBytes(password);
    var md5 = new window.runtime.com.hurlant.crypto.hash.MD5();
    var output = md5.hash(ba);
    logAction("Hash Key Created " + output.toString());
    return output;
}
```

To allow the user to change his password, the use of the reencrypt method of the SQLConnection class is used. This method requires that you pass in the new encryption key and optionally allows you to pass in a responder method. In this case, the createEncryptionKey method is used to generate the new key from the new password field. Also, to know when the process is complete, an event listener is added for the SQLEvent.REENCRYPT event.

The completed application allows for the connection and disconnection of an encrypted database that uses the user-defined password hash for the encryption key. It also allows for the changing of the encryption key:

```
<html>
    <head>
        <title>Encrypted Database Sample</title>
        <script type="text/javascript" src="AIRAliases.js"></script>
          <script type="text/javascript" src="AIRIntrospector.js"></script>
          <script type="application/x-shockwave-flash" src="as3crypto.swf"></script>
        <script type="text/javascript">
            var ENCRYPTED_DB_FILE = "encrypted.db";
            var dbFile;
            var conn;

            function createEncryptionKey(password) {
                var ba = new air.ByteArray();
                ba.writeUTFBytes(password);
                var md5 = new window.runtime.com.hurlant.crypto.hash.MD5();
                var output = md5.hash(ba);
```

```
                        logAction("Hash Key Created " + output.toString());
                        return output;
                }

                function handleConnectClick(event) {
                        logAction("Attempting to Connect to Database");
                        dbFile =
air.File.applicationStorageDirectory.resolvePath(ENCRYPTED_DB_FILE);
                        conn = new air.SQLConnection();
                        conn.addEventListener(air.SQLEvent.OPEN, handleDatabaseOpen);
                        conn.addEventListener(air.SQLErrorEvent.ERROR,
handleDatabaseError);
                        conn.openAsync(dbFile,air.SQLMode.CREATE,null,false,1024,
createEncryptionKey(document.getElementById('password').value));
                }

                function handleDisconnectClick(event) {
                        conn.close();
                        document.getElementById('connectButton').disabled = false;
                        document.getElementById('password').disabled = false;
                        document.getElementById('disconnectButton').disabled = true;
                        document.getElementById('newPassword').disabled = true;
                        document.getElementById('reencryptButton').disabled = true;
                }

                function handleReencryptClick(event) {
                        conn.addEventListener(air.SQLEvent.REENCRYPT,
handleDatabaseReencrypt);
                        conn.reencrypt(createEncryptionKey(document.
getElementById('newPassword').value));
                }

                function handleDatabaseOpen(event) {
                        logAction("Database Connection Successful");
                        document.getElementById('connectButton').disabled = true;
                        document.getElementById('password').disabled = true;
                        document.getElementById('disconnectButton').disabled = false;
                        document.getElementById('newPassword').disabled = false;
                        document.getElementById('reencryptButton').disabled = false;
                }

                function handleDatabaseReencrypt(event) {
                        conn.removeEventListener(air.SQLEvent.REENCRYPT,
handleDatabaseReencrypt);
                        logAction("Reencrypt Successful");
                }

                function handleDatabaseError(event) {
                        logAction("Database Error " +
event.error.detailArguments.toString() );
                }

                function logAction(action) {
                        var resultsDiv = document.getElementById('results');
                        resultsDiv.innerHTML += "[ACTION]: " + action + "<br />";
```

```
                }
        </script>
        <style type="text/css">
                body {font-family: Arial; font-size:12px;padding: 15px;}
                #results {padding: 5px;border: 1px solid #666;}
        </style>
    </head>
    <body>
        <h3>Encrypted By Password</h3>
        <div>
                Connect to Database<br />
                Password
                <input id="password" type="text" />
                <input id="connectButton" type="button" value="Connect"
onclick="handleConnectClick(event)" />
                <input id="disconnectButton" type="button" value="Disconnect"
onclick="handleDisconnectClick(event)" disabled="true" />
        </div>
        <div>
                Change Password / Reencrypt<br />
                New Password
                <input id="newPassword" type="text" disabled="true" />
                <input id="reencryptButton" type="button" value="Change Password"
onclick="handleReencryptClick(event)" disabled="true" />
        </div>
        <br />
        <div>Results:</div>
        <div>
                <div id="results"></div>
        </div>
    </body>
</html>
```

10.7 Creating Tables in a Database

Problem

You want to create a table in the SQLite local database.

Solution

Create tables in a database using the SQLStatement class.

Discussion

To create a table in your database, create an instance of the SQLStatement class. Doing so enables you to execute SQL statements in an open database by using the connection established with the SQLConnection class. The SQLStatement class tells the sqlConnection public property which SQL object to accept to create the connection to the local database file. The SQLStatement's text property, on the other hand, accepts the SQL string to execute, which will work remotely with the database.

To execute the SQL text string, you need to invoke the **execute** method, which executes the specified SQL string in the **text** property of the **SQLStatement** class:

```
var SQLStmsqlStatement:SQLStatement = new SQLStatement();
sqlStatementSQLStm.sqlConnection = conn;
var sqlText:String =
    "CREATE TABLE IF NOT EXISTS students (" +
    "    studentId INTEGER PRIMARY KEY AUTOINCREMENT, " +
    "    firstName TEXT, " +
    "    lastName TEXT, " +
    ")";
sqlStatementSQLStm.text = sqlText;

sqlStatementSQLStm.execute();
```

The **execute** method can be managed in asynchronous mode and will therefore trigger the **RESULT** and **ERROR** events:

```
sqlStatementSQLStm.addEventListener(SQLEvent.RESULT, onStatementResult);
sqlStatementSQLStm.addEventListener(SQLErrorEvent.ERROR, onStatementError);
```

In synchronous execution mode, you manage the execution in a **try...catch** block:

```
try
{
    sqlStatementSQLStm.execute();

}
catch (error:SQLError)
{
    Alert.show("Error message:", error.message);
    Alert.show("Details:", error.details);
}
```

Supported SQL Dialects

Using the SQL language, you can manipulate data inside a database. Adobe AIR supports SQLite database systems and many standard SQL-92 standard SQL dialects. For retrieving, adding, modifying, and removing data from database tables, the following statements are supported:

- SELECT
- INSERT
- UPDATE
- DELETE

For creating, modifying, and removing such database objects as tables, views, indices, and triggers, AIR supports these SQL commands:

- Tables:

```
CREATE TABLE
ALTER TABLE
```

```
              DROP TABLE
```
- Indices:
```
      CREATE INDEX
      DROP INDEX
```
- Views:
```
      CREATE VIEW
      DROP VIEW
```
- Triggers:
```
      CREATE TRIGGER
      DROP TRIGGER
```

In addition, AIR supports clauses and special statements that are extensions to SQL and provided by the runtime, as well as two language elements:

- The COLLATE clause
- The EXPLAIN clause
- The ON CONFLICT clause and conflict algorithms
- The REINDEX statement
- Comments
- Expressions

SQL storage classes represent the actual data types used to store values. AIR supports the following:

- NULL: A NULL value
- INTEGER: A signed integer
- REAL: A floating-point number value
- TEXT: A text string (limited to 256MB)
- BLOB: A raw binary data (limited to 256MB)

BLOB stands for Binary Large Object.

For a complete and detailed overview of SQL support in local databases, you can refer to *http://help.adobe.com/en_US/AS3LCR/Flash_10.0/local DatabaseSQLSupport.html* or *http://help.adobe.com/en_US/AIR/1.5/ jslr/localDatabaseSQLSupport.html*.

To create a table in a database, you use the CREATE TABLE statement:

```
CREATE TABLE TableName ( column-definition )
```

Each column definition represents the name of the column to create, followed by the data type.

ActionScript/Flex

The following ActionScript class modifies the class from Recipe 10.3 and adds an instance of the SQLStatement class to create a table in the database that was opened with the SQLConnection class:

```
package com.oreilly.aircookbook.ch10
{
    import flash.data.SQLConnection;
    import flash.data.SQLStatement;
    import flash.errors.SQLError;
    import flash.events.SQLErrorEvent;
    import flash.events.SQLEvent;
    import flash.filesystem.File;

    import mx.controls.Alert;

    public class CreateTable
    {
        private var _myDB:File;
        private var _isOpen:Boolean = false;

        private var _dbConn:SQLConnection;

        private var sqlString:String;

        public function get myDB():File
        {
            return _myDB;
        }

        public function get isOpen():Boolean
        {
            return _isOpen;
        }


        public function CreateTable()
        {
            createLocalDB();
            sqlString = "CREATE TABLE IF NOT EXISTS Students(" +
                        "stuId INTEGER PRIMARY KEY AUTOINCREMENT, " +
                        "firstName TEXT, " +
                        "lastName TEXT" + ")";
        }

        private function createLocalDB():void
        {
```

```
            var folder:File= File.applicationStorageDirectory.resolvePath( "db" );

            folder.createDirectory();

            _myDB = folder.resolvePath( "myDBFile.db" );
    }

    public function createTableDB(dbFile:File,isAsync:Boolean=true):void
    {
            _dbConn = new SQLConnection();

            if(isAsync)
            {
            _dbConn.openAsync(dbFile);

            _dbConn.addEventListener(SQLEvent.OPEN, openHandler);
            _dbConn.addEventListener(SQLErrorEvent.ERROR, errorHandler);

            }else{

                try
                {
                    _dbConn.open(dbFile);

                    var createStm:SQLStatement = new SQLStatement();
                    createStm.sqlConnection = _dbConn;
                    createStm.text = sqlString;

                    createStm.addEventListener(SQLEvent.RESULT, onStatementResult);
                    createStm.addEventListener(SQLErrorEvent.ERROR,
onStatementError);

                    createStm.execute();
                }
                catch (error:SQLError)
                {
                        trace("Error message:", error.message);
                        trace("Details:", error.details);
                }
            }
    }

    private function openHandler(event:SQLEvent):void
    {

            _isOpen = _dbConn.connected;

            var createStm:SQLStatement = new SQLStatement();
            createStm.sqlConnection = _dbConn;
            createStm.text = sqlString;

            createStm.addEventListener(SQLEvent.RESULT, onStatementResult);
            createStm.addEventListener(SQLErrorEvent.ERROR, onStatementError);

            createStm.execute();
```

```
    }

    private function errorHandler(event:SQLErrorEvent):void
    {
        mx.controls.Alert.show("Error message:", event.error.message);
        mx.controls.Alert.show("Details:", event.error.details);
        _isOpen = _dbConn.connected
    }

    private function onStatementResult(event:SQLEvent):void
    {
        mx.controls.Alert.show("Table created");
    }

    private function onStatementError(event:SQLErrorEvent):void
    {
        mx.controls.Alert.show("Error message:", event.error.message);
        mx.controls.Alert.show("Details:", event.error.details);
    }

    }
}
```

In the constructor of the class, you assign a value to the **String** that contains the SQL statement to create a **Students** table in the database:

```
sqlString = "CREATE TABLE IF NOT EXISTS Students(" +
            "stuId INTEGER PRIMARY KEY AUTOINCREMENT, " +
            "firstName TEXT, " +
            "lastName TEXT" + ")";
```

This string is passed as an argument to the **text** property of the **SQLStatement** instance that has been created as a temporary variable in the **createTableDB** method. This public method opens a connection to the database before creating the table. This is a compulsory step; if you try to create a table in a database without defining any connection, the **SQLErrorEvent.ERROR** class will throw an error.

The ActionScript code that creates the **SQLStatement** class instance passes it the reference to the database connection, and then the SQL statement is written in the **openHandler** event handler, managed by the asynchronous connection mode, as well as in the **try...catch** statement for the synchronous connection to the database. The code is the same for both connections:

```
var createStm:SQLStatement = new SQLStatement();
createStm.sqlConnection = _dbConn;
createStm.text = sqlString;

createStm.addEventListener(SQLEvent.RESULT, onStatementResult);
createStm.addEventListener(SQLErrorEvent.ERROR, onStatementError);

createStm.execute();
```

The following Flex code uses the *CreateTable.as* ActionScript class to create a database and a table at the click of a button:

```
<?xml version="1.0" encoding="utf-8"?>
<mx:WindowedApplication
xmlns:mx="http://www.adobe.com/2006/mxml"
layout="vertical"
initialize="init()">

<mx:Script>
<![CDATA[
    import com.oreilly.aircookbook.ch10.CreateTable;

    private var myDB:File;
    private var myDBclass:CreateTable;

    private function init():void
    {
        createBtn.addEventListener(MouseEvent.CLICK, onClick);
        openBtn.addEventListener(MouseEvent.CLICK, onClickOpen);
    }

    private function onClick(evt:MouseEvent):void
    {
        myDBclass = new CreateTable();
        myDB = myDBclass.myDB;

        openBtn.enabled = true;

        mx.controls.Alert.show("Database File Was Created : \n" + myDB.nativePath );
    }

    private function onClickOpen(evt:MouseEvent):void
    {
        myDBclass.createTableDB(myDB)

        if (myDBclass.isOpen)
        {
            mx.controls.Alert.show("Database File Was Opened and the TABLE was
created" );
        }
    }
]]>
</mx:Script>

<mx:Button id="createBtn" label="Create DB"  />

<mx:Button label="Create a Table" id="openBtn" enabled="false"  />


</mx:WindowedApplication>
```

JavaScript

To create a table in the database using the JavaScript code, follow these basic steps:

1. Create a database.
2. Open a connection to the database.
3. Create a `SQLStatement` instance.
4. In the instance, specify the database in which to create the table by using the `sqlConnection` property.
5. Specify the SQL string to apply on the `text` property.
6. For an asynchronous execution mode, create the event handlers to handle the result of the execute operation.
7. Execute the `execute` method to apply the SQL statements.

The following example creates a database file and executes a connection to this empty database, which it passes onto the `SQLStatement` instance to create a table:

```
// Constants
var DB_NAME = 'db/myDBFile.db';

var SQL_STRING =
"CREATE TABLE IF NOT EXISTS Students (" +
"stuId INTEGER PRIMARY KEY AUTOINCREMENT, " +
"firstName TEXT, " +
"lastName TEXT" +
")";


var myDB;
var dbConn;
var dbStm;
var isAsync;

function createDB()
{
    var folder = air.File.applicationStorageDirectory.resolvePath("db");
    folder.createDirectory();
    myDB = folder.resolvePath(DB_NAME);
    myDB = air.File.desktopDirectory.resolvePath(DB_NAME);

    air.Introspector.Console.log( "Database File was created: " + myDB.nativePath );

}

function openDB(isAsync)
{
    dbConn = new air.SQLConnection();

    if (isAsync)
    {

        dbConn.openAsync(myDB);
```

```
            dbConn.addEventListener(air.SQLEvent.OPEN, onOpenHandler);
            dbConn.addEventListener(air.SQLErrorEvent.ERROR, onErrorHandler);

    }else
    {
        try
        {
            dbConn.open(myDB);
            air.Introspector.Console.log("Database File Was Opened successfully with
                                        a synchronous operation");

            dbStm = new air.SQLStatement();
            dbStm.sqlConnection = dbConn;
            dbStm.text = SQL_STRING;

            dbStm.addEventListener(air.SQLEvent.RESULT, onStatementResult);
            dbStm.addEventListener(air.SQLErrorEvent.ERROR, onStatementError);

            dbStm.execute();

        }
        catch (error)
        {
            air.Introspector.Console.log("Error message:", error.message);
            air.Introspector.Console.log("Details:", error.details);
        }
    }
}

function onOpenHandler(event)
{
    air.Introspector.Console.log("Database File Was Opened successfully");

    dbStm = new air.SQLStatement();
    dbStm.sqlConnection = dbConn;
    dbStm.text = SQL_STRING;

    dbStm.addEventListener(air.SQLEvent.RESULT, onStatementResult);
    dbStm.addEventListener(air.SQLErrorEvent.ERROR, onStatementError);

    dbStm.execute();

}

function onErrorHandler(event)
{
    air.Introspector.Console.log("Error message:", event.error.message);
    air.Introspector.Console.log("Details:", event.error.details);
}

function onStatementResult(event)
{
air.Introspector.Console.log("Table created");
}
```

```
function onStatementError(event)
{
    air.Introspector.Console.log("Error message:", event.error.message);
    air.Introspector.Console.log("Details:", event.error.details);
}
```

The SQL statement is declared as a constant at the beginning of the code. It can be changed at will to carry out other operations or add columns to the table you are creating. Launched when the asynchronous openAsync method is invoked, the onOpenHandler event handler creates the instance of the SQLStatement class. Within this event handler the sqlConnection property is set to the SQLConnection instance, and then the SQL commands are passed to the text property that executes the operations on the database:

```
dbStm = new air.SQLStatement();
dbStm.sqlConnection = dbConn;
dbStm.text = SQL_STRING;
```

Regardless of whether the database has been opened in asynchronous or synchronous mode, the JavaScript code calls the execute method of the SQLStatement.

The HTML page loads the content of the external JavaScript file and invokes the openDB function at the click of a button:

```
<!DOCTYPE html PUBLIC "-//W3C//DTD XHTML 1.0 Transitional//EN"
"http://www.w3.org/TR/xhtml1/DTD/xhtml1-transitional.dtd">
<html xmlns="http://www.w3.org/1999/xhtml">
<head>

<script type="text/javascript" src="frameworks/AIRAliases.js"></script>
<script type="text/javascript" src="frameworks/AIRIntrospector.js"></script>

<script type="text/javascript" src="CreateTableDB.js"></script>

<meta http-equiv="Content-Type" content="text/html; charset=utf-8" />

<title>AIR Cookbook: 10.4 Creating Tables in a Database (JavaScript)</title>
</head>

<body onload="createDB()">
<h1>AIR Cookbook: 10.4 Creating Tables in a Database (JavaScript)</h1>
<p>
  <label>Create a Table in a Database File
  <input type="button" name="openDB" id="openDB" value="Create" accesskey="o"
tabindex="1" onclick="openDB(true);document.getElementById('resultDiv').innerText =
'Database was opened successfully';" />
  </label>
</p>
<p><div id="resultDiv"></div></p>
</body>
</html>
```

After you create the Button to create the table, the following messages appear in the AIR Introspector Console tab when the button is clicked:

[app:/Ch10/createTable.html][19:20:40] Database File was created: C:\Documents and Settings\User\Desktop\db\myDBFile.db
[app:/Ch10/createTable.html][19:20:43] Database File Was Opened successfully
[app:/Ch10/createTable.html][19:20:43] Table created

To visualize the content of a SQLite database, you can use a free SQLite Database Browser application (*http://sqlitebrowser.sourceforge.net*) or the AIR-based SQLite Admin application (*http://coenraets.org/blog/2008/02/sqlite-admin-for-air-10/*).

10.8 Querying a Database Synchronously

Problem

You want to establish synchronous database operations

Solution

Query a database using the `sqlConnection` and `text` properties of the `SQLStatement` class.

Discussion

When working with synchronous operations, you must understand a few concepts regarding how synchronous operations behave when there are two or more actions that are dependent on each other and how they handle errors.

When you need to execute an operation only if a previous operation has been successful, all you need to do is write the code immediately after the operation on which it depends.

When synchronous operations are executed, you use `try...catch...finally` code blocks to handle errors instead of using event handlers.

Don't forget that writing a synchronous database operation could penalize the performance and user experience of the application, which will freeze until the entire cycle of executed operations is complete. The user won't be able to interact with the application in the meantime.

In this solution, you will see how to insert data in a table by using SQL's `INSERT` statement. By creating a SQL string, like the one shown here, you can insert static or dynamic information in the database:

```
sqlString = "CREATE TABLE IF NOT EXISTS Students(" +
"stuId INTEGER PRIMARY KEY AUTOINCREMENT, " +
"firstName TEXT, " +
"lastName TEXT" + ")";

sqlInsert = "INSERT INTO Students (firstName, lastName) " +
"VALUES ('Marco', 'Casario')";
```

The `sqlInsert` string inserts the values `Marco` and `Casario` into the `firstName` and `last Name` columns, respectively.

The database will be opened in synchronous mode with the **open** method so that all the following operations on that database connection will be executed in synchronous mode.

Flex/ActionScript

The *QueryingTableSynch.as* class creates a new SQLite local database, creates a table, and carries out data insertion. All these operations are executed in synchronous mode, because the database has been opened by using the **open** method:

```
package com.oreilly.aircookbook.ch10
{
    import flash.data.SQLConnection;
    import flash.data.SQLStatement;
    import flash.errors.SQLError;
    import flash.events.SQLErrorEvent;
    import flash.events.SQLEvent;
    import flash.filesystem.File;

    import mx.controls.Alert;

    public class QueryingTableSynch
    {
        private var _myDB:File;
        private var _isOpen:Boolean = false;

        private var _dbConn:SQLConnection;

        private var sqlString:String;
        private var sqlInsert:String;

        public function get myDB():File
        {
            return _myDB;
        }

        public function get isOpen():Boolean
        {
            return _isOpen;
        }


        public function QueryingTableSynch()
        {
            createLocalDB();

            sqlString = "CREATE TABLE IF NOT EXISTS Students(" +
                        "stuId INTEGER PRIMARY KEY AUTOINCREMENT, " +
                        "firstName TEXT, " +
                        "lastName TEXT" + ")";
```

```
        sqlInsert = "INSERT INTO Students (firstName, lastName) " +
                    "VALUES ('Marco', 'Casario')";
}

private function createLocalDB():void
{
    var folder:File= File.applicationStorageDirectory.resolvePath( "db" );

    folder.createDirectory();

    _myDB = folder.resolvePath( "myDBFile.db" );

}

public function createTableDB(dbFile:File):void
{
    _dbConn = new SQLConnection();

    try
    {
        trace("Creating Table ....");

        _dbConn.open(dbFile);
        var createStm:SQLStatement = new SQLStatement();

        createStm.sqlConnection = _dbConn;
        createStm.text = sqlString;

        createStm.execute();

            trace("Table created ....");
    }
    catch (error:SQLError)
    {
            trace("Error message:", error.message);
            trace("Details:", error.details);
    }
}

public function insertData(dbFile:File):void
{
    try
    {
        trace("Inserting data ....");

        var createStm:SQLStatement = new SQLStatement();
        createStm.sqlConnection = _dbConn;

        createStm.text = sqlInsert
        createStm.execute();

        trace("Data inserted!");

    }
    catch (error:SQLError)
```

```
        {
            trace("Error message:", error.message);
            trace("Details:", error.details);
        }
    }
  }
}
```

After the database is opened, all the following operations for that connection are automatically executed in synchronous mode. The Students table in the createTableDBB method, with the firstName and lastName columns, is created this way; the execute method of the SQLStatement instance is executed in synchronous mode. The same applies to the insertion of the values with the INSERT SQL statement in the insertData method that executes the following SQL statement:

```
sqlInsert = "INSERT INTO Students (firstName, lastName) " +
            "VALUES ('Marco', 'Casario')";
```

In the synchronous execution mode, the operations are executed line by line in the code. To manage the errors that the application could encounter when it is opening the database or when operations are being executed, the code resides in a try...catch...finally code block.

To use this ActionScript class, you can use the following MXML code, which is written by using the Flex Framework and invokes the public methods to carry out operations on the database in synchronous execution mode:

```
<?xml version="1.0" encoding="utf-8"?>
<mx:WindowedApplication
xmlns:mx="http://www.adobe.com/2006/mxml"
layout="vertical"
    initialize="init()">

<mx:Script>
<![CDATA[
    import com.oreilly.aircookbook.ch10.QueryingTableSynch;

    private var myDB:File;
    private var myDBclass:QueryingTableSynch;

    private function init():void
    {
        createBtn.addEventListener(MouseEvent.CLICK, onClick);
        openBtn.addEventListener(MouseEvent.CLICK, onClickOpen);
        insertBtn.addEventListener(MouseEvent.CLICK, onClickInsert);
    }

    private function onClick(evt:MouseEvent):void
    {
        myDBclass = new QueryingTableSynch();
        myDB = myDBclass.myDB;

        openBtn.enabled = true;
```

```
                mx.controls.Alert.show("Database File Was Created : \n" + myDB.nativePath );
        }

        private function onClickOpen(evt:MouseEvent):void
        {
            myDBclass.createTableDB(myDB);
            insertBtn.enabled = true;
        }

        private function onClickInsert(evt:MouseEvent):void
        {
            myDBclass.insertData(myDB);
            mx.controls.Alert.show("Data was inserted into the database : \n" +
                            myDB.nativePath );
        }
    ]]>
    </mx:Script>

    <mx:Button id="createBtn" label="Create DB"  />

    <mx:Button label="Open DataBase" id="openBtn" enabled="false"  />

    <mx:Button label="Insert Data Asynchronously" enabled="false" id="insertBtn" />

    </mx:WindowedApplication>
```

JavaScript

The following JavaScript code creates a new database, inserts the Students table, and with an INSERT statement inserts a value in the database. The whole operation is executed in synchronous mode.

```
// Constants
var DB_NAME = 'db/myDBFile.db';
var SQL_STRING =
    "CREATE TABLE IF NOT EXISTS Students (" +
    "    stuId INTEGER PRIMARY KEY AUTOINCREMENT, " +
    "    firstName TEXT, " +
    "    lastName TEXT" +
    ")";

var SQL_INSERT = "INSERT INTO Students (firstName, lastName) " +
    "VALUES ('Alessio', 'Casario')";


var myDB;
var dbConn;
var dbStm;

var isAsync;

function createDB()
{
var folder =
air.File.applicationStorageDirectory.resolvePath("db");
```

```
        folder.createDirectory();

        myDB = folder.resolvePath(DB_NAME);
        myDB = air.File.desktopDirectory.resolvePath(DB_NAME);

        air.Introspector.Console.log( "Database File was created: " + myDB.nativePath )
        openDB();
    }

    function openDB()
    {
        dbConn = new air.SQLConnection();

        try
        {
            dbConn.open(myDB);
            air.Introspector.Console.log("Database File Was Opened successfully with
                                  a synchronous operation");

            dbStm = new air.SQLStatement();
            dbStm.sqlConnection = dbConn;
            dbStm.text = SQL_STRING;

            dbStm.execute();

        }
        catch (error)
        {
           air.Introspector.Console.log("Error message:", error.message);
           air.Introspector.Console.log("Details:", error.details);
        }

    }

    function insertData()
    {
        try
        {
            dbStm.text = SQL_INSERT;

            dbStm.execute();

            air.Introspector.Console.log("Data was inserted into the Database");

        }
        catch (error)
        {
           air.Introspector.Console.log("Error message:", error.message);
           air.Introspector.Console.log("Details:", error.details);
        }
    }
```

Both the openDB function and the insertData function manage the operations on the
database in the try...catch statement so as to intercept possible errors. The insert
Data method uses the same instance of the SQLStatement class, dbStm, but the value

passed to the text property has been changed. If the values are in fact inserted, the SQL text that is executed is the text contained in the SQL_INSERT variable, which is specified in the constants at the top of the file:

```
var SQL_INSERT = "INSERT INTO Students (firstName, lastName) " +
    "VALUES ('Alessio', 'Casario')";
```

Here are the messages that appear in the AIR Introspector Console tab:

[app:/Ch10/insertDataSinch.html][16:25:53]   Database   File   was   created:
C:\Documents and Settings\User\Desktop\db\myDBFile.db
[app:/Ch10/insertDataSinch.html][16:25:54] Database File Was Opened successfully with a synchronous operation
[app:/Ch10/insertDataSinch.html][16:26:02] Data was inserted into the Database

The following is the complete HTML page that uses the previous JavaScript code:

```
<!DOCTYPE html PUBLIC "-//W3C//DTD XHTML 1.0 Transitional//EN"
"http://www.w3.org/TR/xhtml1/DTD/xhtml1-transitional.dtd">
<html xmlns="http://www.w3.org/1999/xhtml">
<head>

<script type="text/javascript" src="frameworks/AIRAliases.js"></script>
<script type="text/javascript" src="frameworks/AIRIntrospector.js"></script>

<script type="text/javascript" src="InsertDataSinchInsertDataSync.js"></script>

<meta http-equiv="Content-Type" content="text/html; charset=utf-8" />

<title>AIR Cookbook: 10.5 Querying a Database Asynchronously  (JavaScript)</title>
</head>

<body onload="createDB()">
<h1>AIR Cookbook: 10.5 Querying a Database Asynchronously  (JavaScript)</h1>


<p>
  <label>Create a Table in a Database File
  <input type="button" name="openDB" id="openDB" value="Insert Data"
accesskey="o" tabindex="1"
onclick="insertData();document.getElementById('resultDiv').innerText = 'Data was
added to the database';" />
  </label>
</p>
<p><div id="resultDiv"></div></p>
</body>
</html>.
```

10.9 Querying a Database Asynchronously

Problem

You want to execute database operations asynchronously.

Solution

Use the `openAsync` method of the `SQLConnection` class to query a database asynchronously. Register the event listeners on the `RESULT` event of the `SQLEvent` class and the `ERROR` event of the `SQLErrorEvent` class.

Discussion

The asynchronous operations execute in the background, which allows the user to continue interacting with the application even if the results still haven't been returned. By creating event listeners, which dispatch the `RESULT` event of the `SQLEvent` class and the `ERROR` event of the `SQLErrorEvent`, the end of each operation is managed to establish whether it has been successful or whether errors have occurred.

Before discussing the example, it is important to specify that it isn't possible to change the `text` property of a `SQLStatement` instance if it has already been assigned. As an alternative, AIR lets you create several instances of the `SQLStatement` class that connect to the same database. This way, it is possible to manage several SQL statement operations by creating different instances of the `SQLStatement` class for each of them. For example:

```
var createText:StringsqlString = "CREATE TABLE IF NOT EXISTS Students(" +
        "stuId INTEGER PRIMARY KEY AUTOINCREMENT, " +
        "firstName TEXT, " +
        "lastName TEXT" + ")";

var insertText:StringsqlInsert = "INSERT INTO Students (firstName, lastName) " +
        "VALUES ('Marco', 'Casario')";

var sqlCreate:SQLStatement = new SQLStatement();
sqlCreate.sqlConnection = conn;
sqlCreate.text = createText;
sqlCreate.execute();

var sqlInsert:SQLStatement = new SQLStatement();
sqlInsert.sqlConnection = conn;
sqlInsert.text = insertText;
sqlInsert.execute();
```

This code creates two instances of the `SQLStatement` class: `sqlCreate` and `sqlInsert`. Both instances connect to the same database by using the instance of the `SQLConnection` called `conn`. However, whereas the first instance creates the structure of the database (the `Students` table with the two columns `firstName` and `lastName`), the second `SQLStatement` instance executes an `INSERT` SQL statement by inserting the values in the newly created table.

With this approach, every `SQLStatement` object has its own queue or list of operations that it is instructed to perform. As soon as the first operation of the queue list is executed, it will pass on to the following operations until the queue list is finished.

Flex/ActionScript

In the example, you will create nonglobal variables at the method level, and you can assign different text properties to them:

```
package com.oreilly.aircookbook.ch10
{
    import flash.data.SQLConnection;
    import flash.data.SQLStatement;
    import flash.errors.SQLError;
    import flash.events.SQLErrorEvent;
    import flash.events.SQLEvent;
    import flash.filesystem.File;

    import mx.controls.Alert;

    public class QueryingTableAsynch
    {
        private var _myDB:File;
        private var _isOpen:Boolean = false;

        private var _dbConn:SQLConnection;

        private var sqlString:String;
        private var sqlInsert:String;

        public function get myDB():File
        {
            return _myDB;
        }

        public function get isOpen():Boolean
        {
            return _isOpen;
        }


        public function QueryingTableAsynch()
        {
            createLocalDB();

            sqlString = "CREATE TABLE IF NOT EXISTS Students(" +
                        "stuId INTEGER PRIMARY KEY AUTOINCREMENT, " +
                        "firstName TEXT, " +
                        "lastName TEXT" + ")";

            sqlInsert = "INSERT INTO Students (firstName, lastName) " +
                        "VALUES ('Marco', 'Casario')";
        }

        private function createLocalDB():void
        {
            var folder:File= File.applicationStorageDirectory.resolvePath( "db" );

            folder.createDirectory();
```

```
        _myDB = folder.resolvePath( "myDBFile.db" );
    }

    public function createTableDB(dbFile:File):void
    {
        _dbConn = new SQLConnection();


        _dbConn.openAsync(dbFile);

        _dbConn.addEventListener(SQLEvent.OPEN, openHandler);
        _dbConn.addEventListener(SQLErrorEvent.ERROR, errorHandler);
    }

    public function insertData(dbFile:File):void
    {

        var createStm:SQLStatement = new SQLStatement();
        createStm.sqlConnection = _dbConn;

        createStm.text = sqlInsert;
        createStm.execute();

        createStm.addEventListener(SQLEvent.RESULT, onStatementResult);
        createStm.addEventListener(SQLErrorEvent.ERROR, onStatementError);
    }

    private function openHandler(event:SQLEvent):void
    {
        trace("The Database File " + _myDB.nativePath + " was opened");
        _isOpen = _dbConn.connected;

        var createStm:SQLStatement = new SQLStatement();
        createStm.sqlConnection = _dbConn;
        createStm.text = sqlString;

        createStm.addEventListener(SQLEvent.RESULT, onStatementResult);
        createStm.addEventListener(SQLErrorEvent.ERROR, onStatementError);

        createStm.execute();

    }

    private function errorHandler(event:SQLErrorEvent):void
    {
        mx.controls.Alert.show("Error message:", event.error.message);
        mx.controls.Alert.show("Details:", event.error.details);
        _isOpen = _dbConn.connected
    }

    private function onStatementResult(event:SQLEvent):void
    {
```

```
                    mx.controls.Alert.show("Table created: " + event.type +
                                    event.target.text);
        }

        private function onStatementError(event:SQLErrorEvent):void
        {
            mx.controls.Alert.show("Error message:", event.error.message);
            mx.controls.Alert.show("Details:", event.error.details);
        }

    }
}
```

The following ActionScript in the openHandler event handler, which has been registered on the OPEN event of the SQLConnection openAsync method, creates the table in the newly created and opened database. In fact, the temporary variable createStm executes the SQL string that carries out a CREATE TABLE statement. Being asynchronous operations, the event handlers have to be registered on the RESULT and ERROR events to manage the result data of the operation and possible errors.

Data insertion is carried out on the insertData method using the SQL string contained in the sqlInsert variable as a text property.

In the onStatementResult event handler, you access the text property of the SQLStatement class that has generated the event through the event object, as well as the type of event that has been triggered.

The following is an example of MXML code that uses this ActionScript class to create a local database and to populate a table by executing asynchronous operations:

```
<?xml version="1.0" encoding="utf-8"?>
<mx:WindowedApplication
xmlns:mx="http://www.adobe.com/2006/mxml"
layout="vertical"
    initialize="init()">


<mx:Script>
<![CDATA[
    import com.oreilly.aircookbook.ch10.QueryingTableAsynch;

    private var myDB:File;
    private var myDBclass:QueryingTableAsynch;

    private function init():void
    {
        createBtn.addEventListener(MouseEvent.CLICK, onClick);
        openBtn.addEventListener(MouseEvent.CLICK, onClickOpen);
        insertBtn.addEventListener(MouseEvent.CLICK, onClickInsert);
    }

    private function onClick(evt:MouseEvent):void
    {
        myDBclass = new QueryingTableAsynch();
```

```
        myDB = myDBclass.myDB;

        openBtn.enabled = true;

        mx.controls.Alert.show("Database File Was Created : \n" + myDB.nativePath );
    }

    private function onClickOpen(evt:MouseEvent):void
    {
        myDBclass.createTableDB(myDB);

        insertBtn.enabled = true;

    }

    private function onClickInsert(evt:MouseEvent):void
    {
        myDBclass.insertData(myDB);
        mx.controls.Alert.show("Data was inserted into the database : \n" +
            myDB.nativePath );
    }
]]>
</mx:Script>

<mx:Button id="createBtn" label="Create DB"  />

<mx:Button label="Open DataBase" id="openBtn" enabled="false"  />

<mx:Button label="Insert Data Asynchronously" enabled="false" id="insertBtn" />

</mx:WindowedApplication>
```

JavaScript

In JavaScript, you create two global variables that contain the instance of the
SQLStatement class. Each SQLStatement instance carries out a connection to the same
database and executes a different SQL statement by loading a different SQL string in
its text property:

```
// Constants
var DB_NAME = "db/myDBFile.db";

var SQL_STRING =
    "CREATE TABLE IF NOT EXISTS Students (" +
    "    stuId INTEGER PRIMARY KEY AUTOINCREMENT, " +
    "    firstName TEXT, " +
    "    lastName TEXT" +
    ")";

var SQL_INSERT = "INSERT INTO Students (firstName, lastName) " +
    "VALUES ('Marco', 'Casario')";

var myDB;
var dbConn;
```

```
var dbStmCreate;
var dbStmInsert;

function createDB()
{
    var folder = air.File.applicationStorageDirectory.resolvePath("db");
    folder.createDirectory();

    myDB = folder.resolvePath(DB_NAME);
    myDB = air.File.desktopDirectory.resolvePath(DB_NAME);

    air.Introspector.Console.log( "Database File was created: " + myDB.nativePath );

    openDB();

}

function openDB()
{
    dbConn = new air.SQLConnection();

    dbConn.openAsync(myDB);
    dbConn.addEventListener(air.SQLEvent.OPEN, onOpenHandler);
    dbConn.addEventListener(air.SQLErrorEvent.ERROR, onErrorHandler);
}

function populateDB()
{
    air.Introspector.Console.log("Populating the database with data ..... ");

    dbStmInsert = new air.SQLStatement();
    dbStmInsert.sqlConnection = dbConn;
    dbStmInsert.text = SQL_INSERT;

    dbStmInsert.execute();

    dbStmInsert.addEventListener(air.SQLEvent.RESULT, onStatementResult);
    dbStmInsert.addEventListener(air.SQLErrorEvent.ERROR, onStatementError);

}


function onOpenHandler(event)
{
    air.Introspector.Console.log("Database File Was Opened successfully");

    dbStmCreate = new air.SQLStatement();
    dbStmCreate.sqlConnection = dbConn;
    dbStmCreate.text = SQL_STRING;

    dbStmCreate.execute();

    dbStmCreate.addEventListener(air.SQLEvent.RESULT, onStatementResult);
    dbStmCreate.addEventListener(air.SQLErrorEvent.ERROR, onStatementError);
}
```

```
function onErrorHandler(event)
{
    air.Introspector.Console.log("Error message:", event.error.message);
    air.Introspector.Console.log("Details:", event.error.details);
}

function onStatementResult(event)
{
    air.Introspector.Console.log("The following SQL statement has been executed:"
                                 + event.target.text);
}

function onStatementError(event)
{
    air.Introspector.Console.log("Error message:", event.error.message);
    air.Introspector.Console.log("Details:", event.error.details);
}
```

While the creation of the table happens in the event handler that is triggered on the OPEN event of the asynchronous openAsync method, the data insertion is handled in the second instance of the SQLStatement class, dbStmCreate, which executes the INSERT SQL statement in the public populateDB method.

This JavaScript code manages only one event handler: SQLEvent.RESULT. The SQL statement appears in this event handler and is executed by the SQLStatement object, which has triggered the RESULT event, by accessing the target property of the event object:

```
function onStatementResult(event)
{
    air.Introspector.Console.log("The following SQL statement has been executed:
"  + event.target.text);
}
```

The complete HTML page is as follows:

```
<!DOCTYPE html PUBLIC "-//W3C//DTD XHTML 1.0 Transitional//EN"
"http://www.w3.org/TR/xhtml1/DTD/xhtml1-transitional.dtd">
<html xmlns="http://www.w3.org/1999/xhtml">
<head>

<script type="text/javascript" src="frameworks/AIRAliases.js"></script>
<script type="text/javascript" src="frameworks/AIRIntrospector.js"></script>

<script type="text/javascript" src="InsertDataAsynch.js"></script>

<meta http-equiv="Content-Type" content="text/html; charset=utf-8" />

<title>AIR Cookbook: 10.6 Querying a Database Asynchronously  (JavaScript)</title>
</head>

<body onload="createDB()">
<h1>AIR Cookbook: 10.6 Querying a Database Asynchronously  (JavaScript)</h1>
```

```
<p>
  <label>Create a Table in a Database File
  <input type="button" name="openDB" id="openDB" value="Insert Data"
accesskey="o" tabindex="1"
onclick="populateDB();document.getElementById('resultDiv').innerText = 'Data was
added to the database';" />
  </label>
</p>
  <p><div id="resultDiv"></div></p>
</body>
</html>
```

The following are the messages that will appear in the AIR Introspector Console tab after you click the button in the HTML page:

[app:/Ch10/insertDataAsynch.html][20:21:18] Database File was created: C:\Documents and Settings\User\Desktop\db\myDBFile.db

[app:/Ch10/insertDataAsynch.html][20:21:18] Database File Was Opened successfully

[app:/Ch10/insertDataAsynch.html][20:21:18] The following SQL statement has been executed CREATE TABLE IF NOT EXISTS Students (stuId INTEGER PRIMARY KEY AUTOINCREMENT, firstName TEXT, lastName TEXT);

[app:/Ch10/insertDataAsynch.html][20:21:21] Populating the database with data .....

[app:/Ch10/insertDataAsynch.html][20:21:21] The following SQL statement has been executed: INSERT INTO Students (firstName, lastName) VALUES ('Marco', 'Casario');

10.10 Retrieving Results from a Query

Problem

You want to retrieve data from a database with a SELECT statement.

Solution

Use the SELECT statement with the SQLStatement class to query a database and retrieve data.

Discussion

Creating a database solves two basic needs. The first is to have a robust and well-structured place to store data, and the second is to be able to query the database to retrieve information according to certain search parameters. The search parameters are written by using the SELECT SQL statement that describes the set of data you want to retrieve and examine or edit.

To retrieve data from a database, you have to work with an instance of the SQLStatement class by using the SELECT statement to query the database and make it return zero or more rows of data. The SQL syntax of the SELECT statement is as follows:

```
SELECT [ALL | DISTINCT] result [FROM table-list] [WHERE expr]
[GROUP BY expr-list] [HAVING expr] [compound-op select-statement]*
[ORDER BY sort-expr-list] [LIMIT integer [( OFFSET | , ) integer]]
```

This enables you to write complex and powerful statements to query the database and make it return precise data. For further information, consult the Adobe Help pages regarding local database SQL support (*http://help.adobe.com/en_US/AIR/1.5/jslr/local DatabaseSQLSupport.html#select*).

The SQLStatement class provides the getResult methods, which can access the SQLResult object that contains the results of the SQL statement execution. By invoking this method, the data returned by the SQL statement is retrieved and can be visualized in the application or edited.

With AIR, you can launch the SELECT SQL statement by creating an instance of the SQLStatement class to which you can pass the database connection:

```
var selectStmt:SQLStatement = new SQLStatement();
selectStmt.sqlConnection = dbConn;
selectStmt.text = "SELECT firstName, lastName FROM Students";
```

Then you can register the event handlers to handle the result data or possible errors that could occur, on the RESULT event of the SQLEvent class or on the ERROR event of the SQLErrorEvent class:

```
selectStmt.addEventListener(SQLEvent.RESULT, onResultHandler);
selectStmt.addEventListener(SQLErrorEvent.ERROR, onErrorHandler);
```

Finally, you launch the **execute** method to execute the statement:

```
selectStmt.execute();
```

In the onResultHandler result handler, you invoke the getResult method of the SQLStatement class to retrieve the values and visualize them in the AIR application.

If you open the database with the open method in synchronous mode, you should insert a try...catch block instead of the event handlers registered with the addEventListener method:

```
try
{
    selectStmt.execute();
    // Invoke the selectStmt.getResult();
}
catch (errorsqlError:Error)
{
    // error handling
}
```

ActionScript/Flex

Referring to the ActionScript class you created in Recipe 10.6, you can add a public method to retrieve the data, as well as a variable that will contain the SELECT SQL statement in the constructor of the class.

Here is the complete *SelectDataAsynch.as* class, where the new code is highlighted in bold:

```
package com.oreilly.aircookbook.ch10
{
    import flash.data.SQLConnection;
    import flash.data.SQLResult;
    import flash.data.SQLStatement;
    import flash.events.SQLErrorEvent;
    import flash.events.SQLEvent;
    import flash.filesystem.File;

    import mx.collections.ArrayCollection;
    import mx.controls.Alert;

    public class SelectDataAsynch
    {
        private var _myDB:File;
        private var _isOpen:Boolean = false;

        private var _dbConn:SQLConnection;

        private var sqlString:String;
        private var sqlInsert:String;
        private var sqlSelect:String;

        [Bindable]
        private var _myResultAC:ArrayCollection;

        public function get myDB():File
        {
            return _myDB;
        }

        public function get isOpen():Boolean
        {
            return _isOpen;
        }

        public function get myResultAC():ArrayCollection
        {
            return _myResultAC;
        }


        public function SelectDataAsynch()
        {

            this.createLocalDB();
```

```
            sqlString = "CREATE TABLE IF NOT EXISTS Students(" +
                        "stuId INTEGER PRIMARY KEY AUTOINCREMENT, " +
                        "firstName TEXT, " +
                        "lastName TEXT" + ")";

            sqlInsert = "INSERT INTO Students (firstName, lastName) " +
                        "VALUES ('Katia', 'Casario')";

            sqlSelect = "SELECT * FROM Students";
        }

        private function createLocalDB():void
        {
            _dbConn = new SQLConnection();

            var folder:File=
    File.applicationStorageDirectorydesktopDirectory.resolvePath( "db" );

            folder.createDirectory();

            _myDB = folder.resolvePath( "myDBFile.db" );

            _dbConn.openAsync(_myDB);

            _dbConn.addEventListener(SQLEvent.OPEN, openHandler);
            _dbConn.addEventListener(SQLErrorEvent.ERROR, errorHandler);

        }

        public function insertData(dbFile:File):void
        {
            var insertStm:SQLStatement = new SQLStatement();
            insertStm.sqlConnection = _dbConn;

            insertStm.text = sqlInsert;
            insertStm.execute();

            insertStm.addEventListener(SQLEvent.RESULT, onStatementResult);
            insertStm.addEventListener(SQLErrorEvent.ERROR, onStatementError);
        }

        public function selectData(dbFile:File):void
        {
            var selectStm:SQLStatement = new SQLStatement();
            selectStm.sqlConnection = _dbConn;

            selectStm.text = sqlSelect;
            selectStm.execute();

            selectStm.addEventListener(SQLEvent.RESULT, onSelectResult);
            selectStm.addEventListener(SQLErrorEvent.ERROR, onStatementError);
        }

        private function openHandler(event:SQLEvent):void
```

```
    {
        _isOpen = _dbConn.connected;

        var createStm:SQLStatement = new SQLStatement();
        createStm.sqlConnection = _dbConn;
        createStm.text = sqlString;

        createStm.addEventListener(SQLEvent.RESULT, onStatementResult);
        createStm.addEventListener(SQLErrorEvent.ERROR, errorHandler);

        createStm.execute();
    }

    private function errorHandler(event:SQLErrorEvent):void
    {
        mx.controls.Alert.show("Error message:", event.error.message);
        mx.controls.Alert.show("Details:", event.error.details);
        _isOpen = _dbConn.connected
    }

    private function onStatementResult(event:SQLEvent):void
    {
        mx.controls.Alert.show("Table created:" + event.type +
                                event.target.text);
        SQLStatement(event.target).removeEventListener(SQLEvent.RESULT,
                                                        onStatementResult);
        SQLStatement(event.target).removeEventListener(SQLErrorEvent.ERROR,
                                                        errorHandler);

    }

    private function onStatementError(event:SQLErrorEvent):void
    {
        mx.controls.Alert.show("Error message:", event.error.message);
        mx.controls.Alert.show("Details:", event.error.details);
    }

    private function onSelectResult(event:SQLEvent):void
    {
        var result:SQLResult = event.target.getResult();

        var temp:Array = result.data is Array ? result.data : [{rows:
result.rowsAffected}];

        _myResultAC = new ArrayCollection(temp);

        SQLStatement(event.target).removeEventListener(SQLEvent.RESULT,
onSelectResult);
        SQLStatement(event.target).removeEventListener(SQLErrorEvent.ERROR,
errorHandler);
    }

    }
}
```

The new ActionScript class that implements the SQL operations to retrieve SQL data can be used in an MXML application with the following code:

```
<mx:WindowedApplication
xmlns:mx="http://www.adobe.com/2006/mxml"
layout="vertical"
initialize="init()">


<mx:Script>
<![CDATA[
    import mx.events.CollectionEvent;
    import com.oreilly.aircookbook.ch10.SelectDataAsynch;

    private var myDB:File;
    [Bindable]
    private var myDBclass:SelectDataAsynch;

    private function init():void
    {
        createBtn.addEventListener(MouseEvent.CLICK, onClick);
        openBtn.addEventListener(MouseEvent.CLICK, onClickOpen);
        insertBtn.addEventListener(MouseEvent.CLICK, onClickInsert);
        selectBtn.addEventListener(MouseEvent.CLICK, onClickSelect);
    }

    private function onClick(evt:MouseEvent):void
    {
        myDBclass = new SelectDataAsynch();
        myDB = myDBclass.myDB;

        openBtn.enabled = true;

        mx.controls.Alert.show("Database File Was Created : \n" + myDB.nativePath );
    }

    private function onClickOpen(evt:MouseEvent):void
    {
        insertBtn.enabled = true;
        selectBtn.enabled = true;
    }

    private function onClickInsert(evt:MouseEvent):void
    {
        myDBclass.insertData(myDB);
        mx.controls.Alert.show("Data was inserted into the database : \n" +
                            myDB.nativePath );
    }

    private function onClickSelect(evt:MouseEvent):void
    {
        myDBclass.selectData(myDB);

        myDG.dataProvider = myDBclass.myResultAC;
    }
```

```
]]>
</mx:Script>

<mx:HBox>
    <mx:Button id="createBtn" label="Create DB"  />

    <mx:Button label="Open DataBase" id="openBtn" enabled="false"  />

    <mx:Button label="Insert Data Asynchronously" enabled="false" id="insertBtn" />

    <mx:Button label="Show Data" id="selectBtn" enabled="false" />
</mx:HBox>

<mx:DataGrid id="myDG" width="100%" height="60%"/>

</mx:WindowedApplication>
```

JavaScript

The JavaScript version of this code dynamically creates a ul list HTML element, instead of using a DataGrid control, which will create as many list items as the number of data items returned by the SELECT SQLStatement in a for loop. You can create dynamic HTML elements in JavaScript by using the createElement, createTextNode, and appendChild methods and by inserting the for loop in the event handler of the air.SQLEvent.RESULT event of the SQLStatement instance.

Here is the complete JavaScript file, saved as *RetrieveDataAsynch.js*. The new portions of code are highlighted in bold:

```
// Constants
var DB_NAME = 'db/myDBFile.db';

var SQL_STRING =
    "CREATE TABLE IF NOT EXISTS Students (" +
    "    stuId INTEGER PRIMARY KEY AUTOINCREMENT, " +
    "    firstName TEXT, " +
    "    lastName TEXT" +
    ")";

var SQL_INSERT = "INSERT INTO Students (firstName, lastName) " +
    "VALUES ('Marco', 'Casario')";

var SQL_SELECT = "SELECT * FROM Students";

var myDB;
var dbConn;
var dbStmCreate;
var dbStmInsert;
var dbStmSelect;

function createDB()
{
    var folder =
```

```
air.File.applicationStorageDirectory.resolvePath("db");

folder.createDirectory();

  myDB = folder.resolvePath(DB_NAME);
  myDB =
air.File.desktopDirectory.resolvePath(DB_NAME);

    air.Introspector.Console.log( "Database File was created: " + myDB.nativePath );

    openDB();
}

function openDB()
{
    dbConn = new air.SQLConnection();

    dbConn.openAsync(myDB);
    dbConn.addEventListener(air.SQLEvent.OPEN, onOpenHandler);
    dbConn.addEventListener(air.SQLErrorEvent.ERROR, onErrorHandler);
}

function populateDB()
{
    air.Introspector.Console.log("Populating the database with data ..... ");

    dbStmInsert = new air.SQLStatement();
    dbStmInsert.sqlConnection = dbConn;
    dbStmInsert.text = SQL_INSERT;

    dbStmInsert.execute();

    dbStmInsert.addEventListener(air.SQLEvent.RESULT, onStatementResult);
    dbStmInsert.addEventListener(air.SQLErrorEvent.ERROR, onStatementError);
}

function selectData()
{

    dbStmSelect = new air.SQLStatement();
    dbStmSelect.sqlConnection = dbConn;

    dbStmSelect.text = SQL_SELECT;
    dbStmSelect.execute();

    dbStmSelect.addEventListener(air.SQLEvent.RESULT, onSelectResult);
    dbStmSelect.addEventListener(air.SQLErrorEvent.ERROR, onStatementError);
}

function onOpenHandler(event)
{
    air.Introspector.Console.log("Database File Was Opened successfully");

    dbStmCreate = new air.SQLStatement();
    dbStmCreate.sqlConnection = dbConn;
```

```
    dbStmCreate.text = SQL_STRING;

    dbStmCreate.execute();

    dbStmCreate.addEventListener(air.SQLEvent.RESULT, onStatementResult);
    dbStmCreate.addEventListener(air.SQLErrorEvent.ERROR, onStatementError);
}

function onErrorHandler(event)
{
    air.Introspector.Console.log("Error message:", event.error.message);
    air.Introspector.Console.log("Details:", event.error.details);
}

function onStatementResult(event)
{
    air.Introspector.Console.log("The following SQL statement has been executed: "
+ "\n" +event.target.text);
}

function onSelectResult(event)
{
    var result = dbStmSelect.getResult();
    var numResults = result.data.length;

    var ul = document.createElement('ul');

    for (i = 0; i < numResults; i++)
    {
        var row = result.data[i];

        var x = document.createElement('li');
        x.appendChild(document.createTextNode("Student #"+ row.stuId + ": " +
row.firstName + " " + row.lastName));
        ul.appendChild(x);

            var output = "ID: " + row.stuId;
            output += "; NAME: " + row.firstName;
            output += "; LAST NAME: " + row.lastName;

            air.Introspector.Console.log(output);
    }

    document.getElementById('resultDiv').appendChild(ul);
}

function onStatementError(event)
{
    air.Introspector.Console.log("Error message:", event.error.message);
    air.Introspector.Console.log("Details:", event.error.details);
}
```

The core of this JavaScript code is in the onSelectResult event handler, which is triggered when the SQLStatement has been completed. Inside this event handler, you create a for loop, which uses the length of the items returned by the SELECT statement in the `result.data.length` property as the end of the loop. Create as many `li` elements as there are records in the database; then append them to the `ul` element with the `appendChild` method of the document class.

Furthermore, messages are passed onto the AIR Introspector Console tab, showing the content of the database.

Here is the HTML page that includes and uses the methods of this library:

```
<!DOCTYPE html PUBLIC "-//W3C//DTD XHTML 1.0 Transitional//EN"
"http://www.w3.org/TR/xhtml1/DTD/xhtml1-transitional.dtd">
<html xmlns="http://www.w3.org/1999/xhtml">
<head>

<script type="text/javascript" src="frameworks/AIRAliases.js" />
<script type="text/javascript" src="frameworks/AIRIntrospector.js" />

<script type="text/javascript" src="examples/10/RetrieveDataAsynch.js" />

<meta http-equiv="Content-Type" content="text/html; charset=utf-8" />

<title>AIR Cookbook:  10.7 Retrieving Results from a Query  (JavaScript)</title>
</head>

<body onload="createDB()">
<h1>AIR Cookbook: 10.7 Retrieving Results from a Query  (JavaScript)</h1>


<p>
  <label>Create a Table in a Database File
  <input type="button" name="openDB" id="openDB" value="Insert Data"
 accesskey="o" tabindex="1" onclick="populateDB();document.getElementById('resultDiv').
innerText = 'Data was added to the database';" />
  </label>
</p>

<p>

<label>Select Data in the Database

<input type="button" name="openDB2" id="openDB2" value="Select Data" accesskey="o"
tabindex="1" onclick="selectData();document.getElementById('resultDiv').innerText =
'Data selected';" />

  </label>
</p>

<div id="resultDiv"></div>
</body>
</html>
```

The following are the text messages that are passed onto the AIR Introspector Console tab (they vary according to the content of the database):

[app:/Ch10/selectDataAsynch.html][18:51:20] Database File was created: C:\Documents and Settings\User\Desktop\db\myDBFile.db

[app:/Ch10/selectDataAsynch.html][18:51:20] Database File Was Opened successfully

[app:/Ch10/selectDataAsynch.html][18:51:20] The following SQL statement has been executed CREATE TABLE IF NOT EXISTS Students (stuId INTEGER PRIMARY KEY AUTOINCREMENT, firstName TEXT, lastName TEXT);

[app:/Ch10/selectDataAsynch.html][18:51:22] Populating the database with data .....

[app:/Ch10/selectDataAsynch.html][18:51:23] The following SQL statement has been executed: INSERT INTO Students (firstName, lastName) VALUES ('Marco', 'Casario');

[app:/Ch10/selectDataAsynch.html][18:51:23] ID: 1; NAME: Marco; LAST NAME: Casario

[app:/Ch10/selectDataAsynch.html][18:51:23] ID: 2; NAME: Alessio; LAST NAME: Casario

10.11 Using Parameters in Queries

Problem

You want to use parameters in queries to create a reusable SQL statement and prevent the risk of SQL injection.

Solution

Use the `parameters` property to specify named or unnamed parameters in SQL queries and to create reusable SQL statements.

Discussion

Parameters enable you to create reusable SQL statements to work with the same `SQLStatement` instance and carry out multiple SQL operations. For example, you can use an `INSERT` statement several times during the life cycle of the application to allow the user to insert multiple values in the database that will populate the database with data. This is why it is compulsory to use the parameters approach in SQL statements for the performance of the application itself. Parameters can be declared as named or unnamed parameters.

Named parameters are declared with a specific name, which the database uses as a placeholder in the SQL statement. They can be specified by using the `:` or `@` character. Here's an example where `:name` and `:surname` are two parameters that are inserted in the SQL text statement:

```
var statementInstance:SQLStatement = new SQLStatement();
```

```
var sqlText:String = "INSERT INTO Students (firstName, lastName) VALUES (:name,
:surname)";
statementInstance.parameters[":name"] = "Marco";
statementInstance.parameters[":surname "] = "Casario";


SQL_String = "INSERT INTO Students (firstName, lastName) VALUES (:name, :surname)"
statementIstance.parameters[":name"] = "Marco";
statementIstance.parameters[":surname "] = "Casario";
```

Unnamed parameters, on the other hand, are specified with the ? character in the SQL statement, and they are set by using a numerical index in the same order they are written in the SQL statement:

```
var statementInstance:SQLStatement = new SQLStatement();
var sqlText:String = "INSERT INTO Students (firstName, lastName) VALUES (?, ?)";
statementInstance.parameters[0] = "Marco";
statementInstance.parameters[1] = "Casario";

SQL_String = "INSERT INTO Students (firstName, lastName) VALUES (?, ?)"
statementIstance.parameters[0] = "Marco";
statementIstance.parameters[1] = "Casario";
```

The parameters property is an associative array, and the indices are zero-index based.

Using parameters doesn't enable you only to reuse the same SQL statement; it also makes the application more robust and secure. It's more robust because the parameters are typed substitutions of values and they guarantee the storage class for a value passed into the database. It's more secure because the parameters aren't written in the SQL text and they don't link the user input to the SQL text. Therefore, this prevents possible SQL injection attacks. In fact, when you use parameters, the values are treated as substituted values instead of being part of the SQL text.

It will become necessary to use parameters in SQL statements in most AIR applications. To use parameters, you need to have an instance of the SQLStatement class where you can define the parameters property as an associative array. The SQL text will also have to be changed by defining the placeholder values that will be associated to the parameters of the SQLStatement instance.

In this solution, you will add a public method to the ActionScript and JavaScript class you created in Recipe 10.7 to create a parameterized INSERT SQL operation.

ActionScript/Flex

Use the ActionScript class created in Recipe 10.7 to create an *InsertParam.as* class, making the following changes:

1. Add a private String property called sqlAdd'sqlAdd'.
2. Change the constructor by adding a SQL statement that will use parameters:

    ```
    private var sqlAdd:String;
    ```

```
//...

public function InsertParam()
{
    this.createLocalDB();

    sqlString = "CREATE TABLE IF NOT EXISTS Students(" +
                "stuId INTEGER PRIMARY KEY AUTOINCREMENT, " +
                "firstName TEXT, " +
                "lastName TEXT" + ")";

    sqlInsert = "INSERT INTO Students (firstName, lastName) " +
                "VALUES ('Marco', 'Casario')";

    sqlSelect = "SELECT * FROM Students";

    sqlAdd = "INSERT INTO Students (firstName, lastName)" +
        "VALUES (:name, :surname)";
}
```

3. Write a new public method that will be invoked by the application and that will be responsible for executing the SQL statement and associating the parameters to the SQL text:

```
public function insertParameters (paramName:String, paramLast:String):void
{
    var paramStmt:SQLStatement = new SQLStatement();
    paramStmt.sqlConnection = _dbConn;
    paramStmt.text = sqlAdd;

    paramStmt.parameters[":name"] = paramName;
    paramStmt.parameters[":surname"] = paramLast;

    paramStmt.execute();

    paramStmt.addEventListener(SQLEvent.RESULT, paramAddHandler);

    paramStmt.addEventListener(SQLErrorEvent.ERROR, errorHandler);
}

private function paramAddHandler(event:SQLEvent):void
{
    trace("Data added using parameters");
}
```

The insertParam method accepts two parameters: paramName:String and paramLast:String. These are used by the parameters property of the SQLStatement instance:

```
paramStmt.parameters[":name"] = paramName;
paramStmt.parameters[":surname"] = paramLast;
```

The MXML page that imports the new ActionScript class has a `Form` container with two `TextInput` controls. The text you will insert into these two controls will be passed onto the `insertParam` method, which will use them as parameters in the SQL statement:

```
<?xml version="1.0" encoding="utf-8"?>

<mx:WindowedApplication
xmlns:mx="http://www.adobe.com/2006/mxml"
layout="vertical"
initialize="init()">


<mx:Script>
<![CDATA[
    import com.oreilly.aircookbook.ch10.InsertParam;

    private var myDB:File;
    [Bindable]
    private var myDBclass:InsertParam;

    private function init():void
    {
        createBtn.addEventListener(MouseEvent.CLICK, onClick);
        openBtn.addEventListener(MouseEvent.CLICK, onClickOpen);
        insertBtn.addEventListener(MouseEvent.CLICK, onClickInsert);
        selectBtn.addEventListener(MouseEvent.CLICK, onClickSelect);
        addBtn.addEventListener(MouseEvent.CLICK, onClickAdd);
    }

    private function onClick(evt:MouseEvent):void
    {
        myDBclass = new InsertParam();
        myDB = myDBclass.myDB;

        openBtn.enabled = true;

        mx.controls.Alert.show("Database File Was Created : \n" + myDB.nativePath );
    }

    private function onClickOpen(evt:MouseEvent):void
    {
        insertBtn.enabled = true;
        selectBtn.enabled = true;
    }

    private function onClickInsert(evt:MouseEvent):void
    {
        myDBclass.insertData(myDB);
        mx.controls.Alert.show("Data was inserted into the database : \n" +
                                myDB.nativePath );
    }

    private function onClickSelect(evt:MouseEvent):void
    {
        myDBclass.selectData(myDB);
```

```
            myDG.dataProvider = myDBclass.myResultAC;
        }

        private function onClickAdd(evt:MouseEvent):void
        {
         myDBclass.insertParameters(nameTxt.text, lastTxt.text);
        }

    ]]>
</mx:Script>

<mx:VDividedBox>


<mx:HBox>
<mx:Button id="createBtn" label="Create DB"  />

<mx:Button label="Open DataBase" id="openBtn" enabled="false"  />

<mx:Button label="Insert Data Asynchronously" enabled="false" id="insertBtn" />

<mx:Button label="Show Data" id="selectBtn" enabled="false" />
</mx:HBox>


<mx:DataGrid id="myDG" width="100%" height="60%"/>


<mx:VBox width="100%">
    <mx:Label text="Insert Values into the Database" />
    <mx:Form width="100%">
        <mx:FormHeading label="Heading"/>
            <mx:FormItem label="Name">
            <mx:TextInput id="nameTxt"/>
        </mx:FormItem>
            <mx:FormItem label="Surname">
            <mx:TextInput id="lastTxt"/>
        </mx:FormItem>
        <mx:FormItem >
        <mx:Button label="Insert Values" id="addBtn"/>
        </mx:FormItem>
    </mx:Form>
</mx:VBox>

</mx:VDividedBox>
</mx:WindowedApplication>
```

In the event handler that is triggered with the click of the button, the `insertParam` method of the ActionScript class is invoked, and the values inserted in the two `TextInput` controls are passed onto it.

You can test it by launching the AIR application, inserting values in the text fields, and clicking the button to send the data. This data will be inserted in the database and shown in the `DataGrid` control that is associated with the `ArrayCollection` that contains the `SELECT` SQL statement.

JavaScript

As far as the JavaScript and HTML version is concerned, you can also add a few finishing touches to the JavaScript and HTML files you created in the previous solution to add parameters to a SQL operation. Create a new file called *InsertParam.js* based on the *RetrieveDataAsynch.js* file, and make the following changes:

1. Insert two new variables in the JavaScript file; one will contain the SQL text with specified named parameters, and the other will be the instance of the `SQLState` `ment` with the following parameters:

```
var SQL_ADD =     "INSERT INTO Students (firstName, lastName)" +
    "VALUES (:firstName, :lastName)";

// ...

var dbStmAddParam;

// ...

function addDataParam(name, last)
{
    dbStmAddParam = new air.SQLStatement();
    dbStmAddParam.sqlConnection = dbConn;
    dbStmAddParam.text = SQL_ADD;

    dbStmAddParam.parameters[":firstName"] = name;
    dbStmAddParam.parameters[":lastName"] = last;

    dbStmAddParam.addEventListener(air.SQLErrorEvent. RESULT, onStatementResult);
    dbStmAddParam.addEventListener(air.SQLErrorEvent.ERROR, onStatementError);

    dbStmAddParam.execute();
}
function onSelectResult(event)
{
    selectData();
}
```

The `addDataParam` function accepts two parameters, which it will pass onto the `parameters` property of the `SQLStatement` instance. You launch the `selectData` function in the event handler of the `air.SQLEvent.RESULT` event, which has the role of writing all the records returned by a `SELECT` statement in a `ul` list.

2. Add the `selectData` function. This is the content of the `selectData` function and the `RESULT` event handler:

```
function selectData()
{
```

```
        dbStmSelect = new air.SQLStatement();
        dbStmSelect.sqlConnection = dbConn;

        dbStmSelect.text = SQL_SELECT;
        dbStmSelect.execute();

        dbStmSelect.addEventListener(air.SQLEvent.RESULT, onSelectResult);
        dbStmSelect.addEventListener(air.SQLErrorEvent.ERROR, onStatementError);
    }

    function onSelectResult(event)
    {
        var result = dbStmSelect.getResult();
        var numResults = result.data.length;

        var ul = document.createElement('ul');

        for (i = 0; i < numResults; i++)
        {
            var row = result.data[i];

            var x = document.createElement('li');
            x.appendChild(document.createTextNode("Student #"+ row.stuId + ": " +
    row.firstName + " " + row.lastName));
            ul.appendChild(x);

             var output = "ID: " + row.stuId;
             output += "; NAME: " + row.firstName;
             output += "; LAST NAME: " + row.lastName;

             air.Introspector.Console.log(output);
        }

        document.getElementById('resultDiv').appendChild(ul);
    }
```

The HTML page will contain a Form with two text input controls. The values inserted by the user will be used as parameters of the addDataParam function that is defined in the JavaScript file:

```
<!DOCTYPE html PUBLIC "-//W3C//DTD XHTML 1.0 Transitional//EN"
"http://www.w3.org/TR/xhtml1/DTD/xhtml1-transitional.dtd">
<html xmlns="http://www.w3.org/1999/xhtml">
<head>

<script type="text/javascript" src="frameworks/AIRAliases.js"></script>
<script type="text/javascript" src="frameworks/AIRIntrospector.js"></script>

<script type="text/javascript" src="InsertParam.js"></script>

<script language="javascript" type="text/javascript">
<!--

function sendParam()
{
```

```
    var name = document.simpleForm.firstName.value;
    var last = document.simpleForm.lastName.value;

    addDataParam(name,last);
}
//-->
</script>

<meta http-equiv="Content-Type" content="text/html; charset=utf-8" />

<title>AIR Cookbook:  10.8 Using Parameters in Queries  (JavaScript)</title>
</head>

<body onload="createDB()">
<h1>AIR Cookbook: 10.8 Using Parameters in Queries  (JavaScript)</h1>


<p>
  <label>Create a Table in a Database File
  <input type="button" name="openDB" id="openDB" value="Insert Data" accesskey="o"
tabindex="1" onclick="populateDB();document.getElementById('resultDiv').innerText =
'Data was added to the database';" />
  </label>
</p>
<p>
  <label>Select Data in the Database

<input type="button" name="openDB2" id="openDB2" value="Select Data" accesskey="o"
tabindex="1" onclick="selectData();document.getElementById('resultDiv').innerText =
'Data selected';" />

  </label>
</p>

<p>div>
<form name="simpleForm">
  Insert Name: <input type="text" name="firstName" size="20" /><br />
 Insert Surname:<input type="text" name="lastName" size="20" />
  <br />
  <input type="button" value="Insert Values" onclick="sendParam()" />
</form>
</divp>
<p><div id="resultDiv"></div></p>
</body>
</html>
```

10.12 Including a Database in an Application

Contributed by Luca Mezzalira (http://lucamezzalira.wordpress.com/)

Problem

You want to include an existing SQLite database with Adobe AIR.

Solution

Embed an existing SQLite database in the AIR application, and copy it to another folder to interact with it.

Discussion

Many desktop applications use databases to store data locally on the user's computer. In some AIR applications, you need to embed an existing SQLite database with the packaged .*air* file.

Because the .*air* file is a package with some files inside, when you install an AIR application in your computer, you copy those files into the application folder or in a sub-folder. If you want to include other files in an AIR application, then when you create it, you must package the other files like images, text files, or database files as well. This includes an existing SQLite database (created for another application or with another program). Note that the application folder, `File.applicationDirectory`, is read-only. If you try to work with a database file in this directory, it will fail with a silent error. To make this work, you must copy database file with the `copyTo` method of the `File` class into another folder such as the Documents folder or the desktop folder. When you copy this file into this directory, you can work with your database and can create new records, update records, or delete them.

ActionScript/Flex

In this ActionScript example, the file *software.db* is copied from the application directory of the AIR application to the Documents directory of the user's computer. After the file is copied, you can then interact with it as needed.

```
var dbFile:File = File.applicationDirectory.resolvePath("db/software.db");
var dbWorkFile:File = File.documentsDirectory.resolvePath("software.db");

if(!dbWorkFile.exists){
    dbFile.copyTo(dbWorkedFile);
}
```

JavaScript

In this JavaScript example, the file *software.db* is copied from the application directory of the AIR application to the Documents directory of the user's computer. After the file is copied, you can then interact with it as needed.

```
var dbFile = air.File.applicationDirectory.resolvePath("db/software.db");
var dbWorkFile = air.File.documentsDirectory.resolvePath("software.db");

if(!dbWorkFile) {
    dbFile.copyTo(dbWorkFile);
}
```

10.13 Persisting Application Settings

Contributed by Marin Todorov (http://www.underplot.com/)

Problem

You need to easily persist a group of settings for your JavaScript AIR application.

Solution

Utilize the embedded SQLite database by reading the application settings from it when the application loads.

Discussion

Within an application, some settings may need to persist beyond a single session. For example, you might want the user to be able to select the position of the application windows, the color scheme, or the name of the default user profile. In these cases, the values can be stored in the SQLite database and loaded into the application upon instantiation. By doing this, you allow these values to persist, and when the users open the application again, they will see that their settings have been saved.

JavaScript

To understand how the persistence will work, you can look at the settings database and the JavaScript static class, `Settings`, which performs the loading and setting of the persistent data.

In the database there will be a `name` column and a `value` column. In addition, there will be a `namespace` column, just to be able to group easier similar settings. Finally, there will be a unique index to ensure that there are not duplicate records. Here are the SQL queries to create this database:

```
CREATE TABLE settings (IdSetting INTEGER PRIMARY KEY, name TEXT, namespace TEXT,
value TEXT);
CREATE UNIQUE INDEX [UNIQ] ON [settings]([name] DESC,[namespace] DESC)
```

Table 10-1 lists the initial settings populated in the database, *settings.db*:

Table 10-1. Initial Database Settings

IdSetting	Name	Namespace	Value
1	title	NULL	Set Example
2	x	position	79
3	y	position	305
4	width	size	220
5	height	size	320

In this example, `title` stores the title of the application. The values x and y within the `position` namespace persist the application's position on the screen. Finally, `width` and `height` within the `size` namespace persist the dimensions of the application's window.

In the JavaScript class there are two methods: `load` and `save`. The `load` method reads everything from the database and loads it into the class itself. The `save` method compares the setting values at load time with the setting values when the method was called, and if something was modified, those entries are updated in the database.

```
var Settings = {

    __db: null,
    __result: null,

    __load: function(dbconn) {
        Settings.__db = dbconn;

        var stmt = new air.SQLStatement();
            stmt.sqlConnection = dbconn;
            stmt.text = "select IdSetting, name, value, namespace from settings";
            stmt.execute();

        var result = stmt.getResult().data;

        Settings.__result = result;

        for( var i=0; i<result.length; i++ ){

            if (result[i].namespace!=null) {
                if (!Settings[result[i].namespace]) {
                    Settings[result[i].namespace] = {};
                }
                Settings[result[i].namespace][result[i].name] = result[i].value;
            } else {
                Settings[result[i].name] = result[i].value;
            }
        }
        stmt = null;
        result = null;
    },

    __save: function() {
        var stmt = new air.SQLStatement();
            stmt.sqlConnection = Settings.__db;

        for (var i = 0; i < Settings.__result.length; i++) {

            if (Settings.__result[i].namespace!=null) {
                if (
Settings[Settings.__result[i].namespace][Settings.__result[i].name] !=
Settings.__result[i].value ) {
                    stmt.text = "update settings set value= :value where name=
:name and namespace= :namespace";
                    stmt.parameters[":name"] = Settings.__result[i].name;
```

```
                        stmt.parameters[":value"] =
Settings[Settings.__result[i].namespace][Settings.__result[i].name];
                        stmt.parameters[":namespace"] = Settings.__result[i].namespace;
                        stmt.execute();
                }
        }
            else {
                if (Settings[Settings.__result[i].name] !=
Settings.__result[i].value) {
                    stmt.text = "update settings set value= :value where name=
:name and namespace IS NULL";
                    stmt.parameters[":name"] = Settings.__result[i].name;
                    stmt.parameters[":value"] =
Settings[Settings.__result[i].name];
                        stmt.execute();
                }

        }


        }
        stmt = null;
    }
};
```

In this class, the method names are prefixed with __ to preserve the class namespace, just in case you have settings named load or save (which would overwrite the methods if they didn't have the prefix).

When you call the __load method and provide it with valid database connection, you can read and write settings like this:

```
Settings.namespace.property
```

For properties that are not designated to a namespace, use this:

```
Settings.property
```

For properties that are assigned a namespace, use this:

```
Settings.position.x = 100;
```

In this example, the application persists its window position on the screen, the window dimensions, and the window title:

```
<html>
<head>
    <script type="text/javascript" src="AIRAliases.js"></script>
    <script type="text/javascript" src="Settings.js"></script>
    <script type="text/javascript">
        var db = null;
        var stmt = null;

        //the settings database in the app directory
        var dbFile =
air.File.applicationStorageDirectory.resolvePath("settings.db");
```

```
            //on application load connect to the db
            function onApplicationLoad() {
                //add handler to save the settings
                window.nativeWindow.addEventListener("closing", onWindowClose);

                //open connection to settings.db database
                db = new air.SQLConnection();
                db.addEventListener( air.SQLEvent.OPEN, onDatabaseOpen );
                db.open( dbFile, air.SQLMode.CREATE );
            }

            //read the settings from db
            function onDatabaseOpen(e) {
                Settings.__load(db);

                //set x, y and window title
                window.nativeWindow.x = Settings.position.x
                window.nativeWindow.y = Settings.position.y;
                window.nativeWindow.width = Settings.size.width;
                window.nativeWindow.height = Settings.size.height;
                window.nativeWindow.title = Settings.title;

                //show the window
                window.nativeWindow.visible = true;
                }

            //method to set window's title
            function setTitle() {
                //update window's title
                window.nativeWindow.title = document.getElementById('titleFld').value;

                //update the settings object
                Settings.title = document.getElementById('titleFld').value;
            }

            //read the x and y before the window is closed and save them to db
            function onWindowClose() {
                Settings.position.x = window.nativeWindow.x;
                Settings.position.y = window.nativeWindow.y;
                Settings.size.width = window.nativeWindow.width;
                Settings.size.height = window.nativeWindow.height;

                //save the settings
                Settings.__save();
            }
        </script>
        <style>
            body {padding: 10px; color: #ccc; background: #333;}
            input {width:190px;}
        </style>
    </head>
    <body onload="onApplicationLoad()">
        Change the title of the application:<hr /><br />

        Window title: <br />
```

```
        <input type="text" id="titleFld" /><br />
    <input type="button" value="Change window title" onClick="setTitle()" />

    <br /><br />
    Change window position on the screen, resize it and change the title and
 these settings will be saved for the next time you run the program
</body>
</html>
```

ActionScript/Flex

Although you can persist application settings in ActionScript in many ways, you can use Adobe's ActionScript library, as3preferenceslib. This library, along with code samples, are at the project site at *http://code.google.com/p/as3preferenceslib/*. A sample application is included with the code.

CHAPTER 11

Encrypted Local Store

Adobe AIR offers several ways to store data locally. You have the legacy option of storing data as a shared object, you can also access the local file system to read and write data, and finally you can write to an embedded SQLite database. When it comes to securing pieces of data like passwords or access keys, your best option is to use the built-in encrypted data store, defined by the `EncryptedLocalStore` class.

 If you need to secure sets of structured data, your best option is to use the embedded SQLite database encryption support covered in Recipe 10.5 and Recipe 10.6.

The data within this store is housed within DPAPI on Windows and within Keychain on Mac OS X using AES-CBC 128-bit encryption.

Once data is written to the encrypted local store, it is accessible only by the application that wrote the data. In addition, the data is stored in a user-specific directory, so each user on the operating system will have a different encrypted local store for the application. For even more restrictive security on data, the encrypted local store also offers an option that ensures that any application attempting to get data from `EncryptedLocalStore` not only has the correct publisher ID but also has had no changes made to the application directory.

The recipes in this chapter will demonstrate how to store and retrieve data from `EncryptedLocalStore`.

11.1 Storing Data in the Encrypted Local Store

Problem

You would like your application to store a serial number that will be used to verify the user with your remote server for data retrieval. It is critical that this information be private and secure.

Solution

Use the `EncryptedLocalStore` class, which is the built-in storage solution within AIR for persisting secure information.

Discussion

The `EncryptedLocalStore` class includes methods to save, retrieve, and remove data from the secure local store. To store data to the encrypted local store, you must first convert it to binary. To convert the data to binary, you can use the `ByteArray` class. The `ByteArray` class is located within the `flash.utils` package and contains methods to read and write data of many different data types to the byte stream.

ActionScript/Flex

To convert a simple piece of `String` data to a `ByteArray`, you can use the `writeUTF Bytes` method. The following simple example takes a variable `serialNumber` and converts it to a `ByteArray` using the `writeUTFBytes` method of the `ByteArray` class. For example:

```
var serialNumber:String = "0000-1234-7777-9876"
var bytes:ByteArray = new ByteArray();
bytes.writeUTFBytes(serialNumber);
```

Now that you have the data in the format needed to save to the encrypted local store, you can complete this simple example by including a fourth line of code, which sets the bytes into the encrypted local store:

```
EncryptedLocalStore.setItem("serialNumber", bytes);
```

The following full example shows a simple form where a user can enter a serial number and persist it to the encrypted local store:

```
<?xml version="1.0" encoding="utf-8"?>
<mx:WindowedApplication xmlns:mx="http://www.adobe.com/2006/mxml" layout="absolute">

    <mx:Script>
        <![CDATA[

            private function saveToLocalStore():void{
                var bytes:ByteArray = new ByteArray();
                bytes.writeUTFBytes(serialNumberTxt.text);
                EncryptedLocalStore.setItem("serialNumber", bytes);
            }

        ]]>
    </mx:Script>

    <mx:HBox horizontalCenter="0" y="134">
        <mx:Label text="Serial Number"/>
        <mx:TextInput id="serialNumberTxt"/>
        <mx:Button label="Save to the encrypted local store"
                    click="saveToLocalStore()"/>
```

```
    </mx:HBox>

</mx:WindowedApplication>
```

JavaScript

To convert a simple piece of String data to a ByteArray, you can use the writeUTF Bytes method. The following simple example takes a variable serialNumber and converts it to a ByteArray using the writeUTFBytes method of the ByteArray class:

```
var serialNumber = "0000-1234-7777-9876"
var bytes = new air.ByteArray();
bytes.writeUTFBytes(serialNumber);
```

Now that you have the data in the format needed to save to the encrypted local store, you can complete this simple example by including a fourth line of code, which sets the bytes into the encrypted local store:

```
air.EncryptedLocalStore.setItem("serialNumber ", bytes);
```

The following full example shows a simple form where a user can enter a serial number and persist it to the encrypted local store:

```
<html>
    <head>
    <script src="AIRAliases.js" />
    <script>

        function saveToLocalStore(){
            var bytes = new air.ByteArray();
            bytes.writeUTFBytes(document.theform.serialNumberTxt.value);
            air.EncryptedLocalStore.setItem("serialNumber", bytes);
        }

    </script>
    </head>
    <body>
        <form name="theform">
            Serial Number: <input type="text" size="20" name="serialNumberTxt"/>
            <input type="button" value="Save to the encrypted local store"
                    onclick="saveToLocalStore()"/>
        </form>
    </body>
</html>
```

11.2 Retrieving Data from the Encrypted Local Store

Problem

You need to retrieve secure data you added to the encrypted local store.

Solution

Use the `getItem` function of the `EncryptedLocalStore` class to retrieve your data from the local store.

Discussion

As mentioned in Recipe 11.1, all data stored within the encrypted local store is stored in binary format as a `flash.utils.ByteArray` and assigned a `String` identifier. To retrieve data from the encrypted local store, you need to know the identifier that it was stored with and also be working within the same AIR application that originally stored the data.

ActionScript/Flex

In the following example, which extends Recipe 11.1, the `getItem` method is called with an identifier of `serialNumber` passed in:

```
var data:ByteArray = EncryptedLocalStore.getItem("serialNumber");
```

Now that you have retrieved the data from the encrypted local store, the only thing left to do is to use the correct `ByteArray`retrieving data in encrypted local stores function to parse the data from binary back to a human-readable format.

The following example adds one line of code, which uses the `readUTFBytes` method to parse the data object into a `String`. This method also requires a single argument that passes the length of the data object.

```
var data:ByteArray = EncryptedLocalStore.getItem("serialNumber");
var serialNumber:String = data.readUTFBytes(data.length);
```

Starting with the code from Recipe 11.1, the following example adds the functionality to retrieve the data from the encrypted local store and display it within a `TextInput` control:

```
<?xml version="1.0" encoding="utf-8"?>
<mx:WindowedApplication xmlns:mx="http://www.adobe.com/2006/mxml" layout="absolute">

    <mx:Script>
        <![CDATA[

            private function saveToLocalStore():void{
                var bytes:ByteArray = new ByteArray();
                bytes.writeUTFBytes(serialNumberTxt.text);
                EncryptedLocalStore.setItem("serialNumber", bytes);
            }

            private function retrieveFromLocalStore():void {
                var data:ByteArray = EncryptedLocalStore.getItem("serialNumber");
                serial.text = data.readUTFBytes(data.length);
            }

        ]]>
```

```
    </mx:Script>

    <mx:HBox horizontalCenter="0" y="134">
        <mx:Label text="Serial Number"/>
        <mx:TextInput id="serialNumberTxt"/>
        <mx:Button label="Save to the encrypted local store"
                       click="saveToLocalStore()"/>
    </mx:HBox>

    <mx:Button label="Retrieve from the encrypted local store"
                 click="retrieveFromLocalStore()" x="263" y="181"/>

    <mx:TextInput id="serial" x="41" y="181" width="214"/>

</mx:WindowedApplication>
```

JavaScript

In the following example, which extends Recipe 11.1, the `getItem` method is called with an identifier of `serialNumber` passed in:

```
var data = air.EncryptedLocalStore.getItem("serialNumber");
```

Now that you have retrieved the data from the encrypted local store, the only step left to take is to use the correct `ByteArray` function to parse the data from binary back to a human-readable format.

The following example adds one line of code, which uses the `readUTFBytes` method to parse the data object into a `String`. This method also requires a single argument that passes the length of the data object.

```
var data = air.EncryptedLocalStore.getItem("serialNumber");
var serialNumber = data.readUTFBytes(data.length);
```

Starting with the code from Recipe 11.1, the following example adds the functionality to retrieve the data from the encrypted local store and display it within an `Input` form field:

```
<html>
    <head>
    <script src="AIRAliases.js" />
    <script>

        function saveToLocalStore(){
            var bytes = new air.ByteArray();
            bytes.writeUTFBytes(document.theform.serialNumberTxt.value);
            air.EncryptedLocalStore.setItem("serialNumber", bytes);
        }

        function retrieveFromLocalStore(){
            var data = air.EncryptedLocalStore.getItem("serialNumber");
            document.theform.serialNumber.value =
            data.readUTFBytes(data.length);
        }
```

```
            </script>
        </head>
        <body>
            <form name="theform">
            Serial Number: <input type="text" size="20" name="serialNumberTxt"/>
            <input type="button" value="Save to the encrypted local store"
                        onclick="saveToLocalStore()"/>
            <br/>
            <input type="text" size="20" name="serialNumber"/>
            <input type="button" value="Retrieve from the encrypted local store"
                        onclick="retrieveFromLocalStore()"/>
            </form>
        </body>
    </html>
```

11.3 Removing and Resetting Data in the Encrypted Local Store

Problem

You have data being stored within the encrypted local store that you would like to delete.

Solution

Use either the removeItem method (which will remove the single item) or the reset method (which will clear the entire store) of the EncryptedLocalStore class to remove data from the encrypted local store.

Discussion

Data stored in encrypted local store persists until either the application that created it removes it by identifier or the encrypted local store is reset. Even uninstalling the application will not remove the data that was persisted, so it is up to the developer to remove any data that is no longer necessary.

To remove a single item from the local store, you use the removeItem method. This method accepts a single argument of type String that is the identifier that the data was associated with when persisted.

ActionScript/Flex

The following example removes an item under the identifier serialNumber from the encrypted local store:

```
EncryptedLocalStore.removeItem("serialNumber");
```

The second way to remove data from the encrypted local store is to use the reset method. The reset method will remove all data that is stored within the EncryptedLo calStore that is being stored for the accompanying application.

The following example utilizes the **reset** method to clear all data from the Encrypted LocalStore:

```
EncryptedLocalStore.reset();
```

The following full example includes code to save data to the encrypted local store from Recipe 11.1 and includes code to retrieve data from the encrypted local store from Recipe 11.2. It also adds the functions to remove data or reset the entire encrypted local store data set associated with the application.

Note that if you attempt to retrieve data with an identifier that has been removed or not yet saved, you will get a runtime error (specifically, error #1009: "Cannot access a property or method of a null object reference").

```
<?xml version="1.0" encoding="utf-8"?>
<mx:WindowedApplication xmlns:mx="http://www.adobe.com/2006/mxml"
layout="absolute">

    <mx:Script>
        <![CDATA[

            private function saveToLocalStore():void{
                var bytes:ByteArray = new ByteArray();
                bytes.writeUTFBytes(serialNumberTxt.text);
                EncryptedLocalStore.setItem("serialNumber", bytes);
            }

            private function retrieveFromLocalStore():void {
                var data:ByteArray = EncryptedLocalStore.getItem("serialNumber");
                serial.text = data.readUTFBytes(data.length);
            }

            private function removeFromLocalStore():void{
                EncryptedLocalStore.removeItem("serialNumber");
            }

            private function resetLocalStore():void{
                EncryptedLocalStore.reset();
            }

        ]]>
    </mx:Script>

    <mx:HBox horizontalCenter="0" y="134">
        <mx:Label text="Serial Number"/>
        <mx:TextInput id="serialNumberTxt"/>
        <mx:Button label="Save to the encrypted local store"
                    click="saveToLocalStore()"/>
    </mx:HBox>

    <mx:Button label="Retrieve from the encrypted local store"
                click="retrieveFromLocalStore()" x="263" y="181"/>

    <mx:TextInput id="serial" x="41" y="181" width="214"/>
```

```
    <mx:Button x="153" y="220" label="Remove from the encrypted local store"
        click="removeFromLocalStore()"/>

    <mx:Button x="164.5" y="250" label="Reset the encrypted local store"
        click="resetLocalStore()"/>

</mx:WindowedApplication>
```

JavaScript

The following example removes an item under the identifier `serialNumber` from the encrypted local store:

```
air.EncryptedLocalStore.removeItem("serialNumber");
```

The second way to remove data from the encrypted local store is to use the `reset` method. The `reset` method will remove all data that is stored within the `Encrypted LocalStore` that is being stored for the accompanying application.

The following example utilizes the `reset` method to clear all data from the `Encrypted LocalStore`:

```
air.EncryptedLocalStore.reset();
```

The following full example includes code to save data to the encrypted local store from Recipe 11.1 and includes code to retrieve data from the encrypted local store from Recipe 11.2. It also adds the functions to remove data or reset the entire EncryptedLocalStore.

```
<html>
    <head>
    <script src="AIRAliases.js" />
    <script>

    function saveToLocalStore(){
        var bytes = new air.ByteArray();
        bytes.writeUTFBytes(document.theform.serialNumberTxt.value);
        air.EncryptedLocalStore.setItem("serialNumber", bytes);            }

    function retrieveFromLocalStore(){
        var data = air.EncryptedLocalStore.getItem("serialNumber");
        document.theform.serialNumber.value = data.readUTFBytes(data.length);   }

    function removeFromLocalStore(){
        air.EncryptedLocalStore.removeItem("serialNumber");
    }

    function resetLocalStore(){
        air.EncryptedLocalStore.reset();
    }

    </script>
    </head>
    <body>
        <form name="theform">
```

```
Serial Number: <input type="text" size="20" name="serialNumberTxt"/>
<input type="button" value="Save to the encrypted local store"
        onclick="saveToLocalStore()"/>
<br/>
<input type="text" size="20" name="serialNumber"/>
<input type="button" value="Retrieve from the encrypted local store"
        onclick="retrieveFromLocalStore()"/>
<br/>
<input type="button" value="Remove from the encrypted local store"
        onclick="removeFromLocalStore()"/>
<br/>
<input type="button" value="Reset the encrypted local store"
        onclick="resetLocalStore()"/>
</form>
</body>
</html>
```

11.4 Storing Application-Specific Data in the Encrypted Local Store

Problem

Your client requires more data security than the standard encrypted local store settings enable.

Solution

When adding data to the encrypted local store, set stronglyBound, the optional third argument of the setItem method, to true.

Discussion

Data stored within the encrypted local store is accessible to only the AIR application that originally saved the data because it is bound to the application's publisher ID. However, for an even higher level of security, you can set the stronglyBound argument of the setItem method to true. Setting this property to true within the setItem method binds the data to the actual bits of the application. This ensures that any application that attempts to get data from the encrypted local store not only has the correct publisher ID but also has had no changes made to its application directory.

Be aware, however, that this extra layer of protection comes with some trade-off. Because no changes can be made to the application directory, you will lose any strongly Bound data stored within the encrypted local store when your application is updated to a newer version. To avoid runtime errors, you must account for this when coding your application with stronglyBound data.

ActionScript/Flex

The following example is identical to the one used within Recipe 11.1 with the only change being the optional third argument of the **setItem** method set to **true**. This alters the data being stored within the encrypted local store to be **stronglyBound**.

```
var serialNumber:String = "0000-1234-7777-9876"
var bytes:ByteArray = new ByteArray();
bytes.writeUTFBytes(serialNumber);
EncryptedLocalStore.setItem("serialNumber ", bytes, true);
```

Here is a full example showing a simple form where a user can enter a serial number and persist it to the encrypted local store where the data is **stronglyBound** to the application:

```
<?xml version="1.0" encoding="utf-8"?>
<mx:WindowedApplication xmlns:mx="http://www.adobe.com/2006/mxml"
layout="absolute">

    <mx:Script>
        <![CDATA[

            private function saveToLocalStore():void{
                var bytes:ByteArray = new ByteArray();
                bytes.writeUTFBytes(serialNumberTxt.text);
                EncryptedLocalStore.setItem("serialNumber", bytes, true);
            }

        ]]>
    </mx:Script>

    <mx:HBox horizontalCenter="0" y="134">
        <mx:Label text="Serial Number"/>
        <mx:TextInput id="serialNumberTxt"/>
        <mx:Button label="Save to the encrypted local store"
                        click="saveToLocalStore()"/>
    </mx:HBox>

</mx:WindowedApplication>
```

JavaScript

The following example is identical to the one used within Recipe 11.1 with the only change being the optional third argument of the **setItem** method set to **true**. This alters the data being stored within the encrypted local store to be **stronglyBound**.

```
var serialNumber = "0000-1234-7777-9876"
var bytes = new air.ByteArray();
bytes.writeUTFBytes(serialNumber);
air.EncryptedLocalStore.setItem("serialNumber", bytes, true);
```

Here is a full example showing a simple form where a user can enter a serial number and persist it to the encrypted local store where the data is **stronglyBound** to the application:

```
<html>
    <head>
    <script src="AIRAliases.js" />
    <script>

        function saveToLocalStore(){
            var bytes = new air.ByteArray();
            bytes.writeUTFBytes(document.theform.serialNumberTxt.value);
            air.EncryptedLocalStore.setItem("serialNumber", bytes, true);
        }

    </script>
    </head>
    <body>
        <form name="theform">
            Serial Number: <input type="text" size="20" name="serialNumberTxt"/>
        <input type="button" value="Save to the encrypted local store"
                onclick="saveToLocalStore()"/>
        </form>
    </body>
</html>
```

11.5 Safeguarding Files with Encrypted Local Store

Contributed by Ryan Stewart (http://blog.digitalbackcountry.com/)

Problem

You need to protect entire files inside an AIR application.

Solution

Using the EncryptedLocalStore and the File APIs you can put a file in a safe and secure location.

Discussion

Most people associate the encrypted local store with storing usernames and passwords or other bits of text. But thanks to the fact that EncryptedLocalStore uses instances of the ByteArray class, it's easy to throw all kinds of things in there. This recipe offers two examples for saving data into the encrypted local store and loading it back out.

There are couple of items to keep in mind when working with entire files in Encrypted LocalStore. First, the EncryptedLocalStore is supported only up to 10MB. It can go higher, but you may see performance problems. In addition, the encrypted local store isn't cleared out when the application is uninstalled. You may have to manually clear it out using the reset method.

In this example, two methods handle the interaction with the EncryptedLocalStore: saveFile and loadFile.

The `saveFile` function takes a `File` object (which could be from a drag-and-drop operation or a file open dialog box), and it also contains start a `ByteArray` that will store the file data. Just like any other File API, there needs to be a stream to put the bytes into the `ByteArray`. When that is complete, the application grabs the name of the file so that it can reference it later. It then uses `EncryptedLocalStore.setItem` to add the file data to the encrypted local store.

The next function is the `loadFile` function. It takes the data out of `EncryptedLocal Store` and saves it to the hard drive. It also takes a `File` object so that the application knows where to store the file when it is finished reading it. Just like with any other File API, a `ByteArray` is created that will contain the file bits. Then the `EncryptedLocal Store.getItem` method is called to grab the data out of the encrypted local store. When that is complete, a new `FileStream` is created, and it writes that file data to the file.

If you ever need to clear the encrypted local store, you can just call the `EncryptedLocal Store.reset` function, and that will wipe away the data. The `EncryptedLocalStore` APIs are some of the easiest in AIR, but they allow for the ability to save and protect all kinds of data thanks to the `ByteArray`.

ActionScript/Flex

Here is the completed application in Flex with both the `saveFile` and `loadFile` methods:

```
<?xml version="1.0" encoding="utf-8"?>
<mx:WindowedApplication xmlns:mx="http://www.adobe.com/2006/mxml"
layout="absolute">
    <mx:Script>
        <![CDATA[
            import mx.events.FileEvent;

            public function onSaveClick(event:Event) : void
            {
                // Clear out everything
                EncryptedLocalStore.reset();

                var file : File = new File();
                file.browseForOpen("Save File in Encrypted Local Store");
                // Add the event listener for the selection
                file.addEventListener(Event.SELECT,
                    function onSaveSelect(event:Event) : void
                    {
                        saveFile(event.currentTarget as File);
                    });
            }

            public function saveFile(file:File) : void
            {
                var stream : FileStream = new FileStream();

                var filedataArray : ByteArray = new ByteArray();
                stream.open(file, FileMode.READ);
                stream.readBytes(filedataArray, 0, file.size);
```

```
                    stream.close();
                    // Set the file name so we can pull it out later.
                    fileName = file.name;

                    // Set the item in the Encrypted Local Store
                    EncryptedLocalStore.setItem(fileName,filedataArray);
                }

                public function onLoadClick(event:Event) : void
                {
                    var file : File = File.desktopDirectory.resolvePath(fileName);
                    file.addEventListener(Event.SELECT,
                        function onLoadSelect(event:Event) : void
                        {
                            loadFile(event.currentTarget as File);
                        });
                    file.browseForSave("Load File From Encrypted Local Store");
                }

                public function loadFile(file:File) : void
                {
                    // Create the ByteArray and pull it out of the local store
                    var byteArray : ByteArray = new ByteArray();
                    byteArray = EncryptedLocalStore.getItem(fileName);

                    // Open and write the file using the regular File APIs
                    var stream : FileStream = new FileStream();
                    stream.open(file, FileMode.WRITE)
                    stream.writeBytes(byteArray);
                    stream.close();
                }

                private var fileName : String;

            ]]>
        </mx:Script>
        <mx:Label text="Click the button below to save a file into the
    Encrypted Local Store" />
        <mx:Button id="btnSave" click="onSaveClick(event)" label="Save
     File to Encrypted Local Store" />
        <mx:Label text="Click the button below to save the file from the Encrypted
    Local Store back to your hard drive" />
        <mx:Button id="btnLoad" click="onLoadClick(event)" label="Load File from
    Encrpted Local Store" y="50" />
    </mx:WindowedApplication>
```

JavaScript

Here is the completed application in JavaScript with both the saveFile and loadFile methods:

```
<html>
    <head>
        <title>Encrypted Local Store File Storage</title>
        <script type="text/javascript" src="AIRAliases.js"></script>
```

```
<script type="text/javascript">

      var fileName;

   function onSaveClick(event) {
           // Clear out everything
           air.EncryptedLocalStore.reset();
           var file = new air.File();
           file.browseForOpen("Save File in Encrypted Local Store");
           // Add the event listener for the selection
           file.addEventListener(air.Event.SELECT,onSaveSelect);
      }

      function onSaveSelect(event) {
           saveFile(event.currentTarget);
      }

      function saveFile(file) {
           var stream = new air.FileStream();

           var filedataArray = new air.ByteArray();
           stream.open(file, air.FileMode.READ);
           stream.readBytes(filedataArray, 0, file.size);
           stream.close();
           // Set the file name so we can pull it out later.
           fileName = file.name;
           // Set the item in the Encrypted Local Store
           air.EncryptedLocalStore.setItem(fileName,filedataArray);
      }

      function onLoadClick(event) {
           var file = air.File.desktopDirectory.resolvePath(fileName);
           file.addEventListener(air.Event.SELECT,onLoadSelect);
           file.browseForSave("Load File From Encrypted Local Store");
      }

      function onLoadSelect(event) {
           loadFile(event.currentTarget);
      }

      function loadFile(file) {
           // Create the ByteArray and pull it out of the local store
           var byteArray = new air.ByteArray();
           byteArray = air.EncryptedLocalStore.getItem(fileName);

           // Open and write the file using the regular File APIs
           var stream = new air.FileStream();
           stream.open(file, air.FileMode.WRITE)
           stream.writeBytes(byteArray);
           stream.close();
      }

   </script>
</head>
```

```
<body>
<p>Click the button below to save a file into the Encrypted Local Store</p>
<input type="button" value="Save File to Encrypted Local Store"
onclick="onSaveClick(event)" /><br />
<p> Click the button below to save the file from the Encrypted Local Store back
to your hard drive</p>
<input type="button" value="Load File from Encrpted Local Store"
onclick="onLoadClick(event)" />
</body>
</html>
```

CHAPTER 12

Application and Window Native Menus

Operating systems provide facilities for creating menus; these menus are called *native menus*. Adobe AIR supports working with native menus, and the recipes in this chapter show you how to build several types of native menus. At this writing, AIR supports application, window, context, and pop-up menus. Application and window menus serve the same purpose but on different platforms. Specifically, window menus are available only on Windows, and application menus are available only on Macs. Computer users are familiar with the typical native menus, so the usability of your AIR application improves a lot when you offer users application or window menus.

To create native menus, the Adobe AIR classes to use are `flash.display.NativeMenu` and `flash.display.NativeMenuItem`.

To create context menus, you can also use the classes `flash.ui.ContextMenu` and `flash.ui.ContextMenuItem`.

 AIR enables you to create system tray and Dock icon menus as well. See Chapter 13 for more information on these custom taskbar and Dock menus.

12.1 Creating a Native Menu

Problem

You want to create a menu for your AIR application and present the menu as an application menu or window menu depending on the user's operating system.

Solution

Use the `NativeMenu` constructor to create the base menu, attach child `NativeMenuItem` objects, and then set the top-level base menu as the menu for the AIR application or window depending on your preference or the operating system.

Discussion

When working with the AIR menu API, always keep in mind that menus are platform specific. Table 12-1 points out two important differences between native menus in an AIR application deployed on Windows vs. a Mac.

Table 12-1. Native Menus in an AIR Application: Windows vs. Mac

	Windows	Mac
Supported menu?	Window menu	Application menu
Default menu present?	No	Yes

On Windows, you can create a native window menu that applies only to a particular window and is automatically displayed below the title bar. To add a native menu to a window, create a `NativeMenu` object, and assign it to the `menu` property of the `Native Window` object (covered in Recipe 12.5).

On Mac, you can create a native application menu that applies to the whole application only. Every application running on Mac OS X creates a default application menu to which you can add items, add subitems, or remove existing items.

To add a native menu to your application on a Mac, create a `NativeMenu` object, and assign it to the `menu` property of the `NativeApplication` object (covered in Recipe 12.6).

To create a `NativeMenu` object as the top-level menu for an application or window menu, just use the `NativeWindow` constructor:

```
var baseMenu:NativeMenu = new NativeMenu();
```

ActionScript/Flex

The following code shows the start of a new AIR application that creates a window menu on Windows and an application menu on a Mac:

```
<?xml version="1.0" encoding="utf-8"?>
<mx:WindowedApplication xmlns:mx="http://www.adobe.com/2006/mxml"
    layout="absolute"applicationComplete="init()>
    <mx:Script>
        <![CDATA[

        private function init():void{

            var baseMenu:NativeMenu = new NativeMenu();
            var myMenu:NativeMenu = new NativeMenu();>
            baseMenu.addSubmenu(myMenu, "Example Menu");

            if(NativeApplication.supportsMenu){
                this.nativeApplication.menu = baseMenu;
            }

            if(NativeWindow.supportsMenu){
                this.nativeWindow.menu = baseMenu;
```

```
                }
            }
        ]]></mx:Script>
    </mx:WindowedApplication>
```

ActionScript/Flash

If you are using Flash for your AIR application and windows, you need to set this ActionScript class as the document class for your Flash file:

```
package com.newmovieclip.aircookbook.chapter12{

    import flash.display.*;
    import flash.desktop.*;

    public class Step1 extends Sprite{

        public function Step1():void{
            var baseMenu:NativeMenu = new NativeMenu();
            var myMenu:NativeMenu = new NativeMenu();
            baseMenu.addSubmenu(myMenu, "Example Menu");
            if(NativeApplication.supportsMenu){
                NativeApplication.nativeApplication.menu = baseMenu;
            }
            if(NativeWindow.supportsMenu){
                this.stage.nativeWindow.menu = baseMenu;
            }
        }
    }
}
```

JavaScript

The following code shows the start of a new AIR application that creates a window menu on Windows and an application menu on a Mac:

```
<html>
<head>
<meta http-equiv="Content-Type" content="text/html; charset=utf-8" />
<title>Create Native Menu step 1</title>

<script src="AIRAliases.js" type="text/javascript"></script>
<script type="text/javascript">
function initialize(){
    var application = air.NativeApplication.nativeApplication;

    var baseMenu = new air.NativeMenu();
    var myMenu = new air.NativeMenu();
    baseMenu.addSubmenu(myMenu, "Example Menu");

    if(air.NativeApplication.supportsMenu){
        application.menu= baseMenu;
    }
    if(air.NativeWindow.supportsMenu){
        this.nativeWindow.menu = baseMenu
```

```
        }
    }
    </script>
    </head>
    <body onLoad="initialize()">
    </body>
    </html>
```

Adding Items to the Base Menu

Next, you must add menu items to the top-level menu. To begin, create an instance of the NativeMenuItem class by calling the constructor and passing in the label for the menu item as a parameter. Two methods are available to add a menu item to a menu: addItemAt and addItem. The first way, using addItemAt, allows you to specify the index position where you want to add the menu item, with the position count starting at 0.

In ActionScript/Flex/Flash, the code for this is as follows:

```
<mx:Script>
    <![CDATA[

        private function init():void{

            var baseMenu:NativeMenu = new NativeMenu();

            var menuItemA:NativeMenuItem = new NativeMenuItem("Menu Item A");
            baseMenu.addItemAt(menuItemA,0);


            if(NativeApplication.supportsMenu) {
                this.nativeApplication.menu.addSubmenu(baseMenu, "Example Menu");
            }

            if(NativeWindow.supportsMenu) {
                this.nativeWindow.menu.addSubmenu(baseMenu, "Example Menu");
            }

        }   ]]>
    </mx:Script>

    var menuItemA:NativeMenuItem = new NativeMenuItem("Menu Item A");
    baseMenu.addItemAt(menuItemA,0);
```

In JavaScript, the code is as follows:

```
    var menuItemA = new air.NativeMenuItem("Menu Item A");
    baseMenu.addItemAt(menuItemA,0);
```

The second way to add items to a menu is to use the addItem method. To use this method, you just need to replace the addItemAt method with the addItem method in the previous code examples, but you do not need to provide an index position, because the menu items are placed in the same order as you add them.

You can make your native menus more accessible for the user in two ways. The first is by using keyboard shortcuts, and the second is by setting a mnemonic index.

The first way, adding keyboard shortcuts to your menu, is explained in Recipe 12.9.

The second possibility to make your menu more accessible and usable is by setting a mnemonic index. A *mnemonic* is a memory aid; in `NativeMenuItem` objects in AIR, the *mnemonic index* refers to a character in the menu label at the corresponding position, and in the display, the character at this index is underlined. On Windows, the menu item is accessible by pressing that underlined key when the menu is in focus. On a Mac, this mnemonic index is irrelevant, because the default mnemonic for the menu item is the first letter or two of the menu, followed by pressing the Return key.

If you have more menu items that use the same significant letter on Windows, the user has to press that key as many times as necessary to cycle through the matching items until the desired item is highlighted; then the user presses Enter. For ease of use, a best practice is to try to choose a unique significant letter for every menu item because it makes the user experience more enjoyable.

You can set a significant letter (a mnemonic) using a position index of the label `String`. Keep in mind that the index starts at 0. The following example uses the letter *u* as the mnemonic:

```
var menuItemC:NativeMenuItem = new NativeMenuItem("Menu Item C");
menuItemC.keyEquivalent = "C";

menuItemC.mnemonicIndex=10;
```

By combining key equivalents and mnemonics, you can make your menus more accessible, so it is a best practice to use both methods.

12.2 Responding to Menu Events

Problem

You have created a menu in your AIR application and want to react to the events dispatched by the `nativeMenu` and `NativeMenuItem` objects.

Solution

Add an event listener for selecting and displaying events of the `NativeMenu` or `NativeMenuItem` object.

Discussion

When a user chooses a menu item, the NativeMenuItem dispatches a select event. By registering a listener to the NativeMenuItem object, you can react to the select event.

ActionScript/Flex/Flash

In this example, you first create a new instance of the NativeMenuItem class. Next you add a listener to listen for the select event. When the select event is dispatched by the NativeMenuItem instance, the selectHandler function is executed:

```
var menuItemC:NativeMenuItem = new NativeMenuItem("Menu Item C");
menuItemC.addEventListener(Event.SELECT,selectHandler);

private function selectHandler(event:Event):void{
    trace(event.target.label);
}
```

JavaScript

The following code makes a menu item and attaches a listener to it for the select event:

```
var menuItemC = new air.NativeMenuItem("Menu Item C");
menuItemC.addEventListener(air.Event.SELECT,selectHandler);
```

The selectHandler function in JavaScript looks like this:

```
function selectHandler(event){
    air.trace(event.target.label);
}
```

This example just traces the label, but of course in a real-life situation you would write your specific actions for that menu item in the selectHandler function.

Listening for Select Events

Because select events bubble up to the containing menus, you can also listen for select events on a parent menu.

ActionScript/Flex

This simple menu example traces the label of the selected menu item but registers only one listener to the base menu:

```
<?xml version="1.0" encoding="utf-8"?>
<mx:WindowedApplication xmlns:mx="http://www.adobe.com/2006/mxml"
    layout="absolute"
    applicationComplete="init()"
    >
    <mx:Script>
        <![CDATA[

            private function init():void{
```

```
                var baseMenu:NativeMenu = new NativeMenu();

                var menuItemEng:NativeMenuItem = new NativeMenuItem("English");
                var menuItemEs:NativeMenuItem = new NativeMenuItem("Spanish");
                var menuItemDe:NativeMenuItem = new NativeMenuItem("German");
                var menuItemNl:NativeMenuItem = new NativeMenuItem("Dutch");

                baseMenu.addItem(menuItemEng);
                baseMenu.addItem(menuItemEs);
                baseMenu.addItem(menuItemDe);
                baseMenu.addItem(menuItemNl);

                baseMenu.addEventListener(Event.SELECT,selectHandler);

                if(NativeApplication.supportsMenu){
                    this.nativeApplication.menu = baseMenu;
                }

                if(NativeWindow.supportsMenu){
                    this.nativeWindow.menu = baseMenu;
                }
            }
            private function selectHandler(event:Event):void{
                    trace(event.target.label);
            }
        ]]>
    </mx:Script>
</mx:WindowedApplication>
```

ActionScript/Flash

This simple menu example traces the label of the selected menu item but registers only one listener to the base menu:

```
package com.newmovieclip.aircookbook.chapter12{

    import flash.display.*;
    import flash.desktop.*;
    import flash.events.*;

    public class Step3 extends Sprite{

        public function Step3():void{
            var baseMenu:NativeMenu = new NativeMenu();

            var menuItemEng:NativeMenuItem = new NativeMenuItem("English");
            var menuItemEs:NativeMenuItem = new NativeMenuItem("Spanish");
            var menuItemDe:NativeMenuItem = new NativeMenuItem("German");
            var menuItemNl:NativeMenuItem = new NativeMenuItem("Dutch");

            baseMenu.addItem(menuItemEng);
            baseMenu.addItem(menuItemEs);
            baseMenu.addItem(menuItemDe);
            baseMenu.addItem(menuItemNl);
```

```
            baseMenu.addEventListener(Event.SELECT,selectHandler);

            if(NativeApplication.supportsMenu){
                NativeApplication.nativeApplication.menu = baseMenu;
            }
            if(NativeWindow.supportsMenu){
                this.stage.nativeWindow.menu = baseMenu;
            }
        }
        private function selectHandler(event:Event):void{
            trace(event.target.label);
        }
    }
}
```

JavaScript

This simple menu example traces the label of the selected menu item but registers only one listener to the base menu:

```
<html xmlns="http://www.w3.org/1999/xhtml">
<head>
<meta http-equiv="Content-Type" content="text/html; charset=utf-8" />
<title>Create Native Menu step 3</title>

<script src="AIRAliases.js" type="text/javascript"></script>
<script type="text/javascript">
function initialize(){
    var application = air.NativeApplication.nativeApplication;
    var baseMenu = new air.NativeMenu();

    var menuItemEng = new air.NativeMenuItem("English");
    var menuItemEs = new air.NativeMenuItem("Spanish");
    var menuItemDe = new air.NativeMenuItem("German");
    var menuItemNL = new air.NativeMenuItem("Dutch");

    baseMenu.addItem(menuItemEng);
    baseMenu.addItem(menuItemEs);
    baseMenu.addItem(menuItemDe);
    baseMenu.addItem(menuItemNL);

    baseMenu.addEventListener(air.Event.SELECT,selectHandler);

    if(air.NativeApplication.supportsMenu){
        application.menu= baseMenu;
    }
    if(air.NativeWindow.supportsMenu){
        this.nativeWindow.menu = baseMenu
    }
}
function selectHandler(event){
    air.trace(event.target.label);
}
</script>
</head>
```

```
<body onLoad="initialize()">
</body>
</html>
```

Updating Before Display

Regarding menu display listeners, imagine that you want to update the menu contents or item appearance before the menu is shown to the user. This is where the `displaying` menu event comes in. The `displaying` event is dispatched just before a menu is displayed to the user. For example, in the listener for the displaying event of a History menu, you could change the menu items to reflect the current list of recently viewed documents.

ActionScript/Flex/Flash

The following code shows how to register a listener for the `displaying` event, which is similar to using the `select` event:

```
var baseMenu:NativeMenu = new NativeMenu();
var historyMenuItem:NativeMenuItem = new NativeMenuItem("History");
basemenu.addItem(historyMenuItem);
historyMenuItem.addEventListener(Event.DISPLAYING, displayingHandler);

private function displayingHandler(event:Event):void{

    //update the recently viewed documents
    trace("displaying");
}
```

JavaScript

The following code shows how to register a listener for the `displaying` event, which is similar to using the `select` event:

```
var baseMenu = new air.NativeMenu();
var historyMenuItem = new air.NativeMenuItem("history");
baseMenu.addItem(historyMenuItem);
historyMenuItem.addEventListener(air.Event.DISPLAYING, displayingHandler);

function displayingHandler(event){

    //update the recently viewed documents
    air.trace("displaying");
}
```

12.3 Adding a Menu Separator

Problem

You want to add a menu separator line inside a native menu.

Solution

Instantiate a `NativeMenuItem`, and in the constructor, set the second parameter (`isSeparator`) to true; then add the instance to the `NativeMenu` instance.

Discussion

Adding a menu separator is actually simple; you add it like it is a regular menu item and then specify that it actually is a separator. You can do that in the second parameter of the `nativeMenuItem` constructor. It is not necessary to give the menu item a label because it is not displayed. In following example, the label for the separator is left blank.

ActionScript/Flex/Flash

In ActionScript/Flex/Flash, use the following code:

```
var baseMenu:NativeMenu = new NativeMenu();

    var menuItemEng:NativeMenuItem = new NativeMenuItem("English");
    var menuItemEs:NativeMenuItem = new NativeMenuItem("Spanish");
    var menuItemDe:NativeMenuItem = new NativeMenuItem("German");
    var menuItemNl:NativeMenuItem = new NativeMenuItem("Dutch");
    var mySeparator:NativeMenuItem = new NativeMenuItem("",true);

    baseMenu.addItem(menuItemEng);
    baseMenu.addItem(menuItemEs);

    baseMenu.addItem(mySeparator);

    baseMenu.addItem(menuItemDe);
    baseMenu.addItem(menuItemNl);
```

JavaScript

In JavaScript, use this code:

```
var baseMenu = new air.NativeMenu();

    var menuItemEng = new air.NativeMenuItem("English");
    var menuItemEs = new air.NativeMenuItem("Spanish");
    var menuItemDe = new air.NativeMenuItem("German");
    var menuItemNL = new air.NativeMenuItem("Dutch");

    var mySeparator = new air.NativeMenuItem("",true);

    baseMenu.addItem(menuItemEng);
    baseMenu.addItem(menuItemEs);
    baseMenu.addItem(mySeparator);
    baseMenu.addItem(menuItemDe);
    baseMenu.addItem(menuItemNL);
```

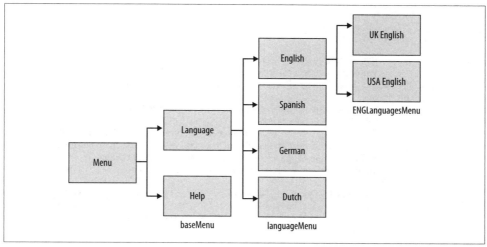

Figure 12-1. Nested menu structure

12.4 Creating Nested Menus

Problem

You want to create a more advanced menu that has a nested menu structure.

Solution

Create a submenu in the given menu item by setting the `submenu` property of the menu item.

Discussion

To create a nested menu structure, you add a `NativeMenuItem` object to the parent menu and then assign the `NativeMenu` object to the menu item's `submenu` property. You can also write it in a shorter way by using the `addSubmenu` method of the `NativeMenu` class.

The following example uses both ways to create the nested menu structure shown in Figure 12-1.

ActionScript/Flex

For a nested menu structure, use this code:

```
<?xml version="1.0" encoding="utf-8"?>
<mx:WindowedApplication xmlns:mx="http://www.adobe.com/2006/mxml"
    layout="absolute"
    applicationComplete="init()"
    >
    <mx:Script>
```

```
<![CDATA[

    private function init():void{

        var baseMenu:NativeMenu = new NativeMenu();
        var languageMenu:NativeMenu = new NativeMenu();
        var engLanguagesMenu:NativeMenu = new NativeMenu();

        var menuItemEng:NativeMenuItem = new NativeMenuItem("English");
        //define submenu items
            engLanguagesMenu.addItem(new NativeMenuItem("UK English"));
            engLanguagesMenu.addItem(new NativeMenuItem("USA English"));
        //add the engLanguagesMenu as submenu of menuItemEng
        menuItemEng.submenu = engLanguagesMenu;

        var menuItemEs:NativeMenuItem = new NativeMenuItem("Spanish");
        var menuItemDe:NativeMenuItem = new NativeMenuItem("German");
        var menuItemNl:NativeMenuItem = new NativeMenuItem("Dutch");

        languageMenu.addItem(menuItemEng);
        languageMenu.addItem(menuItemEs);
        languageMenu.addItem(menuItemDe);
        languageMenu.addItem(menuItemNl);

        //add all the languages as submenu of the baseMenu
        //with a label 'Language'
        baseMenu.addSubmenu(languageMenu,"Language");
        baseMenu.addItem(new NativeMenuItem("Help"));
        baseMenu.addEventListener(Event.SELECT,selectHandler);

        if(NativeApplication.supportsMenu){
            this.nativeApplication.menu = baseMenu;
        }

        if(NativeWindow.supportsMenu){
            this.nativeWindow.menu = baseMenu;
        }
    }
    private function selectHandler(event:Event):void{
            trace(event.target.label);
    }
]]>
    </mx:Script>
</mx:WindowedApplication>
```

ActionScript/Flash

The code for a nested menu structure is as follows:

```
package com.newmovieclip.aircookbook.chapter12{

    import flash.display.*;
    import flash.desktop.*;
    import flash.events.*;
```

```
        public class Step4 extends Sprite{

            public function Step4():void{
                var baseMenu:NativeMenu = new NativeMenu();
                var languageMenu:NativeMenu = new NativeMenu();
                var engLanguagesMenu:NativeMenu = new NativeMenu();

                var menuItemEng:NativeMenuItem = new NativeMenuItem("English");
                //define submenu items
                    engLanguagesMenu.addItem(new NativeMenuItem("UK English"));
                    engLanguagesMenu.addItem(new NativeMenuItem("USA English"));
                //add the engLanguagesMenu as submenu of menuItemEng
                menuItemEng.submenu = ENGLanguagesMenu;
                var menuItemEs:NativeMenuItem = new NativeMenuItem("Spanish");
                var menuItemDe:NativeMenuItem = new NativeMenuItem("German");
                var menuItemNl:NativeMenuItem = new NativeMenuItem("Dutch");

                languageMenu.addItem(menuItemEng);
                languageMenu.addItem(menuItemEs);
                languageMenu.addItem(menuItemDe);
                languageMenu.addItem(menuItemNl);

                //add all the languages as submenu of the baseMenu
                //with label 'Language'
                baseMenu.addSubmenu(languageMenu,"language");
                baseMenu.addItem(new NativeMenuItem("Help"));
                baseMenu.addEventListener(Event.SELECT,selectHandler);

                if(NativeApplication.supportsMenu){
                    NativeApplication.nativeApplication.menu = baseMenu;
                }
                if(NativeWindow.supportsMenu){
                    this.stage.nativeWindow.menu = baseMenu;
                }
            }
            private function selectHandler(event:Event):void{
                trace(event.target.label);
            }
        }
    }
```

JavaScript

To create a nested menu structure, follow this example:

```
<html xmlns="http://www.w3.org/1999/xhtml">
<head>
<meta http-equiv="Content-Type" content="text/html; charset=utf-8" />
<title>Create Native Menu step 3</title>

<script src="AIRAliases.js" type="text/javascript"></script>
<script type="text/javascript">
function initialize(){
    var application = air.NativeApplication.nativeApplication;
    var baseMenu = new air.NativeMenu();
```

```
            var languageMenu = new air.NativeMenu();
            var englLanguagesMenu = new air.NativeMenu();

            var menuItemEng = new air.NativeMenuItem("English");
            //define submenu items
                englLanguagesMenu.addItem(new air.NativeMenuItem("UK English"));
                englLanguagesMenu.addItem(new air.NativeMenuItem("USA English"));
            //add the englLanguagesMenu as submenu of menuItemEng
            menuItemEng.submenu = englLanguagesMenu;
            var menuItemEs = new air.NativeMenuItem("Spanish");
            var menuItemDe = new air.NativeMenuItem("German");
            var menuItemNL = new air.NativeMenuItem("Dutch");

            languageMenu.addItem(menuItemEng);
            languageMenu.addItem(menuItemEs);
            languageMenu.addItem(menuItemDe);
            languageMenu.addItem(menuItemNL);

            //add all the languages as submenu of the baseMenu
            //with label 'language'
            baseMenu.addSubmenu(languageMenu,"Language");
            baseMenu.addItem(new air.NativeMenuItem("Help"));
            baseMenu.addEventListener(air.Event.SELECT,selectHandler);

            if(air.NativeApplication.supportsMenu){
                application.menu= baseMenu;
            }
            if(air.NativeWindow.supportsMenu){
                this.nativeWindow.menu = baseMenu
            }
        }
        function selectHandler(event){
            air.trace(event.target.label);
        }
        </script>
        </head>
        <body onLoad="initialize()">
        </body>
        </html>
```

12.5 Creating a Native Window Menu (Windows)

Problem

You want to create a native window menu that works on the Windows platform.

Solution

Add a native menu to a window by creating a NativeMenu object, and assign it to the menu property of the NativeWindow object.

Discussion

You can check whether the user is on a Mac or Windows platform by using the `NativeWindow.supportsMenu` Boolean value. If that value returns `true`, then you are sure the user is on a Windows platform, because at the time of this writing only the Windows platform will return `true` for this property.

For ActionScript/Flex, use the following lines:

```
if(NativeWindow.supportsMenu){
    this.nativeWindow.menu = baseMenu;
}
```

For ActionScript/Flash, use this variation:

```
if(NativeWindow.supportsMenu){
    this.stage.nativeWindow.menu = baseMenu;
}
```

In JavaScript, follow this example:

```
if(air.NativeWindow.supportsMenu){
    this.nativeWindow.menu = baseMenu
}
```

The native menu called `baseMenu` is the menu you created in Recipe 12.1.

12.6 Creating a Native Window Menu (Mac)

Problem

You want to create a native window menu on the Mac platform.

Solution

Add a native menu to your application by creating a `NativeMenu` object, and assign it to the `menu` property of the `NativeApplication` object.

Discussion

You can check whether the user is on a Mac platform by using the `NativeApplication.supportsMenu` Boolean value. If that value returns `true`, then you are sure the user is on the Mac platform, because at the time of this writing only the Mac platform will return `true` for this property.

For ActionScript/Flex, the code you need is as follows:

```
if(NativeApplication.supportsMenu){
    this.nativeApplication.menu = baseMenu;
}
```

For ActionScript/Flash, use this code:

```
if(NativeApplication.supportsMenu){
    NativeApplication.nativeApplication.menu = baseMenu;
}
```

In JavaScript, follow this example:

```
if(air.NativeApplication.supportsMenu){
    application.menu= baseMenu;
}
```

The native menu called `baseMenu` is the menu you created in Recipe 12.1.

12.7 Creating a Context Menu (ActionScript)

Problem

You want to use ActionScript to create a context menu in your AIR application.

Solution

Assign a `NativeMenu` instance or a `ContextMenu` instance to the `contextMenu` property of one or more display objects.

Discussion

Every display object that inherits from the `InteractiveObject` base class has a `context Menu` property that you can set to a `NativeMenu` or `ContextMenu` object. Just be sure you use `NativeMenuItem` objects with the `NativeMenu` instance and use `ContextMenuItem` objects with the `ContextMenu` objects. You cannot mix those two kinds of menu items. The context menu API in Adobe AIR does not support submenus, so when you need a nested menu as part of a context menu, use a `NativeMenu` menu with `NativeMenuItem` objects, and attach it to your interactive object. In addition, in a context menu, you must add all items to the `customItems` array.

ActionScript/Flex

The following example adds a simple command menu when you right-click the AIR application. Because the example focuses on creating the context menu, the command functionality is not implemented here.

```
<?xml version="1.0" encoding="utf-8"?>
<mx:WindowedApplication xmlns:mx="http://www.adobe.com/2006/mxml"
    layout="absolute"
    applicationComplete="init()"
    >
    <mx:Script>
        <![CDATA[

            private function init():void{
```

```
        //create the contextMenu
        var backgroundColorMenu:ContextMenu = new ContextMenu();

        backgroundColorMenu.customItems.push(new ContextMenuItem("RED"));
        backgroundColorMenu.customItems.push(new ContextMenuItem("GREEN"));
        backgroundColorMenu.customItems.push(new ContextMenuItem("BLUE"));
        backgroundColorMenu.addEventListener(Event.SELECT,selectHandler);

          //attach the contextMenu tot the label component
        myLabel.contextMenu = backgroundColorMenu;

    }
    private function selectHandler(event:Event):void{
        trace("You choose color : " + event.target.label);
    }
]]>
</mx:Script>
<mx:Label x="48" y="43" text="AIR CookBook rocks" id="myLabel"/>
</mx:WindowedApplication>
```

ActionScript/Flash

The following example adds a simple command menu when you right-click the AIR application. Because the example focuses on creating the context menu, the command functionality is not implemented here.

```
package com.newmovieclip.aircookbook.chapter12{

    import flash.display.*;
    import flash.desktop.*;
    import flash.events.*;
    import flash.ui.*;

    public class Step7 extends Sprite {

        public function Step7():void {
            //create red square
            var squareSprite:Sprite = new Sprite();
            squareSprite.graphics.beginFill(0xFF0000,1);
            squareSprite.graphics.drawRect(0,0,100,100);
            squareSprite.graphics.endFill();
            addChild(squareSprite)

             //make contextMenu and attach to the squareSprite
            var backgroundColorMenu:ContextMenu = new ContextMenu();
            backgroundColorMenu.customItems.push(new ContextMenuItem("Red"));
            backgroundColorMenu.customItems.push(new ContextMenuItem("Green"));
            backgroundColorMenu.customItems.push(new ContextMenuItem("Blue"));

            backgroundColorMenu.addEventListener(Event.SELECT,selectHandler);
             //attach contextMenu    tot the red square
            squareSprite.contextMenu=backgroundColorMenu;
        }
        private function selectHandler(event:Event):void{
            trace("You choose color : " + event.target.label);
```

```
        }
    }
}
```

12.8 Creating a Context Menu (JavaScript)

Problem

You want to use JavaScript to create a context menu in your AIR application.

Solution

Create a `NativeMenu` object, attach the `NativeMenuItem` objects or submenus you want, and then display your custom menu in place of the default menu.

Discussion

In JavaScript, the only way to show a custom menu when the user right-clicks an object in your AIR application is to use the `NativeMenu` and `NativeMenuItem` classes.

Start by creating a regular `NativeMenu` as demonstrated in Recipe 12.1. Because you are in an HTML environment, however, you need to make sure the default context menu is not shown. To prevent this, you must write a function that listens to the JavaScript `oncontextmenu` event that is dispatched when the user right-clicks. When the event is received by the handler function, call the event object's `preventDefault` method. Finally, display the custom menu by calling the `display` method of the `NativeMenu` instance. The code looks like this:

```
<html xmlns="http://www.w3.org/1999/xhtml">
<head>
<meta http-equiv="Content-Type" content="text/html; charset=utf-8" />
<title>Create context menu</title>

<script src="AIRAliases.js" type="text/javascript"></script>
<script type="text/javascript">
var backgroundColorMenu;

function initialize(){
    backgroundColorMenu= new air.NativeMenu();
    backgroundColorMenu.addItem(new air.NativeMenuItem("RED"));
    backgroundColorMenu.addItem(new air.NativeMenuItem("GREEN"));
    backgroundColorMenu.addItem(new air.NativeMenuItem("BLUE"));
    backgroundColorMenu.addEventListener(air.Event.SELECT,selectHandler);
}
function showContextMenu(event){
    event.preventDefault();
    //display the contextMenu
    backgroundColorMenu.display(window.nativeWindow.stage,
        event.clientX, event.clientY);
}
function selectHandler(event){
```

```
            air.trace(event.target.label);
    }
    </script>
    </head>
    <body onLoad="initialize()">
    <p oncontextmenu="showContextMenu(event)">AIR Cookbook rocks !</p>
    </body>
    </html>
```

12.9 Assigning Keyboard Shortcuts to Menu Items

Problem

You want to give the user the option to use keyboard shortcuts to control your native menu.

Solution

Set a key equivalent to every menu item that needs a keyboard shortcut by setting the keyEquivalent property of the NativeMenuItem instance.

Discussion

A good way to make your menu more accessible and usable is by using keyboard shortcuts.

To assign a key equivalent to a native menu item in ActionScript/Flex/Flash, use these lines:

```
var menuItemC:NativeMenuItem = new NativeMenuItem("Menu Item C");

menuItemC.keyEquivalent = "c";
```

The code you need in JavaScript is as follows:

```
var menuItemC = new air.NativeMenuItem("Menu Item C");
menuItemC.keyEquivalent = "c";
```

A key equivalent consists actually of two parts: a primary key **String** and an **Array** of modifier keys that also must be pressed. For Windows, the default modifier key is the Ctrl key. For the Mac, it is the Command key.

Because the previous code does not specify any special key modifier, the actual shortcuts will be Ctrl+C on Windows and Command+C on the Mac.

If you want to add the Shift key to the modifier array, simply specify the primary key in uppercase. AIR automatically will add the Shift key to the modifier array. For example, the ActionScript/Flex/Flash code

```
var menuItemC:NativeMenuItem = new NativeMenuItem("Menu Item C");
menuItemC.keyEquivalent = "C";
```

and the JavaScript code

```
var menuItemC = new air.NativeMenuItem("Menu Item C");
menuItemC.keyEquivalent = "C";
```

specify the shortcut Ctrl+Shift+C for Windows and the shortcut Command+Shift+C for the Mac.

The Shift key is always added to a modifier array, even if you define the modifier array yourself. You can define the modifier array in ActionScript/Flex/Flash as follows:

```
var menuItemC:NativeMenuItem = new NativeMenuItem("Menu Item C");
menuItemC.keyEquivalent = "C";
menuItemC.keyEquivalentModifiers = [Keyboard.CONTROL];
```

Or you can define the modifier array in JavaScript as follows:

```
var menuItemC = new air.NativeMenuItem("Menu Item C");
menuItemC.keyEquivalent = "C";
menuItemC.keyEquivalentModifiers = [Keyboard.CONTROL];
```

This code does the same thing as the previous snippet. The only difference is that you now define the Ctrl modifier yourself instead of using the default value.

12.10 Enabling and Disabling Menu Items

Problem

You want to enable or disable menu items at a given moment in your AIR application.

Solution

Set the enabled property of the NativeMenuItem object to true (default) to enable a menu item or false to disable it.

Discussion

When a menu item is disabled, it is grayed out and does not dispatch select events. By setting the enabled property to true or false, you can enable or disable a NativeMenuItem object.

To disable a menu in ActionScript/Flex/Flash, follow this example:

```
var menuItemEs:NativeMenuItem = new NativeMenuItem("Spanish");
menuItemEs.enabled = false;
```

To disable a menu in JavaScript, use the following lines:

```
var menuItemEs = new air.NativeMenuItem("Spanish");
menuItemEs.enabled = false;
```

12.11 Toggling Menu Items

Problem

You want to toggle a menu item in your AIR application to indicate it is checked.

Solution

Set the `checked` property of the `NativeMenuItem` object to `true` to display a check mark next to the menu item label.

Discussion

Every menu item has a built-in checked state. You can use this state to indicate that a `menuItem` is active. When a menu item is checked, a check mark is automatically shown next to the menu item label. The only thing you need to do to display a check mark next to the label is to set the `checked` property of the `NativeMenuItem` object to `true` or `false` depending on whether the item needs to be checked.

To do so in ActionScript/Flex/Flash, use the following:

```
var menuItemEs:NativeMenuItem = new NativeMenuItem("Spanish");
menuItemEs.checked = true;
```

To do so in JavaScript, use the following:

```
var menuItemEs = new air.NativeMenuItem("Spanish");
menuItemEs.checked = true;
```

CHAPTER 13

Taskbar and Dock Integration

By leveraging taskbar and Dock functionality in your AIR application, you can enhance your application's usability. This ability is especially useful when you want to notify the user that an event of interest has occurred.

On Windows, you can place an additional representation of your application (other than the taskbar button) in the form of an icon in the system tray (also called the *notification area*) of the taskbar. On a Mac, you can place an icon referencing your application in the Dock when the application is running. To get the attention of the user when something important happens, you can make a system tray icon flash (Windows) or the Dock icon of your application bounce (Mac).

On both operating systems, you can also add menus to the icons in the system tray or Dock.

Because the implementations in this chapter are operating system specific, it is a best practice to first check which operating system and associated icon is supported on the user's computer. You can check which icon types are supported using the static `NativeApplication` properties: `supportsDockIcon` and `supportsSystemTrayIcon`. Both types of icons support menus and custom images, but Table 13-1 outlines some differences.

Table 13-1. Icon Type Differences

System Tray Icon (Windows)	Dock Icon (Mac)
This icon is visible only when you set an image.	This is always visible, showing the image specified inside the application descriptor, unless you set a different image.
You can set tooltip text.	You cannot set a tooltip text.
You can listen for mouse events dispatched by the system tray icon.	Clicking the Dock icon doesn't dispatch any events; however, you can detect a click on the icon by listening to the invoke event of the NativeApplication object.

The code you need to check the available icon type is as follows:

```
if(NativeApplication.supportsDockIcon){
    //Dock available
```

```
}else if (NativeApplication.supportsSystemTrayIcon){
    // taskbar and system tray available
}
```

13.1 Adding an Icon to the System Tray (Windows)

Problem

You want to add an icon to your application button in the Windows system tray.

Solution

Assign an `Array` containing the new image or images to the `bitmaps` property of the
`icon` object in your `NativeApplication` instance.

Discussion

The `icon` property of `NativeApplication` is an `InteractiveIcon` instance that represents
the application icon(s). The `bitmaps` property of `InteractiveIcon` holds the images that
will be shown inside the system tray on your Windows taskbar. This property expects
an array of several images and enables you to define several sizes of your icon image.
AIR automatically selects the image according to the current display size of the system
tray icon (set on the operating system level). At runtime, AIR will detect the dimensions
of the icons in the array, and the bitmap in the array closest to the display size will be
used and scaled if necessary. Most typical sizes (in pixels) are 16 × 16, 32 × 32, 48 × 48,
and 128 × 128.

 To set the icon in your application's taskbar button, you specify it in
your application descriptor file (see Recipe 2.8).

ActionScript/Flex

This example demonstrates how to add an `Array` of images to the `bitmaps` property of
your application icon. The images you put in the `Array` must be of type `BitmapData`. A
`BitmapData` object represents the pixels of a `Bitmap` object.

The full MXML code for the example is as follows:

```
<?xml version="1.0" encoding="utf-8"?>
<mx:WindowedApplication xmlns:mx="http://www.adobe.com/2006/mxml"
    applicationComplete="init()"
    layout="absolute"
    title="Recipe 13.1: Adding an icon to the Windows taskbar"
    >
    <mx:Script >
```

```
<![CDATA[
    //embed the images to use as icon
    import mx.core.BitmapAsset;

    [Embed(source="app:/assets/icons/flashing/Icon_fl_32.png")]
    public var img32:Class;

    [Embed(source="app:/assets/icons/flashing/Icon_fl_16.png")]
    public var img16:Class;

    //define the bitmapData object

    private var icon32:BitmapAsset;
    private var icon16:BitmapAsset;

    private function init():void{
        //define bitmapData object

        icon32= (new img32()as BitmapAsset);
        icon16= (new img16()as BitmapAsset);
        //assign the bitmapData objects to the icon.bitmaps
        if(NativeApplication.supportsSystemTrayIcon){
            this.nativeApplication.icon.bitmaps =[icon32.bitmapData,
icon16.bitmapData];
        }
    }
]]>
</mx:Script>
</mx:WindowedApplication>
```

You first embed the images in your AIR application by using the Embed directive so that they are available at runtime. You then instantiate the embedded assets and store them in local variables that you can readily access when needed. When the application is fully loaded (as indicated by the dispatch of the applicationComplete event), you make a new instance of every loaded image, which is actually a BitmapAsset instance, so you cast the object to a BitmapAsset object, as shown here:

```
icon32= (new img32() as BitmapAsset);
...
```

Lastly, you can now access the bitmapData property of the Bitmap, so put the image instances in an Array, and assign that Array to the icon.bitmaps property of the NativeApplication object. This example adds four sizes of the icon image:

```
this.nativeApplication.icon.bitmaps =[ icon32.bitmapDta,icon16.bitmapData];
```

JavaScript

This example demonstrates how to add an Array of images to the icon.bitmaps property. The images you put in the Array must be of type BitmapData. A BitmapData object represents the pixels of a Bitmap object.

This is the code when developing AIR applications with JavaScript:

```html
<html >
<head>
<title>Recipe 13.1: Adding an icon to the Windows system tray</title>

<script src="AIRAliases.js" type="text/javascript"></script>

<script type="text/javascript">

var iconLoadComplete = function(event) {
        if (air.NativeApplication.supportsSystemTrayIcon) {
            air.NativeApplication.nativeApplication.icon.bitmaps =
                new runtime.Array(event.target.content.bitmapData);
        }
    }
function init(){
    var iconLoad = new air.Loader();
    iconLoad.contentLoaderInfo.addEventListener(air.Event.COMPLETE,iconLoadComplete);
        iconLoad.load(new air.URLRequest("assets/Icon_16.png"));
}
</script>
</head>
<body onLoad="init()">
</body>
</html>
```

First, define a new `air.Loader` instance to load the icon file. To initiate the loading process, you call the `load` method of the `air.Loader` class. The `load` method needs a `URLRequest` object. This object contains the location information of the image file that needs to be loaded. This example loads one image file (*Icon_16.png*). When the icon is loaded, you assign it to the `icon.bitmaps` property in order for it to show in the system tray.

13.2 Adding a Custom Menu to the System Tray Icon (Windows)

Problem

You want to attach a menu to the system tray icon on Windows.

Solution

Make an instance of the `NativeMenu` class, and assign it to the `icon.menu` property of the `NativeApplication` object. On Windows, the system tray icon is represented by the `SystemTrayIcon` property.

Discussion

To attach a menu to the system tray icon, you use the `NativeMenu` instance. The following examples first embed several sizes of the icon image, read the `bitmapData` of the images, and assign the data to the `icon.bitmaps` property of the `NativeApplication` object. This approach is similar to Recipe 13.1, but this time you using only two sizes of the icon image.

ActionScript/Flex

The example code in bold indicates the line where you instantiate a new `NativeMenu` object and attach one item to that menu with the label "Close." To know when the menu item is clicked, you add a listener for the `Event.SELECT` event. Finally, you attach the menu to the `SystemTrayIcon.menu` property. When you run the example and right-click the system tray, your custom menu will pop up. When you click the close menu item, the `nativeApplication` is exited (`NativeApplication.exit`).

The example code is as follows:

```
<?xml version="1.0" encoding="utf-8"?>
<mx:WindowedApplication xmlns:mx="http://www.adobe.com/2006/mxml"
    applicationComplete="init()"
    layout="absolute"
    title="Recipe 13.2: Adding a custom menu to the systemtray icon (windows)"
    >
    <mx:Script >
        <![CDATA[
            //embed the images to use as icon
            import mx.core.BitmapAsset;

            [Embed(source="app:/assets/icons/flashing/Icon_fl_32.png")]
            public var img32:Class;

            [Embed(source="app:/assets/icons/flashing/Icon_fl_16.png")]
            public var img16:Class;

            //define the bitmapData object

            private var icon32:BitmapAsset;
            private var icon16:BitmapAsset;

            private function init():void{
                //define bitmapData object

                icon32= (new img32()as BitmapAsset);
                icon16= (new img16()as BitmapAsset);
                //assign the bitmapData objects to the icon.bitmaps
                if(NativeApplication.supportsSystemTrayIcon){
                    this.nativeApplication.icon.bitmaps
=[icon32.bitmapData,icon16.bitmapData];
                }


                var myMenu:NativeMenu = new NativeMenu();
                myMenu.addItem(new NativeMenuItem("Close",false));
                myMenu.addEventListener(Event.SELECT,closeApp);
```

```
                //add the menu to the system tray icon
                if(NativeApplication.supportsSystemTrayIcon){
                    SystemTrayIcon(NativeApplication.nativeApplication.icon).menu
= myMenu;
                }
            }
            private function closeApp(event:Event):void{
                this.nativeApplication.exit();
            }
        ]]>
    </mx:Script>
</mx:WindowedApplication>
```

JavaScript

In this example, you first load the icon file as you did in Recipe 13.1. Next you create a new air.NativeMenu object with one air.NativeMenuItem object. When the user clicks the application, the closeApp function is called:

```
var myMenu = new air.NativeMenu();
myMenu.addItem(new air.NativeMenuItem("Close application",false));
myMenu.addEventListener(air.Event.SELECT,closeApp);
```

The closeApp function calls the exit method of the NativeApplication class to close the application.

To attach the menu to the system tray icon, set your custom menu as the value for the icon.menu property of the NativeApplication instance. Before you do so, however, check that the guest operating system supports system tray icons using the air.NativeApplication.supportsSystemTrayIcon property of the NativeApplication class:

```
//set the menu of the system tray icon
if (air.NativeApplication.supportsSystemTrayIcon) {
    air.NativeApplication.nativeApplication.icon.menu = myMenu;
}
```

The full example JavaScript code is as follows:

```
<html >
<head>
<title>Recipe 13.2: Adding a custom menu to the systemtray icon (windows)</title>

<script src="AIRAliases.js" type="text/javascript"></script>

<script type="text/javascript">

var iconLoadComplete = function(event) {
        if(air.NativeApplication.supportsSystemTrayIcon) {
            air.NativeApplication.nativeApplication.icon.bitmaps =
            new runtime.Array(event.target.content.bitmapData);
        }
    }
function init(){
    var iconLoad = new air.Loader();
```

```
    iconLoad.contentLoaderInfo.addEventListener(air.Event.COMPLETE,iconLoadComplete);
        iconLoad.load(new air.URLRequest("assets/Icon_16.png"));
    //define a menu
    var myMenu = new air.NativeMenu();
    myMenu.addItem(new air.NativeMenuItem("Close application",false));
    myMenu.addEventListener(air.Event.SELECT,closeApp);
    //set the menu of the system tray icon
    if (air.NativeApplication.supportsSystemTrayIcon) {
        air.NativeApplication.nativeApplication.icon.menu = myMenu;
    }
}
function closeApp(event){
    air.NativeApplication.nativeApplication.exit();
}
</script>
</head>
<body onLoad="init()">
</body>
</html>
```

13.3 Adding a Custom Menu to the Dock Icon (Mac)

Problem

You want to attach a menu to the Dock icon on a Mac.

Solution

Make an instance of the `NativeMenu` class, and assign it to the `icon.menu` property of the `NativeApplication` object. The Dock icon is represented as an instance of the `DockItem` class.

Discussion

The technique you use to attach a menu to the Dock icon on a Mac is the same as demonstrated in Recipe 13.2. You will, however, need to check for Dock icon support on the user's operating system.

ActionScript

To check that the Dock icon is supported, test the Boolean value of `NativeApplication.supportsDockIcon`. If it is supported, you can copy the example from Recipe 13.2 in full and change the `if` structure to this:

```
//add the menu to the system tray icon
if(NativeApplication.supportsDockIcon){
    DockIcon(NativeApplication.nativeApplication.icon).menu = myMenu;
}
```

JavaScript

To check that the Dock icon is supported, you test the Boolean value of `air.NativeAp`
`plication.supportsDockIcon`. You will copy the example code from Recipe 13.2 and
change the `if` structure according to the following code:

```
//set the menu of the Dock icon
if (air.NativeApplication.supportsDockIcon) {
   air.NativeApplication.nativeApplication.icon.menu = myMenu;
}
```

13.4 Changing the System Tray or Dock Icon

Problem

You want to change the system tray or Dock icon at runtime.

Solution

Assign an `Array` containing the new icon image (or several icon images with different
sizes) to the `icon.bitmaps` property of the `NativeApplication` object.

Discussion

Changing the system tray icon or Dock icon is as easy as assigning a new icon image to
the `icon.bitmaps` property of the `NativeApplication` object.

 You cannot change the icon image used for your application on the
taskbar button of your application window (on Windows). That image
is always the image you specified as the icon image in your application
descriptor file (see Recipe 2.8).

The following example creates an animated system tray or Dock icon (depending on
the user's operating system) by constantly changing the icon at a given time interval,
similar to the way a traditional GIF animation works, sequencing images over time.

As you did earlier, you first load the different sizes of the primary icon image. This time
you load a second set of icon images with the slightly altered versions of the primary
icon with some color changes. When you continuously change the icon to one of those
two icon images, the user has the illusion that the icon is flashing in your system tray
or Dock.

ActionScript/Flex

You implement the "flashing icon" behavior by using a `Timer` object with a timer interval
set to 500 milliseconds. The `Timer` class gives you the possibility of running code on a
specific time sequence. You have to set up an event listener for the `TimerEvent.TIMER`

event, and then at each interval, the changeIcon function is executed that assigns the new array of images to the icon.bitmaps property. These parts of the code are highlighted in bold.

Here is the full MXML code:

```
<?xml version="1.0" encoding="utf-8"?>
<mx:WindowedApplication xmlns:mx="http://www.adobe.com/2006/mxml"
    applicationComplete="init()"
    layout="absolute">


    <mx:Script >
        <![CDATA[
            import mx.core.BitmapAsset;
            [Embed(source="app:/assets/icons/flashing/Icon_fl_128.png")]
            public var img128:Class;

                [Embed(source="app:/assets/icons/flashing/Icon_fl_48.png")]
            public var img48:Class;

                [Embed(source="app:/assets/icons/flashing/Icon_fl_32.png")]
            public var img32:Class;

            [Embed(source="app:/assets/icons/flashing/Icon_fl_16.png")]
            [Bindable]
            public var img16:Class;
            [Embed(source="app:/assets/icons/Icon_128.png")]
            [Bindable]
            public var imgfl128:Class;
            [Embed(source="app:/assets/icons/Icon_48.png")]
            [Bindable]
            public var imgfl48:Class;
            [Embed(source="app:/assets/icons/Icon_32.png")]
            [Bindable]
            public var imgfl32:Class;
            [Embed(source="app:/assets/icons/Icon_16.png")]
            [Bindable]
            public var imgfl16:Class;

             private var iconfl128:BitmapData
             private var iconfl48:BitmapData
             private var iconfl32:BitmapData
             private var iconfl16:BitmapData
             private var icon128:BitmapData
             private var icon48:BitmapData
             private var icon32:BitmapData
             private var icon16:BitmapData

            private function init():void{
                //define bitmapData object
                icon128= (new img128()as BitmapAsset).bitmapData;
                icon48= (new img48()as BitmapAsset).bitmapData;
                icon32= (new img32()as BitmapAsset).bitmapData;
                icon16= (new img16()as BitmapAsset).bitmapData;
```

```
                    iconfl128= (new imgfl128()as BitmapAsset).bitmapData;
                    iconfl48= (new imgfl48()as BitmapAsset).bitmapData;
                    iconfl32= (new imgfl32()as BitmapAsset).bitmapData;
                    iconfl16= (new imgfl16()as BitmapAsset).bitmapData;
                    //define timer object

                    var tmr:Timer = new Timer(500);
                    tmr.addEventListener(TimerEvent.TIMER,changeImage);
                    tmr.start();
                }

                private function changeImage(event:TimerEvent):void{
                    if(event.target.currentCount%2){
                        this.nativeApplication.icon.bitmaps
=[icon128,icon48,icon32,icon16];
                    }else{

                        this.nativeApplication.icon.bitmaps
=[iconfl128,iconfl48,iconfl32,iconfl16];
                    }
                }
            ]]>
        </mx:Script>
</mx:WindowedApplication>
```

JavaScript

In JavaScript, you use an `air.Timer` object to create the illusion of a flashing icon. Every time the `air.TimerEvent.TIMER` event is dispatched, you execute the `changeImage` function that assigns one of the two icons to the `icon.bitmaps` property of the `air.NativeApplication.nativeApplication` instance.

```
<html >
<head>
<title>Recipe 13.4: CHANGING THE DOC OR TASKBAR ICON</title>

<script src="AIRAliases.js" type="text/javascript"></script>

<script type="text/javascript">

var iconsNormal = ["Icon_16.png","Icon_32.png"];
var iconsFlashing = ["Icon_fl_16.png","Icon_fl_32.png"];

//arrays that hold the icons there bitmapdata
var bitmapDataArrNormal =[];
var bitmapDataArrFlashing =[];

function iconNormalComplete(event) {
        bitmapDataArrNormal.push(event.target.content.bitmapData);
}
function iconFlashingComplete(event) {
        bitmapDataArrFlashing.push(event.target.content.bitmapData);
}
function init(){
```

```
        //load the icons
        loadIcons(iconsNormal,0);
        loadIcons(iconsFlashing,1)
        //start a new timer to change the icon
        //every 500 miliseconds
        var tmr = new air.Timer(500);
        tmr.addEventListener(air.TimerEvent.TIMER,changeIcon);
        tmr.start();
}

function changeIcon(event){
    //
    if(event.target.currentCount%2){
        air.NativeApplication.nativeApplication.icon.bitmaps =
bitmapDataArrNormal;
    }else{
        air.NativeApplication.nativeApplication.icon.bitmaps =
bitmapDataArrFlashing;
    }
}
function loadIcons(arr,flag){
    for(var i=0;i<arr.length;i++){
        //define the loader
        var iconLoad = new air.Loader();
        //register the right listener
        if(flag){
            iconLoad.contentLoaderInfo.addEventListener(air.Event.COMPLETE,iconFlashingComplete);
        }else{
            iconLoad.contentLoaderInfo.addEventListener(air.Event.COMPLETE,iconNormalComplete);
        }
        //load the icon image
            iconLoad.load(new air.URLRequest("assets/"+ arr[i]));
    }
}
</script>
</head>
<body onLoad="init()">
</body>
</html>
```

13.5 Notifying the User Through the Dock (Mac)

Problem

You want to attract the user's attention through the Dock.

Solution

If the operating system supports window-level notification, you can make the Dock icon "bounce" by calling the DockItem.bounce method.

Discussion

You can pass a `NotificationType` to the `bounce` method to inform the user that something critical has happened (the application continuously bounces until the application is in the foreground) or just to give the user some information (a single bounce). The two appropriate `NoticationType` constants are `NotificationType.CRITICAL` and `NotificationType.INFORMATIONAL`. To determine whether the operating system has this notification capability, you access `NativeWindow.supportsNotification`.

ActionScript

The following example shows a small application that has two buttons defined. When clicked, the buttons notify the user in either a critical or informational way. After checking that the operating system supports Dock icons, you can cast the `NativeApplication.icon` property to an instance of the `DockIcon` class.

```
<?xml version="1.0" encoding="utf-8"?>
<mx:WindowedApplication xmlns:mx="http://www.adobe.com/2006/mxml"
    layout="vertical"
    title="Recipe 13.5: Bouncing the dock icon (MAC)"
    deactivate="bounce()" >

   <mx:Script >
      <![CDATA[

          private function bounce():void
          {
              if (NativeApplication.supportsDockIcon)
              {
                  var myIcon:DockIcon = NativeApplication.nativeApplication.icon
as DockIcon;
                  var type:String = critical.selected ? NotificationType.CRITICAL
: NotificationType.INFORMATIONAL;
                  myIcon.bounce(type);
              }
          }

      ]]>
   </mx:Script>
   <mx:RadioButtonGroup id="notificationType" />
   <mx:RadioButton id="critical" group="{notificationType}" label="NOTIFY THE USER
CRITICAL" selected="true"/>
   <mx:RadioButton id="informational" group="{notificationType}" label="NOTIFY THE
USER INFORMATIONAL"/>
</mx:WindowedApplication>
```

JavaScript

In AIR, you define the notification types in the `air.NotificationType` class. You can bounce the icon of the `air.NativeApplication` instance by calling the `bounce` method:

```
<html >
    <head>
```

```
<title>Recipe 13.5: Bouncing the dock icon (MAC)</title>
<script src="AIRAliases.js" type="text/javascript"></script>
<script type="text/javascript">

    function notify()
    {
        if (air.NativeApplication.supportsDockIcon)
        {
            var critical = document.getElementById("critical");
            var type = (critical.checked ? air.NotificationType.CRITICAL :
air.NotificationType.INFORMATIONAL);
            if (air.NativeApplication.supportsDockIcon)
            {
                air.NativeApplication.nativeApplication.icon.bounce(type);
            }
        }
    }

    function setListener()
    {
        nativeWindow.addEventListener('deactivate', notify);
    }

    </script>
</head>
    <body onload="setListener()">
        <form >
            <div><input id="critical" type="radio" name="notify" value="NOTIFY THE
USER CRITICAL" checked="checked" />NOTIFY THE USER CRITICAL</div>
            <div><input id="information" type="radio" name="notify" value="NOTIFY THE
USER INFORMATIONAL" />NOTIFY THE USER INFORMATIONAL</div>
        </form>
    </body>
</html>
```

13.6 Notifying the User Through the Taskbar (Windows)

Problem

You want to attract the user's attention through the taskbar.

Solution

If the operating system supports window-level notification, you can make the taskbar
and window flash by calling the `NativeWindow.notifyUser` method.

Discussion

You can pass a `NotificationType` to the `notifyUser` method to inform the user that
something critical has happened (the taskbar flashes until the application is in the foreground) or just to give the user some information (the taskbar and window flashes only

ones). The two appropriate `NoticationType` constants are `NotificationType.CRITICAL` and `NotificationType.INFORMATIONAL`. To determine whether the operating system has this notification capability, you access `NativeWindow.supportsNotification`.

ActionScript

The following example shows how to implement this notification with the `Native Window` class. When the application window is deactivated (is not on the foreground), the taskbar and window flash to get the attention of the user:

```
<?xml version="1.0" encoding="utf-8"?>
<mx:WindowedApplication xmlns:mx="http://www.adobe.com/2006/mxml"
    layout="vertical"
    title="Recipe 13.6: Flashing the window/taskbar (WINDOWS)"
    deactivate="notify()"
    >


    <mx:Script >
        <![CDATA[

            private function notify():void{
                if(NativeWindow.supportsNotification &&
NativeApplication.supportsSystemTrayIcon){
                    var type:String = critical.selected ? NotificationType.CRITICAL
: NotificationType.INFORMATIONAL;
                    this.nativeWindow.notifyUser(type);
                }
            }
        ]]>
    </mx:Script>

    <mx:RadioButtonGroup id="notificationType" />
        <mx:RadioButton id="critical" group="{notificationType}" label="NOTIFIY THE
USER CRITICAL"
            selected="true"/>
    <mx:RadioButton id="informational" group="{notificationType}" label="NOTIFIY
THE USER INFORMATIONAL"/>

</mx:WindowedApplication>
```

JavaScript

The following example shows how to implement the notification with the `air.Native Window` class. When the application window is deactivated (is not on the foreground), the taskbar and window flash to get the attention of the user:

```
<html >
<head>
<title>Recipe 13.6: Flashing the system tray icon (WINDOWS)</title>
<script src="AIRAliases.js" type="text/javascript"></script>
<script type="text/javascript">

function notify(){
    if(air.NativeApplication.supportsSystemTrayIcon &&
```

```
air.NativeWindow.supportsNotification) {
        var critical = document.getElementById('critical');
        var type = (critical.checked ?  air.NotificationType.CRITICAL
  : air.NotificationType.INFORMATIONAL);
        nativeWindow.notifyUser(type);
    }
}
function setListener(){
    nativeWindow.addEventListener('deactivate',notify);
}
</script>
</head>
<body onLoad="setListener()">
<form >
 <div><input id="critical" type="radio" name="notify" value="NOTIFY THE USER
CRITICAL" checked="checked" />NOTIFY THE USER CRITICAL</div>
 <div><input id="information" type="radio" name="notify" value="NOTIFY THE USER
INFORMATIONAL" />NOTIFY THE USER INFORMATIONAL</div>
</form>
</body>
</html>
```

CHAPTER 14

File Types

When a file type is associated with your AIR application, then every associated file of that type will open itself in your AIR application. This gives you great opportunities to work with external files in your AIR application. Recipe 14.1 discusses how to register a file type with your AIR application.

Before you begin, you should note that you make associations for an AIR application when installing the application, not at compile or debug time. This means you can't test file associations until you package and install your application. When your application is packaged, the application descriptor XML file is read, and the file associations are set. This is not automatically done if another application on the system is already the default application; in other words, the AIR application install process does not override an existing file type association. If you want to take over the association from another application, take a look at Recipe 14.3.

14.1 Registering Custom File Types

Problem

You want to register a custom file type so that the operating system will associate it with your AIR application.

Solution

Use the `fileTypes` element in the application descriptor file to declare the file types associated with your AIR application.

Discussion

Associations between your application and a file type must be declared in the application descriptor file. Depending on your environment and compiler settings, this descriptor file is typically the *-app.xml* file in your Adobe AIR project, characterized by the `application` root nodes. In that XML file, you can manipulate, for example, the initial, minimum, and maximum width and height; the initial position of your main AIR application window (see Chapter 2); and the file type associations.

An empty `fileTypes` node in the application descriptor file typically looks like this:

```
<fileTypes>
      <fileType>

            <name></name>
            <extension></extension>
            <description></description>
            <contentType></contentType>
            <icon>
                  <image16x16></image16x16>
                  <image32x32></image32x32>
                  <image48x48></image48x48>
                  <image128x128></image128x128>
            </icon>
      </fileType>
</fileTypes>
```

For each file type you want to register, you need to define a `fileType` node in the `fileTypes` element in your application descriptor XML file. The `name` and `extension` values are required, but the `description` and `contentType` values are optional. The `name` value is the name the system displays for the registered file. The `extension` is the extension for the file (not including the preceding period). You can use the same `name` for multiple extensions.

The `description` is shown to the user by the operating system user interface, such as when the user looks at the file properties.

The `contentType` property helps the operating system locate the best application to open a file in some special circumstances, such as when the extension is not recognized. The `contentType` property is required for any `fileType` property defined in the application descriptor file. The value of the `contentType` node is the name of the MIME type for the files.

 MIME stands for *Multipurpose Internet Mail Extensions*, and MIME types form standard ways of classifying file types. You can find an overview of common MIME types and their corresponding file extensions at *http://www.webmaster-toolkit.com/mime-types.shtml*.

Last but not least, you can also specify an `icon` for the file extension. The icon files must be included in the AIR installation file because they are not packaged automatically.

Setting an icon for the file extension is also optional. The path specified is relative to the installed AIR application root directory at runtime. Icon files must be in the PNG format, but you can specify different icon sizes. When all sizes are not provided, the closest size is scaled to fit for a given use of the icon by the operating system.

The following example shows a full `fileTypes` node from an application descriptor XML file:

```
<fileTypes>
    <fileType>
        <name>Example.myOwnFileType</name>
        <extension>koen</extension>
        <description>This is a custom fileType that has my name
        </description>
        <contentType>text/plain</contentType>
        <icon>
            <image16x16>KOEN16.PNG</image16x16>
            <image32x32>KOEN32.PNG</image32x32>
            <image48x48>KOEN48.PNG</image48x48>
            <image128x128>KOEN128.PNG</image128x128>
        </icon>
    </fileType>
</fileTypes>
```

According to the previous `fileTypes` node, if the user double-clicks a file called *file.koen*, then the associated AIR application will launch.

To retrieve the path to the specific file, you need to write a handler function for the `InvokeEvent` object dispatched by the `NativeApplication` object. The `NativeApplication` object represents the AIR application, and it can dispatch application-level events. If you want to open the file, you can use that specific path.

When the AIR application is invoked a second time, another instance of the application is not started. Instead, the first instance receives an additional invoke event.

If your AIR application is already running when the user double-clicks the associated file, AIR will immediately dispatch the `InvokeEvent` object to the running AIR application.

ActionScript

The following code illustrates how your AIR application can handle an invoke event dispatched by the runtime when an associated file is opened:

```
<?xml version="1.0" encoding="utf-8"?>
<mx:WindowedApplication xmlns:mx="http://www.adobe.com/2006/mxml"
    layout="absolute"
    applicationComplete="init()"
    >

    <mx:Script >
        <![CDATA[

            private function init():void{
                this.nativeApplication.addEventListener(InvokeEvent.INVOKE,invokeHandler);

            }
            private function invokeHandler(event:InvokeEvent):void{
                pathLabel.text = event.arguments[0];
```

```
                }

            ]]>
        </mx:Script>
        <mx:Label id="pathLabel" x="86" y="97" text="" fontSize="15"/>
    </mx:WindowedApplication>
```

JavaScript

The following code shows how your AIR application can handle the invoke event that is dispatched by AIR when an associated file is opened:

```
<html >
<head>
<title>Recipe 14.1: File association</title>

<script src="AIRAliases.js" type="text/javascript"></script>

<script type="text/javascript">

function init(){
    air.NativeApplication.nativeApplication.addEventListener
(air.InvokeEvent.INVOKE,invokeHandler);

}

function invokeHandler(event){
    document.getElementById("textOutput1").innerHTML = event.arguments[0];
}

</script>
</head>
<body onLoad="init()">

<div id="textOutput1">...</div>

</body>
</html>
```

 Keep in mind that you can test this file association functionality only by effectively making a release build of your AIR application and installing it on your system.

14.2 Determining Whether an Application Is the Default Application for a File Type

Problem

You want to check whether an AIR application is (still) the default application for a given file type on the user's computer.

Solution

Use the `isSetAsDefaultApplication` method from the `NativeApplication` class.

Discussion

The AIR application installer does not override existing file associations, and file associations on a user's system can change at any time (for example, when another program is installed). The best practice, therefore, is to verify that the expected file associations are in place when your application starts.

To determine whether an AIR application is the default application for a file type, you have to check the `Boolean` return value from the `isSetAsDefaultApplication` method. This method is part of the `NativeApplication` object that represents the AIR application.

ActionScript

The following code implements this little check mechanism. This code is placed into a function that is executed when the application is completely loaded:

```
private function init():void{

    if (NativeApplication.nativeApplication.isSetAsDefaultApplication("koen")){
        // *.koen files are already associated with this AIR app
    }else{
        //ask user to associate *.koen files  with this AIR app
    }

}
```

JavaScript

The following code implements this little check mechanism. This code is placed into a function that is executed when the application is completely loaded:

```
function init(){

    if (air.NativeApplication.nativeApplication.isSetAsDefaultApplication("koen")){
        // *.koen files are already associated with this AIR app
    }else{
        //ask user to associate *.koen files  with this AIR app
    }

}
```

14.3 Setting and Removing an Application as the Default Application for a File Type

Problem

You want to set or remove an AIR application as the default application for a file type.

Solution

Use the `setAsDefaultApplication` or `removeAsDefaultApplication` method from the `NativeApplication` class.

Discussion

AIR applications can manage associations for the file types that were originally declared in the application descriptor file (Recipe 14.1). Even if a user has manually created an association between a file type and your AIR application, trying to set it as the default application will result in a runtime exception.

Suppose you declared a file type association in the descriptor file but the association is broken because another installed application took over the association. Because you originally defined the association, you can now set your AIR application as the default application.

To do this, you call the `setAsDefaultApplication` method and pass the file type extension as a parameter. This is a method of the `nativeApplication` object that represents the AIR application.

In the same way, you can remove an existing file type association by using the `removeAsDefaultApplication` method.

ActionScript

The following code shows how `removeAsDefaultApplication` and `setAsDefaultApplication` work. By using these two file type management methods, you can make sure your AIR application is always able to open the right files.

To set your AIR application to the default application for a file type, use the following code:

```
this.nativeApplication.setAsDefaultApplication("koen");
```

To remove your AIR application as the default application for a file type, use the following code:

```
this.nativeApplication.removeAsDefaultApplication("koen");
```

In Recipe 14.4 you can see a full ActionScript example that also shows these two file type management methods.

JavaScript

The following code shows how `removeAsDefaultApplication` and `setAsDefaultApplica`
`tion` work. By using these two file type management methods, you can make sure your
AIR application is always able to open the right files.

To set your AIR application as the default application for a file type, use the following code:

```
air.NativeApplication.nativeApplication.setAsDefaultApplication("koen");
```

To remove your AIR application as the default application for a file type, use the following code:

```
air.NativeApplication.nativeApplication.removeAsDefaultApplication("koen")
```

In Recipe 14.4 you can see a full JavaScript example that also shows these two file type
management methods.

14.4 Getting the Path of the Default Application for a File Type

Problem

You want to know the path of the default application that is currently associated with
a given file type.

Solution

Use the `getDefaultApplication` method from the `NativeApplication` class.

Discussion

If you want to know the path to the application that is associated with a given file type,
you can pass the extension of that file type to the `getDefaultApplication` method from
the `nativeApplication` object.

In ActionScript, to get the path of the default application, use the following code:

```
var path:String = this.nativeApplication.getDefaultApplication("koen");
```

In JavaScript, to get the path of the default application, use the following code:

```
var path = air.NativeApplication.nativeApplication.getDefaultApplication("koen");
```

Keep in mind, however, that this function works only on file types that are defined in
the application descriptor file.

ActionScript

The following code combines all the recipes from this chapter in one example:

```
<?xml version="1.0" encoding="utf-8"?>
<mx:WindowedApplication xmlns:mx="http://www.adobe.com/2006/mxml"
```

```
layout="vertical" applicationComplete="init()">
    <mx:Script>
        <![CDATA[

            private const FILE_EXTENSION:String = "acbtest";

            private function init():void
            {
                trace("[ch14] app init : start");

                this.nativeApplication.addEventListener(
                    InvokeEvent.INVOKE,
                    invokeHandler);

                textOutput1.text = "nativeApplication.isSetAsDefaultApplication : " +
                    this.nativeApplication.isSetAsDefaultApplication(FILE_EXTENSION);

                textOutput2.text = "File.applicationDirectory.nativePath : " +
                    File.applicationDirectory.nativePath;

                if (this.nativeApplication.isSetAsDefaultApplication(FILE_EXTENSION))
                {
                    // remove the association
                    this.nativeApplication.removeAsDefaultApplication(FILE_EXTENSION)
                }
                else
                {
                    //set this app as default
                    this.nativeApplication.setAsDefaultApplication(FILE_EXTENSION);
                }

                textOutput3.text = "nativeApplication.isSetAsDefaultApplication : " +
                    this.nativeApplication.isSetAsDefaultApplication(FILE_EXTENSION);

                textOutput4.text = "nativeApplication.getDefaultApplication : " +
                    this.nativeApplication.getDefaultApplication(FILE_EXTENSION);
            }

            private function invokeHandler(event:InvokeEvent):void
            {
                trace("[ch14] invokeHandler : " + event.arguments[0]); // trace the path
            }

        ]]>
    </mx:Script>


    <mx:Label id="textOutput1" />
    <mx:Label id="textOutput2" />
    <mx:Label id="textOutput3"/>
    <mx:Label id="textOutput4" />

</mx:WindowedApplication>
```

JavaScript

The following is the JavaScript:

```
<html>
<head>
<title>AIRCookbook CH14</title>

    <script src="AIRAliases.js" type="text/javascript"></script>
    <script type="text/javascript">

  var FILE_EXTENSION = "koen";

  function init()
  {
      air.trace("[ch14] app init : start");

      air.NativeApplication.nativeApplication.addEventListener(
          air.InvokeEvent.INVOKE,
          invokeHandler);

      document.getElementById("textOutput1").innerHTML =
"nativeApplication.isSetAsDefaultApplication : " +
          air.NativeApplication.nativeApplication.isSetAsDefaultApplication(FILE_EXTENSION);

      document.getElementById("textOutput2").innerHTML =
"air.File.applicationDirectory.nativePath : " +
          air.File.applicationDirectory.nativePath;

      if (air.NativeApplication.nativeApplication.isSetAsDefaultApplication(FILE_EXTENSION))
      {
        // remove the association
        air.NativeApplication.nativeApplication.removeAsDefaultApplication(FILE_EXTENSION)
      }
      else
      {
        //set this app as default
        air.NativeApplication.nativeApplication.setAsDefaultApplication(FILE_EXTENSION);
      }

      document.getElementById("textOutput3").innerHTML =
"nativeApplication.isSetAsDefaultApplication : " +
          air.NativeApplication.nativeApplication.isSetAsDefaultApplication(FILE_EXTENSION);

      document.getElementById("textOutput4").innerHTML =
"nativeApplication.getDefaultApplication : " +
          air.NativeApplication.nativeApplication.getDefaultApplication(FILE_EXTENSION);
    }

        function invokeHandler(event)
        {
            air.trace("[ch14] invokeHandler : " + event.arguments[0]); // trace the path
        }
</script>
```

```
</head>
<body onload="init();">
    <div id="textOutput1">...</div>
    <div id="textOutput2">...</div>
    <div id="textOutput3">...</div>
    <div id="textOutput4">...</div>
</body>
</html>
```

CHAPTER 15

Service Monitor Framework

For desktop applications, you often need the ability to detect the status of network connectivity and monitor its changes. Some applications require a constant Internet connection, while others, called *occasionally connected applications*, can work offline as well as online by caching the offline content. Adobe AIR can detect network connectivity changes, thereby enabling you to plan the behavior of the application based on its status.

15.1 Including the Service Monitor Framework in an Application (JavaScript)

Problem

You want to use the service monitor framework with JavaScript to detect the status of network connectivity.

Solution

Import the service monitor framework into the AIR application.

Discussion

The service monitor framework is a separate framework from the standard AIR framework. To be able to use the service monitor framework, you need to import the *servicemonitor.swf* file into your HTML and JavaScript application. You can find this file in the AIR SDK's frameworks folder. Copy *servicemonitor.swf* into the directory of your AIR project.

To import the file, use the `script` tag. The tag's `type` attribute specifies the scripting language of the element's contents and overrides the default scripting language. Set the `type` attribute to the `application/x-shockwave-flash` value, as shown here:

```
<script type="application/x-shockwave-flash"
src="frameworks/servicemonitor.swf"></script>
```

In the previous line of code, the *servicemonitor.swf* file resides in the frameworks folder of the AIR project root. The following is a simple example of a complete HTML page that contains this import:

```
<html xmlns="http://www.w3.org/1999/xhtml">
<head>

<script type="application/x-shockwave-flash"
src="frameworks/servicemonitor.swf"></script>

</head>

<body></body>
</html>
```

Now the AIR application is ready to use the service monitor framework to monitor the status of network connectivity.

It is also good practice to import the *AIRAliases.js* file from the frameworks folder of the AIR SDK into the project directory of any AIR applications developed with HTML and JavaScript. Once you've imported it into the HTML page, you can access the AIR APIs without using the fully qualified package name of the class, saving you some typing. In fact, the *AIRAliases.js* file includes aliases for commonly used package-level functions. If you open the *AIRAliases.js* file, you will find the definitions of the aliases for all the AIR APIs. For example, for the `File` class, you'll find the following definitions:

```
air.File = window.runtime.flash.filesystem.File;
air.FileStream = window.runtime.flash.filesystem.FileStream;
air.FileMode = window.runtime.flash.filesystem.FileMode;
```

Therefore, instead of accessing the `File` class by going through the `runtime` property on the HTML `window` object, like so:

```
var myFile = new runtime.flash.filesystem.File("app:/myFile.txt");
```

these aliases allow you to access the `File` class with the shortest syntax that doesn't use the fully qualified package name, like so:

```
var myFile = new air.File("app:/myFile.txt");
```

The `app:/` prefix refers to the application directory of the application and is an alternative to using the `static` property on the `File` class.

 AIR defines the `runtime` property on the HTML `window` object; `runtime` provides access to the AIR classes using the fully qualified package name of the class.

You can import *AIRAliases.js* into the HTML page using the `script` tag:

```
<script type="text/javascript" src="frameworks/AIRAliases.js">
</script>
```

The HTML page, complete with the importation of the service monitor framework and AIR aliases, therefore becomes the following:

```
<!DOCTYPE html PUBLIC "-//W3C//DTD XHTML 1.0 Transitional//EN"
"http://www.w3.org/TR/xhtml1/DTD/xhtml1-transitional.dtd">

<html xmlns="http://www.w3.org/1999/xhtml">
<head>

<script type="application/x-shockwave-flash"
src="frameworks/servicemonitor.swf"></script>

<script type="text/javascript" src="frameworks/AIRAliases.js">
</script>

<meta http-equiv="Content-Type" content="text/html; charset=utf-8" />
<title>AIR Cookbook: Including the Service Monitor Framework in an
 Application (JavaScript)</title>
</head>

<body>

</body>
</html>
```

Monitoring Network Status with Adobe AIR

Two objects let you check the network connection status: the `networkChangeEvent` event and the `ServiceMonitor` class.

The `networkChangeEvent` event is one of the events of the `NativeApplication` class, which is a singleton object that dispatches application-level events.

 A *singleton* object is a design pattern that is used to restrict the instantiation of a class to one object. It is useful when exactly one object is needed to coordinate actions across the system.

The AIR application dispatches the `networkChangeEvent` event when a new network connection becomes available or an existing network connection is lost. This event informs you only that the status of the connection has changed; it does not provide information about the cause. With all the different types of connections available nowadays (Internet, VPN, wireless connection, UMTS, and so on), the `networkChangeEvent` event is limited in its scope. It is almost impossible to be sure that you have access to a certain resource by using this event only.

This is where the service monitor framework, based on the `ServiceMonitor` class, comes into play. You can use the `ServiceMonitor` class to control and monitor whether the AIR application can actually reach a specific service.

AIR's service monitor framework provides the classes and methods to execute controls on the status of network connectivity.

The ServiceMonitor class is a dynamic class that acts as a base class for all the other service monitor objects; it resides in the air.net package and dispatches the following events related to network connectivity:

- activate (an inherited event from the EventDispatcher class): This event is dispatched when the AIR application gains operating system focus and becomes active.

- deactivate (an inherited event from the EventDispatcher class): This event is dispatched when the AIR application loses operating system focus and is becoming inactive.

- status: This event is dispatched when the service status has changed.

This class is a base class for another two subclasses: URLMonitor and SocketMonitor. These are the two classes, with their related methods, that you will use most of the time to detect the status of the service.

The URLMonitor class, which is part of the air.net package, controls the availability of HTTP (or HTTPS) services, such as Representational State Transfer (REST) services.

> *REST* describes an interface that transmits domain-specific data over HTTP without using an additional messaging layer such as SOAP (which is used by web services).

The SocketMonitor class, on the other hand, controls the availability of the connection against a TCP socket, such as a mail or FTP server.

> A *TCP socket* is an endpoint for communication, and it consists of an <IP Address,Port> pair.

15.2 Including the Service Monitor Framework in an Application (Flash)

Problem

You want to use the service monitor framework with Adobe Flash to detect the status of network connectivity.

Solution

Import the `ServiceMonitorShim` library to detect the status of network connectivity.

Discussion

The service monitor framework is a separate framework from the standard AIR framework. To use the `ServiceMonitor` classes, you have to import the *ServiceMonitor Shim.swc* file into your AIR application first. The `ServiceMonitorShim` component is installed in the environment of Adobe Flash CS4 Professional when you install the Adobe AIR update for the software. With the Adobe AIR update installed, Adobe Flash CS4 Professional adds the necessary features to develop, compile, and distribute Adobe AIR applications with Flash. You can download the Adobe AIR update for Adobe Flash CS4 Professional in the Downloads section of the Adobe Flash Support Center (*http://www.adobe.com/support/flash/downloads.html*).

 Before installing the Adobe AIR update, you need to have installed the Adobe Flash Player update for Flash CS3 Professional (9.0.2). You can find this update to download in the same Downloads section.

Launch Flash CS4 Professional, and then choose Window→Components Panel to open the Components panel. Alternatively, you can press Ctrl+F7 (Windows) or Command +7 (Mac OS). You will notice a new category among the standard list of Flash components: AIR Service Monitor. Expand this category to find the `ServiceMonitorShim` component. To use the service monitor framework, you only have to drag this component from the Components panel into the Library. If you prefer, you can drag it directly on the Stage outside the visible area, and it will automatically be added to the Library (Figure 15-1).

With the `ServiceMonitorShim` component in your Flash project's Library, you can use the classes in the `air.net` package in Flash to add the `import` statement to your Action-Script 3 code:

```
import air.net.*;
```

For example, now you can to monitor the connection to a URL using the `URLMonitor` class (see Recipe 15.3), which is one of the classes in the `air.net` package:

```
import air.net.URLMonitor;
```

15.3 Monitoring the Connection to a URL

Problem

You need to check and monitor the availability of an HTTP- or HTTPS-based service.

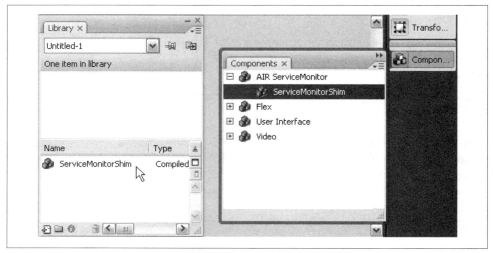

Figure 15-1. Dragging the ServiceMonitorShim *component from the Components panel into the Library*

Solution

Use the URLMonitor class to get the status of and monitor changes on the HTTP (or HTTPS) requests that can be made to a certain address.

Discussion

To be sure that a remote service can be reached, you can call that service to determine the status. The class you need for the job is URLMonitor, which is a subclass of Service Monitor.

The constructor of the class accepts two parameters: urlRequest, which is an instance of the URLRequest class that specifies the service or the URL to call, and acceptableSta tusCodes, which is typed as an Array and specifies the numeric status codes of the result. The acceptableStatusCodes parameter isn't compulsory, and if it isn't specified, the following values will be recognized as status codes:

- 200 (OK)
- 202 (Accepted)
- 204 (No content
- 205 (Reset content)
- 206 (Partial content in response to request with a Range header)

To create a URLMonitor object that determines the status of an HTTP (or HTTPS) service, it is sufficient to pass its constructor a URLRequest object with the URL to connect to. In ActionScript, you have to import the class from the air.net package and write the following:

```
import air.net.URLMonitor;
private var urlRequest : URLRequest = new
URLRequest( "http://www.comtaste.com" );
private var HTTPMonitor : URLMonitor = new URLMonitor( urlRequest );
```

With JavaScript, you have to import the *servicemonitor.swf* file to use the service monitor framework (see Recipe 15.1) and then write the following:

```
<script src="servicemonitor.swf" type="application/x-shockwave-flash">
</script>

<script type="text/javascript">
function init()
{
var urlRequest = new air.URLRequest( "http://www.comtaste.com" );
var httpMonitor = new air.URLMonitor(urlRequest);
}
</script>
```

In both cases, this code specifies only the HTTP (or HTTPS) service to which the call
must be directed to test its availability. No test is carried out until the start method of
the URLMonitor class has been executed. You can also create an event listener for the
StatusEvent.STATUS event and intercept the code property in the event object. The code
property of the STATUS event contains the description of the object's status:

```
httpMonitor .addEventListener( StatusEvent.STATUS, onStatusEvent );
httpMonitor .start();
```

Once the start method has launched the URLMonitor instance, this object keeps monitoring every change in the network. You can set the pollInterval property of the
ServiceMonitor to check connectivity at a specified interval in milliseconds.

When this change happens, you can also use the URLMonitor.available property, which
returns true or false according to the availability of the network. The initial value is
false until something changes in the network activity that sets the property to true:

```
httpMonitor.available
```

ActionScript/Flex

You can create an ActionScript class that verifies the availability of an HTTP service
and keeps monitoring changes in the network. The following code creates a class named
CheckURL and saves it in the com.oreilly.aircookbook.ch15 package:

```
package com.oreilly.aircookbook.ch15
{
    import air.net.URLMonitor;

    import flash.events.StatusEvent;
    import flash.net.URLRequest;
    import mx.controls.Alert;

    public class CheckURL
    {
```

```
private var urlMonitor:URLMonitor;
private var _isConnected : String;

public function CheckURL(urlRequest:URLRequest,
                         acceptableStatusCodes:Array=null)
{
    urlMonitor = new URLMonitor(urlRequest);
    urlMonitor.start();
    urlMonitor.addEventListener( StatusEvent.STATUS, onStatusEvent );
}

private function onStatusEvent( event:StatusEvent ) : void
{
    // it returns a Boolean
    isConnected = urlMonitor.available.toString();

    // it returns Service.available
    // isConnected = event.code;

    // If you're using the Flex SDK
    Alert.show( isConnected );

    // If you're using the Flash IDE
    trace( isConnected );
}

public function get isConnected():String
{
    return _isConnected;
}

[Bindable]
public function set isConnected(_isConnected:String):void
{
    this._isConnected = _isConnected;
}

    }
}
```

In the previous example, you declared the private property _isConnected in the class, and you specified the setter/getter methods for it. This is the property that will contain the status of network connectivity.

In the constructor class in the previous code, you created an instance of the URLMonitor class, which has the urlRequest and acceptableStatusCodes parameters set. The URLMonitor instance uses these two parameters, of which only the first is compulsory, to carry out the tests on the HTTP (or HTTPS) service. To launch the checking process, you executed the start method and created an event listener for the StatusEvent.STATUS event, which is registered in the onStatusEvent event handler.

The onStatusEvent event handler sets the isConnected property to the value contained in the urlMonitor.available property. This event handler is invoked every time the StatusEvent.STATUS event is triggered or every time the network connectivity changes.

If you re-create the example using the Adobe Flash IDE, remember to insert the ServiceMonitorShim component in the Library (see Recipe 15.3). If, on the other hand, you are using Flex Builder, the service monitor framework is automatically added as a library to the Flex project.

Furthermore, make sure the StatusEvent.STATUS event is dispatched even if, for example, only the access to the new connection is made.

JavaScript/HTML

In JavaScript, using the URLMonitor class is only slightly different. You first have to import *servicemonitor.swf* into the page (see Recipe 15.2).

The following example creates an AIR application that uses the URLMonitor class to verify that the image at *http://www.comtaste.com/img/logoComtaste.gif* is reachable. If the available property returns as true and therefore the service can be reached, you will load the remote image in a div placeholder and load the entire *http://www.comtaste .com* home page in the application. Here is the complete code for this example:

```
<!DOCTYPE html PUBLIC "-//W3C//DTD XHTML 1.0 Transitional//EN"
"http://www.w3.org/TR/xhtml1/DTD/xhtml1-transitional.dtd">
<html xmlns="http://www.w3.org/1999/xhtml">
<head>

<!-- Include service monitor framework -->
<script src="frameworks/servicemonitor.swf" type="application/x-shockwave-
flash"></script>

<script type="text/javascript" src="frameworks/AIRAliases.js"></script>
<script type="text/javascript" src="frameworks/AIRIntrospector.js"></script>

<script type="text/javascript">


var HTTPMonitor = null;

function checkConn()
{
    var req = new air.URLRequest("http://blog.comtaste.com/atom.xml");
    HTTPMonitor = new air.URLMonitor( req );
    HTTPMonitor.addEventListener(air.StatusEvent.STATUS, announceStatus);
    HTTPMonitor.start();
}

function announceStatus(e)
{

    if (HTTPMonitor.available)
```

```
    {
        document.getElementById("resultDiv").innerText = HTTPMonitor.available;
        loadImage();

    } else {
     document.getElementById("resultDiv").innerText = "Can't connect to the
URL. The connection is unavailable";
    }
}


function loadImage()
{
    myImg = document.createElement('img');
    myImg.src = "http://www.comtaste.com/img/logoComtaste.gif"
    document.getElementById("placeholder").appendChild(myImg);
    document.getElementById("htmlFrame").src = "http://www.comtaste.com/";
    document.getElementById("htmlFrame").onload = sizeFrame;
}

function sizeFrame(evt)
{
    document.getElementById("resultDiv").innerText = "The url: "
+evt.currentTarget.src +
    " has been loaded !";
}

</script>

<meta http-equiv="Content-Type" content="text/html" />
<title>AIR Cookbook: Including the Service Monitor Framework in an Application
(JavaScript)</title>

</head>

<body onload="checkConn()">

<div id="resultDiv">Checking .... </div>

    <div id="placeholder" > </div>

    <iframe id="htmlFrame" frameborder="0" width="600" height="450"/>

</body>
</html>
```

The JavaScript example invokes the checkConn method when the application starts up upon the onload event of the body. The checkConn method creates the instance of the URLMonitor class and verifies whether the image at *http://www.comtaste.com/img/logo Comtaste.gif* is reachable. An event listener is created for the STATUS event and registered to the announceStatus event handler. Finally, the HTTPMonitor object is executed by launching the start method.

The result of the HTTP (or HTTPS) service is returned by the `URLMonitor.available` property when the `STATUS` event is triggered. The `announceStatus` event handler tells the application to invoke the `loadImage` function or to alert the user with an error message.

The error message is written in the `div` element of the application with an `ID` equal to `resultDiv`. By using the `getElementById` method, you point to this node of the document, and by using the `innerText` property, you write the following error message: "Can't connect to the URL. The connection is unavailable."

If, on the other hand, the `available` property returns `true`, a call to the `loadImage` function is invoked. This function loads the remote image in an `img` dynamically created and loads the *http://www.comtaste.com* home page into an `iframe` tag.

15.4 Reading Only the Head of a URL

Problem

You need to check the availability of an HTTP service to download only the HTTP headers.

Solution

Use `method`, which is a public property of the `URLRequest` class (part of the `flash.net` package), to check only the HTTP header for an HTTP service.

Discussion

Sometimes you may have to manage several instances of the `URLMonitor` or `SocketMonitor` class to test whether the application can access different services. A good rule to follow is to test and verify the availability of a network service before using it. You must be careful, however, to use the connection tests wisely so as to not waste bandwidth. By taking advantage of the `method` property of the `URLRequest` object, you can optimize the data requests to the server.

ActionScript/Flex

Recipe 15.3 used the `URLMonitor` class to check the availability of an HTTP service. This class accepts two parameters to pass to the constructor: a `URLRequest` object and an `Array`:

```
URLMonitor(urlRequest:URLRequest, acceptableStatusCodes:Array = null)
```

In the first parameter, you specify a URL, creating an instance of the `URLRequest` class:

```
var checkConn:URLMonitor;
checkConn = new URLMonitor(new URLRequest('http://www.comtaste.com/index.php'));
```

With this code, the `URLMonitor` object checks the availability of the access to the *index.php* page on the *http://comtaste.com* domain, downloading the entire contents of the PHP page. For an application that has to verify more than one HTTP service, the operation could be bandwidth-intensive.

As an alternative, you can specify the `method` property of the `URLRequest` object to the `URLMonitor` object so that it downloads only the HTTP header information. This check is, in fact, sufficient to check the connection to that service.

Before passing the entire URL to check onto the constructor of the `URLMonitor` class, create a data type variable as `URLRequest`, and set the method value to the public constants available in the `URLRequestMethod` class:

```
var urlCheck:URLRequest = new URLRequest("http://www.comtaste.com/index.php");
urlCheck.method = URLRequestMethod.HEAD;

var checkConn:URLMonitor = new URLMonitor(urlCheck);
```

The `URLRequestMethod` class, when used in web applications in Flash Player, provides values that specify whether the `URLRequest` object should use the `POST` method or the `GET` method. This class, however, also shows the public static constant `HEAD`.

HTTP headers contain all the information of an HTTP request and are very important in an HTTP response. This is an example of an HTTP response header for the *http://www.comtaste.com* URL request:

HTTP Status Code: HTTP/1.1 200 OK
Server: Microsoft-IIS/5.0
Date: Sat, 07 Jun 2008 13:15:21 GMT
X-Powered-By: ASP.NET
Connection: close
X-Powered-By: PHP/5.1.6
Content-type: text/html

JavaScript/HTML

You can find the `URLRequest` class in the `air.URLRequest` package, and you can access it with the following:

```
request.method = air.URLRequestMethod.HEAD;
```

Otherwise, using the `method` property of the `URLRequest` property is similar to the ActionScript approach. Here's the complete example that uses the static `HEAD` constant:

```
<!DOCTYPE html PUBLIC "-//W3C//DTD XHTML 1.0 Transitional//EN"
"http://www.w3.org/TR/xhtml1/DTD/xhtml1-transitional.dtd">

<html xmlns="http://www.w3.org/1999/xhtml">
<head>

<script type="application/x-shockwave-flash"
src="frameworks/servicemonitor.swf"></script>

<script type="text/javascript" src="frameworks/AIRAliases.js"></script>
```

```
<script type="text/javascript">

        var checkURL = null;

        function init()
        {
            var request = new air.URLRequest( 'http://www.comtaste.com/' );
            request.method = air.URLRequestMethod.HEAD;

            checkURL = new air.URLMonitor( request );
            checkURL.addEventListener(air.StatusEvent.STATUS, announceStatus);
            checkURL.start();

        }

        function announceStatus(e)
        {
            if (HTTPMonitor.available)
            {
                document.getElementById("resultDiv").innerText =
                HTTPMonitor.available;

            } else {

                document.getElementById("resultDiv").innerText =
                "Can't connect to the url. The connection is unavailable";
            }
        }

</script>

<meta http-equiv="Content-Type" content="text/html; charset=utf-8" />
<title>AIR Cookbook:Reading only the HEAD of a URL (JavaScript)</title>
</head>

<body onload='init()'>

    <div id="resultDiv">Checking .... </div>

</body>
</html>
```

The init function is called upon the onload event of the application body. In this function, a URLRequest object is created, and its method property is set to the static constant
air.URLRequestMethod.HEAD.

15.5 Monitoring the Connection to a Specific Port on a Server

Problem

You want to monitor the connection to a network resource at a specific port.

Solution

Use `SocketMonitor`, which is a subclass of the `ServiceMonitor` class, to check and monitor the connections to a specific port on a server.

Discussion

Checking that you have the necessary authorizations to connect to a specific port on a server is crucial because firewalls or default network routers often restrict access to ports to guarantee network safety. That authorization is especially important for desktop applications that need to connect to a specific port of a server. For example, an application might have to send an email using the Simple Mail Transfer Protocol (SMTP), which initiates a TCP connection to the server's port 25.

Adobe AIR supports the `SocketMonitor` class in the service monitor framework, which allows the developer to check and monitor a specified TCP endpoint. This class is similar to the `URLMonitor` class (see Recipe 15.4), and its constructor has the following syntax:

```
SocketMonitor(host:String, port:int)
```

Set as type `String`, the `host` parameter specifies the host being monitored. The value assigned to `host` can be a domain name (such as *http://www.comtaste.com*) or an IP address (194.242.61.188). Set as type `int`, the `port` parameter specifies the port being monitored.

ActionScript/Flex

This example establishes a connection to a specific port. To check, monitor, and establish a connection to a specific port, create an instance of the `SocketMonitor` class, and specify the port to detect in the second parameter:

```
import air.net.SocketMonitor;
        private var monitor:SocketMonitor;
        private var conn:Socket;
        private var isConnected:String;

        public function checkPort(); void
        {
            // Create the istance of the Socket class
            conn = new Socket();

            // Create the istance of the SocketMonitor class
            //    to monitor port 25 on localhost server
            monitor = new SocketMonitor( " www.comtaste.com", 25 );

            conn.addEventListener(Event.CONNECT, onConnect);
            monitor.addEventListener(StatusEvent.STATUS, onSocketStatus);

            // To start the SocketMonitor class
```

```
        monitor.start();
    }
```

 If you are using the Adobe Flash IDE to create an AIR application, you need to import the *ServiceMonitorShim.swc* file into the Library of the Flash project in your AIR application package (see Recipe 15.2).

The checkPort method checks the availability of the connection to the *http://www.com taste.com* site over port 25, and if the connection has been successful, it connects to the server.

Then create two event listeners on the events of Event.CONNECT for the Socket class and on the events of StatusEvent.STATUS for the SocketMonitor class. In the event handler of the STATUS event, the available property is checked, and it returns a Boolean according to the result obtained by the connection test:

```
private function onConnect(event:Event):void
    {
        trace( "Connection to port 25 established !" );
        // You are now ready to send and receive data

    }

    private function onSocketStatus(e:StatusEvent):void
    {
        // it returns a Boolean
        isConnected = monitor.available.toString();

        // it returns Service.available
        // isConnected = event.code;

        if (monitor.available)
        {
            conn.connect("www.comtaste.com", 25 );

        } else {

            // If you're using the Flex SDK
            //Alert.show( "Connection to port 25 NOT established !" );

            // If you're using the Flash IDE
            trace( "Connection to port 25 NOT established !" );
        }
    }
```

JavaScript/HTML

In JavaScript, the operations to check and monitor the connection against a specific port are similar to those for ActionScript. The class you use is the same: the SocketMo nitor that can be instanced only after having imported the service monitor framework.

To import the service framework, you need to import the *servicemonitor.swf* file with a `script` tag in the page:

```
<!-- Include service monitor framework -->
<script src="frameworks/servicemonitor.swf" type="application/x-shockwave-flash" />
```

The example uses this component and its methods to detect connectivity changes to a URL connection on port 25:

```html
<!DOCTYPE html PUBLIC "-//W3C//DTD XHTML 1.0 Transitional//EN"
"http://www.w3.org/TR/xhtml1/DTD/xhtml1-transitional.dtd">
<html xmlns="http://www.w3.org/1999/xhtml">
<head>

    <!-- Include service monitor framework -->
    <script src="frameworks/servicemonitor.swf" type="application/x-shockwave-
flash"></script>

    <script type="text/javascript" src="frameworks/AIRAliases.js"></script>
    <script type="text/javascript" src="frameworks/AIRIntrospector.js"></script>

<script type="text/javascript">

    var checkSocket = null;
    var host = 'www.comtaste.com';
    var port = 25;

    function checkConn()
    {
        checkSocket = new air.SocketMonitor( host, port );
        checkSocket.addEventListener(air.StatusEvent.STATUS, announceStatus);
        checkSocket.start();
    }

    function announceStatus(e)
    {
        if (checkSocket.available)
        {
            document.getElementById("resultDiv").innerText = checkSocket.available;
        } else {
            document.getElementById("resultDiv").innerText = "Can't connect to port 25.
            The connection is unavailable";
        }
    }

</script>

<meta http-equiv="Content-Type" content="text/html; charset=utf-8" />
<title>AIR Cookbook: Monitoring the Connection to a Specific Port on a Server
(JavaScript)</title>
</head>

<body onload="checkConn()">

    <div id="resultDiv">Checking .... </div>
```

```
</body>
</html>
```

The SocketMonitor class accepts two parameters in the constructor: host and port. These two parameters are declared in the global variables in the script block and then used in the checkConn function and invoked on the onload event of the body.

 In addition to monitoring the connection to a server, AIR gives Java-Script developers the ability to communicate with a server on a specific port with the Socket and XMLSocket classes.

CHAPTER 16

Application Updates

In the past when a bug was found or an enhancement was needed, developers working on Internet-based applications enjoyed the simplicity of quickly and seamlessly updating the application running on their servers. This metaphor changes when developing applications for the desktop on Adobe AIR; under this model, updates now need to be distributed to the complete user base.

Now that your application resides in an environment you do not "own," you must take additional measures. To maintain the ability to perform seamless updates, you must include update procedures in your application before it goes into the wild so that it can "phone home" to get updates if and when needed.

16.1 Creating Applications with Update Capabilities

Problem

You are creating an AIR application that you plan to distribute and want to build in the ability to upgrade your users to new versions quickly.

Solution

Use the Adobe AIR Update Framework library, which is new to AIR 1.5 and makes it easier for applications to handle the various update scenarios that may arise.

Discussion

The Adobe AIR Update Framework library offers you all the functionality you need to create AIR applications that can remotely update themselves. The framework retrieves specifics about the available update from a *remote* XML file. This file contains versioning information, as well as the location of the update files. This file is accessed whenever the application makes a request to check for an update. Consider the following example called *update.xml*:

```
<?xml version="1.0" encoding="utf-8"?>
<update xmlns="http://ns.adobe.com/air/framework/update/description/1.0">
```

```
    <version>1.1</version>
    <url>http://mydomain.com/air/myapplication.air</url>
    <description><![CDATA[ Various Bug Fixes ]]></description>
</update>
```

The nodes of this XML file are as follows:

- version: The newest version available
- url: The URL to download the AIR package
- description: Additional text to provide the user with a description of what the update contains

You can also provide language-specific descriptions by adding a text subnode to the description node. Here's an example of this:

```
<description>
    <text xml:lang="en">English description</text>
    <text xml:lang="it">Italian description</text>
</description>
```

The Adobe AIR Update Framework supports a second, optional XML configuration file packaged with the application that you can use to set additional configuration properties that dictate the operations of the updating process at runtime. These configuration properties will instruct the framework on which dialog boxes to show to the user during the update process. You also can choose to set these properties manually on the ApplicationUpdaterUI class, but a best practice would be to include an XML file, such as *updaterConfig.xml* shown here, within your application distribution, so you can change configuration information within the XML file without having to recompile the application:

```
<?xml version="1.0" encoding="utf-8"?>
<configuration xmlns="http://ns.adobe.com/air/framework/update/configuration/1.0">
    <url>http://mydomain.com/myairapp/update.xml</url>
    <delay>1</delay>
    <defaultUI>
        <dialog name="checkForUpdate" visible="true" />
        <dialog name="downloadUpdate" visible="true" />
        <dialog name="downloadProgress" visible="true" />
        <dialog name="installUpdate" visible="true" />
    </defaultUI>
</configuration>
```

The nodes of this file are as follows:

- url: This is the path to the *update.xml* file (the remote XML file containing application version information).
- delay: This is the interval in which the Adobe AIR Update Framework checks whether updates are available. This is configured in days, so 1 represents one day. A value of .04 is approximately one hour.
- defaultUI: The dialog nodes within the defaultUI node allow you to show or hide specific sections of the Adobe AIR Update Framework user interface. By default,

they will all show. These dialog boxes are shown in Figure 16-1–Figure 16-4 later in this chapter.

Because you will be using the built-in updater interface of the `ApplicationUpdaterUI` class, you must make sure you have *applicationupdater_ui.swc* linked to your project.

To use this updater class, you create an instance of the `ApplicationUpdaterUI` class and set the path to the *updaterConfig.xml* file. Finally, you need to initialize the updater. The following examples show how to create an instance of the `ApplicationUpdaterUI` class, set the path to the *updaterConfig.xml* file, and initialize the updater. Consult the version appropriate for your application language.

Upon initialization of the `ApplicationUpdaterUI` instance, the `UpdateEvent.INITIAL IZED` event will fire, and you can check several properties of the instance. These properties include the following:

- `isFirstRun`: This is `true` only if this is the first run since an update has occurred.
- `previousVersion`: This contains the previous version information only if `isFirstRun` is `true`.
- `currentVersion`: This always contains the version information of the currently running application.

Because you set the delay to `1` in *updaterConfig.xml*, the updater will not automatically check until the application has been open for a full day. So, the updater also provides a way for you to manually check for updates by calling the `checkNow` method.

The `ApplicationUpdaterUI` class handles all the functionality of the update process. For information on how to create your own updater with a custom interface, please check out Recipe 16.2.

Flex/ActionScript

This example sets the path to the configuration file, instantiates an `ApplicationUpda terUI` instance, listens for the `UpdateEvent.INITIALIZED` event, and then initializes the updater on `creationComplete` of the application. Finally, when the initialize handler `updaterInitialized` is called, the event's properties are displayed onscreen.

 You need to have the *applicationupdater_ui.swc* file included in your Flex build path. This file can be found in the frameworks directory of the Adobe AIR 1.5 SDK.

```
<?xml version="1.0" encoding="utf-8"?>
<mx:WindowedApplication xmlns:mx="http://www.adobe.com/2006/mxml" layout="absolute"
    creationComplete="init()">
    <mx:Script>
    <![CDATA[
```

```
import air.update.events.UpdateEvent;
import air.update.ApplicationUpdaterUI;

private var updater:ApplicationUpdaterUI = new ApplicationUpdaterUI();

private function init():void{
    updater.configurationFile = new File("app:/config/updaterConfig.xml");
    updater.addEventListener(UpdateEvent.INITIALIZED, updaterInitialized);
    updater.initialize();
}

private function updaterInitialized(event:UpdateEvent):void{
    isFirstRun.text = event.target.isFirstRun;
    previousVersion.text = event.target.previousVersion;
    currentVersion.text = event.target.currentVersion;
}

]]>
</mx:Script>

<mx:Canvas width="300" height="200" horizontalCenter="0" verticalCenter="0">
    <mx:Label text="isFirstRun:" x="80" y="45"/>
    <mx:Text id="isFirstRun" x="180" y="45"/>
    <mx:Label text="previousVersion:" x="78" y="75"/>
    <mx:Text id="previousVersion" x="180" y="75"/>
    <mx:Label text="currentVersion:" x="78" y="105"/>
    <mx:Text id="currentVersion" x="180" y="105"/>
    <mx:Button click="updater.checkNow();" label="Check for Update"
    x="88" y="135"/>
</mx:Canvas>

</mx:WindowedApplication>
```

JavaScript

This example sets the path to the configuration file, instantiates an `ApplicationUpda`
`terUI` instance, listens for the `UpdateEvent.INITIALIZED` event, and then initializes the
updater when the `onLoad` event of the `body` tag is called. Finally, when the `updaterIni`
`tialized` method is called, the event's properties are displayed onscreen.

> You need to have the *applicationupdater_ui.swf* file included via a script
> as an include to your file, as shown next. This can be found in the
> frameworks directory of the AIR 1.5 SDK.

```
<!DOCTYPE html PUBLIC "-//W3C//DTD HTML 4.01//EN">
    <html>
    <head>
    <title>Update framework Sample</title>
    <script src="AIRAliases.js" type="text/javascript" charset="utf-8">
    </script>
    <script src="applicationupdater_ui.swf" type="application/x-shockwave-flash">
    </script>
```

```
<script>
var updater;
function initialize() (
    updater  = new runtime.air.update.ApplicationUpdaterUI();
    updater.configurationFile = new   air.File("app:/config/updaterConfig.xml");
    updater.addEventListener(
                  runtime.air.update.events.UpdateEvent.INITIALIZED,
                  function(event){updaterInitialized()}
      );
      updater.initialize();
}

function updaterInitialized(event) (
    document.getElementById('isFirstRun').innerHTML =
                          updater.isFirstRun;
    document.getElementById('previousVersion').innerHTML =
                          updater.previousVersion;
    document.getElementById('currentVersion').innerHTML =
                          updater.currentVersion;
}
</script>
</head>

<body onLoad="initialize()">
    isFirstRun: <span id="isFirstRun"></span><br/><br/>
    previousVersion:<span id="previousVersion"></span><br/><br/>
    currentVersion: <span id="currentVersion"></span><br/><br/>
    <input type="button" onClick="updater.checkNow()"
        value="Check for updates" />
</body>
</html>
```

In this recipe, the default `ApplicationUpdaterUI` class was used. Figure 16-1 through Figure 16-4 show various screens of the default user interface.

Specifically, Figure 16-1 shows the dialog box presented to the user when `checkForUp date` is set to `true` in *updaterConfig.xml*.

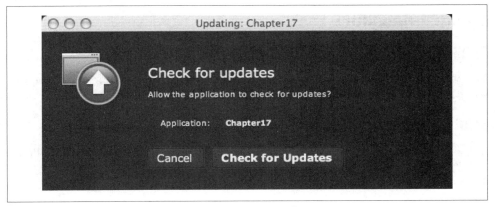

Figure 16-1. Step 1 of the default ApplicationUpdaterUI class

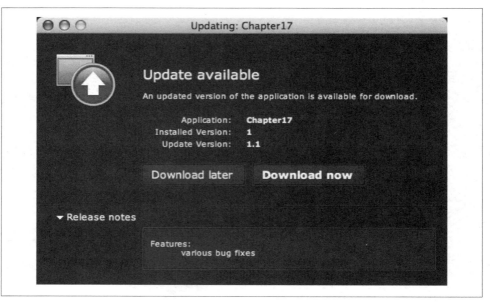

Figure 16-2. Step 2 of the default `ApplicationUpdaterUI` *class*

Figure 16-2 shows the dialog box presented to the user when `downloadUpdate` is set to true in *updaterConfig.xml*.

Figure 16-3 shows the dialog box presented to the user when `downloadProgress` is set to true in *updaterConfig.xml*.

Figure 16-4 shows the dialog box presented to the user when `installUpdate` is set to true in *updaterConfig.xml*.

16.2 Creating Custom Update Interfaces for Applications with Update Capabilities

Problem

You want to use the Adobe AIR Update Framework; however, your client requires specific information to appear in the updater dialog box.

Solution

Use the Adobe AIR Update Framework's *applicationupdater.swc/applicationupdater.swf* file, which does not include a user interface for the updater dialog box, and create a custom updater interface.

This is not the complete list of events available for the Adobe AIR Update Framework. It does include all the events necessary to create the custom updater interface in the following examples.

With an understanding of the events that will be listened for, you're ready to investigate the flow of the update process.

Flex/ActionScript

This sample consists of two files: the main MXML file based on the `WindowedApplication` file and a `Window` component that acts as the user interface for the update process. The `Window` component is referred to as `UpdateWindow` throughout the rest of this recipe and resides in the root directory along with the main MXML file. The main application window simply contains a single `Button` component that, when clicked, launches a new window. The code for the main application window is as follows:

```
<?xml version="1.0" encoding="utf-8"?>
<mx:WindowedApplication xmlns:mx="http://www.adobe.com/2006/mxml" layout="absolute"
    title="Adobe AIR Update Framework">

    <mx:Script>
        <![CDATA[

            private function openUpdateWindow():void{
                var updateWindow:UpdateWindow = new UpdateWindow();
                updateWindow.open();
            }
        ]]>
    </mx:Script>
    <mx:Button click="openUpdateWindow()" label="Open Update Window"
        horizontalCenter="0" verticalCenter="0"/>

</mx:WindowedApplication>
```

`UpdateWindow` is the guts of this example because it contains all the methods and event listeners to handle each step of the update process. This component contains five different states that contain the controls and feedback to give the user full control over the update. Each following section will contain only the methods necessary to interact with the Adobe AIR Update Framework. The full source code for `UpdateWindow` is available later in this recipe.

Upon `creationComplete` of the window, the `init` method is called. This method creates a new instance of the `ApplicationUpdater` class, sets the `delay` property of the updater to 0, sets the updater's `updateURL`, adds six different event listeners, and then calls the `initialize` method on new instance of the `ApplicationUpdater` class.

The UpdateWindow defaults to the Main state, which shows the user information about the currently installed application including the updater's isFirstRun, previousVersion, and currentVersion properties. It also contains a Button component, which allows the user to check to see whether an update is available.

Because the delay property is set to 0 in this example, the updater never automatically checks for an update. When the user clicks the Check for Update button, the updater's checkNow method is called. Figure 16-5 shows the results of the checkNow method.

```
private function init():void{
    updater = new ApplicationUpdater();
    updater.delay = 0;
    updater.updateURL = "http://mydomain.com/myairapp/update.xml";
    updater.addEventListener(UpdateEvent.INITIALIZED,
                             updaterInitialized);
    updater.addEventListener(StatusUpdateEvent.UPDATE_STATUS,
                             statusUpdate);
    updater.addEventListener(StatusUpdateErrorEvent.UPDATE_ERROR,
                             statusUpdateError);
    updater.addEventListener(UpdateEvent.DOWNLOAD_START,
                             downloadStarted);
    updater.addEventListener(ProgressEvent.PROGRESS,
                             downloadProgress);
    updater.addEventListener(UpdateEvent.DOWNLOAD_COMPLETE,
                             downloadComplete);
    updater.addEventListener(DownloadErrorEvent.DOWNLOAD_ERROR,
                             downloadError);
    updater.initialize();
}

private function updaterInitialized(event:UpdateEvent):void{
    isFirstRun.text = event.target.isFirstRun;
    previousVersion.text = event.target.previousVersion;
    currentVersion.text = event.target.currentVersion;
}
```

The checkNow method dispatches the StatusUpdateEvent.UPDATE_STATUS event, which then calls the statusUpdate method. If the available property of this event is true, the state of the UpdateWindow is set to Available. If there is no update available, the state is set to None, and the user is shown a message stating this.

```
private function statusUpdate(event:StatusUpdateEvent):void{
    event.preventDefault();
    if(event.available){
        currentState="Available";
        version.text =  event.version;
        details.text = String(event.details);
    } else {
        currentState="None";
    }
}
```

If an update is available, the user sees the Available state, information about the update is displayed, and the user can choose to cancel or download the update (Figure 16-6).

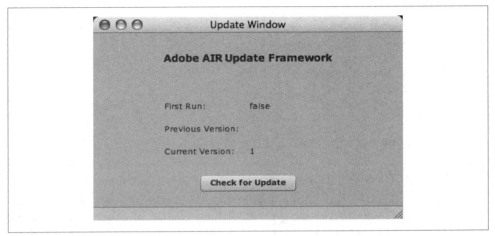

Figure 16-5. *UpdateWindow shows the updater's properties for the first run and the current version.*

Figure 16-6. *UpdateWindow shows that an update is available.*

If the user clicks the Download Now button, the downloadUpdate method is called on the ApplicationUpdater instance. The ApplicationUpdater instance then attempts to download the new AIR file from the URL that has been supplied in the *update.xml* file. If the ApplicationUpdater instance is able to begin the download, the UpdateEvent.DOWN LOAD_START event is dispatched, and the downloadStarted method is called, which changes UpdateWindow to the Downloading state. If the ApplicationUpdater instance cannot begin the download, the DownloadErrorEvent.DOWNLOAD_ERROR event is dispatched, which calls the downloadError method. The downloadError method simply alerts the user that a problem occurred when attempting the download.

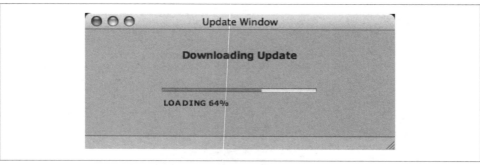

Figure 16-7. UpdateWindow shows the download progress.

Assuming that the download has started correctly, the `ProgressEvent.PROGRESS` event begins to be dispatched as the file is downloading. This event calls the `downloadPro gress` method, which updates a progress bar that is part of the `Downloading` state. Figure 16-7 shows the download progress being displayed to the user.

```
private function downloadStarted(event:UpdateEvent):void{
    currentState="Downloading";
}

private function downloadError(event:DownloadErrorEvent):void{
    currentState="";
    Alert.show("An error has occurred while downloading the update",
                        "DownloadErrorEvent.DOWNLOAD_ERROR");
    close();
}

private function downloadProgress(event:ProgressEvent):void{
    dBar.setProgress(event.bytesLoaded, event.bytesTotal);
}
```

Upon completion of the download, the `UpdateEvent.DOWNLOAD_COMPLETE` event is dispatched, which calls the `downloadComplete` method. If this event is ignored, the `ApplicationUpdater` automatically begins the install of the new AIR application. In this example, the `preventDefault` method is called on the `UpdateEvent`, and the state of `UpdateWindow` is set to `InstallNow`. The `preventDefault` method halts the automatic install by the `ApplicationUpdater` instance (Figure 16-8).

```
private function downloadComplete(event:UpdateEvent):void{
    event.preventDefault();
    currentState="InstallNow";
}
```

The `InstallNow` state gives the user the option to cancel or install the update. If the user chooses to install the update, the `installUpdate` method is called on the `Application Updater` instance. At this time, the application closes, installs the new AIR application, and relaunches. Upon relaunch, if the user launches `UpdateWindow`, the `isFirstRun` property shows as `true`, and the new version information is displayed (Figure 16-9).

Figure 16-8. *UpdateWindow* asks the user whether they want to install the update.

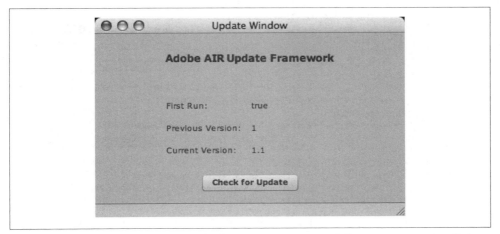

Figure 16-9. *UpdateWindow* shows that the first run is now **true** and the new version is installed.

The full source code for UpdateWindow is as follows:

```
<?xml version="1.0" encoding="utf-8"?>
<mx:Window xmlns:mx="http://www.adobe.com/2006/mxml" width="400" height="300"
    creationComplete="init()" layout="absolute" currentState="Main"
    title="Update Window">

    <mx:states>
        <mx:State name="Available">
            <mx:AddChild position="lastChild">
                <mx:Text id="version" x="181.5" y="64"/>
            </mx:AddChild>
            <mx:SetProperty target="{mainTitle}" name="text"
                value="There is an update available"/>
            <mx:AddChild position="lastChild">
                <mx:Label x="98.5" y="64" text="New version:"/>
            </mx:AddChild>
```

```
                    <mx:AddChild position="lastChild">
                        <mx:Label x="98" y="90" text="Details:"/>
                    </mx:AddChild>
                    <mx:AddChild position="lastChild">
                        <mx:TextArea x="181" y="89" id="details" width="174"
                            height="126" editable="false"/>
                    </mx:AddChild>
                    <mx:AddChild position="lastChild">
                        <mx:Button x="181" y="223" label="Cancel" click="close()"/>
                    </mx:AddChild>
                    <mx:AddChild position="lastChild">
                        <mx:Button x="246" y="223" label="Download Now"
                            click="updater.downloadUpdate();"/>
                    </mx:AddChild>
            </mx:State>
            <mx:State name="Downloading">
                <mx:SetProperty target="{mainTitle}" name="text"
                    value="Downloading Update"/>
                <mx:AddChild position="lastChild">
                    <mx:ProgressBar x="99" y="78" id="dBar" mode="manual"/>
                </mx:AddChild>
            </mx:State>
            <mx:State name="None">
                <mx:AddChild position="lastChild">
                    <mx:Button label="Close" click="close();"
                        y="81" horizontalCenter="0"/>
                </mx:AddChild>
                <mx:SetProperty target="{mainTitle}" name="text"
                    value="You already have the most current version"/>
            </mx:State>
            <mx:State name="InstallNow">
                <mx:SetProperty target="{mainTitle}" name="text"
                    value="Would you like to install the update now?"/>
                <mx:AddChild position="lastChild">
                    <mx:Button x="190.5" y="94"
                        label="Install Now" click="updater.installUpdate();"/>
                </mx:AddChild>
                <mx:AddChild position="lastChild">
                    <mx:Button x="117.5" y="94" label="Cancel" click="close()"/>
                </mx:AddChild>
            </mx:State>
            <mx:State name="Main">
                <mx:AddChild position="lastChild">
                    <mx:Label x="90" y="90" text="First Run:"/>
                </mx:AddChild>
                <mx:AddChild position="lastChild">
                    <mx:Label x="90" y="120" text="Previous Version:"/>
                </mx:AddChild>
                <mx:AddChild position="lastChild">
                    <mx:Label x="90" y="150" text="Current Version:"/>
                </mx:AddChild>
                <mx:AddChild position="lastChild">
                    <mx:Text x="200" y="90" id="isFirstRun"/>
                </mx:AddChild>
                <mx:AddChild position="lastChild">
```

```
                    <mx:Text x="200" y="120" id="previousVersion"/>
            </mx:AddChild>
            <mx:AddChild position="lastChild">
                    <mx:Text x="200" y="150" id="currentVersion"/>
            </mx:AddChild>
            <mx:AddChild position="lastChild">
                    <mx:Button y="190" label="Check for Update" horizontalCenter="0"
                        click="updater.checkNow()"/>
            </mx:AddChild>
        </mx:State>
</mx:states>

<mx:Script>
        <![CDATA[

            import mx.controls.Alert;
            import air.update.events.StatusUpdateErrorEvent;
            import air.update.events.StatusUpdateEvent;
            import air.update.events.DownloadErrorEvent;
            import air.update.events.UpdateEvent;
            import air.update.ApplicationUpdater;

            public var updater:ApplicationUpdater

            private function init():void{
                updater = new ApplicationUpdater();
                updater.delay = 0;
                updater.updateURL = "http://mydomain.com/myairapp/update.xml";
                updater.addEventListener(UpdateEvent.INITIALIZED,
                                        updaterInitialized);
                updater.addEventListener(StatusUpdateEvent.UPDATE_STATUS,
                                        statusUpdate);
                updater.addEventListener(StatusUpdateErrorEvent.UPDATE_ERROR,
                                        statusUpdateError);
                updater.addEventListener(UpdateEvent.DOWNLOAD_START,
                                        downloadStarted);
                updater.addEventListener(ProgressEvent.PROGRESS,
                                        downloadProgress);
                updater.addEventListener(UpdateEvent.DOWNLOAD_COMPLETE,
                                        downloadComplete);
                updater.addEventListener(DownloadErrorEvent.DOWNLOAD_ERROR,
                                        downloadError);
                updater.initialize();
            }

            private function updaterInitialized(event:UpdateEvent):void{
                isFirstRun.text = event.target.isFirstRun;
                previousVersion.text = event.target.previousVersion;
                currentVersion.text = event.target.currentVersion;
            }


            private function statusUpdate(event:StatusUpdateEvent):void{
                event.preventDefault();
                if(event.available){
```

```
                                currentState="Available";
                                version.text =  event.version;
                                details.text = String(event.details);
                        } else {
                                currentState="None";
                        }
                }


            private function statusUpdateError(event:StatusUpdateErrorEvent):void{
                currentState="";
                        Alert.show("An error has occurred while checking for updates",
                                    "StatusUpdateEvent.UPDATE_STATUS");
                        close();
                }

            private function downloadStarted(event:UpdateEvent):void{
                        currentState="Downloading";
                }

            private function downloadError(event:DownloadErrorEvent):void{
                        currentState="";
                        Alert.show("An error has occurred while downloading the update",
                                    "DownloadErrorEvent.DOWNLOAD_ERROR");
                        close();
                }

            private function downloadProgress(event:ProgressEvent):void{
                        dBar.setProgress(event.bytesLoaded, event.bytesTotal);
                }

            private function downloadComplete(event:UpdateEvent):void{
                        event.preventDefault();
                        currentState="InstallNow";
                }

        ]]>
    </mx:Script>

    <mx:Label y="24" text="Adobe AIR Update Framework"
            horizontalCenter="0" width="100%"
            textAlign="center" fontWeight="bold" fontSize="13" id="mainTitle"/>

    </mx:Window>
```

JavaScript

This sample consists of two files: the main *Index.html* file that acts as the main application window and a `Window` component (called `UpdateWindow` throughout this recipe) that contains the *UpdateWindow.html* file and acts as the user interface for the update process. The main application window contains a single `Button` that, when clicked, launches a new window. The code for *Index.html* file is as follows:

```
<!DOCTYPE html PUBLIC "-//W3C//DTD HTML 4.01//EN">
    <html>
    <head>
    <title>Adobe AIR Update Framework</title>
    <script>
          function openUpdateWindow(){
                var updateWindow = window.open('UpdateWindow.html',null,
                                    'width = 220, height = 250');
          }
    </script>
    </head>
    <body>
    <div align="center">
          <input type="button" onClick="openUpdateWindow()"
                value="Open Update Window" />
    </div>
    </body>
</html>
```

UpdateWindow is the guts of this example because it contains all the methods and event listeners to handle each step of the update process. This file contains five different divs that contain the controls and feedback to give the user full control over the update.

When the *UpdateWindow.html* file loads into Window, the body tag's onLoad event calls the initialize method, which creates a new instance of the ApplicationUpdater class. It also sets the delay property of the updater to 0, sets the updater's updateURL, adds six different event listeners, and then calls the initialize method on the new instance of the ApplicationUpdater.

UpdateWindow defaults to showing only the Main div, which shows the user information about the currently installed application including the updater's isFirstRun, previous Version, and currentVersion properties. It also contains a Button, which allows the user to check to see whether an update is available.

Because the delay was set to 0 in this example, the updater will never automatically check for an update. When the user clicks the Check for Update button, the updater's checkNow method is called (Figure 16-10).

The checkNow method dispatches the StatusUpdateEvent.UPDATE_STATUS event, which then calls the statusUpdate method. If the available property of this event is true, the state of the UpdateWindow is set to Available. If there is no update available, the state is set to None, and the user is shown a message stating this.

If an update is available and the user is now seeing only the Available div, information about the update is displayed, and the user is given the option to cancel or download the update (Figure 16-11).

If the user has clicks the Download Now button, the downloadUpdate method is called on the ApplicationUpdater. The ApplicationUpdater then attempts to download the new AIR file from the URL that has been supplied in the *update.xml* file. If the ApplicationUpdater is able to begin the download, the UpdateEvent.DOWNLOAD_START

Figure 16-10. UpdateWindow shows the updater's properties for the first run and the current version.

Figure 16-11. UpdateWindow shows that an update is available.

event is dispatched, and the downloadStarted method is called, which changes the UpdateWindow component to show only the Downloading div. If the ApplicationUpdater cannot begin the download, the DownloadErrorEvent.DOWNLOAD_ERROR event is dispatched, which calls the downloadError method. The downloadError method simply alerts the user that a problem occurred when attempting the download.

Assuming that the download has started correctly, the ProgressEvent.PROGRESS event begins to be dispatched as the file is downloading. This event calls the downloadProgress method, which updates the Downloading div and shows the percent of download completed (Figure 16-12).

Upon completion of the download, the UpdateEvent.DOWNLOAD_COMPLETE event is dispatched, which calls the downloadComplete method. If this event is ignored, the ApplicationUpdater automatically begins the install of the new AIR application. In this example, the preventDefault method is called on the UpdateEvent, and the Update Window is set to show only the InstallNow div (Figure 16-13). The preventDefault method will halt the automatic install by the ApplicationUpdater.

The InstallNow state gives the user the option to cancel or install the update. If the user chooses to install, the installUpdate method is called on the ApplicationUpdater. The

Figure 16-12. UpdateWindow shows the download progress.

Figure 16-13. UpdateWindow asks user whether they want to install the update.

Figure 16-14. UpdateWindow shows that the first run is now true and the new version is installed.

application closes, installs the new AIR application, and relaunches. Upon relaunch, if the user launches UpdateWindow, the isFirstRun property shows as true, and the new version information is displayed (Figure 16-14).

The full source code for UpdateWindow (*UpdateWindow.html*) file is as follows:

```
<!DOCTYPE html PUBLIC "-//W3C//DTD HTML 4.01//EN">
    <html>
```

```
<head>
<title>Update Window</title>
<script src="AIRAliases.js" type="text/javascript" charset="utf-8">
</script>
<script src="applicationupdater.swf" type="application/x-shockwave-flash">
</script>
<script>

var updater;

function showDiv(divName){
    document.getElementById('Available').style.visibility = 'hidden';
    document.getElementById('Downloading').style.visibility = 'hidden';
    document.getElementById('InstallNow').style.visibility = 'hidden';
    document.getElementById('Main').style.visibility = 'hidden';
    document.getElementById('None').style.visibility = 'hidden';
    document.getElementById(divName).style.visibility = 'visible';
}

function initialize(){
    showDiv('Main');
    updater = new runtime.air.update.ApplicationUpdater();
    updater.delay=0;
    updater.updateURL = "http://mydomain.com/myairap/update.xml";

updater.addEventListener(runtime.air.update.events.UpdateEvent.INITIALIZED,
                         function(event){updaterInitialized(event);}
                         );

updater.addEventListener(runtime.air.update.events.StatusUpdateEvent.UPDATE_STATUS,
                         function(event){statusUpdate(event);}
                         );

updater.addEventListener(runtime.air.update.events.StatusUpdateErrorEvent.UPDATE_ERROR,
                         function(event){statusUpdateError(event);}
                         );

updater.addEventListener(runtime.air.update.events.UpdateEvent.DOWNLOAD_START,
                         function(event){downloadStarted(event);}
                         );

updater.addEventListener(air.ProgressEvent.PROGRESS,
                         function(event){downloadProgress(event);}
                         );
updater.addEventListener(runtime.air.update.events.UpdateEvent.DOWNLOAD_COMPLETE,
                         function(event){downloadComplete(event);}
                         );

updater.addEventListener(runtime.air.update.events.DownloadErrorEvent.DOWNLOAD_ERROR,
                         function(event){downloadError(event);}
                         );

    updater.initialize();

}
```

```
function updaterInitialized(event){

    document.getElementById('isFirstRun').innerHTML =
                                    updater.isFirstRun;

    document.getElementById('previousVersion').innerHTML =
                                    updater.previousVersion;

    document.getElementById('currentVersion').innerHTML =
                                    updater.currentVersion;
    showDiv('Main');

}

function statusUpdate(event){
    event.preventDefault();
    if(event.available){
        showDiv('Available');
        document.getElementById('version').innerHTML =
                                    event.version;
        document.getElementById('details').innerHTML =
                                    event.details;
    } else {
        showDiv('None');
    }
 }

function statusUpdateError(event){
    alert('statusUpdateError');
}

function downloadStarted(event){
    showDiv('Downloading');
}

function downloadError(event){
    showDiv('Main');
    alert('An error has occurred while downloading the update');
    window.close();
}

function downloadProgress(event){
    document.getElementById('progress').innerHTML =
        Math.ceil((event.bytesLoaded/event.bytesTotal)*100) + "%";
}

function downloadComplete(event){
    event.preventDefault();
    showDiv('InstallNow');
}

</script>
```

```
<style>
    div{
        position:absolute;
    }
</style>

</head>

<body onLoad="initialize()">

    <div id="Available" align="center">
    <h3>There is an update available</h3>
    New Version: <span id="version"></span><br/><br/>

    Details:<span id="details"></span><br/><br/>
    <input type="button" onClick="window.close()"
        value="Cancel" />
    <input type="button" onClick="updater.downloadUpdate()"
        value="Download Update" />
    </div>

    <div id="Downloading" align="center">
    <h3>Downloading Update</h3>
    Progress: <span id="progress"></span>
    </div>

    <div id="InstallNow" align="center">
    <h3>Would you like to install the update now?</h3>
    <input type="button" onClick="window.close()"
        value="Cancel" />
    <input type="button" onClick="updater.installUpdate()"
        value="Install Update" />
    </div>

    <div id="Main" align="center">
    <h3>Adobe AIR Update Framework</h3>
    isFirstRun: <span id="isFirstRun"></span><br/><br/>

    previousVersion:<span id="previousVersion"></span><br/><br/>

    currentVersion: <span id="currentVersion"></span><br/><br/>

    <input type="button" onClick="updater.checkNow()"
        value="Check for Updates" />
    </div>

    <div id="None" align="center">
    <h3>You already have the most current version</h3>
    <input type="button" onClick="window.close()"
        value="Cancel" />
    </div>

</body>
</html>
```

CHAPTER 17

AIR Application Distribution with the Browser API

After you create your AIR application, you will need a reliable means of distributing your application to its potential users. The AIR Browser API enables developers to distribute their applications via the browser so that the install process is as seamless as possible for the end user. When you use the Browser API, you can prevent a user from having to install AIR separately from your application. This means the user can install your application without ever leaving your site and in as few steps as possible.

In addition, the Browser API provides functionality beyond installation. For example, you can launch an AIR application from the browser. Additionally, you can determine valuable pieces of information about the user's environment including whether the user has AIR installed, whether the user has your application installed, and what version of your application is installed.

17.1 Including the Browser API

Problem

You need to include the Browser API in a Flash movie to interact with an AIR application from the Web.

Solution

Include the Browser API SWF in your application to gain the needed functionality.

Discussion

To utilize any of the Browser API functionality, it must first be included in your application. Adobe hosts the SWF for the Browser API at *http://airdownload.adobe.com/air/browserapi/air.swf*. You can load this SWF into your Flash, Flex, or SWF-based AIR application to provide the Browser API functionality.

This snippet demonstrates how to include the Browser API SWF in your application:

```
private const BROWSERAPI_URL_BASE: String =
"http://airdownload.adobe.com/air/browserapi";

private var _loader:Loader;
private var _air:Object;

public function handleCreationComplete():void {
    _loader = new Loader();
    var loaderContext:LoaderContext = new LoaderContext();
    loaderContext.applicationDomain = ApplicationDomain.currentDomain;
    _loader.contentLoaderInfo.addEventListener(Event.INIT, onInit);
    _loader.load(new URLRequest(BROWSERAPI_URL_BASE + "/air.swf"), loaderContext);
}

private function onInit(e:Event):void {
    _air = e.target.content;
}
```

17.2 Detecting the Installed Version of AIR

Problem

You need to determine which version of AIR is installed on the user's computer.

Solution

Access the `runtimeVersion` property of the `NativeApplication` instance to determine which version of AIR is installed.

Discussion

There are times when you want to determine which version of AIR is running on the user's computer. While technically part of the Browser API, this can allow you to warn the user if the updated version of your application will require an update to the runtime as well. The `NativeApplication` class instance that is at `NativeApplication.nativeApplication` contains a property, `runtimeVersion`, that contains the current runtime on the user's computers. In addition, there is also a property, `runtimePatchLevel`, that will return just the patch level for the current version. The `runtimeVersion` property contains both the major release version as well as the patch level.

ActionScript/Flex

In this example, a Flex application detects the version of AIR that is installed on the user's computer:

```
<?xml version="1.0" encoding="utf-8"?>
<mx: Application
    xmlns:mx="http://www.adobe.com/2006/mxml"
```

```
    layout="vertical"
    horizontalAlign="center"
    verticalAlign="middle">

    <mx:Label text="Installed AIR Version:
        {NativeApplication.nativeApplication.runtimeVersion}"
        fontWeight="bold" />

</mx: Application>
```

JavaScript

In this example, a JavaScript application detects the version of AIR that is installed on the user's computer:

```html
<html>
 <head>
        <title>Application Sandbox sample</title>
        <script type="text/javascript" src="AIRAliases.js"></script>
        <script type="text/javascript">
            function getAIRVersion() {
                var version = document.getElementById("version");
                version.innerHTML =
                    air.NativeApplication.nativeApplication.runtimeVersion;
            }
        </script>
 </head>
    <body onload="getAIRVersion()">
        <h3>AIR Version</h3>
        <div id="version"></div>
    </body>
</html>
```

17.3 Launching an AIR Application from the Browser

Problem

You need to be able to launch an AIR application from your website.

Solution

Use the Browser API's `launchApplication` method to launch an approved AIR application from the browser.

Discussion

The Browser API gives you the ability to launch an AIR application from a web-based SWF, but this method has a few limitations. First, this functionality works only on AIR applications that allow it. If the `allowBrowserInvocation` setting in the application descriptor file (see Chapter 2) is set to `true`, then the application can be launched from the browser. If it is not set to `true` (it defaults to `false`), the invoked application will never launch. Second, the launching of the application must be triggered by a user gesture (in most cases a mouse click). This is a purposeful limitation that keeps SWFs from launching an AIR application without the user's knowledge.

You can launch applications by using the Browser API's `launchApplication` method. To use this approach, you will need two pieces of information: the application ID of the AIR application and the publisher ID of the AIR application.

Finding the Publisher ID

The publisher ID is defined only when an application is packaged and is always `null` when launching your application from `adl`. You can determine this value in two ways. You can check `NativeApplication.nativeApplication.publisherID` for the publisher ID at runtime; alternatively, any time after the application is installed, you can navigate to the installation directory and consult the *META-INF/AIR/publisherid* file, which contains the publisher ID.

This recipe's examples use a sample AIR application. This application has no real UI or controls; rather, it just displays "Application Launched" when the application opens. For this sample, the application ID is `com.oreilly.aircookbook.as.17.3`, and the publisher ID is `9F542B7BA834BBBF0CA61BF006C9E4312C42DDE6.1`. If you want to see the sample work with your application, be sure to modify these parameters accordingly.

Using the Browser API

To use the Browser API to launch an AIR application, you first have to load the Browser API into your application. Next, you need to call the `launchApplication` method, which takes three parameters: the application ID, the publisher ID, and an array of arguments. The first two parameters are required, but you are not obligated to pass in any arguments.

In this example, the user interface consists of a single button that launches the application. This button is enabled once the Browser API SWF is loaded.

```
<?xml version="1.0" encoding="utf-8"?>
<mx:Application xmlns:mx="http://www.adobe.com/2006/mxml"
    layout="absolute"
    creationComplete="handleCreationComplete()">

    <mx:Script>
        <![CDATA[

            private const BROWSERAPI_URL_BASE: String =
"http://airdownload.adobe.com/air/browserapi";

            private var _loader:Loader;
            private var _air:Object;

            public function handleCreationComplete():void {
                _loader = new Loader();
```

```
                var loaderContext:LoaderContext = new LoaderContext();
                loaderContext.applicationDomain =
ApplicationDomain.currentDomain;
                _loader.contentLoaderInfo.addEventListener(Event.INIT, onInit);
                _loader.load(new URLRequest(BROWSERAPI_URL_BASE + "/air.swf"),
loaderContext);
            }

            private function onInit(e:Event):void {
                _air = e.target.content;
                launchButton.enabled = true;
            }

            private function handleClick( event:MouseEvent ):void {
                _air.launchApplication( "com.oreilly.aircookbook.as.17.3",
                        "9F542B7BA834BBBF0CA61BF006C9E4312C42DDE6.1" );
            }

        ]]>
    </mx:Script>

    <mx:Button id="launchButton" label="Launch Application" enabled="false"
click="handleClick(event)" />

</mx:Application>
```

Here is the code to build a sample AIR application that offers its publisher ID for use in the previous example:

```
Decscriptor:
<?xml version="1.0" encoding="UTF-8"?>
<application xmlns="http://ns.adobe.com/air/application/1.5">
    <id>com.oreilly.aircookbook.as.17.3</id>
    <filename>aircookbook.17.3</filename>
    <name>aircookbook.as.17.3</name>
    <version>v1</version>
    <initialWindow>
        <content>ch17_3.swf</content>
    </initialWindow>
    <allowBrowserInvocation>true</allowBrowserInvocation>
</application>

The application code:
<?xml version="1.0" encoding="utf-8"?>
<mx:WindowedApplication xmlns:mx="http://www.adobe.com/2006/mxml" layout="vertical">
 <mx:Text text="THIS IS AN EXAMPLE APPLICATION" />
 <mx:Text text="{NativeApplication.nativeApplication.publisherID}" />
</mx:WindowedApplication>
```

17.4 Installing an AIR Application from the Browser

Problem

You want to implement a custom installation solution in the browser, such as a one-click install from an online Flash or Flex application.

Solution

Use the install method found in the Browser API to attach the installation of an AIR application to a Flex or Flash UI control.

Discussion

The easiest means of installing an AIR application from the browser is using one of the install badges, which use the Browser API to perform the installation (for more information on the install badges, see Recipe 17.5). In cases where you want to customize the experience beyond the standard install badge, though, you can utilize the Browser API to provide similar functionality.

After you include the Browser API in your application, the three methods you need to use are `getStatus` to determine whether AIR is installed (or available for the operating system), `getApplicationVersion` to determine which (if any) version of the application is installed on the operating system, and `installApplication` to perform the actual installation.

The `getStatus` method returns a string that indicates the status of AIR on the user's machine. It returns three possible values:

- `installed`: Indicates that AIR is already installed on the user's machine
- `available`: Indicates that AIR is not installed on the user's machine but it is available for the user's platform
- `unavailable`: Indicates that AIR is not installed on the user's machine and there is not a current version of the runtime for the user's platform

The `installApplication` method takes three parameters: the absolute URL for the packaged AIR file, the version of AIR that is required, and an array of arguments. The arguments are optional and are passed to the application's install process if present. If the user does not have AIR installed, it will be installed with the AIR application. However, you will want to be sure that AIR is available for the user's platform to prevent any unwanted errors from being displayed. It is best to call the `getStatus` method if you are planning to call the `installApplication` method.

The `getApplicationVersion` method takes three parameters. First, you pass in the application ID. Second, you pass in the publisher ID. Finally, you pass in a callback method that will be executed when the value is returned. The callback method will be passed the application version as a string.

In this example, a sample application is located at *http://www.davidtucker.net/staging/ TargetApplication.air*. The application ID and publisher ID are also included in the code. The user interface for this example consists of a button that triggers the application installation and a label that indicates the status to the user. First, the Browser API is loaded. Then, upon initialization, the getStatus method is called. If the status (and, consequently, AIR) is installed or available, the install button is enabled. If the AIR status is installed, the application also calls the getApplicationVersion method to determine whether the application has already been installed.

```
<?xml version="1.0" encoding="utf-8"?>
<mx:WindowedApplication xmlns:mx="http://www.adobe.com/2006/mxml"
    layout="vertical"
    horizontalAlign="center"
    verticalAlign="middle"
    creationComplete="handleCreationComplete()">

    <mx:Script>
        <![CDATA[

            private const BROWSERAPI_URL_BASE: String =
"http://airdownload.adobe.com/air/browserapi";

            private var _loader:Loader;
            private var _air:Object;

            public function handleCreationComplete():void {
                _loader = new Loader();
                var loaderContext:LoaderContext = new LoaderContext();
                loaderContext.applicationDomain =
ApplicationDomain.currentDomain;
                _loader.contentLoaderInfo.addEventListener(Event.INIT, onInit);
                _loader.load(new URLRequest(BROWSERAPI_URL_BASE + "/air.swf"),
loaderContext);
            }

            private function onInit(e:Event):void {
                _air = e.target.content;
                var airStatus:String = _air.getStatus();
                switch( airStatus ) {
                    case "installed":
                        _air.getApplicationVersion(
"com.oreilly.aircookbook.as.17.3", "9F542B7BA834BBBF0CA61BF006C9E4312C42DDE6.1",
handleApplicationVersion );
                        break;
                    case "available":
                        statusLabel.text = "AIR will need to be installed for
this application";

                        installButton.enabled;
                        break;
                    case "unavailable":
                        statusLabel.text = "AIR is not available for your platform";
                        break;
                }
            }
```

```
                private function handleApplicationVersion( version:String ):void
                {
                    if( version != null ) {
                        statusLabel.text = "Version Installed: " + version;
                        installButton.enabled = false;
                    } else {
                        statusLabel.text = "Application Not Installed";
                        installButton.enabled = true;
                    }
                }

                private function handleClick( event:MouseEvent ):void
                {
                    _air.installApplication(
"http://www.davidtucker.net/staging/TargetApplication.air", "1.5" );
                }

            ]]>
        </mx:Script>

        <mx:Button id="installButton" label="Install Application" enabled="false"
click="handleClick(event)" />

        <mx:Label id=" statusLabel " />

    </mx:WindowedApplication>
```

Remember that the installation *must* be triggered by a user gesture. In this case, you couldn't call the `installApplication` method at any point; it has to be on the mouse click. This is a security feature baked into the Browser API that prevents you from launching or installing an application without the user's knowledge or consent.

17.5 Using the Included Seamless Install Badge

Problem

You need a prebuilt and easy-to-implement way to install an AIR application from the browser.

Solution

Use the seamless install badge from Adobe.

Discussion

An *install badge* allows any user with Flash Player version 9.0.115 or newer installed to install an AIR application from the Web. In addition, if the user does not have AIR installed, AIR automatically installs with the application. When paired with the Flash

Player Express Install functionality, install badges enable users to upgrade Flash Player to the needed level before attempting to install the AIR application.

 At the time this book was being written, Adobe had just released a new AIR application that simplifies the creation of a customized install badge. This application is called Badger, and more information can be found here: *http://www.adobe.com/devnet/air/articles/badger_for_air _apps.html*

The entire install badge process is outlined clearly at the Adobe AIR Developer Center. The article located at *http://www.adobe.com/devnet/air/articles/air_badge_install.html* includes sample code that will be used in this entry. The code includes the badge items as well as the SWF files needed for the express installation process. To follow along, download the exercise files that are included with the article.

 In addition to the install badge included with the Adobe AIR SDK, a second badge is available on the Adobe AIR Developer Center site at *http://www.adobe.com/devnet/air/articles/badge_for_air.html*.

Configuring the Install Badge

First, be sure you have downloaded the files from the Adobe AIR Developer Center article mentioned earlier. To insert the install badge into a page, you need to extract all the files from the expressInstallDirectory directory into the folder where your page will reside. One of the files in the expressInstallDirectory is a sample *index.html* file that, among other things, defines the settings for the install badge (see Figure 17-1). You can edit these settings, found at the top of the file, to be specific to your AIR application.

The badge allows you to define an image that will be displayed as a preview of your application. You must also define the URL of your application and the required version of AIR for your application.

```
<script language="JavaScript" type="text/javascript">
<!--
// ---------------------------------------------------------------------------
// Globals
// Major version of Flash required
var requiredMajorVersion = 9;
// Minor version of Flash required
var requiredMinorVersion = 0;
// Minor version of Flash required
var requiredRevision = 115;
// AIR Version Required
var airVersion = "1.5";
// AIR Application Name
var airApplicationName = "Sample Application";
// AIR Application URL
```

```
var airApplicationURL = "http://www.davidtucker.net/staging/TargetApplication.air";
// AIR Application Image
var airApplicationImage = "sample.jpg";
// -------------------------------------------------------------------------
// -->
</script>
```

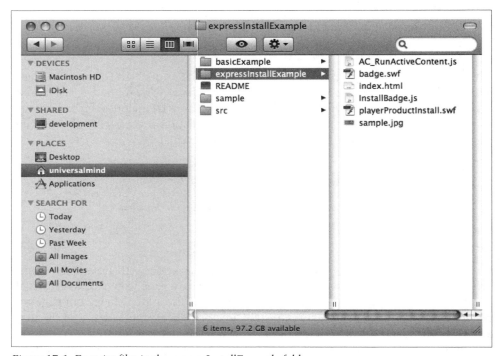

Figure 17-1. Exercise files in the expressInstallExample folder

In addition, you will need to edit the *index.html* file's **noscript** code block and update
it with the values for your application:

```
<!-- Noscript Block for users with JavaScript Disabled -->
<noscript>
<table id="AIRDownloadMessageTable">
    <tr>
        <td>
        Download <a
href="http://www.davidtucker.net/staging/TargetApplication.air">Sample
Application</a> now.<br /><br />
        <span id="AIRDownloadMessageRuntime">
        This application requires the Adobe&#174; AIR&#8482; runtime to be
installed for <a href="http://airdownload.adobe.com/air/mac/download/1.5/
AdobeAIR.dmg">Mac OS</a> or <a href="http://airdownload.adobe.com/air/win/
download/1.5/AdobeAIRInstaller.exe">Windows</a>.</span>
        </td>
    </tr>
```

```
</table>
</noscript>
```

Figure 17-2. Adobe AIR install badge

Once this code is in place, the AIR badge (Figure 17-2) should now be properly configured for your application.

For reference, the following is the completed *index.html* file in its entirety. For this code to work properly, you must be sure the needed SWF and JavaScript files are included in the same directory as your *index.html* file.

```
<!DOCTYPE html PUBLIC "-//W3C//DTD XHTML 1.0 Transitional//EN"
  "http://www.w3.org/TR/xhtml1/DTD/xhtml1-transitional.dtd">
<html xmlns="http://www.w3.org/1999/xhtml" xml:lang="en" lang="en">
<head>
<meta http-equiv="Content-Type" content="text/html; charset=iso-8859-1" />
<title>Adobe AIR Application Installer Page</title>
<script language="JavaScript" type="text/javascript">
<!--
// ----------------------------------------------------------------------------
// Globals
// Major version of Flash required
var requiredMajorVersion = 9;
// Minor version of Flash required
var requiredMinorVersion = 0;
// Minor version of Flash required
var requiredRevision = 115;
// AIR Version Required
var airVersion = "1.5";
// AIR Application Name
var airApplicationName = "Sample Application";
// AIR Application URL
var airApplicationURL = "http://www.davidtucker.net/airtips/sampleApplication-1.air";
// AIR Application Image
var airApplicationImage = "sample.jpg";
// ----------------------------------------------------------------------------
// -->
</script>
</head>
<body>
<div id="flashContent">

    <!-- Insert the Installer JavaScript -->
```

```
<script src="AC_RunActiveContent.js" language="javascript"></script>

<script src="InstallBadge.js" language="javascript"></script>

<!-- Noscript Block for users with JavaScript Disabled -->
<noscript>
<table id="AIRDownloadMessageTable">
    <tr>
        <td>
        Download <a
href="http://www.davidtucker.net/airtips/sampleApplication.air">Sample
Application</a> now.<br /><br />
        <span id="AIRDownloadMessageRuntime">
        This application requires the Adobe&#174; AIR&#8482; runtime to
be installed for <a href="http://airdownload.adobe.com/air/mac/download/1.5/
AdobeAIR.dmg">Mac OS</a> or <a href="http://airdownload.adobe.com/air/win/
download/1.5/AdobeAIRInstaller.exe">Windows</a>.</span>
        </td>
    </tr>
</table>
</noscript>

</div>
</body>
</html>
```

Index

We'd like to hear your suggestions for improving our indexes. Send email to *index@oreilly.com*.

deleting files or directories, 194
detecting installed version of AIR, 397
directory aliases, 191
disabling menu items, 326
displaying HTML content, 110
displaying prompt before closing windows, 83
drag and drop support, 179, 182, 185–187
encrypting SQL databases, 241
full-screen windows, 65
initial window settings, 33
installation folders, 34
launching native windows, 56
launching windows, 56–58
lightweight windows, 64
loading PDF documents, 149
localization information, 45
menu events, 312
menu separators, 316
minimizing, maximizing and restoring window controls, 78
monitoring connections to server ports, 369
monitoring URL connections, 363
moving files or directories, 198, 200
multiple windows, 68
nested menus, 319
notifications through Doc, 340
notifications through the taskbar, 342
paths for default applications for file type, 353
PDF support, 148
persisting application settings, 286
positioning windows, 95, 97
querying SQL databases, 257, 273, 282
reading data from files, 204
reading heads of URLs, 366
removing and resetting data in encrypted local stores, 298
resizing windows, 80
retrieving data from clipboard, 165
retrieving data in encrypted local stores, 295
safeguarding files in encrypted local stores, 303
screen positioning, 100
selecting files or directories, 202
service monitor framework, 355–358
SQL database in applications, 285

storing application data in encrypted local stores, 300
storing data in encrypted local stores, 293
toggling menu items, 327
writing data to files, 205

K

keyboard shortcuts
  menu items, 325
keys
  storing, 233

L

language-specific AIR installations, 44
launchApplication method, 398
launching
  applications from browsers, 40, 397–399
  native windows, 50
  windows, 49–58
libraries
  ActionScript library, 142–145
  Adobe AIR Update Framework library, 373
lightweight windows
  creating, 50, 61
load method, 287
loading
  HTML content, 112
  PDF documents, 148
  SWF files, 51
loadString method, 139
local stores (see encrypted local stores)
localization
  languages, 44
locationChange ActionScript event, 104
logging
  Introspector console, 8

M

Mac
  application icons, 38
  checking whether user is using Mac or Windows, 321
  copyright information and application filename, 30
  Doc, 329–343
  menus, 308
  native menus, 321
  window chrome, 50

main application windows
    changing, 47
maximizing windows, 76
MD5 hashing
    as3corelib library, 206
menu events, 311–315
menu separators, 315
menus
    adding custom menus to Doc Icons, 335
    adding to Windows system tray, 332–335
    native menus, 307–327
Microsoft Windows (see Windows)
migrating serialization changes, 213–215
minimizing windows, 76
mnemonic indexes, 311
modes (see transfer modes)
monitoring
    network communication, 11
    network status, 357
    server ports, 367–371
    URL connections, 359–365
monitors (see screens)
moving files or directories, 197, 199
MXML
    changing system tray or Doc icons, 337
    connecting to SQL databases, 229
    custom chrome, 72
    drop shadows, 87
    HTML container history list, 132

N

name spaces (see XML namespaces)
names
    applications and files, 25–28
native menus, 307–327
    context menus, 322–325
    creating, 307–311, 320
    enabling and disabling menu items, 326
    keyboard shortcuts, 325
    menu events, 311–315
    menu separators, 315
    nested menus, 317–320
    responding to, 311–315
    toggling menu items, 327
native windows
    launching, 50, 56
NativeApplication class, 396
NativeWindow class, 49, 77
NativeWindow.startResize method, 78

nested menus
    creating, 317–320
nesting
    Window component, 53
networkChangeEvent events, 357
networks
    connectivity events, 358
    controlling connectivity status, 358
    monitoring communications, 11
    monitoring status, 357
nodes
    initialWindow nodes, 48
    systemChrome nodes, 54
notifications
    Dock, 339
    taskbar, 341–343

O

onSelectResult event handler, 275
open method, 221
openAsync method, 226
openMode:String parameter, 221
operating system clipboard (see clipboard support)
operating systems (see Mac; Windows)
originalUrl property, 130

P

pages (see HTML content)
pageSize:int parameter, 222
parameters
    in SQL queries, 277–284
passwords
    encrypting SQL databases, 237–243
paths
    applications, 34
    default applications for file types, 351
    Flex build path, 375
    retrieving for files, 347
PDF support, 147–158
    availability, 147
    communication between PDF and AIR, 150–158
    loading PDF documents, 148
performance
    autoCompact operation and SQL database, 222
    transparent windows, 71

persisting application settings, 286
Pixel Bender Toolkit, 90
ports
    authorizations for connecting to, 368
    monitoring connections to, 367–371
power saving
    videos disabling, 67
previousVersion property, 375, 380
programming
    SQL databases, 217–290
    synchronous versus asynchronous, 19–21
ProgressEvent.PROGRESS event, 380
prompts
    displaying before closing windows, 81–83
publisher IDs
    finding, 398

Q

queries
    SQL databases, 253–284

R

reading
    data from files, 203
    URL heads, 365
reencrypt method, 238
reference:Object parameter, 221
registering
    custom file types, 345–348
removing
    data in encrypted local stores, 296–299
    default application status, 350
rendering
    clipboard data, 169
    transparent windows, 71
resetting data in encrypted local stores, 296–299
resizing windows, 78–80
REST (Representational State Transfer)
    transmitting domain-specific data over HTTP, 358
restoring
    windows controls, 77
retrieving
    data from clipboard, 164
    data from encrypted local stores, 293–296
    paths for files, 347
    query results, 267–276

running
    AIR applications, 2–7
    applications, 3, 5, 7
runtime
    application versions, 43

S

sandboxes
    bridging content from, 134–138
save method, 287
Screen class, 93
screen savers
    videos disabling, 67
Screen.screens arrays, 95
screens
    positioning windows, 93–101
scripting
    DOM from ActionScript, 119–128
scroll ActionScript event, 104
scrollBarsVisible parameter, 58
scrolling
    HTML content, 141
SDK (see AIR SDK)
seamless install badge, 402–406
searching
    for files, 208–213
security
    bridging content between sandboxes, 134–138
select events, 312
SELECT statement, 267
selecting
    files or directories, 201
serialization class
    migrating changes, 213–215
servers
    monitoring connection to ports, 367–371
    port authorizations, 368
service monitor framework, 355–371
    applications, 355–359
    monitoring server ports, 367–371
    monitoring URL connections, 359–365
    reading URL heads, 365
ServiceMonitor class, 357, 358
ServiceMonitorShim component, 359
setData method, 162
setDataHandler method, 169
settings, 23–45
    allowBrowserInvocation, 397

AIR and Adobe Flash Player, 359
    applications, 41, 373–394
UpdateWindow component, 381, 389
url node, 374
url property, 130
URLMonitor class, 358, 360
URLRequestMethod class, 366
URLs
    monitoring connections to, 359–365
    reading heads, 365
userDirectory alias, 189
utility windows
    creating, 59

V

VeriSign, 19
version property, 380
versions
    Adobe Acrobat or Adobe Reader, 148
    Adobe Flash Player, 359
    AIR, xvii, 23, 396
    applications, 28
    SQL database dialects, 244
    versioning information, 373
videos
    disabling screen savers and power saving,
        67
visible parameter, 58
visibleBounds variable, 94

W

Window.open method, 57
windowInitOptions parameter, 58
windows, 47–92
    closing, 81–86
    creating, 59–67, 70–76
    custom chrome, 86–92
    full-screen windows, 64
    launching, 49–58
    lightweight windows, 50, 61
    main application windows, 47
    minimizing and maximizing, 76
    multiple, 67–70
    positioning, 93–101
    resizing, 78–80
    setting, 32–34
    utility windows, 59
Windows

application icons, 38
checking whether user is using Mac or
        Windows, 321
default Programs menu folders, 36
menus, 308
native menus, 320
taskbar, 329–343
window chrome, 50
writing data to files, 204

X

XML namespaces
    referencing, 24
XMLHTTPRequest
    monitoring requests, 11

Colophon

The animal on the cover is a marsh harrier.

The cover image is from Wood's Animate Creation. The cover font is Adobe ITC Garamond. The text font is Linotype Birka; the heading font is Adobe Myriad Condensed; and the code font is LucasFont's TheSansMonoCondensed.

SAME CODE, NEW TURF

x x x x x x x x x x x x x x x x x x x x x x x x x x x x x x x x x x x x x x x x x x x x x x x x x x x x x

ADOBE® AIR™ COOKBOOK

Created in partnership with O'Reilly Media, the online Adobe AIR cookbook is where Flash®, Flex®, and Ajax developers come together to find and share code recipes for common development tasks. In fact, some of the recipes you'll find in this book came from the website. So visit the Adobe AIR cookbook site today to find solutions and share your own. Bask in the glow of helping fellow Flash, Flex, and Ajax developers, and start building and deploying better rich Internet applications to the desktop—faster. Who knows, some of your recipes could even end up in these pages.

ON.

GET COOKING TODAY > www.adobe.com/go/air_cookbook